Southern Trident

*Strategy, History and the Rise of
Australian Naval Power*

Edited by David Stevens and John Reeve

ALLEN & UNWIN

First published in 2001

Copyright © in this collection Commonwealth of Australia 2000
© in the pieces remains with the individual authors

All rights reserved. No part of this book may be reproduced or transmitted in any form or by any means, electronic or mechanical, including photocopying, recording or by any information storage and retrieval system, without prior permission in writing from the publisher. *The Australian Copyright Act* 1968 (the Act) allows a maximum of one chapter or 10% of this book, whichever is the greater, to be photocopied by any educational institution for its educational purposes provided that the educational institution (or body that administers it) has given a remuneration notice to Copyright Agency Limited (CAL) under the Act.

Allen & Unwin
83 Alexander Street
Crows Nest NSW 2065
Australia
Phone: (61 2) 8425 0100
Fax: (61 2) 9906 2218
E-mail: frontdesk@allen-unwin.com.au
Web: http://www.allenandunwin.com

National Library of Australia
Cataloguing-in-Publication entry:

> Southern trident: strategy, history and the rise of Australian naval power.
>
> Includes index.
> ISBN 1 86508 462 X.
>
> 1. Australia. Royal Australian Navy – History. 2. Sea-power – Australia – History. 3. Australia – History, Naval. I. Stevens, David, 1958– . II. Reeve, John, 1956– .
>
> 359.00994

Set in 10/11.5pt Times by Midland Typesetters, Maryborough, Victoria
Printed by South Wind Productions, Singapore

10 9 8 7 6 5 4 3 2 1

Dedicated to the memory of Admiral Sir George King-Hall, KCB, CVO, Commander-in-Chief Australia Station, 1911–13

George King-Hall was appointed to the Command of the Australia Station at the age of 60 and soon perceived that the situation surrounding the establishment of an Australian navy was far more a national than simply a naval one. After his arrival in Sydney he made up his mind that his work was not only to help in establishing the Royal Australian Navy, but also to shepherd it into the ambit of the Imperial Fleet and to have the same White Ensign covering both British and Australian men-of-war. Perhaps the most popular British admiral to serve on the Australia Station, King-Hall displayed an extraordinary sympathy with the aspirations and ideals of the Australian people. This sympathy was of immense value to Australia at a very critical time, helping to overcome opposition to the new fleet and bringing it to birth. Admiral King-Hall retired from the Royal Navy in 1913 and died in 1939.

Foreword

I am delighted to provide the foreword to this collection of essays. It marks the maturing of a joint initiative of the Royal Australian Navy and the School of History of the University of New South Wales at the Australian Defence Force Academy to remedy the lack of naval historical studies within this country by the establishment of the Osborne Fellowship. That this initiative has already been an enormous success has been demonstrated in the excellent results achieved within the naval history courses now being conducted at both undergraduate and postgraduate levels. I am particularly pleased that these courses are being undertaken by cadets and commissioned officers of all three services and I am sure that the increased levels of understanding of our naval history and of maritime strategic issues in general will bear fruit in the years ahead. It seems to me that there is as much a vocational as an educational benefit in the raising of awareness of our naval past amongst the officers who will one day lead the Australian Defence Force.

I want to dwell on this question of 'awareness', because it is one that I need to make a priority for myself and for the navy as a whole in the years ahead. That it was necessary to take the step of funding an appointment in naval history is a reflection of a larger problem within Australia and one that is very much my contemporary concern as the Chief of Navy. This is the existence of a syndrome, which in another country was aptly called 'sea blindness'. Australia is an island continent, its discovery and settlement from Europe was by sea, and its economic and military security have always depended, and still depend absolutely, upon our ability to move shipping upon it. Nevertheless, our thoughts as a nation either turn inwards or, perhaps worse, look on the oceans around us simply as a playground and the backdrop for another coastal resort development. We have truly been called a maritime power with continental preoccupations.

The picture is improving, I believe, with regard to maritime affairs in general. Partly this has been driven by the increased national consciousness of the importance of exports to the Australian economy. Offshore resource exploitation, the law of the sea and environmental concerns have also played their part. So, too, have the incursions into Australian territory of seaborne drug smugglers and illegal immigrants. Nevertheless, despite the RAN's active role in much of this surveillance and enforcement activity, and its search and rescue activities, I do not feel that the navy and its roles as a warfighting organisation are well understood. One of my major priorities must be to improve that understanding.

We need to do more to explain what it is that the navy and maritime forces do within the context of Australia's Strategic Policy, because that policy is very much one which enunciates a Maritime Strategy. Australia is an island continent, the ocean is our major highway of international trade and the natural impediment to others reaching our nation in force. Being able to control this natural barrier is fundamental to our long-term prosperity and security. We therefore need to develop an improved awareness of the way in which the emerging concepts of Australian manoeuvre warfare point inevitably towards a truly joint *maritime* approach to operations for the defence of Australia and our regional interests.

Whether Australia will need to stand alone, or whether it operates within the framework of an alliance or a coalition, our circumstances dictate that the context will be maritime and it will be joint. I particularly welcome the Australian Army's current debate on its roles within such a concept of strategy, and I believe that we are at the beginning of a new understanding of the co-operative efforts which will be possible across the environments in future warfighting. At every level of warfare, within a region such as ours, seaborne forces are already key enablers for both offensive and defensive action. Emergent technology would suggest that there is considerable potential for markedly increasing our capabilities to provide direct support of land forces within the littoral—and for the synergies of airborne and seaborne forces to be improved as well. In sum, I believe that the navy faces enormous challenges, but I am also convinced that it possesses the tools and the human talent necessary to meet those challenges. The facts of both our responsibilities for Australian security and our capabilities in meeting them need to be 'sold' to the Australian public as a whole and our decision-makers in particular.

I do not look upon this as an exercise in sheer propaganda. The Australian Navy has made its share of mistakes over the last hundred years and we need recognise and understand them if we are to develop and survive as a professional organisation. But I am absolutely convinced that the contribution of the naval services to Australia's history and its development has been vital, that this contribution is constantly underestimated or misunderstood, and that there will be grave implications for Australia's security if this situation is allowed to continue. Because if it does, then the support of the electorate will diminish to the point at which it will become unwilling to fund a combat-oriented navy.

Abraham Lincoln remarked that it is possible to fool all of the people some of the time and some of the people all of the time, but that you cannot fool all of them all of the time. We cannot be in the business of 'fooling' the electorate, but it is very much our business to ensure that they are properly informed of what it is that navies do and how they do it. We have been slow in the navy to recognise that it is our duty to inform and to do our best to increase the sophistication of the debate, which must always be in progress in any healthy democracy, over the level and form of the national security effort. My own feeling is that this is one of the implications of the drive to 'self-reliance' with which we are only now coming fully to terms. In the context of our history, an enormous amount has been achieved in the understanding of Australia's naval heritage over the last decade. I look to this effort being continued and extended by books such as this, not only for its own sake, but because I believe such work lays the foundations for the development and the enunciation of the contemporary 'naval case' which I believe to be so vital.

Perhaps one of the less well comprehended implications of our acceptance of so much of the form and substance of the Royal Navy within the organisation and ethos of the Royal Australian Navy was that we have not pressed harder for our place within Australian society as a whole to be recognised by Australians for what it is and should be—something unique and something essential. Part of that recognition must derive from an understanding of the history of maritime security and maritime strategy in the context of Australia's progress towards true independence and sovereignty. Many of the chapters contained in this volume dwell upon the conflict between Australia's own security requirements and those of the British Empire as a whole and the differing strategic perceptions of Melbourne and Whitehall. That such matters were a vital concern from the beginnings of Federation has been recognised by this book's endorsement as a Centenary activity by the National Council for the Centenary of Federation.

I conclude by drawing the reader's attention to the dedication of this collection to Admiral Sir George King-Hall. If such a memorial tends to emphasise our links with the Royal Navy, it is because King-Hall, last British Commander-in-Chief on the Australia Station, was one of the few people in the period before the First World War who fully recognised the potential which the new navy represented. He did much to protect the emerging RAN from shortsighted attempts by both local and imperial authorities to interfere with what, in hindsight, was a remarkable innovation which exactly matched the strategic imperatives of August 1914 and afterwards. He 'sold' the vital message that the navy mattered and that it could do the job that needed to be done—for that we must be very grateful. But more than that, we have to continue in exactly the same vein.

Vice Admiral David Shackleton, RAN
Chief of Navy

Contents

Foreword	v
Vice Admiral David Shackleton, RAN	
Notes on contributors	xi
Illustrations, maps and tables	xvi
Abbreviations	xviii
Acknowledgements	xx
Introduction	1
David Stevens and John Reeve	

PART I   CONCEPTS AND APPROACHES TO MARITIME STRATEGY

1	The rise of modern naval strategy c. 1580–1880 *John Reeve*	7
2	Sea power in modern strategy *Colin Gray*	24
3	History and theory: the Clausewitzian ideal and its implications *Jon Sumida*	40
4	Imperial naval defence—a model for transnationalism: a Canadian perspective *Nicholas Tracy*	55
5	Maritime forces and expeditionary strategies: we are all Corbettians now *Peter Hore*	72
6	Strategic culture and the Australian way of warfare: perspectives *Michael Evans*	83

PART II PERSPECTIVES ON IMPERIAL AND AUSTRALIAN NAVAL DEFENCE

7   Australia, the *Trent* crisis of 1861 and the strategy of imperial defence   99
    Andrew Lambert
8   New Zealand's naval defence, 1854–1914   119
    Richard Jackson
9   Colonial naval forces before Federation   125
    Bob Nicholls
10 'A vigorous offensive': core aspects of Australian maritime defence concerns before 1914   140
    Peter Overlack
11 'The view from Port Phillip Heads': Alfred Deakin and the move towards an Australian navy   160
    Colin Jones
12 'A sea of troubles': the Great White Fleet's 1908 war plans for Australia and New Zealand   174
    James R. Reckner
13 A.W. Jose in the politics and strategy of naval defence, 1903–1909   197
    Ross Lamont
14 Sir John Fisher, the fleet unit concept, and the creation of the Royal Australian Navy   214
    Nicholas Lambert
15 'Defend the north': Commander Thring, Captain Hughes-Onslow and the beginnings of Australian naval strategic thought   225
    David Stevens
16 Divergent paths: problems of command and strategy in Anglo–Australasian naval operations in the Asia–Pacific (August–November 1914)   242
    Geoffrey McGinley
17 A strategy for the lower deck of the early Royal Australian Navy   262
    Kathryn Spurling
18 The Royal Australian Navy, the Constitution and the law— then and now   276
    David Letts
19 A fleet not a navy: some thoughts on the themes   291
    James Goldrick

Notes   296
Index   352

Notes on contributors

DR MICHAEL EVANS is a Senior Research Fellow in the Australian Army's Land Warfare Studies Centre, Duntroon. He is a graduate in history and war studies of the Universities of Rhodesia, London and Western Australia. He did national service in the Rhodesian Army and was later a regular officer in the Zimbabwe Army, where he headed that army's war studies program. He has a strong interest in maritime, amphibious and joint force strategy and doctrine. His most recent publications include *The Role of the Australian Army in a Maritime Concept of Strategy* (LWSC Working Paper, No. 101, 1998), *Conventional Deterrence in the Australian Strategic Context* (LWSC Working Paper No. 103, 1999) and as editor, *Changing the Army: The Roles of Doctrine, Development and Training* (1999).

CAPTAIN JAMES GOLDRICK, RAN, joined the RAN College in 1974 and went on to graduate from the University of New South Wales (UNSW) at the end of 1978. He has since commanded two ships and assumed the post of Director General Maritime Studies Program at the beginning of 1999. He has lectured in naval history and contemporary naval affairs at many institutions. Published works as author or editor include *The King's Ships Were at Sea: The War in the North Sea August 1914–February 1915* (1984), *With the Battle Cruisers* (1986), *Reflections on the Royal Australian Navy* (1991), *Mahan Is Not Enough* (1993) and *No Easy Answers: The Development of the Navies of India, Pakistan, Bangladesh and Sri Lanka* (1997).

PROFESSOR COLIN GRAY is a political scientist with broad interests in national security policy, strategic theory and military history. He was educated at the King's School, Rochester, at the University of Manchester and at Lincoln College, Oxford University. He is Professor of International

Politics and Strategic Studies at the University of Reading, and is a senior associate to the National Institute for Public Policy, Fairfax, VA. He is the author of many books including *The Leverage of Sea Power: The Strategic Advantage of Navies in War* (1992), *Weapons Don't Make War: Policy, Strategy, and Military Technology* (1993), *The Navy in the Post-Cold War World* (1994), *Explorations in Strategy* (1996), *Modern Strategy* (1999) and *The Second Nuclear Age* (1999).

CAPTAIN PETER HORE, RN, recently retired as the Royal Navy's Head of Defence Studies. He was originally a logistics specialist and during the Falklands War was the Joint Logistics Commander on Ascension Island. Since promotion to captain he has served mainly in central defence appointments helping to define defence and naval strategy, and the effects of changing concepts, technology and geopolitics. As Head of Defence Studies he directed the Royal Navy's non-technical research and founded the Maritime Strategic Studies Institute. He is the author of many reviews, articles and chapters and has co-edited *Dimensions of Sea Power: the strategy of choice* (1998) and *Maritime Aviation: light and medium aircraft carriers in the 21st century (1999)*.

COMMANDER RICHARD JACKSON, RNZN (Rtd), joined the RNZN in 1968. He has served in a variety of sea and shore postings including an exchange post at US Pacific Command's Intelligence Centre, and command of the patrol craft HMNZS *Rotoiti*, and the Naval Radio Station HMNZS *Irirangi*. He later served in Defence Headquarters and on the Naval Staff in Wellington during which time he gained a Masters in Public Policy at Victoria University. He was a founder writer for *New Zealand Defence Quarterly* and has also contributed to many other professional journals in New Zealand and overseas.

COLIN JONES is a retired public servant who has spent many years of part-time research into naval subjects. He lives in Melbourne. As an observer of the naval scene, rather than a practitioner, he thinks of himself often as a person who takes in a 'view from Port Phillip Heads'. Had we not won the Battle of the Coral Sea, he would have been evacuated to the country as a babe in arms. He was educated in Brisbane and has a degree in history and philosophy from the University of Queensland. His books include *Australian Colonial Navies* (1986) and *Wings and the Navy* (1997).

PROFESSOR ANDREW LAMBERT is Professor of Naval History in the Department of War Studies, King's College, London. Before that he held teaching positions at the Royal Naval College Greenwich, and the Royal Military Academy at Sandhurst. He is also Secretary of the Navy Records Society, Chairman of the Publications Committee of the Society for

Nautical Research, Vice President of the British Commission for Maritime History and a Fellow of the Royal Historical Society. His books include *The Crimean War: British Grand Strategy against Russia 1853–1856* (1990), *The Last Sailing Battlefleet: Maintaining Naval Mastery 1815–1850* (1991), and *The Foundations of Naval History: John Knox Laughton, the Royal Navy and the Historical Profession* (1998).

DR NICHOLAS LAMBERT completed his undergraduate and graduate degrees at Oxford University. Since then he has held an Olin post-doctoral fellowship at Yale University, a Hartley visiting fellowship at Southampton University and the Charter fellowship at Wolfson College, Oxford. His first monograph, *Australia's Naval Inheritance: Imperial Maritime Strategy and the Australia Station 1880–1909* was published in 1999 by the RAN's Maritime Studies Program, while his second, *Sir John Fisher's Naval Revolution*, was recently published in the USA by the University of South Carolina Press.

ROSS LAMONT took a first degree in Arts at the University of Queensland and a licentiate in theology at St Francis's Theological College, Brisbane. In London, he graduated with honours in history from Birkbeck College, then completed an MA in international history at the London School of Economics and Political Science. In 1967 he was appointed a lecturer in history at the University of New England where he taught German history. He is now an Honorary Fellow in the history department of that university. His publications include entries on A.W. Jose and W.H.C.S. Thring for the *Australian Dictionary of Biography* and the introduction to the 1987 edition of the *Royal Australian Navy* volume in the *Official History of Australia in the War of 1914–1918*.

COMMANDER DAVID LETTS, CSM, RAN, joined the RAN College in January 1982 and graduated with a Commerce Degree from UNSW in December 1984. Following service as a supply officer he undertook legal studies completing a Masters of Laws, specialising in International Law, at the Australian National University. In 1997 he was assigned to the Directorate of Discipline Law in the Defence Legal Office and in 1999 became Fleet Legal Officer in Maritime Headquarters. He was awarded the Conspicuous Service Medal in recognition of his service as Supply Officer HMAS *Brisbane* in the 1997 Queen's Birthday Honours list.

SUB-LIEUTENANT GEOFFREY MCGINLEY, RAN, joined the RAN in 1996 and graduated from the Australian Defence Force Academy (ADFA) in 1998 with a BSc majoring in Computer Science and History. In 1999 he completed a History Honours Thesis at ADFA on Australian Naval and Military Operations in the Pacific to 1914. He started his training as a seaman officer in 2000.

BOB NICHOLLS turned to writing after relinquishing a naval career that included service in three navies and stretched over four decades. He has had seven books published, including *Bluejackets and Boxers* (1986) and *Statesman and Sailors* (1995), and is at present working on a study of the breastwork monitor *Cerberus*. He lives in the Southern Highlands of New South Wales, about half way between Canberra and Sydney.

DR PETER OVERLACK held a DAAD (German Academic Exchange Scholarship) and completed his doctoral thesis at the University of Queensland in 1995 on the East Asiatic Cruiser Squadron as an instrument of German 'world policy'. He has since had articles published in *Australian Journal of Politics and History, Journal of Australian Studies, Journal of Military History* (USA), *Journal of Pacific History, Journal of Strategic Studies* (UK), *Journal of the Australian Naval Institute, The Historian* (USA), *War & Society*, and has contributed to several books. He teaches at St Edmund's College, Ipswich, Australia.

DR JAMES R. RECKNER joined the US Navy in 1958 and spent twenty years as seaman, petty officer and officer, including two years with the South Vietnamese Navy's riverine forces during the Vietnam War. Upon retirement in 1978, he emigrated to New Zealand, where he earned a BA, MA (Hons) and PhD in history from the University of Auckland. Since 1988 he has taught military and naval history at Texas Tech University, where he also serves as Director of The Vietnam Center. He is the author of *Teddy Roosevelt's Great White Fleet* (1989), has held the US Secretary of the Navy's Research Chair in Naval History, and serves as a member of the US Secretary of the Navy's Advisory Subcommittee on Naval History.

DR JOHN REEVE is Senior Lecturer and Osborne Fellow in Naval History at UNSW, ADFA. A graduate of Melbourne University (MA) and Cambridge (PhD), he has taught at Cambridge, Yale (as a Fulbright Fellow), Hong Kong, and Sydney Universities. His interests include great power rivalry and diplomacy, naval strategy, and the historical context of sea power. His recent publications include a chapter on foreign policy and war in *The Oxford Illustrated History of Tudor and Stuart Britain* and an essay on Mahan, Corbett and modern maritime strategy in Hugh Smith (ed.), *The Strategists* (Australian Defence Studies Centre, Canberra, forthcoming). He is currently researching studies of Asia–Pacific naval strategy and of the rise of Britain as a great power, and is an Associate Editor of the British *New Dictionary of National Biography*.

DR KATHRYN SPURLING received her PhD from UNSW in 1999 with a dissertation entitled 'Life in the Lower Deck of the Royal Australian Navy, 1911–1952'. She has worked as an historian, researcher and consultant on several projects, and has published widely on the subject of women in the Australian Public Service, women in sport, and those who have served in the Royal Australian Navy.

DR DAVID STEVENS is a graduate of the UNSW and the Australian National University and has been the Director of Naval Historical Studies within the Maritime Studies Program since retiring from the RAN in 1994. He is the author or editor of several books on maritime strategy and naval history including *Maritime Power in the Twentieth Century: The Australian Experience* (1998), *U-Boat Far From Home* (1997), *In Search of a Maritime Strategy* (1997) and *The Royal Australian Navy in World War II* (1996).

ASSOCIATE PROFESSOR JON TETSURO SUMIDA is a graduate of the Universities of California and Chicago and is currently Visiting Professor at the US National War College. He has received the Moncado Prize from the Society of Military History in 1993 and 1995 and the prize as Naval History Author of the Year from the United States Naval Institute in 1996. His publications include *Inventing Grand Strategy and Teaching Command: The Classic Works of Alfred Thayer Mahan Reconsidered* (1997, paperback 1999), *In Defence of Naval Supremacy: Finance, Technology and British Naval Policy, 1889–1914* (1989, paperback, 1993).

DR NICHOLAS TRACY is Adjunct Professor of History at the University of New Brunswick, Canada. He has published extensively in the fields of naval history and foreign policy, with a special interest in the strategic role of naval forces in international relations. Parallel to this work has been study of naval tactics in the age of sail. His most recent publication has been a modern, consolidated edition in five volumes of the *Naval Chronicle*, the most important published primary source for the naval wars against the French Revolution and Empire.

Illustrations, maps and tables

Illustrations

Entry of the Fleet, 1913	2
Horatio Nelson	11
The blockade of Cadiz	16
Alfred Thayer Mahan	28
Sir Julian Corbett	28
HMAS *Sydney* in the North Sea	30
Carl von Clausewitz	41
1902 Imperial Conference	56
Battle cruisers at Jutland	74
Australian Naval and Military Expeditionary Force	76
Destruction of *Emden*	79
Sea Dogs of Australia	88
Re-enactment of Gallipoli landing	91
HMS *Galatea*	105
Trent and *San Jacinto*	109
Flying Squadron in Port Phillip Bay	117
HMS *New Zealand*	124
German gunboat *Eber*	132
The Victorian Navy, 1886	134
Cairns Naval Brigade	137
A colonial commodore and British midshipman	138
Captain William Rooke Creswell	144
'The Fight of the Shepherds'	156
Gayundah and *Paluma*	162

ILLUSTRATIONS, MAPS AND TABLES   xvii

Submarine miners	163
Countess of Hopetoun	167
Welcome to our American comrades	182
USN bluejackets	192
Alfred Deakin	201
'The Peace Rainbow'	204
The Japanese armoured cruiser *Nissin*	212
Sir John Fisher	218
HMS *Pioneer* at Hobart	221
HMS *Invincible* at the Battle of the Falklands	223
Captain Hugh Thring	227
The Australian Commonwealth Naval Board	230
Chart of Sewa Bay	239
The German East Asiatic Squadron	245
The capture of German New Guinea	257
HMAS *Tingira*	268
The ship's company of HMAS *Yarra*	270
The ship's company of HMAS *Sydney*	272
HMA Ships *Parramatta* and *Yarra*	281
Royal Australian Naval College	283
The Australian Fleet Unit, 1913	293

Maps

Map 12.1	Attack plan for Auckland	186
Map 12.2	Attack plan for Sydney	189
Map 12.3	Attack plan for Melbourne	193
Map 16.1	The movements of the German East Asiatic Squadron, July–December 1914	248

Tables

Table 9.1	Australian colonies, men available for naval service, 1892	135
Table 11.1	Australasian floating defences, 1905	161
Table 11.2	Australian military and naval manpower, 1906	164
Table 12.1	The Defence Force of New Zealand, 1908	187

Abbreviations

ACNB	Australian Commonwealth Naval Board
ADF	Australian Defence Force
ADFA	Australian Defence Force Academy
ANZAC	Australia and New Zealand Army Corps
AWM	Australian War Memorial
BL	breech-loading
C4I	command, control, communications, computers and intelligence
CANUS	Canada–United States continental defence arrangements
CDC	Colonial Defence Committee
CFSP	Common Foreign and Security Policy
CGICC	Coast Guard Intelligence Coordination Center
CinC	Commander-in-Chief
CID	Committee of Imperial Defence
COS	Chief of the War Staff
CPP	Commonwealth Parliamentary Papers
DOD	Director of the Operations Division
EC	electro-contact (mine)
EMS	electromagnetic spectrum
EO	electro-observation (mine)
ESDI	European Security and Defence Identity
EUROMARFOR	European Maritime Force
GDP	Gross Domestic Product
GPS	Global Positioning System
HMAS	His (Her) Majesty's Australian Ship
HMS	Her (His) Majesty's Ship
HQAST	Headquarters Australian Theatre
ICBM	inter-continental ballistic missile
MCJO	Maritime Contribution to Joint Operations
MOLE	Maritime Operations in a Littoral Environment
MTR	military–technical revolution
NAA	National Archives of Australia
NATO	North Atlantic Treaty Organisation
NORAD	North American Air Defence Agreement
NWC	Naval War College
ONI	Office of Naval Intelligence
PfP	partnership-for-peace
PRO	Public Record Office, London

ABBREVIATIONS

QF	quick-firing
RAAF	Royal Australian Air Force
RAC	Rear Admiral Commanding the Australian Fleet
RAF	Royal Air Force
RAN	Royal Australian Navy
RCN	Royal Canadian Navy
RGF	Royal Gun Factory
RMA	revolution in military affairs
RN	Royal Navy
RNZN	Royal New Zealand Navy
SDR	Strategic Defence Review (UK, 1998)
SDSC	Strategic and Defence Studies Centre
SIAF	Spanish–Italian Amphibious Force
SLOC	sea lines of communication
SS	steamship
UAV	unpiloted aerial vehicle
UKNLAF	UK–Netherlands Amphibious Force
UN	United Nations
UNSW	University of New South Wales
USMC	United States Marine Corps
USN	United States Navy
USS	United States Ship
WEU	Western European Union
W/T	wireless telegraphy

Acknowledgements

The essays contained in this book originated at the inaugural King-Hall Naval History Conference held in Canberra in July 1999 and are here published in an expanded and enhanced form. This book could not have been produced without the assistance and support, not only of the contributors, but of a considerable number of individuals and organisations. Particular thanks are due to Joe Straczek, David Griffin, Brett Mitchell, David Wilson, Jason Sears, Bernadette McDermott, Julie Cassell, the National Council for the Centenary of Federation, Tenix Defence Systems Pty Ltd and LOPAC PTY LIMITED.

Introduction

On the morning of 4 October 1913 the battle cruiser HMAS *Australia*, flying the flag of Rear Admiral Sir George E. Patey and accompanied by the light cruisers *Melbourne*, *Sydney* and *Encounter*, and the destroyers *Warrego*, *Parramatta* and *Yarra*, entered Sydney Heads. The spring weather was perfect, and the long grey line of ships of the Australian Fleet Unit had materialised punctually from out of a thinning sea mist in the east. Hundreds of small craft provided an eager escort, while hundreds of thousands of sightseers crammed the many headlands to stare at the imposing passage of one of the largest warships ever to enter Port Jackson. Waiting off Fort Denison to return the fleet's salute was the second-class protected cruiser HMS *Cambrian*, last flagship of the Australia Station, and on board was Admiral Sir George King-Hall, ready to haul down his flag as the last Commander-in-Chief.

Sydney Harbour was no stranger to imperial and foreign warships, but the battle cruiser, both majestic and forbidding at the same time, was something different. It was the embodiment of the Commonwealth's own sea power, and unquestionably superior to every other European warship in the Pacific. Already described as a 'living sentient thing' *Australia*'s entering at the head of the fleet evoked a nationalistic euphoria never before experienced. 'The sight of the Fleet meant more to the Australian people than the visit of any foreign fleet. It was our expression of patriotism, ships of defence bought in love of country and empire . . .' wrote the *Sydney Mail*, while the Australian Defence Minister, Senator Edward Millen, remarked:

> Since Captain Cook's arrival, no more memorable event has happened than the advent of the Australian Fleet. As the former marked the birth of Australia, so the latter announces its coming of age, its recognition of the growing responsibilities of nationhood, and its resolve to accept and

A picture taken from HMAS *Australia* showing the rest of the RAN Fleet Unit entering Port Jackson on 4 October 1913. (RAN)

discharge them as a duty both to itself and to the Empire. The Australian Fleet is not merely the embodiment of force. It is the expression of Australia's resolve to pursue, in freedom, its national ideals, and to hand down unimpaired and unsullied the heritage it has received, and which it holds and cherishes as an inviolable trust. It is in this spirit that Australia welcomes its Fleet, not as an instrument of war, but as the harbinger of peace.[1]

Notwithstanding these inspiring words, the acquisition of an independent Australian navy had not been without anguish. The concept of a federated Australian nation was still new, local thoughts and feelings had not always been well understood by British authorities, and even within the Commonwealth many financial, social and political interests remained in conflict. Indeed, although the Royal Australian Navy's initial makeup was essentially part of an imperial design, its existence as an independent force represented a significant departure from the British Empire's long-standing diplomatic and strategic principles. Nevertheless, within a year the Empire would be engulfed in a great war. The Australian Fleet's subsequent operations both to protect local interests and maintain imperial maritime strategic linkages would more than fulfil the expectations of those who had fought so long for its establishment.

In spite of the somewhat impoverished (and indeed erroneous) tradition that Australian naval and military history began at Gallipoli, much scholarly work has increased our understanding of Australian, regional, and international security issues at the era of Federation. Recent research dealing with national interests and strategic threats and purposes has shed light on many of these defining factors. The issues thus raised not only provide the necessary context for re-evaluating the formation of the Royal Australian Navy, but also help better understand problems faced by the Commonwealth's defence planners today.

Certainly the fleet's arrival in 1913 represented far more than a practical expression of Australian nationalism. Navies are not such simple institutions. As the chapters in this volume show, a credible Australian Fleet was rather the culmination of a series of interrelated and often revolutionary developments in a number of diverse fields. These changes encompassed diplomatic and economic issues as well as emerging technologies and questions of strategy. Such developments were ultimately global, and important decisions were often taken in Britain with little or no reference to Australian concerns. It took a statesman of Deakin's ability and vision to mediate between national and imperial aspirations for an Australian Fleet. In this context, issues of maritime strategy provide a particularly important backdrop to the fleet's creation. The Royal Australian Navy inherited a great naval strategic tradition, which reached back many centuries. Yet the practical realities of Australia's regional environment imposed their own priorities not always fully reconcilable with that tradition. The interaction of local and global requirements became the most persistent theme in the development of Australian naval policy.

Certain themes run through this book. The first is the value of sea power—for centuries the friend of free societies—as an essential strategic asset. Two-thirds of the globe is still connected water, and the sea remains the most efficient form of heavy transport—both commercial and military. The strategic potential of sea power thus remains unrivalled, and navies have a strategic significance out of all proportion to the numbers of people they involve. Australia's national environment remains predominantly maritime, and its interests stretch far beyond its territorial dry land.

Second, this book is underpinned by a belief in the fundamental links between history and strategy. Naval history of course predates—as well as includes—the twentieth century, as the classical maritime strategists Mahan and Corbett showed. And the best maritime strategy continues to be historically literate. History, furthermore, is an intellectual training in the complexities of social and international life, as well as a source of corporate experience of enduring relevance. More specifically in this context, the story of the rise of Australian naval power raises issues of contemporary importance. These include the value of a balanced, integrated and interoperable fleet; the need to envisage both regional and out-of-area operations; the role of naval power in alliance-building and diplomacy; the need for a balanced view of the value of people and technology; the nature of the Asia–Pacific region as a land–sea interface bordered by oceans and affected by vast distances; the need to be able to project power from the sea to the land; and the indispensability of protecting the maritime communications of a maritime nation, which means controlling the surface of the sea when and where necessary.

The contributors to this book represent a wide range of service, academic and professional backgrounds, and many are the leading authorities in their areas of expertise. Their willingness to give of their time and wisdom is an excellent opportunity to place the story of Australian naval power in context and perspective. There is not always agreement here, but that is as it should be: our aim has been stimulation and understanding.

The Australian Navy of today goes about its vital business largely unrecognised by the general public, and its operations evoke far less patriotic fervour than a century ago. But Australia's geostrategic environment is enduring, the Commonwealth's maritime responsibilities are vast, and hence the maritime dimension of national defence remains essential for the protection of our regional and global interests. As we move forward to meet the uncertainties of the twenty-first century and the new millennium it behoves us to reflect upon the circumstances and difficulties faced by Australia's first defence planners and strategists. The insights will not only help us to see how we have arrived at the present, but will also assist us in facing the future with confidence. This is surely an appropriate sentiment for the year of the centenary of Federation.

David Stevens and *John Reeve*

PART I

CONCEPTS AND APPROACHES TO MARITIME STRATEGY

1 The rise of modern naval strategy c. 1580–1880
John Reeve

The subject of the rise of modern naval strategy c. 1580–1880 calls for a few words by way of introduction. This chapter is written from an historical point of view, both in terms of naval strategy and of the role of sea power within a wider historical context. But it is also predicated on a belief in the value of distilled historical lessons in strategic discussion. Its purpose is therefore twofold. First it deals with the early modern background to twentieth-century naval strategy as something of intrinsic historical interest, and as the strategic legacy which the early twentieth-century naval world—and the RAN—inherited (both in terms of professional habits and theoretical concepts: concepts mediated in the main by the classical maritime strategists Mahan and Corbett).[1] Secondly and more strategically, it treats early modern naval history as a source of valuable corporate experience of use in strategic debate. The chapter will pursue these two purposes to a degree simultaneously. A few words follow on the approach the chapter will take, on strategy, and on the early modern naval era. The chapter will then set the scene by discussing the strategic structure of the early modern period, will seek to elucidate themes in early modern naval strategy, will make some remarks about Mahan, Corbett and the early modern strategic legacy, and finally will offer some general reflections on the early modern era as strategic experience and food for strategic thought.

On approach

Since the chapter will make reference to a fairly long sweep of naval history, which must necessarily be highly selective, its approach will be thematic rather than chronological, seeking to deal with aspects and lessons of strategic activity, rather than the long and complex story of the conflicts of the era. It will also deal mainly, although not exclusively, with the British case study as an obvious one. Insofar as the chapter deals with state navies and with command it will do so in the context of strategy.

In terms of chronology, the sixteenth century is a logical beginning. The turn of the fifteenth century saw the coming of the modern naval fighting vessel, equipped as a gun platform and with long-range oceanic reach. The early modern military revolution, with the coming of gunpowder, thus went to sea.[2]

This was the beginning of the great age of sea power: an age which has never ended. With European warships making sustained contact with other regions of the world, this was also the beginning of globalised international relations, strategy and war: the world in which we still live—the Mahanian world in which the sea serves as a great global strategic highway. All that was needed was the creation both of merchant fleets and state navies of sufficient size—which occurred during the sixteenth and seventeenth centuries—for the arrival of modern fleet strategy: the use of military force at sea with sufficient critical mass to influence events on land and the international balance of power. In the words of an adviser to the French chief minister Richelieu in the seventeenth century: 'Whoever is master of the sea has a great power over the land'.[3]

Why begin effectively in about 1580? The age of Drake was in various ways the take-off point for the trends described above. The rise of the Elizabethan navy with its race-built galleons, the deterioration of Anglo-Spanish relations in the Atlantic, the decision of Queen Elizabeth to send troops to aid the Dutch revolt against Spain, and the sending of the Spanish Armada of over 100 vessels in 1588 (the largest fleet seen in the Christian world at that time)—to conquer England and knock her out of the war—and the fleet actions the English fought against it: all this starts to place us in the modern naval strategic world.

Why end in about 1880? The late nineteenth century saw certain changes occurring in the areas of technology, of international relations, and of strategic ideas which make it a suitable *terminus ad quem*. With the coming of modern battleships and other weapons such as the locomotive torpedo; the emergence of naval challengers to British dominance—France, Russia and Germany; the formulation of strategic ideas, especially by Mahan, of blue-water battlefleet strategy as part of a theory of sea power; together with concepts of *guerre de course* (commerce war) on the part of the French *Jeune école*; as well as the development of railways and the potential challenge of continental power: all these are things which set the stage for the twentieth-century naval and international world.

On strategy

On the question of strategy, we may well ask what is it? There are many credible modern definitions by commentators such as Liddell Hart.[4] In a sense strategy is in the eye of the beholder. Like pornography, we know it when we see it. We are aware that it merges with operational and tactical issues on one side and higher policy issues on the other. One is inclined to reject (humbly) Mahan's view of tactics as the business of being in contact with the enemy.[5] Many tactical decisions in naval warfare, such as those of Nelson, are highly strategic. We can loosely define naval strategy as the use of military force at sea to serve the ends of policy. One may also suggest that strategy is an art, not a system, and more precisely it is *the making of choices conditioned by contexts*. We should not of course define strategy too narrowly or rigidly. Are there principles of naval strategy? This chapter will reject the view that there are unchanging principles of naval strategy save in all but the very broadest sense, and will argue that strategy is always evolving within the changing context of history.[6] If history teaches anything it is the permanent nature of change, as well as its interaction with continuity. Thus there are patterns in strategic history which we can detect if we do so carefully, with respect to historical particularity.

It is sometimes argued cogently that history and strategy do not mix. Corbett would not have agreed, for Corbett was a great strategist because he was first a great historian. Colin Gray has pointed out in his writings that historians and strategists have valuable things to say to each other.[7] Indeed one could argue that the two fields are intimately connected. As intellectual cultures they both deal with the relationships between particular and contextual phenomena, and between empirical and theoretical material. Both are highly complex, and are ultimately unverifiable, dealing as they do with unpredictable human agents, an infinite number of contingent variables, and in general with Clausewitzian friction. Both deal with relations and conflicts between states and societies, and with relevant political, economic, cultural and technological factors. At the very least, history is an excellent intellectual training for strategic thought, but it can also be a school of strategic experience. Above all it enlarges our frame of reference, which is a critical strategic asset, since the best strategy is usually born of lateral thinking. This last is particularly important today in an era when strategic threats are unclear. Intellectually, a solution is more difficult to establish when the problem itself is ill-defined.

On early modern naval history

Early modern naval history has been dignified by the work of a series of famous and distinguished scholars: Mahan, Corbett, Richmond,[8] John Hattendorf[9] and Nicholas Rodger[10] come readily to mind. The early modern naval era is valuable in at least four ways. First, there is its intrinsic historical fascination. It involves the story of the greatest imperial sea power which has ever existed—a power which created the strategic context and traditions for the RAN and other modern world navies. Second, it constitutes the historical basis of the ideas of Mahan and Corbett, without which we cannot properly understand them any more than we can Clausewitz without a knowledge of the Napoleonic wars. Third, the early modern era remains a tool of professional officer education, which casts light on the nature of state navies by studying their origins, and which offers great lessons in leadership, particularly in the age of Nelson. Fourth, the era is valuable for its strategic raw material. Colin Gray[11] and Nicholas Tracy[12] have utilised its long chronological range in discussing naval strategy in general and trade warfare in particular. We can draw major parallels between earlier British naval hegemony and US and Western hegemony today.

The early modern era is immensely useful, but it was and to an extent still is mythologised in various ways. Corbett, for example, criticised the way in which the divine status attributed to Nelson had enshrined the idea of decisive fleet action beyond the strategic context of which Nelson was very aware.[13] Military services are like churches, with their ranks and hierarchies, ceremonies and traditions, doctrines and heresies, sinners and saints. Historians must continue to demythologise early modern naval history so as to elucidate its lessons.

The strategic structure of the period

It is important to underline the connection between the emerging state navies of this period and the new European state system of which they were a part. It was the European—especially the western European—world of competitive states which provided the infrastructure and resources required by navies and the national purposes they served. We can conveniently describe naval strategic traditions, as they had evolved by the early nineteenth century, in terms of the British Royal Navy and the rest. British naval power was supreme by 1815. But the extended series of wars with France during the 'long' eighteenth century (1689–1815) largely shaped the early modern strategic legacy. We shall return to the nineteenth century, but first describe the era which ran up to 1815.

The Royal Navy

The sixteenth century saw a lack of coherent English naval strategy.[14] This was largely owing to an ethos of plunder and privateering, and to the relatively small number of English ships and their technical limitations. But in this, the era of Drake, with its piracy, raiding and coastal defence (against Spanish armadas), and with the use of the ship as a tactical gun platform, the seeds of later strategic ploys were sown. We can see the origins of the anti-invasion guard, of blockade, of fleet action, of power projection, and of *guerre de course*, despite their being in primitive and partial form. Elizabethan aggression at sea also suggested the inherently offensive nature of naval strategy.

The advent of a modern state navy by the late seventeenth century—public, permanent, professional, bureaucratic, blue-water-oriented and strategically co-ordinated, together with the expansion of trade and the

Horatio Nelson (1758–1805) by Lemuel Abbot painted *c*. 1798–99.
A charismatic leader and a genius of naval warfare, Nelson was the subject of a posthumous cult which emphasised sea battle and profoundly influenced early twentieth-century navies. (National Maritime Museum, Greenwich)

acquisition of colonies and overseas bases, all this allowed a more sophisticated program of strategy. The late seventeenth century saw more continual fleet presence in the Mediterranean, the Atlantic, and the West Indies, and the stationing of the pivotal western squadron at the approach to the Channel.[15]

By the time of Nelson and the French wars (1793–1815) a regular although flexible system of fleet dispositions was well in place. The Channel fleet was still the main station, with over 60 ships (mostly of the line, the rest being frigates), covering Brest and the French Atlantic ports. The Mediterranean fleet (a prestigious command) covered Toulon and Cadiz. Other stations were Ireland and the Channel Isles, the Baltic, the North Sea, the West Indies, North America, the African Cape and the East Indies.[16]

This structure of British naval dispositions, while often a balancing act, provided a guard against invasion, protection of trade, a threat to enemy commerce, and cover for landward power projection both in Europe and overseas.[17] The Royal Navy's strategy was integral to a system of economic warfare against France which, as Nicholas Tracy[18] has shown, was mercantilist rather than logistical in its operation: less concerned with stopping vital commodities than diminishing enemy trade revenue and enhancing one's own, resulting in tax revenues which funded the navy, the limited army, and the continental allies.

Other navies

French strategy had gone on to the defensive following England's victories in fleet actions in the 1690s, resorting to the use of a fleet-in-being, of invasion threat and of commerce raiding. So it essentially remained up to the end of the Napoleonic wars. The French Navy did engage in fleet actions in the eighteenth century, and was capable of victory when the Royal Navy was not at its best, notably at the Chesapeake in 1781—an action critical in the outcome of the American War of Independence.

Spanish strategy had evolved from the great imperial days of the sixteenth and seventeenth centuries and the Atlantic treasure convoys, adjusting to Spain's reduced international status. The Spanish Navy worked in convoys during the Napoleonic wars, and conducted imperial defence while conforming to the strategy of France, its ally.

The smallness of the new American Navy conditioned its strategy. That strategy revolved around coastal defence, privateering, and trade protection.

Eighteenth-century Holland was no longer the great commercial power which had won independence from Spain and fought a succession of trade wars with England. The Dutch, as a smaller power, defended their trade and fought unsuccessfully against the Royal Navy at Camperdown in 1797.[19] Let us now consider the main strategic functions of navies up to 1815.

Fleet engagement

Early modern naval battles inspired dramatic works of art and still sell books, but they were not the sole or even essential ingredient of sea power, even in Nelson's day (Nelson was continually at sea for two years before Trafalgar, performing the vital, exhausting tasks of sea control and blockade). In 1588 it was storms, as much as the English fleet, which defeated the Spanish Armada. The Anglo–Dutch wars of the seventeenth century saw many fleet actions over control of trade, and those actions were significant in terms of the balance of power.[20] But defensive line ahead tactics had created stalemate in battle by the end of the seventeenth century. During the Revolutionary and Napoleonic wars decisive fleet actions were very rare, even for Nelson, although navies had to be ready to fight them. Military power is of course relative, and fleet action was frequently unnecessary for the Royal Navy to keep its strategic advantage. Victory in battle had of course to be capitalised upon to be at all decisive, and the French had failed to do this after Beachy Head in 1690.

The Royal Navy was happier than the French to fight fleet actions, especially Nelson's generation, which took sailing ship technology to its most lethal extent when aided by an adequate signalling system. Nelson's role in this was critical for two reasons. First, Nelson, like Clausewitz on land, realised that war was changing both materially and psychologically and indeed helped to change it, seeking a total victory of annihilation. His reported injunction to a midshipman to 'hate a Frenchman as you do the devil' is not a sentiment of limited war.[21] As Brian Lavery has recently written, the Nile in 1798 was the first naval battle of annihilation, in which the balance of global power changed virtually overnight.[22]

Second, Nelson's hunger for total victory was ultimately strategic. His tactical genius and his personal cult have tended to obscure his strategic purposes—purposes which Corbett understood.[23] Trafalgar was decisive not simply in the negative sense of destroying a potential invasion threat, but also in terms of future British strategic opportunities. After Nelson's victory, Britain was freer to build on the advantages of maritime power, to translate commercial wealth into coalition building and continental power projection; these were the forces which defeated Napoleon. Nelson cast a long shadow over Mahan, his contemporaries, and the early years of the twentieth century, but he was extremely difficult to emulate.

Blockade

Blockade, not fleet action, was the main strategic weapon of the eighteenth-century Royal Navy. As Brian Lavery has observed, for every hour in battle, weeks and months were spent on blockade. This was demanding work which wore down ships and men. But it undermined the morale and seamanship of the French while effectively denying them a naval strategy.[24] The British aims were sea control, defence against invasion, and protection of trade.[25] Within the Royal Navy, opinions differed as to whether the blockade should be close or distant, locking the French up or enticing them out to fight. Distant blockade carried the risk of French escape with serious consequences, as with the Brest blockade during the American War of Independence.[26] Much depended on the weather, the alertness and luck of frigate captains, and chance intelligence, and risks had to be calculated. Nelson, seeking battle in 1805, conducted distant blockade of Toulon, but the French escaped into the Atlantic before their eventual defeat at Trafalgar.

Commerce war

There is no scholarly consensus on the effectiveness of early modern commerce war, although Nicholas Tracy has provided a sophisticated guide.[27] The value of *guerre de course* is one of the most debatable issues in maritime strategic history, having so many variables. English and Dutch raiders found Spanish treasure fleets well guarded and very elusive, only succeeding on rare occasions as in 1628, when ships of the Dutch West India Company took the whole Spanish American *flota* off Cuba.[28] Modern commerce war dates from its adoption by France in the 1690s, but state-organised French privateering declined during the eighteenth century.[29]

It is possible to argue for the efficacy of the *guerre de course* and Colin Gray maintains that its value has been underrated.[30] Spain, when badly overstretched in the early seventeenth century, was forced to spend more on Atlantic defence.[31] The French attacks in squadron after 1692, while not fully pressed home, were damaging to England.[32] Conversely, convoys were highly effective: a lesson which down the ages has had to be relearnt. This historical myopia surely owes much to the posthumous cult of Nelson and decisive battle. It may also be that the power of the Spanish treasure fleets has been understated by Protestant historians of the Elizabethan sea dogs. Convoying of British ships was law by 1793. Less than 1 per cent of convoyed British ships were lost between 1793 and 1815.[33]

The objective value of commerce war remains unproven (and it was certainly unproven to Mahan's generation). It has only arguably ever been decisive in the hands of a strong sea power against a weaker.[34] One might also argue that it worked better against a maritime commercial state such as the Dutch in the seventeenth century, as opposed to an agricultural subsistence economy such as pre-industrial France.

Power projection and amphibious warfare

Modern naval power projection has its origins in the time of Drake. His pre-emptive raid on Cadiz in 1587 delayed the Armada, and raids on the coast of Spain in the 1590s were damaging. As always with amphibious warfare, the potential gain could be enormous and the temptation therefore great, but failure could be spectacular. The capture of Quebec by Wolfe and Saunders in 1759, which led to the fall of French Canada, is a classic case of enormous significance. In such an instance it is tempting to consider the concept of 'decisive power projection'. MacArthur used the case of Quebec to justify his planned attack at Inchon during the Korean War.[35]

Early modern naval power could significantly assist land operations. The Royal Navy's capture of Emden in 1759 covered the Prussian flank.[36] The British campaigns in the Peninsula—Napoleon's 'Spanish ulcer'—were facilitated by sea power. An amphibious threat could conceivably tie down troops in defence. Napoleon wrote: 'With 30 000 men in transports at the Downs, the English can paralyse 300 000 of my army, and that will reduce us to the rank of a second-class power'.[37] Navies also have an ability—invaluable when employed—to rescue defeated armies, such as Moore's at Corunna in 1809: a Napoleonic Dunkirk.

Amphibious power projection was notably difficult without a sympathetic local population. We can compare the successful Dutch invasion of England in 1688,[38] and the Peninsula War, with the failed Jacobite invasions of the British Isles and the loss of the American colonies. Above all, power projection could not succeed without sea control. The Spanish Armada of 1588 and Napoleon's plans in 1805 failed for this fundamental reason.

Naval diplomacy

There is an intimate and longstanding link between naval power and diplomacy. Persuasion and deterrence are about creating an image. Warships were and are well suited to creating the image and symbolism of power in the minds of the international community.[39] Naval strategy and

The Royal Navy's blockade of Cadiz in 1797 by Thomas Butterworth. Blockade, not sea battle, was the main strategic weapon of the Royal Navy in achieving command of the sea during the early modern era.
(National Maritime Museum, Greenwich)

diplomacy were together an effective English weapon in creating the alliance against France during the War of the Spanish Succession at the beginning of the eighteenth century.[40] Conversely, the French decision in favour of *guerre de course* in the 1690s resulted in a loss of international influence.[41] Diplomacy could serve strategy, as with Portugal's entry into the grand alliance in 1703, which gave the Royal Navy access to the port of Lisbon. Strategy could also serve diplomacy. Victory at the Nile in 1798 facilitated the new coalition against France.[42] In a true sense naval warfare is always coalition warfare, given the need for a maritime power to have allies on land, and naval strategy is therefore commonly combined with diplomacy.

Industrial revolution and Pax Britannica

The nineteenth century saw a changing strategic context for naval power, primarily as a result of new technology. The major developments were steam power, iron ships, and long-range guns. The industrial revolution, on one level, transformed naval capabilities. Commanders could plan precisely on the basis of sailing schedules. There was more immunity to weather conditions. There was greater speed and mobility for warships in action. Navies had increased power in littoral regions against coastal forts and harbours, and an ability to penetrate river systems. The submarine telegraph meant that the British battlefleet, kept in home waters, could be rapidly dispatched when and where needed overseas. Steam-powered ships, however, needed regular coaling and were thus more dependent on a global system of bases. It had been predicted that steam would level the playing field by enhancing the power of weaker navies. In the event it reinforced the strategic status quo. Britain still had the benefit of its maritime tradition, as well as being at the forefront of industrial change. The socio-economic context was therefore decisive. Britain continued to enjoy the naval supremacy won against Napoleon, and the Royal Navy became, in Andrew Lambert's phrase, the shield of Empire. Technological change enabled more effective pursuit of the traditional British strategies of sea control, blockade, and power projection.[43] There are parallels between the naval Pax Britannica of the nineteenth century and the post-Cold War era. The mid-nineteenth century saw a hegemonic power, faced with sometimes unclear threats (witness the Russian war scares), engaging in littoral warfare and power projection from the sea.

Themes in early modern naval strategy

It is possible to discern a number of significant themes in early modern naval strategy.

The silence of naval power

The axiom that naval power is silent, even imperceptible, is an old but largely valid one. Mahan called silence 'the most striking and awful mark of the working of Sea Power'.[44] Naval strategy worked (and works) indirectly and prospectively, and in conjunction with land power, diplomacy, and economic forces. (One reason why sea power is often difficult to comprehend is that it is effective without being in itself strategically conclusive.) It also works best having excluded rival naval power from the waters it controls. At its most effective, therefore, it is least visible and virtually silent. A case in point is the War of the Spanish Succession after 1705, when the grand alliance had command of the sea and used it.[45] At such times naval power can arguably alter the meaning of time in war, in favour of the counter-offensive, such as during the War of the Second Coalition after the Nile, and between Trafalgar in 1805 and Wellington's landing in Portugal in 1808.[46]

Strategic geography

The great mobility afforded by the sea enabled early modern naval power to capitalise on the opportunities of geography. Naval power, in conjunction with diplomacy, has a strategic capacity to encircle enemy configurations, as Britain did the continent to a greater or lesser extent during the Anglo–French wars. Early modern naval history revolved significantly around control of maritime choke points: focal areas still of great strategic importance, in particular Gibraltar, the Dardanelles, the Malacca Strait, and the Persian Gulf. There was (and is) great value in controlling both sides of strategic waterways such as the English Channel, which was an early modern British priority. In terms of sea control, it is notable that early modern naval strategy was necessarily offensive. Without such sea control—the prerogative to use its primary strategic environment—a maritime power is defeated.[47] The great admirals knew this: Drake in striking at Cadiz in 1587, Tromp in defeating the Spaniards at the Downs in 1639, and Nelson at Trafalgar in 1805.

Ocean and continent

Early modern land and sea power were inextricably connected. Landward defeat, for example, could impact on the naval balance of power, as when the American victory at Saratoga in 1777 led to French entry into the American War of Independence.[48] Naval defeat could also impact on land war, as did the French victory at the Chesapeake prior to the British surrender at Yorktown. The influence of a land–sea alliance and of continental commitment by a sea power is very clear, as with the Anglo–Dutch alliance during the 1690s. Britain's European continental commitment accelerated its rise as a great power, and the Anglo–Prussian alliance during the Seven Years War was rightly a famous combination. British continental strategy could create a French grand strategic problem as to whether to fight by land or sea. This was the case after the British victory at Quiberon Bay in 1759. After 1689, Britain was in a sense a continental power by virtue of possessing Holland and then Hanover.

Paul Kennedy argues persuasively that Britain's striking of a balance between ocean and continent was the key to its power and success.[49] Despite the wisdom of Frederick the Great in saying that he who defends everything defends nothing—meaning that strategy is always about choices—the hedging of bets in strategy, where possible, is always wise. One never knows exactly what kind of war will arise or how it will evolve.

Queen Elizabeth, often to the despair of her military advisers, walked a tightrope between maritime and continental strategies in a world of greater powers.[50] Conversely, fundamental problems arose for France as a continental power with a land frontier which was often distracting.[51] The European state system had virtually ensured this problem, which reduced the potential for a continental power to translate its assets into maritime leverage. The influence of the land–sea interface therefore played to British natural advantage and to French vulnerability.

The human factor

As always in naval history, the human factor was a force multiplier in the areas of command, morale, and strategic and tactical effectiveness. Trafalgar was effectively won before it was fought by a powerful combination of these elements directed against superior numbers. Nelson, like Cunningham and Nimitz after him, was a people person; it was part of his professionalism.

Nelson—a subject in himself—is of perennial fascination as a charismatic leader and a genius of naval warfare.[52] He remains to this day a model of leadership in war, combining creativity and ruthlessness in a way great commanders have always done. Above all, he allowed strategy to dictate the tactical aim. He then sought battle with knowledge of the enemy, brilliant innovation, and moral courage in calculating risk. He was well aware of the chaotic nature of battle, and of the impossibility of micro-managing amidst it. Preparation, delegation, simplicity, surprise, and inspiration, together with the technical excellence of sailors and subordinate commanders, were the keys to victory in advance. In his person and effect on others he exemplified the human factor in naval warfare. Nelson was a creation of the Royal Navy as well as a creator: an extraordinary man, like a great artist, perhaps impossible outside of his times.

Naval history, like all history, is also made by the interaction of generations, and rebellion and initiative must always be in dialogue with the status quo and occasionally overturn it. Human beings are naturally creatures of habit, and it is often initiative which counts. Nelson's generation progressively freed themselves from strategically indecisive line ahead tactics. They were also tempered by defeat in the American War—Britain's eighteenth-century Vietnam.

We may note three further points about the human factor. When considering the issue of command, it is worth remembering that great admirals could fail. Drake did at Lisbon in 1589, Tromp at the Gabbard in 1653, and Nelson at Tenerife in 1797. No human talent is ultimately proof against the circumstances and friction of war, nor against misjudgement.

Second, early modern naval strategy was sometimes made well by civilians, at least at the grand strategic level: Queen Elizabeth, Pitt the elder and Pitt the younger are cases in point. Third, the relatively small number of persons serving in the early modern Royal Navy (and all navies) is deceptive. The strategic value and significance of naval power is out of all proportion to the number of people it involves. Hence also its economy of human life and ability to make major strategic gains with far fewer casualties in comparison to land war. Ultimately the human factor was (and is) vital because strategy is an art, not a science.[53] It is about creating and exploiting possibilities, balancing risks and resources, and combining the big picture with detail. No one knew better than Nelson that war is not a bureaucratic system, but rather about seizing opportunities in a highly uncertain environment.

Choice and risk

Strategy is always about choices in relation to risks. Even Britain, as a great naval power by the late eighteenth century, was not immune to this problem. Britain's inability to help Prussia early in the Seven Years War put a strain on the alliance.[54] The Royal Navy, needing to concentrate in home waters, had insufficient ships for a Baltic fleet. Limitations on naval strategy are thus quantitative as well as qualitative. Risks must of course be calculated. The decision to send Nelson to the Mediterranean in 1798 was such a risk, depriving the home fleet of its strategic reserve.[55] Part of the Admiralty's approach to risk from the late seventeenth century was to preserve a balanced fleet, as between line of battle ships, frigates, and flotilla.[56] Different ship types, as Corbett knew, represent different ideas and possible strategic combinations, and a balanced fleet thus enhances strategic options.[57] It is a rare luxury to get the war one expects, and risks can be great. The American War of Independence evolved out of British control, and became—through loss of command of the sea—a grand strategic disaster.[58]

Strategy and context

Strategy and operations are dramatic and fascinating, but they are always conditioned by the contexts in which strategic choices are made, be those contexts political, ideological, economic, or otherwise.[59] Paul Kennedy's outstanding history of British sea power, *The Rise and Fall of British Naval Mastery*, a book which pioneered modern contextual naval history, focuses not on battles but on economics. Early modern strategy had its deeply economic context in relation to commerce war. The feasibility of the French *guerre de course*, for example, declined as colonial trade became more profitable than privateering. Ideological contexts should not be forgotten. The religious factor in sixteenth-century warfare is arguably reflected in the ferocity of the Armada battles.[60] The end of religious warfare produced a more multipolar Europe, and underlined the link between strategy and diplomacy in coalition building. Strategy is always formulated in a political context. This was certainly the case in eighteenth-century Britain, when ideas of blue-water strategy and continental commitment were inextricably bound up with party politics.[61]

Mahan, Corbett and the early modern strategic legacy

The classical strategists and their influence are a subject in themselves. Indisputably, however, the early twentieth century and the RAN at its birth were the inheritors of the early modern strategic legacy—especially that of the Royal Navy—both as tradition and as concepts mediated by Mahan and to a lesser extent Corbett. Australia was itself a major product of the British maritime diaspora. The great American naval historian Samuel Eliot Morison believed that the strategic traditions of the eighteenth century (in the forms of convoy, blockade, and amphibious warfare) had shaped early twentieth-century naval strategy, not least through Corbett's history of the Seven Years War.[62]

In the specifically Australian context, certain strategic themes clearly had early modern roots: a blue-water orientation and participation in global designs; sea control and trade defence; fleet action; power projection; a role in the land–sea interface; continental commitment even far from home; and possession of a balanced fleet. Essentially this was a compendium of early modern Royal Naval practice (which Corbett was in the process of codifying), popular Mahanian ideas, and Nelsonian hero-worship. It is an Anglo-Australian strategic profile, arguably not shared in the round by any other early twentieth-century navy save that of the United States. It set the scene for the Australian naval strategic tradition. The colonial apples do not fall far from the imperial tree.

The early modern era as strategic experience

At this point we must admit the devil's advocate to the discussion. Surely today we live in a different world, and surely technology has changed the strategic game out of recognition? To the question about a different world, the answer must be yes. Ours is, by and large, a decolonised international environment, which in this sense is removed from the naked power plays of the early modern era and of Mahan's generation (he died in 1914). Our world also evidences a different global balance of power, with greater wealth and influence rooted in the Asia–Pacific region. Our world is dependent upon oil as a vital industrial–strategic commodity. Our world is politically transformed, with powerful public opinion wanting quick, cheap victories, and impatient of the time involved in a naval strategy such as blockade. New zones of maritime territoriality are now impinging on the traditional high seas. Today there is internationalised flagging of vessels involved in maritime transport. None of these phenomena, however, necessarily negates the strategic value of navies and some indeed enhance it.

How far has the picture changed in terms of technology? To take one example (and probably the major one), we can consider air power. It has certainly changed the context in which naval strategy is formulated by introducing a new dimension, and in so doing helping to solve the problem of locating an enemy at sea (although other methods also now exist). It has greatly enhanced sea control and power projection capabilities, and radically altered the context of amphibious warfare. Such technology can alter the nature of strategic geography. The task of guarding the English Channel and employing it as an anti-invasion moat was complicated by air power. But as the German *Kriegsmarine* knew, the *Luftwaffe*'s strategic mission in 1940 was to achieve control of the air so as to neutralise the Royal Navy, without which precondition no invasion could be launched.[63] British air power in this instance admirably served traditional maritime strategy.

Strategy is of course evolutionary—food for thought in the age of the much-discussed 'Revolution in Military Affairs' (RMA).[64] The implications of the RMA will of course be profound, but we have lived through military revolutions before: the coming of gunpowder and sail, the coming of the line of battle ship, the coming of steam and iron, of submarine, air, and nuclear weaponry and power. The longer sweep of history cautions against the elevation of new and supposedly 'revolutionary' technology as a factor which will change everything. Monocausality is suspect as much in strategy as history. All wars are different, but many are similar. History is a school of loosely evolving strategic patterns, of change and continuity, both of which we neglect at our peril both intellectually and strategically.

What then are the continuing legacies and what is the continuing relevance of early modern strategy? These are less in the area of fleet engagement, and more in the value of a balanced fleet, and in the areas of blue-water sea control, trade protection and blockade, coastal defence, power projection, and naval diplomacy (witness the Taiwan Strait incident of 1996).⁶⁵ Certain themes are also highly pertinent: the use of strategic geography and choke points, the role of the land–sea interface, the vital human factor, the balance of choice and risk, and the importance of contexts. The ability of naval power to gain time, help structure a conflict and enable a counter-offensive was still evident in the Persian Gulf in 1990–91.⁶⁶

Why is this general legacy still relevant? Two-thirds of the globe is still connected water, and that water is still the primary means of heavy transport. National interests are still regional and global. The state system is still competitive and Hedley Bull's 'anarchical society'⁶⁷ and Michael Howard's 'rough world'⁶⁸ are still with us. War is still governed by friction; strategy is still about choices conditioned by unpredictable contexts; and naval power still affords an impressive variety of strategic options. And while Corbett is the theoretical ancestor of new doctrine for power projection from the sea, there has also been recent speculation that we may be entering a new Mahanian age—predicated on a globalising economy dependent upon sea transport and perhaps upon maritime resources.⁶⁹

Early modern history, with its continuing resonances, suggests credibly that sea power is the most successful strategic springboard in history. Throughout modern times, for five centuries, it has never been on the losing side of a major conflict, and this is surely food for thought. The way in which navies have acted as force multiplying factors for demographically small powers—Portugal, Holland, England—is also a lesson for Australia. On the other hand history, and early modern history, are of course irrelevant if one enjoys reinventing the wheel.

2 Sea power in modern strategy
Colin Gray

The nature of war does not change over time, but its character most certainly does. Similarly, the function and purpose of strategy effectively is eternal, but its tactical 'grammar' alters radically with technological, political, economic, and social developments.[1] It is my task, within the framework provided by the assumption that war and strategy are persistent in their nature, to examine the strategic significance of sea power in modern strategy, directly posed as questions. First, how important has sea power been in the strategic history of the twentieth century? Second, does that strategic history carry powerfully plausible implications for the probable importance of sea power in the twenty-first century?

I must begin by alerting the reader to a vital distinction drawn nearly a hundred years ago by Admiral Sir Reginald Custance, RN, between people of a 'materialist', and people of a 'historical', persuasion.[2] The 'materialists' are those who discern the possibility of strategic, even anti-strategic, transformation in every major change in material condition. To such people, history is a matter of antiquarian interest. To the 'historical' school, in contrast, each emerging military–technical revolution (MTR) can alter only the character of war, its grammar that is. I confess to being a card-carrying member of the 'historical' school—as defined by Admiral Custance—and I believe that war and strategy can be understood as well from Roman, Crusader, or Napoleonic, cases, as it can from NATO's trauma in the Balkans over the Wars of Yugoslavian Succession in the 1990s.

It is customary, indeed it is academically polite, to build a case and only then, eventually, to reveal that 'sea power', 'air power', 'cyberspace', or whatever, was the agent of victory or the culprit. I shall abandon custom and, instead, expose immediately the more key among the elements in my argument and also my conclusions. This chapter has a clear track of argument, so there is no special virtue in my attempting to pretend that everything is obscure until the Great Detective reveals all in the final scene of the final act. Notwithstanding some qualifications necessary for fit with time, place, and specific belligerent, this chapter suggests the following:

- Sea power sustained much of its relative strategic significance from 1900 to 2000. This claim is perhaps remarkable, given the pace and extensive domain of technological innovation in the twentieth century. Of course, this is not to deny that the relative significance of sea power is always specific to the actual historical case at issue. Sea power will count for more in some conflicts than in others.
- Sea power, in common with land power, has somewhat changed in its technical, tactical, and operational meaning, from 1900 to 2000. I will argue that both sea power and land power, though especially sea power, have adapted to changing circumstances very largely by co-opting new capabilities.
- By and large, the reasons why sea power was strategically and politically potent in 1900 persist to the year 2000, and—dare we venture the speculation—are likely to persist to the year 2100 also.
- In practice, cumulatively radical, even non-linear, changes in the character of modern warfare have not sidelined sea power. Sea power has not merely survived technical–tactical and operational challenge, rather it has embraced that challenge to make more of itself.
- The twentieth century in one sense has seen a rise in continental-based power. But a strategic lesson of this century now all but passed is that sea power deriving from a continental scale of resources enjoys a systemic advantage over continental land power. If continental-scale powers triumphed in the twentieth century, they triumphed quite substantially through the agency of sea power resting upon a continental fund of assets.
- There are few, if any, conflicts that sea power can wage and win effectively unaided by substantial support from land, air, space, or cyberspace. Indeed, so imperial has first-class military sea power become that it can be difficult to see the seams between sea power, air power, land power, and so forth. Sensibly viewed, there is no trend extant today that suggests a decline in the strategic importance of sea power.

My argument, at core, is that strategic history shows a growing complexity, as additional geographical environments are exploited. In the twentieth century the strategist has had to adjust to exploit no fewer than three new environments for war: the air, space, and the electromagnetic spectrum (EMS), or if you prefer, the 'ether', and cyberspace. Moreover, that move from an 1899 with just two environments—the land and the surface of the sea—to a 1999 with no fewer than five, ignores the added challenge of sub-surface warfare, and the wild card of weapons of mass destruction. As if all this were not complicated enough even as simply posed, there is the fact that the new environments for war—air, space, and the EMS—have strategic effect not only in their own right, but also by their implication for the potency or otherwise of land power and sea power. The other, no less essential, thread to my argument is that the many linear, and even non-linear, changes in strategic affairs in the twentieth century have produced what amounts to a progressive layering of factors.

Properly viewed, I suggest that the strategic history of this past century has registered a succession of revolutions in military affairs (RMA)—certainly a succession of MTRs—that have not *superseded* each other.[3] The artillery-led combined arms military revolution of 1916–18 was not really superseded by an air revolution, a revolution led by armoured/mechanised forces, a nuclear revolution, a missile revolution, or an information revolution. Instead, what we have at the beginning of a new century is a military environment that from the high end to the low end of capability contains virtually all of the additions of the previous century, but which has retired scarcely anything. Military historians are fairly persuasive when they argue that 'modern warfare' was invented and first practised in 1916–18.[4] But they are also persuasive when they argue that 'modern warfare' was invented in 1807–09, or was it in 1861–65?[5] You will have to define for yourself what it is that makes for 'modernity' in war. What I am offering now is a restatement of the earlier cited opposition between so-called 'materialist' and 'historical' schools of thought. Those among us of an 'historical' persuasion can grant readily the probable reality of new military–technical accomplishment. But we are not about to concede that strategic affairs can be transformed or revolutionised by new equipment.[6] Let me illustrate my arguments with reference to events a century apart.

In 1899, Great Britain, for the British Empire, mismanaged a major regional war in Southern Africa.[7] In 1999, Great Britain took a politically leading, and militarily no less than second, place in a conflict at least as badly misdirected as was the Second Boer War. Fortunately, Boer strategy and Serb strategy were only slightly superior to, respectively, British and NATO strategy; a fact which meant that the much bigger battalions had to win. In the Second Boer War of 1899–1902, sea power was the great enabler of British military power projection into Southern Africa. In 1999 over Kosovo, NATO's exclusive maritime dominion was a fact of only minor significance. That was not because trends in relative military effectiveness have been disadvantageous to sea power. Rather, sea power played only modestly in 1999 because of the unique geopolitics of that particular conflict, and because of some poor strategic choices made by NATO.

Any and every generalisation about sea power and strategy theoretically has to be subject to qualification for authority by reference to specific historical and geographical contexts. That is unarguable; it is also a matter of only secondary moment. Far more important is the fact that to date sea power, even naval power narrowly, has resisted successfully every implicit and explicit challenge to its relevance. Just possibly, there may be some political, economic, social, or more likely technological development lurking in ambush for sea power, or naval power, in the twenty-first century. We can prove, and disprove, nothing about a future which, by definition, has yet to happen. Nonetheless, today I am willing to venture the prediction that strategic analysts in the year 2099 will regard commercial and military sea power very much as I do now. Of course, this is a personally safe prediction!

Bearing in mind that this is a volume on naval history, I devote the main body of this chapter to our strategic experience with sea power in the twentieth century. I shall return to the future prospects for sea power towards the end of my remarks.

Mahan was (mainly) right

The strategic experience of the twentieth century has demonstrated that Rear Admiral Alfred Thayer Mahan, USN, was wiser than his critics. Indeed, Mahan is a serious candidate for nomination as the most underrated theorist of modern strategy. No less a historian than Paul M. Kennedy, in a book chapter entitled 'Mahan versus Mackinder', arguably misunderstands Mahan and the common and uncommon elements in the strategic ideas of the two theorists, miscasting the strategic history of this century: perhaps surprising for such a prominent contemporary historian of sea power.[8]

Contrary to Kennedy's argument, as geopolitical and geostrategic thinkers both Sir Halford Mackinder and Mahan are more correct than in error, and their strategic theories generally are complementary. Mahan was right to emphasise the strength of the influence of sea power upon history.[9] But Mackinder was right to predict that the pecking order in world power among polities was shifting in favour of great continental states as a consequence of the revolution in convenience of ground transportation effected first by the railway and then by the internal combustion engine.[10]

Far from eclipsing sea power, however, the rise of great unified and cohesive continental powers, especially the United States, has resulted in Mackinder's 'Columbian Era' (c. 1500–c. 1900) being extended indefinitely.[11] A small insular power such as Britain (notwithstanding its Empire upon which the sun never set) could not compete alone against a very

Rear Admiral Alfred Thayer Mahan, USN (1840–1914) (left) and Sir Julian Corbett (1854–1922) have proved two of the most enduring philosophers of sea power. Unfortunately, like most prophets they are both more often quoted than read. (NH 48056-KN, RAN)

large continental power with mature land communications. But, except from 20 June 1940 until 22 June 1941, Britain was not obliged to stand alone in a stark confrontation between dominant land power and dominant sea power.

The careful reader of a substantial fraction of Mahan's writings, particularly if augmented by acquaintance with the histories and theoretical texts of Sir Julian Corbett, would be well equipped to understand both sea power in strategic history in general, and the prospective advantages and limitations of sea power in the twenty-first century.[12] Sea power, especially naval power, certainly does not enjoy today the kind of unique prominence in public strategic and politically symbolic regard that obtained a century ago. Nonetheless, even though the growing complexity of the grammar of strategy requires modern sea power to compete for attention with weapons of mass destruction, with very smart weapons deliverable by air power, and with information warfare, it has proved more than equal to the challenge. If great navies, in particular the greatest of navies, lost strategic significance relative to the other services as the twentieth century advanced—a debatable proposition, at best—still they reached century's end with the stamp of strategic indispensability upon them. The predictions of a century ago that sea powers would be overwhelmed by land powers have been shown to be as unfounded as were the predictions in midcentury to the effect that air power in general, and atomic-armed air (and missile) power in particular must consign military sea power to the column of yesterday's instruments of war.

It is of the essence of sea power to function as a great enabling instrument of strategy, to be adaptable to evolving technological and tactical conditions, and to function at all levels of conflict with enormous flexibility.[13] Sea power is no longer *the* enabling instrument that once it was prior to the development of air power; indeed modern sea power both incorporates, and itself is enabled to operate by, air power. Nonetheless, the significance of sea power for modern strategy is well captured in parallel claims made by Admiral Sir Herbert Richmond and by the historian Correlli Barnett. Richmond writes of World War II that although '[s]ea power did not win the war itself: it enabled the war to be won'.[14] Barnett offers the judgement that '[f]or the Western Allies, therefore, sea power remained as ever the midwife of victory on land'.[15] Generically similar, if weaker, claims can be advanced for the strategic enabling contributions of sea power towards the Western victories of 1918 and 1989. In the two World Wars and the Cold War the Western Allies functioned as a maritime alliance, which is to say that the principal lines of communication among allies were maritime rather than continental.

Sea power in all its forms, military and civilian, played critical strategic enabling roles in the years 1914–18, 1939–45, and for NATO and the defence of Japan and other East Asian friends and allies of the West from 1949 until 1989.[16] From 1940 until 1944 for war in Europe, and necessarily for the whole of the Pacific War, the Western Allies were obliged by geostrategic circumstances to adopt a maritime strategy in the strictest of the senses conveyed by Corbett. He wrote: '[b]y maritime strategy we mean the principles which govern a war in which the sea is a substantial factor'.[17] The expulsion of the BEF from the continent in May–June 1940 meant that the eventual Allied return to the European land war could be achieved only by amphibious operations on the grandest of scales. The years 1943 and 1944 witnessed the exercise of an amphibious maritime strategy with a vengeance indeed.[18]

The operational and strategic contexts of World War I and the Cold War were radically different for the Western Allies from the circumstances of 1940–44. In both 1914–18 and 1947–89, Western–Allied sea power sustained, enabled perhaps, respectively an extant or a potential fighting front on land. Neither in World War I, nor in the Cold War, was amphibious strategy ever a major enterprise, let alone the main event. Military planners during the Cold War generally were unimpressed by the

HMAS *Sydney* patrolling the North Sea with elements of the British 4th Battle Squadron during the Great War. Australian warships usually operated as an integral part of the Royal Navy, sustaining the maritime strategic links between the Allied nations which allowed the war on land to continue. (RAN)

operational practicability of amphibious action in the face of nuclear threat. In addition, deep uncertainties pervaded maritime operations in the context of a possible World War III. Should Soviet forces well on the road to Calais after only four or five days of fighting have triggered a nuclear response by NATO, and had that nuclear response tripped the switches for a general nuclear 'exchange', it is difficult to understand how sea power could have played its traditional strategic enabling role.

The adaptability characteristic at least of a well-funded navy helps explain why sea power broadly, and navies narrowly, have not been eclipsed in tactical, operational, strategic, or political relevance by the grammar of modern strategy. Navies responded to each of the more significant military developments of the twentieth century with a strategy of co-option. Far from threatening the strategic integrity of sea power, or navies, the emergence of air power, the maturing of the nuclear revolution, the arrival of space power, and most recently the proclaimed dawning of the Tofflers' 'Third Wave' of warfare (information war and information-led war),[19] have been exploited so that powerful navies can become still more powerful. In modern strategy thus far, at least, the ever changing grammar of war has yet to sound the death knell either for navies writ large, or even for surface naval vessels as major combatants. Small, or technically or tactically inferior fleets, find it more and more difficult to operate at sea in the face of the instruments for oceanic surveillance and transparency owned by the leading navies. That condition of operational disadvantage, however, in principle is long familiar.

The flexibility of sea power derives from the fact that the world's land area is essentially insular in geostrategic character (and much of that land area is penetrated by navigable rivers). Seventy-one per cent of the surface of the earth is water, a significant percentage of the world's population lives within 200 kilometres of the sea, and naval power can loiter with variable menace for long periods without intruding into geography owned by friends or potential foes.[20] For the swift obliteration of a roguish foe and its neighbourhood it would be difficult to improve upon employment of nuclear-armed ICBMs. For the precise and rapid bombardment of an enemy there is no plausible alternative to air, or air-breathing missile, strikes. But, for evidence of resolve that translates into the operational ability to loiter for a long time in the region of interest without leaving one's sovereign bases, and to project power of all kinds across the shore (from raiding parties to nuclear strikes), balanced naval power is the military instrument of first choice. A navy can provide the presence that expresses national concern, without necessarily threatening a potential adversary provocatively. The reason why naval power is so preferred is because it offers prudent policymakers optimum flexibility.

Some of the advantages of sea power also can be viewed as limitations, or indeed are strictly chimerical for many second-class navies. Notwithstanding the occasional feasibility of cunning stratagems and devilish devices that can offset brute superiority, the sea, in common with the air and earth orbit, is unforgiving of weakness. The substantially uniform aspects to those geographical environments deny the second-class navy, air force, or space force, anywhere in which to hide with confidence. There can be no fortifiable refuges at sea (though the undersea realm is something of a sanctuary), in the air, or in space at all analogous to the defensibility of city rubble, triple cover jungle, or mountains. The tactical value of humanly altered and natural terrain varies with technology and political context, but overall it continues to offer assistance to those who are at a disadvantage in open and regular land warfare.

Clausewitz insisted plausibly that 'defence is the stronger form of waging war' *on land*.[21] At sea, as Mahan noted in contrast, the offence has a systemic advantage.[22] On land, the side on the tactical offensive has to expose itself as it moves, while the tactical defensive can prepare the ground and remain more or less under cover. At sea, in the air, and in space, the reality of strategy's grammar is that both tactical offence and defence must expose themselves.

Sea power offers the inherent advantages of adaptability, flexibility, and mobility on, under, and over the environment that covers most of the surface of the earth and which surrounds the continental islands. If sea power characteristically continues to be a—though no longer *the*—great strategic enabler, that quality is a limitation as well as a source of advantage. Except for those rare strategic contexts wherein war at sea, relatively small-scale power projection across the shore, or coercive diplomacy by naval means alone, can generate adequate strategic effect for war termination, sea power can be only an enabler.[23] It is a limitation of sea power that it cannot come to grips with a great continental power with a realistic prospect of success. Strategic history has registered several notable contexts of stalemate between the 'whale and the elephant' (or 'the tiger and the shark').[24] Superior sea power enables some other kind of (military) power to win a war. Britain's Royal Navy alone could not defeat Napoleonic France or Wilhelmine or Nazi Germany. Furthermore, that Royal Navy could not even compel the navies of France and Germany to put to sea so that they could be sunk.

In addition to the limitation that sea power, even at its most competent, usually can only enable other military instruments to win wars, it is important to recognise just how slowly sea power generates its strategic effect. It is paradoxical that although naval battles in modern history have lasted only for hours, the benefits (or the disadvantages) of victory (or defeat) can require years to yield their full crop of strategic consequences. The prudent grammar of strategy for war at sea can oblige both sides to conduct a long campaign; witness the two 'Battles' of the Atlantic waged in this century. However, the mighty significance of the technical vehicle for navies—even though, tactically speaking, the human dimension remains critical[25]—translates as a sovereignty of costs that confines fighting fleets to modest numbers of 'capital' ships.[26] A handful of combat events thus can transform the condition of naval balance. So, although maritime geography is merciless on numerically disadvantaged navies, it also is the case that naval superiority for control of the sea is ever likely to be fragile.[27] In modern times the cutting edge of the combat prowess of the US Navy has resided in no more than ten to fifteen discrete vehicles, the fleet aircraft carriers.

It is not a sensible criticism of sea power to note that it functions strategically only slowly; such is its strategic nature. Understanding of the grammar of strategy has to include recognition that for all its advantages in flexibility, adaptability, global mobility, and as a great enabler, sea power is constrained systemically by its dominant need to operate successfully in the maritime environment. In other words, sea power first has to earn the right through combat at sea, before it can work as a strategic instrument to help decide whether a war will be won. The issue, therefore, has to be allowed to descend from the abstractions of sea power and sea lines of communication, down to the historical specificity of actual navies with ships, aircraft, and other weapon systems (e.g., mines, coastal artillery).[28]

As Mahan observed on the fundamentals, 'the sea ... is the great highway', or 'a wide common', and 'both travel and traffic by water have always been easier and cheaper than by land'.[29] These fundamentals, which remained valid throughout the twentieth century, help explain the strategic advantages of sea power as a flexible, adaptive, and mobile, 'enabler'. But, is the grammar of strategy for sea power the same for maritime, as for continental, powers? Do second- and third-class navies sail in the same waters of theory and military practice as do the navies of the first rank in combat prowess? Few are the Anglo–American theorists who have recognised this question as referring to a potentially serious strategic challenge. Two exceptions, writing 90 years apart, are Charles E. Callwell and N.A.M. Rodger. In 1905, Callwell observed that

> We [British] with our vast naval resources and noble traditions of the sea, are inclined to regard the noble art of maritime war solely from the point of view of the stronger side. We are prone to forget that when in any set of operations the conditions dictate the adoption of an aggressive attitude to one belligerent, those conditions may dictate the adoption of a Fabian policy [i.e., a policy of evasion and delay] to the other belligerent. It is often forgotten that the destruction of a hostile navy cannot easily be accomplished, even when that navy represents only a relatively speaking feeble fighting force, unless it accepts battle in the open sea.[30]

The difficulty the Royal Navy was to find in bringing German major fleet units to battle in 1914–18, and again in 1939–45 attests to the wisdom in Callwell's cautionary judgement.

A much more general variant upon Callwell's theme is recorded by Rodger when he offers the following conclusion upon the naval writings of the twentieth century:

> The experience of a century of naval war has taught us many ways in which Mahan's ideas were inadequate and superficial, but it cannot be said that we have today any general explanation of how naval power works and why it is important which can credibly be applied to many different nations and navies (not just the British and the Americans) in the circumstances of the past and the present.[31]

Mahan's ideas were far from 'superficial' and were to prove no more 'inadequate' than one could reasonably expect of a single theorist.

Rodger is right in flagging the absence of a truly general theory of 'naval power ... which can credibly be applied to many different nations and navies', but it is distinctly possible that he has misunderstood the real problem. It is, after all, in the nature of sea power—let alone naval power, more narrowly—that explanation of its working and strategic effect can constitute only a partial theory of strategy and war. When Corbett advised that '[b]y maritime strategy we mean the principles which govern a war in which the sea is a substantial factor', he all but invited misunderstanding by his readers. The fact is that great continental powers such as Germany and Russia, notwithstanding the traditional primacy of land power in their dominant theories of war, have been obliged to find a maritime strategy, even in Corbett's British sense of the concept.

From the 1850s until the end of the 1980s, both Russia and Germany waged conflicts in which 'the sea is a substantial factor'. Specifically, Russia's foes in 1854–56, 1904–05, and 1947–89, and Germany's foes in 1914–18 and 1939–45, were countries or coalitions strategically dependent upon the exercise of sea power. Russia and Germany had no strategic need to use the seas as did their essentially maritime opponents, but that is not the point. The point is that Russia and Germany repeatedly had the most pressing need to deny their foes the ability to use the seas at will.

The quest for a theory of naval power that, following Rodger, accommodates the different circumstances among navies of varying purpose, scale, and competence, still probably should look no further than to Mahan, Corbett, and the Anglo–American tradition of theory of dominant sea power. Three theoretical points are central. First, 'the function of the fleet in war', to deploy Corbett's famous formula,[32] must always depend upon the general strategy pursued: to repeat, belligerents wage war, not sea war. Second, the significance of the strategic effect of a belligerent's sea power relative to its land, air, space, or cyber power must vary with the details of particular conflicts. Third, war at, and from, the sea, is a unity; navies of different levels of military effectiveness are not at liberty to pick the rules of engagement that suit them best while remaining competitive in the maritime sphere. A second-class navy can choose not to risk surface battle, but it cannot so choose and expect to be able to use the seas for positive purposes. Mahan was right. Small, perhaps smaller, navies are of course not only at liberty, they are maximally motivated to discover and exploit operational, tactical and technical terms of engagement for the advantageous conduct of asymmetrical war at sea. For example, if the Royal Navy's battlefleet cannot be challenged to trial by combat by the like French or German battlefleets, then the French or German naval authorities will endeavour to defeat the Royal Navy's battlefleet in detail by maritime 'ambush', or will seek to evade its military authority by striking at British trade with the waging of *guerre de course*.[33]

To date, with the interesting and arguably sole exception of the United States submarine campaign against the sea lines of communication of

Imperial Japan,[34] the hunt for ways to evade the Mahanian logic of success in war at sea have not been well rewarded. That logic emphasised the role of the battlefleet to fight for command. If sea power is a great strategically enabling agent for maritime-oriented coalitions, then it has to follow that the rivals of those coalitions, be they similarly maritime or be they continental in primary focus, have to find ways to disable that otherwise enabling hostile sea power. The efforts at disablement do not have to take maritime form. In common with Alexander the Great, one might disable, indeed annihilate, an enemy's superior sea power by taking its naval bases from the landward side.[35] Alternatively, one might seek to defeat superior sea power politically and strategically. For example, Hitler's Germany sought to defeat superior Anglo (–American) sea power primarily by achieving so extensive and conclusive a range of continental conquest in the East that Britain would judge further conduct of hostilities futile. In addition, Hitler calculated that the defeat of the USSR would so liberate Japan to expand in the Asia–Pacific region that the United States would be distracted from Europe for years to come by that challenge. Bearing in mind the enabling character of sea power, there was indeed strategic reason behind Hitler's move to deprive Britain of a (Soviet) continental sword. Napoleon had entertained the same thought, had let theory be his guide, and made the same mistake with his crossing of the Niemen and drive on Moscow. In the expansive and overambitious words of the Emperor: '*Je veux conquérir la mer par la puissance de terre*'.[36]

Mahan advised that sea power was critical to world power, that the core of sea power was the battlefleet, and that offence was the best defence at sea.[37] Modern strategic history has shown that belligerents dominant at sea consistently have been successful in regular forms of major war, and that attempts by disadvantaged navies to evade the problems posed by a superior enemy battlefleet have not succeeded. Mahan's reputation as a theorist was long overdue for the kind of favourable reappraisal effected recently by Jon Sumida. Unlike Corbett, Mahan did not exaggerate the strategic merit in an amphibiously British way in warfare; also unlike Corbett, wisely he saw continuing value in the practice of convoy.[38] Above all else, perhaps, Mahan grasped the point that a belligerent who must control the sea in order to use it—as contrasted with a belligerent who must seek only to deny such control—has to be willing and able to give battle on demand.

Because sea power is only an enabling instrument of strategy, prominent among the conditions for success in its exercise is a conflict of sufficient duration for its working to be strategically effective. There is nothing magically effective about superior sea power for war as a whole, even for a war of long duration. The United States was unchallenged at sea during the war in Vietnam, but the dominance of the US Navy—

a navy that truly fused the capabilities of sea power and air power—did not enable victory to be won. The American war effort on land in Vietnam proved to be beyond help from the sea, no matter how magnificently the sea was commanded. An enemy such as North Vietnam, with a long coastline in a long war, should be notably vulnerable to the strategic effect that sea power can generate. In practice, though, the vital qualification *ceteris paribus* intrudes to upset the apparent logic of maritime-friendly geostrategy. For political as well as military reasons, the world's premier navy and marine corps was unable credibly so to menace action across the foe's homeland shore that North Vietnam would have been obliged to retain its army entirely north of the seventeenth parallel. Countries with long coastlines are not always vulnerable to power projection from the sea, because the details of particular conflicts yield exceptions to general rules.

For another example, Mahan was right, in general, with his claim that the *guerre de course* does not work as an alternative to a quest after sea control via decisive battle.[39] But, no general rule can be entirely proof against operational and tactical folly. The Imperial Japanese Navy inadvertently did all that it could to ensure the success of the US Navy's submarine campaign against its always overstretched merchant marine.

The technical and tactical conditions for war at sea have changed in modern times, but it is less obvious that revolution has attended the course of modern sea power operationally or strategically. That judgement may appear unduly conservative. After all, a century ago navies anticipated the conduct of war at sea with terms of engagement, or the declining of such by the weaker fleet, not radically dissimilar from those of the great war against France. 'Ships of the line', reclassified as battleships or capital ships, would deploy with careful choreography in line ahead to contend for the decision by means of gunnery.[40] This one-dimensional tactical context was increasingly complicated first by the menace of surface torpedo boats, next by the threat of submarine mines, and then by the peril posed by submarines. If there is little surprise that the Battle of Jutland on 31 May 1916 was primarily a brief passage of arms between the great guns of two lines of battleships, with hindsight it is perhaps strange to recollect that as late as 4 June 1942 Admiral Yamamoto intended to use the gun power of his nine battleships to conclude business with the US Pacific Fleet at Midway.[41]

The detail of sea warfare, the grammar of strategy for war at sea, has been manifestly transformed by the maturing of mine, torpedo, and submarine technologies, by the appearance and development of radio communications, radar and electronic and counter-electronic warfare, by the development of air power, by the appearance of missiles for offence and defence, by the arrival, and now apparent departure (for the US, if not the

Russian, fleet), of nuclear armament, by the systematic availability (in times of peace and crisis, at least) of assistance to communicate, navigate, target, and predict the weather from space systems, and finally by the exploitation of cyberspace for the conduct of information-led, network-centric warfare at and from the sea.[42] What do those changes mean for the strategic significance of sea power and navies?

The grammar of strategy for sea warfare matters critically, because tactical, technical, or operational misunderstanding of the true terms of contemporary military engagement can be strategically fatal. No matter what the theoretical benefits of superior sea power may be, if that sea power is expended witlessly in tactically hopeless operations of war, its strategic leverage will be strictly moot. Having granted the vital importance of military competence in the tactical conditions that obtain, still it must be said that the evolution in those conditions has not translated into a strategic revolution. With the sole exception of nuclear peril, the myriad and synergistic changes in the grammar of strategy as it bears upon sea power have left navies today strategically very much where they were 50 or even 100 years ago. A powerful navy at the beginning of the twenty-first century functions as an enabling instrument of national or coalition strategy. It knits together by means of cost-effectively maritime 'lines' of communication the global resources of allies. It can project military power against and across the shore; and it provides these services flexibly and adaptably.[43] Today, such sea power includes air power, amphibious striking power, some space power, and awesome capability in electronic and counter-electronic warfare. The grammar of strategy for modern sea power, however, for all its often frenetic pace of technical and tactical change, continues to be broadly compatible with ideas on its leverage that require scant amendments for changing eras.

Sea power and war in the twenty-first century: concluding thoughts

Far from heralding and sealing the demise of 'the Columbian Era', the twentieth century witnessed successive strategic (political and commercial) triumphs for maritime power, *and for maritime powers*. In fact, today, at the start of a new century, both American and British military postures and policies are acquiring an ever more classically maritime cast to them. The British Labour Government's Strategic Defence Review—only recently completed—explicitly announces a shift of strategic emphasis in favour of a maritime expeditionary tilt.[44] Liberated from near total focus upon NATO's Central Front along the erstwhile inner German border, and from the need to protect the North Atlantic logistic bridge, the British armed forces are thinking in some suitably classic (perhaps nineteenth-century) ways about how amphibious (now triphibious) power can serve foreign policy. Currently, the leading British military policy issues pertain to the undue heaviness of their land forces, to the shortage of numbers of light infantry battalions, and to the prospect of their forces actually being equipped as they should be. The relative importance of maritime power is not an issue in Britain today. The issue, to repeat, is whether the current, and future, government will actually buy enough of it.

If we turn to consider the United States at century's beginning, as in the British case we find no very noteworthy debate about the significance of maritime power, sea power, or naval power narrowly. Rather do the more hotly debated issues relate to the wisdom of planning a reduction in major surface combatant numbers down to 116, eventually perhaps sinking into the high 90s,[45] and—the driving reason behind that reduction—the wisdom of investing strictly in high-tech, most expensive equipment. With reference to policy, strategy, and ultimately force structure, questions persist about the character of war at and from the sea in the twenty-first century.[46] Necessarily, those questions must transcend technical debate about the cost and effectiveness of network-centric warfare capabilities, and slide into political futurology about possible or probable adversaries at sea. Who will be America's, indeed the West's, (maritime) foes 20, 30, and 40 years from now—and *where do they live*? Is there an open-ocean/ blue-water threat likely to be of strategic concern to us within the lifespan of the fleet that currently we say we will acquire? The two large (40 000– 50 000 ton, 50-aircraft) carriers that the British Royal Navy has been promised could, if ever constructed, launched and commissioned, still be in active service in the 2050s and even 2060s. Naturally, one's grasp of the details of military maritime security 60 years hence is more than a little tenuous.

I began this chapter by posing two extremely broad questions: First, how important has sea power been in the strategic history of the twentieth century; second, does that strategic history carry powerfully plausible implications for the probable importance of sea power in the twenty-first century? I believe that I have answered the first question directly by showing how sea power has adapted successfully to a changing context, and has co-opted technical–tactical rivals. There is much debate today about how much navy we need, and what it should be required to be able to do. But to the best of my knowledge there is no—repeat *no*—debate of interest anywhere on the proposition that naval power narrowly, let alone sea power writ large, is being sidelined by the course of history.

My second question, concerning sea power and naval power in the future, I believe I have answered indirectly, though largely by plain inference. Let me be more direct and offer some predictions.

- The many uses of the sea are increasing, not decreasing, in absolute importance (these uses include trade, fisheries, sea-based resources, and leisure, as well as military battlespace).[47]
- Global geography and the laws of physics oblige security communities to exploit the sea militarily. Of course, we can bombard from altitude, but bombardment is not synonymous with war. This is not to deny that sea-based forces have some, though only some, advantage over land, air, and space-based forces, for the conduct of aerial assault. (In fact, because of the nature of ships and the basic elements of geography, there is always the risk that navies are regarded too much as instruments of power projection *as mobile fire bases alone*).
- The strategic demand for naval power nested in military power overall is not, alas, going to dry up in the twenty-first century.[48] Some scholars and other pundits in the 1990s—as in earlier post-war eras—have speculated in praise of sundry transformational myths. I must advise that the social institution of war is, as Clausewitz noted, a true chameleon,[49] if anything even more adaptable than is naval power to changing times. Major war is neither obsolete nor obsolescent.[50] Claims to the contrary reflect either tortured definitions of key terms or a lack of empathy for the true inhumanity of humanity.[51] Armed conflict in the near future, as today, may resemble an odd mixture of Homer and Tom Clancy, but it will still be armed conflict—pre-modern, modern, and postmodern.
- Finally, the warfare that assuredly will threaten and occur in the twenty-first century will not be of a kind that retires naval power. Yes, in principle ships, especially surface ships, will be vulnerable in the future. But ships have always been vulnerable, just as aircraft and armoured fighting vehicles, and indeed human beings, are vulnerable. Warfare is dangerous. It was always so. Vulnerability is neither a matter of simple either/or, nor is it an existential technical–tactical fact for a whole era. The details of political, strategic, operational, tactical, and technical choices really count. There is a constant tactical dialogue between offence and defence, and hiding and finding, just as it is in the nature of conflict to be paradoxical as two or more adversaries seek to impose their will.[52] One can always sink navies, *notionally*, with extraordinary out-of-context menace (barrage fire by nuclear-armed missiles, for example). But strategic history to date has seen off every one such.

I have no hesitation in concluding this chapter with the dual conservative and radical prediction that navies will remain in the new century much as they have done in the previous one, only with some different equipment. No revolution in political affairs, strategic affairs, or technology, is going to leave sea power or naval power irrelevantly on the beach.

3 History and theory: the Clausewitzian ideal and its implications
Jon Sumida

> Clausewitz's work stands out among those very few older books which have presented profound and original insights that have not been adequately absorbed in later literature.
>
> Bernard Brodie, 1976

In the opening sentences of *Some Principles of Maritime Strategy*, Julian Corbett, Britain's most important historian and theorist of naval conflict, expressed views on the value of war theory that were similar to those of Carl von Clausewitz, the author of *On War*. 'At first sight,' he observed,

> nothing can appear more unpractical, less promising of useful result, than to approach the study of war with a theory. There seems indeed to be something essentially antagonistic between the habit of mind that seeks theoretical guidance and that which makes for the successful conduct of war. The conduct of war is so much a question of personality, of character, of common-sense, of rapid decision upon complex and ever-shifting factors, and those factors themselves are so varied, so intangible, so dependent upon unstable moral and physical conditions, that it seems incapable of being reduced to anything like true scientific analysis.[1]

Corbett went on to quote Clausewitz's views on the proper role of theory not as a prescriber of conduct in battle, but as a guide to self-education.

HISTORY AND THEORY

Carl von Clausewitz (1780–1831) at age 50. (RAN)

But Corbett then proceeded to describe roles for theory that in effect called for the creation of a system of rules and carefully defined language. He maintained that properly contrived theory disseminated throughout the officer corps would ensure that directives from the commander-in-chief would be correctly understood and implemented and, even more importantly, such theory would provide the senior naval and military officers in the field or at sea on the one hand, and their naval, military, and civilian superiors 'at the Council table at home' on the other, with a structured form of discourse that would minimise confusion and thus expedite deliberations.[2] Aware that this contradicted Clausewitz's position, Corbett found it necessary to observe that this use of theory could be over-valued and that 'a strategical maxim' was not to be 'trusted in action'.[3] He then went on, however, to argue that the purpose of theory was to 'determine the normal' in order to have a basis for identifying and evaluating exceptional cases, and concluded with a specific strategic recommendation for a maritime power.[4]

Corbett's approach was in fact inherently prescriptive. His disclaimers notwithstanding, he was a builder of systems, however qualified and sophisticated. Moreover, Corbett rejected the possibility of theory engaging the question of decision-making by commanders in the war crisis, which was one of Clausewitz's primary concerns. 'Theory is in fact,' Corbett wrote, 'a question of education and deliberation, and not of execution at all. That depends on the combination of intangible human qualities which we call executive ability.'[5] Corbett, in other words, used theory to deal with strategic planning while excluding the question of war command. Such an approach seems to have alienated a good number of his pupils at the Royal Navy's war college, a response that Clausewitz would have regarded as appropriate. The German author had written in *On War* about military theory that dealt with planning as opposed to command: 'What is the practical value of those obscure, partially false, confused and arbitrary notions? Very little—so little that they have made theory, from its beginnings, the very opposite of practice, and not infrequently the laughing stock of men whose military competence is beyond dispute.'[6]

Establishing that Corbett and Clausewitz differed fundamentally with respect to the value of prescriptive war theory is one thing. Identifying exactly what Clausewitz thought non-prescriptive war theory was is another. The purpose of this chapter is to explain clearly what Clausewitz's thinking about the latter was, and by so doing to demonstrate that Corbett's historical and theoretical writing cannot be characterised, as has sometimes been the case, as Clausewitzian.[7] More generally, this chapter's findings are intended to challenge the basic outlook of previous studies on *On War*. The author is not a specialist on Clausewitz, German military history, or strategic theory, and his knowledge of *On War* is based upon reading it in translation. Charges of impudence, therefore, would not lack foundation. That being said, I am comforted by Isaiah Berlin's observation, under somewhat similar circumstances, that 'where more than twenty interpretations hold the field, the addition of one more cannot be deemed as impertinence'.[8]

'War,' wrote Prussian Major-General Carl von Clausewitz, 'is merely the continuation of policy [politics] by other means'.[9] Although *On War*, the book from which the famous aphorism comes, is about many important things, the adjective 'Clausewitzian' invariably refers to the concept of war as an instrument of policy.[10] This proposition is commonly interpreted as having two major aspects. In the first place, use of armed force should have well-defined and attainable ends—that is, the resort to and direction of war should be rational. In the second place, the regime of rationality could dictate that an act that was advantageous from a purely military standpoint might justifiably be rejected on political grounds. Viewed in these terms, Clausewitz serves as a patron of reason and restraint, attractive qualities in a century that has experienced two catastrophic world wars and faced the possibility of nuclear destruction.

Clausewitz used the concept of war as an instrument of policy to explain how the capacity of states to wage war was affected by changes in the political consciousness of their societies, to explore the relationship between political aims and military operations, and to justify his view of the primacy of the state over its military organs.[11] Clausewitz believed that the second of these aspects in particular was inadequately addressed in an early draft of *On War*. In July 1827, he thus added a note to the manuscript in which he suggested readers should keep the idea that '*war is nothing but the continuation of policy with other means* ... firmly in mind throughout' in order to 'greatly facilitate' study and that so acting would make the whole 'easier to analyse'.[12] The force of this injunction was magnified by a second note—previously thought to have been written in 1830—which stated that only the first chapter of the book was in its final form and indicated deep dissatisfaction with the balance of the text. The first chapter culminated in a discussion of the famous dictum, which was characterised as a critical element of the foundation of theory.[13]

The foregoing explains why a great deal of scholarly analysis of *On War* has been focused on Clausewitz's discussion of the relationship between war and politics. His study, however, is much more than an essay on a single major theme. In addition to dealing with the linkage between politics and armed conflict, Clausewitz put forward a number of propositions that he believed were easily demonstrable and significant. These were that defence was a stronger form of war than offence, major successes brought forth minor ones, victory required the destruction of the enemy both physically and morally, military effect was always greatest at the point of victory, and every attack lost force as it progressed.[14] Clausewitz also invented the notion of friction in war as a device to explain the great difficulties that attended the execution of any complex military operation, and treated seriously the distinction between limited and unlimited war.[15] Most of *On War* is devoted to the matters just described. Moreover, their connections to the issues raised by the famous dictum are not always strong or clear.

Recent scholarship has demonstrated that the note thought to have been written in 1830 was produced at a much earlier date, and that *On War* is a more finished work than has been supposed. This being the case, the text as it stands cannot be dismissed as an artefact of early drafting and provisional thinking whose content would have changed fundamentally had the author lived to revise the manuscript. Clausewitz in fact worked out most of his new ideas on the relationship of war and politics in the last section of *On War*.[16] Moreover, even before he had done so, Clausewitz in his note of 1827 stated his belief that an open-minded reader would be capable of comprehending his main argument. On the other hand, he at the same time conceded that his volume could with justice be regarded as 'a shapeless mass of ideas' that would be 'liable to endless misinterpretation'.[17] As Clausewitz feared, *On War*, though respected as a profound work, has defied satisfactory explanation as a coherent whole, being widely regarded as disjointed, contradictory, or otherwise perplexing.[18]

Careful study of the second of the eight books that make up *On War* reveals that conceptual unity exists, and is to be found in Clausewitz's method of applying several general ideas to particular cases rather than in his advancement of a single major proposition. In book two, Clausewitz explained the operation of this synthetic mechanism in his exploration of the nature and proper relationship of history with respect to the understanding of decision-making by senior commanders. Previous major treatments of the history and theory question have been compromised by incomplete analysis of book two.[19] Peter Paret's exploration of Clausewitz's use of history and theory in an essay of 1992 was tentative and general—with commendable candour he conceded that 'the relationship between theory and history in Clausewitz's thought has been barely studied'.[20]

This chapter will present a detailed analysis of *On War*, book two, and discuss its implications. The main argument is that Clausewitz did not use ideas alone to explain the phenomenon of armed conflict, but called for the use of ideas in conjunction with historical knowledge to develop a sense of the nature of high command, which he regarded as the prerequisite to the comprehension of war. Clausewitz was convinced that reliable and complete evidence concerning the influence of politics and other factors on the mindsets of the leaders of armies was likely to be nonexistent or unobtainable. Their effects had, therefore, to be constructed theoretically and then mated to known facts about past events in order to achieve a sound understanding of the motives that lay behind the conduct of major military operations. Such engagement with a more complete picture than was achievable by conventional history alone, Clausewitz believed, was essential for anyone who lacked actual experience but wished to understand war. In addition, it was good preparation for officers who might some day have to direct the deployment of armies in real hostilities.[21]

Book two of *On War* is entitled 'On Theory'. In the first chapter, Clausewitz divided the phenomenon of war into two parts, fighting and preparation for fighting. The latter, he argued, was essentially a matter of administrative technique, and thus he excluded it from further serious consideration. The former was divided into two subjects: tactics, which '*was the use of armed forces in the engagement*' and strategy, which was '*the use of engagements for the object of the war*'.[22] In the opening of the second chapter, tactics was characterised as amounting to little more than fighting technique rather than a 'creative intellectual activity'.[23] Clausewitz noted that early attempts to formulate general systems of theory on war were concerned mainly with tactics; in chapter four, he returned to this theme, arguing that while method and routine were useful and even essential at the level of tactics, they were not at the level of strategy.[24] But in the absence of 'an intelligent analysis of the conduct of war', Clausewitz warned, decision-making at the strategic level was almost bound to be taken over by method and routine, with potentially disastrous results.[25]

In chapters one, two, and four, Clausewitz made clear that his main concern was with command decision-making at the strategic level—that is, the province of choosing major courses of action from a range of alternatives. Clausewitz insisted that in such matters a workable positive doctrine—that is, a prescriptive code—was unattainable.[26] He thus condemned all past military theory on the general grounds that it attempted to do that which was impossible. Specifically, Clausewitz criticised existing theories of war for dealing only with 'physical matters and unilateral activity'.[27] The former referred primarily to troop deployments and dispositions, the latter to recommended actions that took no account of the fact that real war was highly dynamic and contingent.

Clausewitz believed that the will of the commander to make decisions in the face of incomplete and misleading information, fear of failure, and the unpredictable major and minor difficulties that could arise in any military operation were no less important than troop strength and movement. And the fact that action by one's own forces could prompt a reaction by the enemy that might change the basic conditions of the engagement in highly favourable or unfavourable ways meant that uncertainty, and unanticipated opportunity or adversity, were inherent to the environment of war. Clausewitz argued, therefore, that the problem with past theorising about war was that it 'did not yet include the use of force under conditions of danger, subject to constant interaction with an adversary, nor the efforts of spirit and courage to achieve a desired end'.[28]

In effect, the exclusion of the moral—that is, the non-physical—dimension of war and the factoring out of enemy response made a complex phenomenon deceptively simple and eliminated the need to address the problem of contingency. This facilitated the development of theory that codified war command through rules, principles, and even systems. Clausewitz conceded that the order produced by these structures was useful as a counter to a 'maelstrom of opinion' whose chaotic effects were 'intellectually repugnant'.[29] But because this approach 'failed to take adequate account of the endless complexities involved' it set up an 'irreconcilable conflict' between theory and practice.[30] 'It is only analytically', Clausewitz argued, that these attempts at theory can be called advances in the realm of truth; synthetically, in the rules and regulations they offer, they are absolutely useless. They aim at fixed values; but in war everything is uncertain, and calculations have to be made with variable quantities. They direct the inquiry exclusively toward physical quantities, whereas all military action is intertwined with psychological forces and effects. They consider only unilateral action, whereas war consists of a continuous interaction of opposites.[31]

Following his critique of conventional theorising, Clausewitz analysed systematically the three fundamental factors whose unquantifiability made the construction of any code of directives an invalid approach to the problem of decision-making by the high command. The first was the critical role of moral force—that is, emotion, of which the most important was courage; this was a quality that not only varied from person to person, but could be different in the same person at one time as opposed to another, and in any case was something difficult to measure. The second was that war consisted of a series of actions and reactions by two or more adversaries, whose course was inherently unpredictable. And the third was the fact that the information upon which actions on both sides were based was bound to be uncertain, and the degree of uncertainty yet another value that was difficult to quantify.[32]

As an alternative to 'positive doctrine', Clausewitz maintained that the function of proper war theory was to examine what others called 'genius'—that is, whatever constituted effective command capability under the most difficult circumstances—which by its very nature *'rises above all rules'*.[33] One way to understand what such a theory might be about was to imagine it as something that was 'meant to educate the mind of the future commander, or, more accurately, to guide him in his self-education, not to accompany him to the battlefield . . .'[34] Clausewitz's distinction between theory as a teacher and theory as a guide to self-education is important because it defined a facilitating role for theory in a larger process of learning in which other things external to theory were the main matter. Theory, in other words, did not contain its whole meaning within itself, but only through conjunction—and indeed only after being transmuted through combination—with something else (later explained to be history). It was this process of connection and transformation that ensured that the gap between theory and practice that other theoreticians regarded as unavoidable, but which Clausewitz deplored, was never, for him, allowed to come into being.

The ultimate goal of the kind of self-education proposed was the development of a capability. The acquisition of a highly subjective kind of knowledge was an important part of this process: grasp of the higher affairs of state and associated policies, the ability to judge issues and leading personalities, understanding of the abilities of subordinates, and comprehension of the performance capabilities of the army to be commanded. 'This type of knowledge', Clausewitz observed, 'cannot be forcibly produced by an apparatus of scientific formulas and mechanics; it can only be gained through a talent for judgment, and by the application of accurate judgment to the observation of man and matter'.[35] 'Natural talent' was schooled by actual war, but in the absence of such, Clausewitz believed that the talent of a senior commander could be enhanced artificially 'through the medium of reflection, study and thought'.[36]

Clausewitz intended his discussion of the creation of command capability by a particular individual as a device to clarify the nature of the problem of theory. He did not exclude persons who were not commanders-in-chief in waiting from his audience,[37] but asked them to understand that any proper theory of war had to make the consciousness of the human executor of high command and human relations its focal points. Clausewitz believed that war was not just an activity performed by humans, but a purely human activity, which meant that it was essential to understand the nature of the agents of action as well as dealing with the actions themselves. Thus he observed that war existed not in the realms of science or art but was rather a 'part of man's social existence'.[38] This being the case, Clausewitz argued that the human dynamics of war could accurately be compared to those of commerce and especially politics, which was to say that certain aspects of ordinary life could serve as a starting point for understanding the nature of armed conflict.

But Clausewitz believed that for those who lacked first-hand experience of war, the main stimulus to the development of understanding about human behaviour and the effects of environmental forces such as time of day, terrain, and weather in a real conflict was the study of the past.[39] Knowledge of history was to be achieved through 'critical analysis', which had three aspects. These were establishing a truthful basic narrative, explaining causation, and evaluating the soundness of actions, or as Clausewitz put it, historical research, critical analysis proper, and criticism proper.[40] Historical research was essential to exclude falsehood, because error would skew all subsequent deliberations. But Clausewitz was acutely aware that crucial information about military operations often did not exist. In war, he wrote, 'facts are seldom fully known and the underlying motive even less so' because they may have been 'intentionally concealed by those in command, or, if they happen to be transitory and accidental, history may not have recorded them at all'.[41]

Incomplete evidence was a fundamental obstacle, but by no means the only one to an accurate comprehension of past events and their meaning. 'Effects in war', Clausewitz maintained, 'seldom result from a single cause; there are usually several concurrent causes'.[42] In addition to multiple causation, establishing the relationship between cause and effect was not easy for three reasons. In the first place, actions had unintended as well as intended effects. In the second place, Clausewitz recognised that circumstances could multiply the force of trivial initial happenings. In war, he observed, 'as in life generally, all parts of a whole are interconnected and thus the effects produced, however small their cause, must influence all subsequent military operations and modify their final outcome to some degree, however slight'.[43] And in the third place, the assessment of causation became increasingly difficult as the level of analysis was shifted from battle to campaign, and from campaign to war, because the number of influential factors and their possible interactions increased with each expansion of scale and complexity.

Clausewitz knew that the difficulty of command was in large part a problem of choosing the right course at the right time. Sound evaluation of particular decisions, therefore, required the consideration of a range of alternative options and the reasons for their rejection as well as the rationale for the action actually taken. 'A great many assumptions', Clausewitz thus argued, 'have to be made about things that did not actually happen but seemed possible, and that, therefore, cannot be left out of account'.[44] 'Critical analysis is not just an evaluation of the means actually employed', he added later, 'but of all possible means—which first have to be formulated, that is, invented'.[45] Once the various command possibilities were identified and described, criticism proper would assess their relative worthiness by 'taking each of the means and assessing and comparing the particular merits of each in relation to the objective'.[46]

The mixture of surmise and fact, and the multitude of issues that had to be taken into account, exposed the approach recommended by Clausewitz to charges of either arbitrariness or incompleteness. He thus insisted that a strong claim to intellectual legitimacy be established by the rigour of the theory that governed the process of reasoning. 'We must never stop at an arbitrary assumption that others may not accept', Clausewitz wrote, 'lest different propositions, equally valid perhaps, be advanced against them; leading to an unending argument, reaching no conclusions, and resulting in no lesson'.[47] He insisted, moreover, on similar grounds, upon the need for what all would recognise as an appropriate critical method. 'A working theory,' Clausewitz maintained, 'is an essential basis for criticism. Without such a theory it is generally impossible for criticism to reach that point at which it becomes truly instructive—when its arguments are convincing and cannot be refuted.'[48]

Systematic examination of a military problem, as it presented itself to the commander in all its complexity and difficulty, did not mean the need to adopt his perspective completely. While Clausewitz expected the critic to 'reduce to factual knowledge' the 'essential interconnections of genius [of the commander]'[49] he also held that the external event—that is, the success or non-success of the operational happenings resulting from the commander's decisions—was germane to the proper assessment of decision-making, however unquantifiable this aspect of evaluation might be. Clausewitz noted that

> the critic, then, having analysed everything within the range of human calculation and belief, will let the outcome speak for that part whose deep, mysterious operation is never visible. The critic must protect this unspoken result of the workings of higher laws against the stream of uninformed opinion on the one hand, and against the gross abuses to which it may be subjected on the other. Success enables us to understand much that the workings of human intelligence alone would not be able to discover. That means that it will be useful mainly in revealing intellectual and psychological forces and effects, because these are least subject to reliable evaluation, and also because they are so closely involved with the will that they may easily control it.[50]

Clausewitz's approach to self-education thus had two distinct modes. On the one hand, there was the use of precise language to establish clearly the relationship of many things in proper proportion. This was, in his own words, supposed 'to illuminate the connections which link things together and to determine which among the countless concatenations of events are the essential ones'.[51] On the other hand, there was a more allusive approach that took account of the critically important role of the commander's mindset—that is, the conscious and unconscious mentality that reacted to events. The second mode was no less important than the first, and the deployment of both together—which precluded the creation of formal bodies of law and attendant technical jargon—was probably what Clausewitz meant when he spoke of natural as opposed to elaborate scientific observation. If it is, he insisted, 'never necessary or even permissible to use scientific guidelines in order to judge a given problem in war, if the truth never appears in systematic form, if it is not acquired deductively but always *directly* through the natural perception of the mind, then that is the way it must also be in critical analysis'.[52]

The object to be perceived through 'natural perception of the mind' was past events. 'Historical examples clarify everything', Clausewitz wrote, 'and also provide the best kind of proof in the empirical sciences'.[53] That being said, he then warned that 'historical examples are, however, seldom used to such good effect'; indeed, Clausewitz complained, 'the use of them by theorists normally not only leaves the reader dissatisfied but even irritates his intelligence'.[54] Historical example was an appropriate instrument when dealing with the explanation of an idea or the application of an idea, or in support of the possible—as opposed to certain—validity of a statement. But the kind of simple narratives or anecdotes that were the usual form of historical evidence were almost always incapable of providing a complete proof of a major theoretical conclusion. 'The sheer range to be covered,' Clausewitz wrote, 'would often rule this out; and, apart from that, it might be difficult to point to actual experience on every detail . . .'[55]

The complex authenticity required to demonstrate the validity of a general truth could only be achieved through the examination of a single case about which a great deal was known and whose nature could be further explicated through the application of the critical analytical techniques that compensated for what could not be established unequivocally from the historical record. Clausewitz was open to the use of several cases when knowledge of a single one was inadequate, but warned that 'this is clearly a dangerous expedient, and is frequently misused'.[56] He saw little value and even pernicious effect in examining an event about which information was sparse, such as a battle or campaign in the distant past. 'An event that is lightly touched upon, instead of being carefully detailed', Clausewitz wrote, 'is like an object seen at a great distance: it is impossible to distinguish any detail, and it looks the same from every angle'.[57]

From the standpoint of methodological tactics, Clausewitz's ideal was to use a properly conceived theory to redress certain unavoidable gaps in the historical record in a way that amplified with minimal distortion the practical instructional value of an extensive body of detailed information about a past event. From the standpoint of pedagogical strategy, the Clausewitzian ideal was to teach war command using *only* a body of work produced by correct methodological tactics; such an approach, he wrote in the words of the *Code Napoléon*, would amount to the presentation of nothing less than '*the truth, the whole truth, and nothing but the truth*'.[58] Clausewitz believed the first was not only achievable, but in fact obligatory though extremely challenging. He was less sanguine about the immediate attainability of the second. It would take time to create the literature required, and without it his pedagogical ideal would remain no more than its name—a distant beacon rather than a practical source of illumination.

In 1827, Clausewitz suspended labour on *On War* and turned his attention to writing the kind of analytical historical studies called for in book two. These were on the Italian campaigns of 1796 and 1799, and the campaign of 1815. In 1830, Clausewitz was recalled to active service in the field when Prussia mobilised in response to the French Revolution of that year. In 1831, shortly after resuming light administrative duty that would have allowed him to carry on his literary endeavours, Clausewitz died from the effects of cholera. When published posthumously, Clausewitz's historical writing of 1827–30 came to 1500 printed pages, which took up four out of the ten volumes of his collected works. This has yet to be translated into English.[59]

Nearly all major treatises on war have either derived theory from history, or used historical examples to illustrate aspects of theory. In book two of *On War*, Clausewitz presented a different approach. His own extensive experience as an officer during the French Revolution and Empire[60] equipped him with knowledge about the difficulty and complexity of war command and, no less importantly, about the incompleteness of the historical record with respect to its actual operation in the past. He thus formulated a body of important ideas for which there was nor could there be any hard evidence, and insisted that these factors had to be imagined and related to known historical facts in order to comprehend the process of war command in particular. In other words, a critically important component of the larger theoretical edifice presented in *On War* defined the terms of synthesis of that for which there was no record, and thus neither summarised nor distilled history, but complemented it.

This aspect of Clausewitzian theory consisted of instructions for dealing with the following issues. First, there were the fundamental psychological factors affecting the state of mind of the commander, which were emotion, contingency, and uncertainty. Second, there were the subjective material factors that informed the commander's judgement, which were his knowledge of policy and politics, assessments of people and issues, and comprehension of the quality of the forces he commanded. Third, there was the multitude of operational facts and motives for action of many individuals that were either never known or if known never recorded or even intentionally obscured. Fourth, there was the peculiar nature of the relationship between cause and effect in war, whose character was affected by the play of unintended consequences and complexity. Fifth, there was the fact that in war commanders were confronted by a range of options, and that assessment of the quality of the decision actually made required consideration of the possible alternatives. And sixth, the success or failure of the operation had to be given a measure of significance when considering the rightness or wrongness of decision-making by way of acknowledging the effects of unknown and perhaps even unknowable factors.

The high degree of subjectivity and surmise introduced by Clausewitz's theoretical dimension was counterbalanced by two injunctions. The first was that the execution of the theoretical instructions be intellectually rigorous, and the second that the historical cases investigated be ones about which a very great deal was known in order to keep the play of surmise about matters of objective and subjective fact to a minimum. For Clausewitz, the end product of theory and its integration with known history was, if not truth, something much closer to the truth than history alone. This truth, moreover, was a thing which was felt as much as thought—a form of consciousness rather than a body of knowledge. The goal of intensive engagement through study and reflection with a combination of fact and surmise, in other words, was not erudition, but the replication of the effects of actual experience. This was done in order to induce the formation of a sensibility that could facilitate effective decision-making in war.

Clausewitz's method of combining theory and history offered authenticity as well as realism. Manoeuvres, hypothetical cases or wargaming provided verisimilitude with regard to specific military circumstances, but not the conditions of danger and the human response to it, especially critically debilitating fear.[61] History provided a better point of departure for the imagination of these factors because empathy with actual participants—whose general character and personal idiosyncrasies could be established by autobiography and perceptive biography—offered a more direct path to the realm of emotions than the invention of fictional sentiments. It was the special function of history, in other words, to evoke the moral dimension of war.[62] History properly deployed in conjunction with sound theory ensured that the student of command was not merely a detached witness to a mental re-enactment of the past, but a virtual participant in its experience. The objective of such involvement was to induce understanding that command at the strategic level was not so much asserted or exercised as expressed.

For Clausewitz, engagement with a single properly presented historical case was preferable to the study of multiple conventional accounts of past campaigns. By the same token, Clausewitz probably believed that his pedagogical objectives could be achieved through the study of only a few events. He did not require, in other words, a comprehensive survey of major recent military happenings; a selection would do. And because ordinary life also involved engagement with complexity, uncertainty, and the risk of negative consequences in the event of error—risk which was sufficient to prompt debilitating apprehension—Clausewitz observed that it too could serve similarly as a source of insight into the nature of command in war. Of course, the critical difference between decision-making in war and ordinary life lay in the far greater magnitude of responsibility in the case of the former, which meant that military crisis was bound to generate commensurately higher levels of fear. War, Clausewitz thus might have said, was like ordinary life, only much more so.

In book one of *On War*, Clausewitz defined major terms and introduced important concepts, including the famous aphorism, but it was essentially a taxonomic prelude to book two. It was in book two that Clausewitz dealt with the problematical nature of armed conflict between nation-states by inventing the means with which such a subject had to be engaged in the absence of actual experience of it. Having presented his method of study, Clausewitz then devoted the remainder of his treatise to the investigation of important issues which needed to be taken into account when employing the method provided in book two: strategy in general, the nature of a military engagement and of military forces, the nature of defence and offence, and finally war planning. When considered as a whole and in terms of intellectual sequence, there can be little doubt that book two—whose title *On Theory* specified Clausewitz's creative objective—is the conceptual pivot of *On War*.

Nothing could be more misleading, therefore, than to reduce Clausewitz's thought to a single sentence about war and politics. The term 'Clausewitzian', if used at all, should refer to the German author's most important and distinctive contribution to the consideration of the phenomenon of war: the invention of a way of attenuating the very serious drawbacks of reductionist theorising and incomplete history by combining theory and history so that each performed functions that the other could or should not perform. It was this conception that Clausewitz probably had in mind when he wrote that his 'basic ideas' would perhaps bring about 'a revolution in the theory of war'.[63] The term 'Clausewitzian' should refer to a particular way of seeing, imagining, and learning, not to a view of the inter-relationship of phenomena. It does not make sense, therefore, to criticise *On War* as an incomplete analysis of the total phenomenon of armed conflict.[64] Such criticism does not reflect its purpose, and such an analysis if attempted would have defeated Clausewitz's principal aim of laying bare '*the hidden processes of intuitive judgment*'.[65]

To engage Clausewitz's argument requires practice of a method, not the acceptance of a body of thought. Clausewitz rejected the notion that war could be understood through comprehension of a description or an explanation. To come to terms with war demanded a strenuous mental re-enactment of decision-making at the strategic level. Such a re-enactment of the past was intended to keep the focus of self-education on the process of human action—that is, command—rather than on military planning as known through the outcomes of human action—that is, strategy. Clausewitz was interested in the induction of experience of high command, not the teaching of strategic lessons. This characteristic of *On War* thus anticipates certain important ideas of the English philosopher and historian R.G. Collingwood (1889–1943).

Collingwood rejected in principle the notion that history could be used to construct general laws and, like Clausewitz, specifically excluded the legitimacy of doing so with regard to the conduct of warfare.[66] Collingwood also maintained that knowledge of past events was always incomplete in significant ways, observing of the Battle of Hastings that 'no one knows, no one ever has known, and no one ever will know what exactly it was that happened'.[67] 'Of what can there be historical knowledge?' he thus asked, to which he replied 'that which can be re-enacted in the historian's mind', which 'must be experience'.[68] To this he added 'the historian's thought must spring from the organic unity of his total experience, and be a function of his entire personality with its practical as well as its theoretical interests'.[69] This affinity between the views of Collingwood and Clausewitz deserves more extended treatment than is possible here. Suffice to say that Clausewitz engaged with questions subsequently central to serious inquiry into the philosophy of history.

As we have seen, Clausewitz asserted, in his conclusions to the first chapter of *On War*, that the concept that 'all wars can be considered acts of policy' must be a major component of the 'foundations of theory'.[70] Clausewitz's view of the relationship between theory and history, however, conditioned the function of his dictum on war and policy. The concept served as the most important of the subjective factors—the second category of his theoretical instructions—which shaped the judgement of military leaders but it was a concept too often overlooked for want of evidence or understanding of its significance in accounts of past wars. It was less an axiom for statesmen and generals, for whom it could hardly come as news,[71] than one of a number of tips for laymen and officers lacking experience and studying history, or for would-be analysts writing it. The famous phrase may legitimately provoke thought about important questions without regard to its intended meaning, but it cannot stand as the epitome of Clausewitz, the philosopher of war—if indeed he can be characterised as such—without betraying Clausewitz, the philosopher of history.

Three major conclusions therefore seem inescapable. In the first place, Clausewitz's main influence on those who followed him was unintended—significant theorists such as Julian Corbett incorporated elements of *On War* in their work,[72] but they did not fully comprehend and thus could not correctly deploy his approach to the study of command. Second, future analysis of *On War* should incorporate Clausewitz's conception of the proper combined uses of history and theory so as to understand properly his treatment of important issues such as the relationship between war and politics and the differing natures of limited and unlimited war. Finally, implementing Clausewitzian ideas about history and theory would introduce radical change in and, arguably, greatly improve the writing of military history and the educating of military officers. Which is to say that, nearly 200 years after it was written, *On War* is not just a classic text, but insofar as the study of military decision-making is concerned, is still in advance of the state of the art.

4 Imperial naval defence—a model for transnationalism: a Canadian perspective
Nicholas Tracy

The development in the twentieth century of a collective system of naval defence for the British Empire was an unprecedented effort to find a compromise between strategic ideals and political realities which would enable freely associated, and eventually legally sovereign, political entities to meet the needs of collective defence. The road followed was one of technical unity, and a community of interest, without a machinery for more than consultation on matters of foreign policy. It is easy to point to the limitations of the structure, but impossible to deny that it resisted the centrifugal political forces of nationalism enough to survive the horrors of the Second World War. The model it provided for the later formation of NATO and other institutions of collective defence is not hard to see and, for better or for worse, can be seen in the operations of the WEU and NATO in the Balkans. Given the limitations of the United Nations, transnationalism is the best that is available for the defence of civilised values, and has been tried in the furnaces of twentieth-century history.

At the turn of the century, the prevailing strategic idea dominating thinking about naval defence was that unity of control and freedom of movement were essential to ensure that overwhelming force could be brought to bear at the decisive battle which would determine the outcome of a war. Centralisation was also valued because it was feared that small fleets could not be efficient. At the 1902 Imperial Conference, the assembled prime ministers were given a memorandum on 'Sea-Power and the Principles Involved' in which they were told that

> The immense importance of the principle of concentration and the facility with which ships and squadrons can be moved from one part of the world to another . . . points to the necessity of a single navy, under one control, by which alone concerted action between the several parts can be assured.[1]

The requirements of operational efficiency conflicted with, and inevitably always will conflict with, the political requirements of a system of collective defence. The Royal Navy satisfied the strategic ideas, but it was not really an imperial force, because it was the instrument of the British Government. In the winter of 1906–07, Rear Admiral Charles Ottley, Director of Naval Intelligence, wrote several assessments of the problem of developing an effective system of collective naval defence of the Empire in which he was scathing about the influence on Australian policy of local naval officers who stood most to gain by the creation of an Australian navy. On the other hand, he admitted that the Admiralty did not like the Australian naval agreement by which the Australian

At the 1902 Imperial Conference the Admiralty countered colonial criticism of its refusal to strengthen fleets on distant stations by arguing that the concentrated battlefleet was the ultimate deterrent. Colonial leaders (front row, from left): Sir R. Bond (Newfoundland), R.J. Seddon (New Zealand), Sir Wilfred Laurier (Canada), Joseph Chamberlain (Secretary of State for the Colonies), Sir Edmund Barton (Australia), Sir A.H. Hume (Natal) and T.E. Fuller (representing Cape Colony). (National Library of Australia)

Commonwealth financed a Royal Navy squadron based in Australian waters, and he sympathetically noted that the Empire was a voluntary association of peoples which derived its strength from the freedom of their choice. The creation of local navies was a necessary attribute to the ability of colonies to leave the association should they so wish.[2]

Nationalist political forces, whether they should be viewed as 'irrational' or 'essential', had to be taken seriously if a system of defence were to be constructed. This reality was recognised by the Liberal Prime Minister of Canada, Sir Wilfred Laurier, and by the Conservative Opposition Leader, Sir Robert Borden. In 1910 Borden, in defending to Parliament his decision to support the government's formation of an independent navy for Canada, said that the arguments for the strategic value of a unified imperial navy were strong, but that 'from a constitutional and political standpoint' he was opposed:

> In the first place I do not believe it would endure. In the second place it would [be] a source of friction . . . It would conduce, if anything could conduce, to severing the present connection between Canada and the Empire.[3]

The experience of total war from 1914 to 1918 was to make it evident even to naval planners in London, but only after a struggle, that, at least in peacetime, operational inefficiencies had to be tolerated in order to obtain the more vital requirement of public political support. In 1919 an Admiralty memorandum on 'Imperial Naval Defence', observed that:

> Discussion as to the best form of co-operation is, in fact, somewhat academic because the statements of Dominion statesmen make it clear that future co-operation from Canada and New Zealand will eventually follow the Australian model. Quite irrespectively, then, of the advantages of this system, the Admiralty will be required to assist in the development of these navies, and to find a place for them in a comprehensive system of Imperial defence.[4]

For the 1921 Imperial Conference the Admiralty prepared a paper on the development and co-ordination of independent naval forces, but made it clear it did not consider the development of Dominion navies 'the ideal policy, which would be a unified navy under a single command'.[5] Two years later, however, Captain Dudley Pound, Admiralty Director of Plans and from 1939 to 1943 First Sea Lord, drew the necessary conclusion when he put up a paper to outline the progression of Admiralty policy vis-a-vis the Dominions, and to detail the means which had been established for co-ordinating the naval policies of the Empire. 'Wars', he wrote, are no longer waged by Navies and Armies alone, but by nations in arms. The success or failure of any measure of defence rests ultimately on the sanction of the people . . . It is for this reason that public interest is placed first in the list of requirements to be fulfilled.[6]

Apart from nationalist politics, there was an incentive for the development of national naval forces, because of the reality that the Royal Navy could not always be used effectively to protect local interests without unnecessary conflict with other great powers. This difficulty especially affected Canadian interests. Shortly after the turn of the century, it was recognised in London that the Royal Navy could no longer guarantee Canadian defence against the United States, and it followed that Royal Navy intervention in Canadian–American maritime disputes might well not be in the interest of Canada, let alone Great Britain. In the 1870s disputed fisheries jurisdiction on the east coast, and the need of the Empire to walk softly in the relations with the post–Civil War United States, had brought the Canadian Government to acquire ships with some degree of naval status.[7] At the turn of the century, the Alaska boundary dispute, and the Straits of Juan de Fuca demarcation dispute, strongly brought home the problem of depending entirely on the support of British forces, which the United States considered had no legitimacy in North American waters.

In the first decades of the century, whatever their wishes might be, the Dominions could only opt out of the common foreign policy of the Empire if foreign countries chose to overlook the juridical unity of the Empire under the Crown.[8] For Canada, it was primarily the attitude of the United States which would determine its capacity to adopt a quasi-neutrality. For the same reason, there were great difficulties in the way of according the Dominions a right to carry out independent military action outside their own territorial seas. In 1908 it was pointed out in the report of the Interdepartmental Conference on the Status of Dominion Ships of War that 'under international law there is only one executive authority in the British Empire capable of being recognized by foreign States; Colonial ships of war cannot operate independently of the Royal Navy'.[9] A memorandum prepared by the Admiralty in 1910 for the Committee of Imperial Defence (CID) noted that the problem of arranging for peacetime control was more difficult politically than was that of making arrangements for wartime co-operation, but that it had to be borne in mind that

> Wars arise out of acts done in times of peace . . . It must be recognized that international difficulties of a very grave nature may arise, owing to the fact that a mobile armed force has been established, over whose action the Central Government would have no control, though the ultimate responsibility would rest with them.[10]

Logically, the solution to the problem of operational and strategic control of the naval forces of the Empire could have been solved by the development of effective means of collectively formulating a common foreign policy. During the first 40 years of the century a great deal of effort was put into the attempt, but the actors in the drama were distracted by a multiplicity of motives, and fell short of reaching a satisfactory solution to the problem.[11] The machinery for managing the external relations of the Empire in the interest of all its constituent parts, inchoate in the first quarter of the century, was crushed eventually by the weight of nationalist perspective.

The compromise solution reached before the First World War to the problem presented by the need to reconcile constitutional autonomy with centralised strategic control and the juridical unity of the Empire was for the Dominions to accept the operational authority of the British Admiralty and its commanders-in-chief when operating outside their own areas of national responsibility. The same principle applied when Royal Navy ships were attached to the Canadian Atlantic and Pacific stations or to the Australian station, within which areas the Dominion governments were held to represent the interests of the entire Empire.[12] Each of the Dominions passed its own code of discipline, which closely mirrored that of the Royal Navy, and so permitted interoperability and common training. For very practical reasons, the Dominion navies purchased British naval equipment. To ensure wartime operational efficiency, Laurier's naval bill adopted the same formula as had the Australians, permitting the government to transfer control to the Admiralty. It did not, however, arrange for automatic transfer upon the outbreak of hostilities.[13]

Canadians were not very happy with this arrangement, but could not agree on a better one. Canadian ultra-nationalists objected that the Liberals were in fact creating a rod for their own backs, whatever their intentions. Mr Monk condemned the idea of 'a navy which will be Canadian when it has to be paid for, in order to be Imperial when it is required for use'.[14] Henri Bourassa, the leader of the Nationalist Party, objected that if Canada constructed a navy of value to the Empire it would be impossible for Canadians to resist the request for military assistance even if they disagreed with Britain's policy at the time. On that platform the Nationalists defeated the Liberals in Quebec, and the argument resonated in Canada's strategic debate over the rest of the twentieth century.

The Dominion governments were invited to attend meetings of the CID, but the Canadian Government refused on the grounds that it was a committee controlled by the British Prime Minister. Participation in the formation of strategic policy, but without much prospect of being able to change it, would make it impossible for Canada to stand aside from policies with which it disagreed. The Dominions were also encouraged to let their officers serve on the naval staff in London, where their perspective would be useful in the development of collective plans. Suspicious nationalism was limited by a willingness to participate in Commonwealth Conferences, and by an underlying belief that the cultural and family ties of the Commonwealth were so strong that they could overcome political suspicions.

At the 1923 Imperial Conference, Liberal Prime Minister William Lyon Mackenzie King commented on the influence the United States had on Canadian opinions, but added: 'If a great and clear call of duty comes, Canada will respond, whether or not the United States responds, as she did in 1914'.[15] The Canadian Government endorsed the resolution of the conference that the security of the territory and trade of all the Dominions was the responsibility of all parts of the Empire, a formula which was later employed in NATO. Commitments were made that the dockyards at Halifax and Esquimalt would be available for the Royal Navy in the event of Britain going to war, regardless of Canadian policies at the time, and Canada undertook to store the equipment in Canada for the conversion into armed merchant cruisers of liners running out of Vancouver.[16] In 1926, however, the Statute of Westminster formally separated the Dominions from Britain's foreign policy.

These pragmatic compromises provided the political formula which ensured that the British Commonwealth, with the military and naval forces which they had developed, responded collectively in 1914 and 1939 on the outbreak of war. It also enabled the Dominions to meet local problems, such as that in the Canadian fisheries, without turning such episodes into major issues between the Empire and other great powers. Where it was inadequate was in the management of crises leading up to war. As the Imperial Chiefs of Staff put it in October 1930:

> the extent of co-operation by the Dominion forces, even where it is assumed that the latter would be co-operating, cannot be gauged, and the Dominion forces have to be regarded largely as an extra asset not to be taken into account.[17]

The visit to Canada in 1936 by Sir Maurice Hankey, the Secretary to the British Cabinet and to the CID, convinced him that the Canadian Government could not be depended upon. Even in 1938–39, the Admiralty did not know how much it could count on from Canada.[18] In May 1938 Hankey wrote Sir Edward Harding, the Permanent Undersecretary of State for Dominion Affairs: 'It would be clearly disastrous if we laid our plans on the assumption that we could count upon Canada, and then when the day comes we found that we had been building on false premises'.[19] Hankey, however, advised against even talking about what to do if the

Dominions chose to keep out of a war; the prospect was too awful, and thinking about it too demoralising. Concern about political attitudes in the Dominions was a factor in Britain's weak policy in the Munich crisis, although Canada, the other Dominion governments, and the government of India did their best to support the needs of collective defence during the crisis.

The political limitations of the system of imperial defence were reflections of the strategic stress which was placed on it by the growing power of the United States and Japan. Before the Great War, the greatest conflict between the strategic requirements of the Empire as a whole, and those of its component parts, was that affecting relations with the United States. The Empire was not able to provide Canada with local security, employing the same operational means as served for the other Dominions and for the mother country. Following the Great War, it was to be the Antipodean Dominions and colonies which found that measures of general security were inadequate for their local needs.

The weakness of the structure of imperial defence in the Pacific had begun to be recognised with Jellicoe's far from encouraging threat assessments during the 1919 Empire tour. On his way to India he had drawn up a general paper on 'Post-War Naval Requirements' which looked at the none-too-attractive prospect of having to match post-war US naval expansion. In Australia he had felt obliged to raise the spectre of a Japanese war because, as he explained in a letter to the First Lord, Lord Long, otherwise he could not have advised any standard for Australian fleet strength. In doing so, of course, he was echoing opinion already held in the Antipodes.[20] The effort made in the 1920s and 1930s to meet this danger was the greatest challenge to the structure of imperial defence, and was in fact to prove its nemesis.

Jellicoe's indication, in his reports to the Australian and New Zealand governments in 1919, that a British Pacific fleet would have to be formed was highly embarrassing to a British Government committed to economy. Clearly, in the light of Japan's naval building program, something had to be done to provide for naval defence in the Pacific. Equally clearly, the only hope lay in collective action, and for very real financial and technical reasons, the Royal Navy could not keep up anything like a war fleet in the Pacific. The plan eventually adopted, of course, was that in the event of anticipated hostilities naval forces in the Eastern theatre should be concentrated at Singapore, there to await the arrival of the main fleet dispatched from Europe.[21] The Imperial Conference considered the problem of naval defence, especially in the Pacific, on 4 July 1921 and Earl Beatty, now the First Sea Lord, iterated the importance of developing a defended dockyard at Singapore. The next day the leaders met at the Admiralty and the fundamentals of interwar strategy were discussed and agreed to.

The limitations of imperial government, and the weaknesses which post-war national budgets had to face, seriously affected this effort at defence co-operation. The New Zealand Government voted £100,000 to support the construction of a base at Singapore, but at the 26th meeting of the Imperial Conference the Secretary of State for India made it clear that the money India spent on its army, which was important throughout the region, precluded any subsidy of the Singapore project. If any money became available, India would prefer to use it to develop a Royal Indian Navy. The Prime Minister of Canada, Sir Arthur Meighen, rejected the appeal for a common perspective on imperial defence in the Pacific, on the grounds that the Canadian public could never be brought to agree.[22]

The Royal Navy's Director of Plans, Barry Domvile, completed on 3 November 1921 a memorandum on 'Plans for War in the Far East', which outlined the problems of conducting war in the Pacific, and suggested that 'the best way to provide a skilled and an adequate war staff at Singapore would be to transfer a large part of the Admiralty to Singapore'. He even suggested that the Chief of Naval Staff should himself be prepared to relocate. British policy, however, was inconsistent, tormented by considerations of economy and the hope that the League of Nations would obviate the need for substantial defence initiatives. The Singapore plan was shelved, producing a very strong objection on 11 March 1921 from Admiral Jellicoe, who had been appointed Governor of New Zealand and was unofficially acting as that government's defence adviser. The Australian government was also strongly against the decision. The Canadian government, however, refused to make any comment, and the government of South Africa approved of 'the great cause of appeasement and conciliation', which might be undermined by the pursuit of security by military means. British Prime Minister Ramsay Macdonald made good use of these later in presenting his decision to the House.[23] The decision to reduce the scale of effort in developing Singapore into a naval base was endorsed at the 1930 Imperial Conference, but only after a strong protest from the New Zealand government.[24] It wasn't until 1933, after the Japanese occupation of Shanghai, that serious work was recommenced on the Singapore base.[25] Inevitably the Pacific Dominions began to look over their shoulders.

The Munich crisis made it all too apparent that the Singapore strategy was built on sand. The Australians and New Zealanders became increasingly sceptical of Britain's ability, or will, to deploy naval forces to the Pacific with an armed and hostile Germany and Italy making threatening noises, and doubted that Britain would really be willing to leave her interests in the Eastern Mediterranean undefended so as to respond to dangers in the Pacific.[26] A year later, the bankruptcy of naval strategy for the Pacific was transparent, and the best that could be done following the outbreak of war in Europe was to increase the provision allowance for the Singapore garrison in the hope that it could hold out for six months should Japan go to war.

Internationalist values

Great as were the consequences of the failure to perfect the Singapore strategy, the imperfections of the structure of imperial defence had compensatory advantages. Indeed, it can be argued that the limitations on centralised decision-making were vital to the survival of the British Commonwealth in the new geopolitical conditions produced by the rise of American and Japanese power. Perhaps it is not too much to say that the fragmentation of imperial defence structures was an important consideration in making possible the linkage with the United States: while the Empire proved capable of uniting for an obvious and unavoidable defensive purpose, it was clearly incapable of a collective act of aggression.

This was not an accident of history. The determination of Britain, and, I might add, of Canada, from the turn of the twentieth century to appease the American colossus, and transform the United States into a fellow traveller down the path of international security, was one of the great decisions of history. The care with which the Empire addressed American defence and foreign policy concerns, even to the extent of overriding defence advice in order to conclude the 1930 London naval arms limitation treaty, was to prove of decisive importance in the outcome of the war. For its part, Canada was never prepared to make any defence commitment which could endanger her neighbourly relationship with the United States, even when the United States was proving to be a rather difficult neighbour.

Compromise in command

The Canadian experience during the Second World War has established a level of expectation for transnationalism in defence. Despite its best efforts, the Canadian Government had not in fact gained much ability to stand aside from imperial foreign policy, and had forfeited any ability to influence it. In May 1939 Skelton, the Anglophobe Undersecretary of State for External Affairs, had noted caustically that

> The first casualty of this war has been Canada's claim to control over her own destiny. If war comes to Poland and we take part, that war comes as a consequence of commitments made by the Government of Great Britain,

about which we are not in one iota consulted, and about which we were not given the slightest inkling of information in advance.[27]

During the Second World War, strategic direction of allied effort was controlled at the outset by the British and French, and later by the British, Americans and Russians. Mackenzie King complained about the lack of consultation, but was more concerned about appearances than substance, and found that it was better to avoid situations which emphasised his inability.[28] Lester Pearson, then a junior officer in the Canadian High Commission in London, wrote in his diary at the end of April 1940 that

> there are people in Ottawa who would prefer to be left in ignorance and without influence rather than agree to the setting up of some Imperial machinery which might, in their suspicious minds, start a centralizing development which would continue after the war.

From 1942 the new Undersecretary of External Affairs, Norman Robertson, and his deputy Hume Wrong, laboured to establish what became known as the 'functionalist' principle which would accord to nations making major contributions to international efforts a proportionate voice in its direction. The new dimension was that the Canadian Government was prepared to accept the responsibilities that were implied by its representation.[29] Strategic direction of military operations, however, was not an area Canada sought to influence.

Ottawa was more interested, and successful, in establishing its authority over operational control, motivated by a concern to ensure that Canadian forces were used intelligently so as to avoid high casualty rates and futile engagements. Sir Robert Borden's experience in the Imperial War Cabinet, and the Battle of Passchendaele, were the origin of a neurosis which continues to influence Canadian defence policy. At the beginning of hostilities in 1939 the Canadian Navy had been ordered to 'cooperate to the fullest extent with the forces of the Royal Navy', but operational control of the Canadian fleet was not transferred to the Admiralty as it had been in the First World War. Canadian naval officers assumed an increasing role in the direction of naval operations in the Western Atlantic. New strategic realities had to be accommodated. In August 1941, when the US Navy became unofficially involved in the Battle of the Atlantic, Canadian forces were arbitrarily consigned to an American commander with no practical experience of trade defence. When the Japanese attack on Pearl Harbor led to the redeployment of the bulk of American naval forces to the Pacific, this arrangement became even less defensible. In March 1943, however, the Canadian Navy was finally granted operational control of escort forces in the Western Atlantic.[30]

Despite the best efforts of the Canadian Government, and its determination to emphasise technical arms, the Canadian neurosis was further fed by the events of the Second World War. The Canadian Army's first encounter with the enemy, in August 1942, was a disastrous raid on German positions in Dieppe against which unseasoned troops were thrown in a frontal amphibious assault on unbroken defences. Of the nearly 5000 Canadian soldiers sent into action less than half were withdrawn at the end of the day, and over 900 were killed. More Canadians were taken prisoner in nine hours' fighting than were to be lost during the 11-month Normandy campaign or the 20-month Italian campaign. The outbreak of war in the Pacific had already led the Canadian Army into yet another disaster when two battalions were sent to defend Hong Kong despite the fact that London considered the place indefensible against Japan. The deployment had been made as part of a strategy of deterrence at a time when few thought Japan would risk a war against the United States. These experiences exercised a strong influence on Canadian military diplomacy in the post-war years.

Canada's cautious defence policy during the interwar years had had nearly disastrous technical consequences. Canada's naval forces, like the Royal Navy, had paid little attention to submarine warfare in the interwar period, and they suffered from the rate at which they had had to expand from the 1930s establishment. Canadian industry was not geared to complex production, and technical liaison with the British defence industry was poor. The corvettes, intended for coastal escort but pressed into service as ocean escorts, lacked gyro compasses and high frequency radio direction finders, were fitted with an obsolescent sonar, and when radar was retrofitted it was a primitive model which could not provide all-round surveillance. Canadian escort groups lacked the tactical intelligence necessary for planning defensive action against U-boat attacks, but because they were predominantly made up of slow corvettes they were given the more difficult task of escorting slow convoys. The result was that in the second half of 1942, the four Canadian escort groups working in the mid-Atlantic amounted to 35 per cent of allied forces but suffered 80 per cent of the merchant-ship losses. The performance of Canadian escort groups was so poor that in early 1943 they had to be redeployed away from the critical mid-Atlantic area.

The Cold War order

As the war came to an end, and when it became evident that the United States would be accepting responsibility for leadership of the defence structure which developed following the war, it was a matter of priority for Commonwealth statesmen that the precedents which had been established in the context of imperial defence should be respected in the new partnerships led by the United States—partnerships which could not be based on common history and juridical union. Each of the Commonwealth countries trod similar paths, with variations determined by differences in geography and power. Britain's transformation from Imperial Metropolitan to satellite Dominion has been the most dramatic, involving the greatest alteration. Canada, on the other hand, was the Dominion best placed to make an orderly transition to the American orbit, but also the Dominion which would find it most difficult to draw effective lines in the sands. In 1945 the Canadian Government's Advisory Committee on Post-Hostilities Problems warned that

> the United States may be expected to take an active interest in Canadian defence preparations in the future. Moreover, that interest may be expressed with an absence of the tact and restraint customarily employed by the United Kingdom in putting forward defence proposals.[31]

The Second World War had made it evident to many in Ottawa that the compromise between autonomy and strategic effectiveness would have to be recast, with greater emphasis on the latter part of the equation. The greatest danger to Canadian sovereignty lies in the concept of 'Fortress America' which inevitably includes Canada in its glacis, and which demonstrated its limitations in the 1920s and 1930s for addressing problems in the world order. In the immediate post-war years the economic re-orientation of Canada towards the United States, due to the staggering cost to Britain of the two world wars, was unavoidable.

The possibly negative implications of this for Canadian foreign policy, however, were avoided, thanks to the scale of the Soviet threat and the consequential need to develop a strong structure of alliances between sovereign states. The need to respond to the Soviet peril to Europe, and through Europe to Canada, was a grim necessity. It also, however, provided a way of controlling the defence relationship with the United States. In the words of Hume Wrong, Deputy to the Undersecretary of State for External Affairs:

> if the North Atlantic is bridged by a new defensive alliance, the problems of North American defence would become a small part of the larger plan, the purpose of which would be the means of defeating the larger enemy.[32]

There was a strong move in Washington to insist on European unification, which would have left Canada as a minor adjunct to American power. This peril was avoided and the form the alliance finally took, of reciprocal guarantees between sovereign states, better served the Canadian need.[33] The European alliance was a moderating force in Canadian–American relations because of its effect on the strategic environment, permitting the United States to draw its defensive perimeter well beyond Canadian territory.

Canada's policy towards NATO was at once an attempt to avoid the dangers of non-commitment, and a continuation of the effort to preserve Canada's freedom of choice. Lester Pearson, who had moved into politics and become Minister of External Affairs, and Brooke Claxton, Minister of National Defence, exerted themselves in 1950 to establish the principle that when plans were being developed for the employment of the forces or the territory of any member nation, its government would have to be invited to participate in planning discussions of NATO's 'Standing Group' which was formed to provide continuity for the Military Committee of NATO Chiefs of Staff which met bi-annually.[34] This arrangement addressed the fear of Canadian forces being used in dangerous ways. On the other hand, Canada did not lobby for a seat on the Standing Group because it was feared that if Canadians were singled out for participation in the central control of NATO planning it would be impossible for Canada to retain its freedom of decision.[35] The focus continued to be on operational control and technical integration, accepting as unavoidable that the great powers would dominate strategic direction. The principle of consultation was built into the treaty, however, and the Canadian Government was careful to establish that the forces it earmarked for NATO became available to a NATO commander only on authority from Ottawa.

Canada's nationalist reaction

As late as January 1963 Canada was viewed by General Norstad, retiring Supreme Allied Commander Europe, as 'one of the two, perhaps three, countries who have done their best in meeting their commitments in every sense'.[36] NATO, however, was not in fact a complete answer to the problem of managing the Canadian–American defence relationship. The US Joint Chiefs of Staff were determined that continental defence should be independent of the multi-lateral alliance which Americans, and most Europeans, regarded as exclusively for the defence of Europe. Co-operative arrangements concluded between the Royal Canadian Navy (RCN) and the US Navy were not formally stated in any document considered by the political leadership. When the North American Air Defence Agreement (NORAD) was concluded in 1958, the Canadian Diefenbaker administration insisted on inclusion of a statement that the two countries would consult, and insisted that the NORAD Agreement was an integral part of the NATO defence system, which acknowledged the right of member states to determine whether their own forces should be engaged in collective action. However, the Secretary General of NATO, General Paul-Henri Spaak, told a Canadian press conference that the North American Air Defence Command should not be regarded as a NATO command, and the final text of the NORAD Agreement carefully avoided any form of words which would clearly establish such a linkage.[37]

Strategically this was illogical. At least from the mid-1950s, Canada's rationale for exposing itself to attack by participating in continental defence arrangements was to enhance deterrence by ensuring the survival of the American nuclear arsenal, primarily with the objective of making the nuclear guarantee of Europe more credible. Juridically, it was also incoherent. The operational arrangements for continental defence were technical realisations of the alliance relationship Canada and the United States shared through NATO, and only differed from other alliance arrangements because they were not part of the military organisation of NATO. France was later to establish a similar relationship with its NATO allies.

As they were understood in the United States, the Canada–United States (CANUS) continental defence arrangements conflicted with Ottawa's longest held political objective and made Canada automatically an accomplice to American foreign policy. The separation of Canadian–American defence arrangements from the consultative structure of NATO resembles in some respects the transfer of strategic discussion from Imperial Conferences to the CID. In both cases, the superpower preferred to deal individually with subordinates rather than risk their developing common positions in general session.

The NORAD Agreement, while it did commit the Americans to consultation with Canada, did not in fact provide for the intervention of the Canadian political leadership before air defence arrangements were put into effect. This defect became all too apparent in 1962 when the American government did not consult with Canada before seeking to implement the arrangements during the Cuban missile crisis. Diefenbaker refused to be stampeded into a state of apprehended war, and the precautionary alert requested by President Kennedy was eventually ordered by the Minister of National Defence, Douglas Harkness, on his own authority. Canadian maritime forces carried out extensive anti-submarine operations in conjunction with the US Navy initially on the authority of Rear Admiral K.L. Dyer, RCN, Flag Officer Atlantic Coast. Eventually Diefenbaker bowed to the pressure of circumstances and authorised the necessary military measures, recognising that the Canadian Government had no power to formulate an independent policy. In all this there was some parallel to the manner in which the Canadian Navy had acted in the Munich crisis. In both crises the Canadian military responded positively to the requirements of collective defence despite irregularities in political protocol. The outcome in 1962, however, was less fortunate. The domestic politico-military crisis, and Canadian–American misunderstanding, was to be a major formative force on Canadian defence policy for the next decade and a half.[38] Lester Pearson's Minister of National Defence, Paul Hellyer, drove many of his senior officers into early retirement in order to push through a policy of unification of the armed services. It is probable that the motive is to be found in the willingness they displayed during the Cuban missile crisis to co-operate with American forces in a near-war situation in the absence of political direction, and in the subsequent military intervention in Canadian politics.[39] In the following years, the increasing involvement of the United States in a major war in Vietnam, and the pressure that Washington put on the Canadian Government to provide a token military contribution to that campaign, added to the reasons for reassessing Canada's military strategy. Canada's forces were restricted to an extent which reduced the incentive of the United States Government to pressure Canada for active commitment to a campaign in which it was clear Canada would have no strategic control.[40] Pierre Elliott Trudeau, who replaced Pearson as head of the Liberal Party and Prime Minister in 1968, two months after Paul Hellyer's unification bill became law, declared the need for a defence policy that was a product of foreign policy, rather than a foreign policy which was the unavoidable product of defence commitments.[41]

In seeing the danger that participation in collective defence could make it difficult for the Canadian government to act independently in international affairs, Trudeau was an heir not only of Mackenzie King and Laurier, but also of the Nationalists. It cannot be coincidental that in the late 1960s and early 1970s Canada's relative military contribution to international security, measured quantitatively, fell to the point where, within the NATO alliance, only Luxembourg and Iceland were behind Canada in the proportion of their Gross Domestic Product (GDP) spent on defence. The need to influence the strategic plans of Canada's allies continued to be recognised, but in the immediate circumstances it appeared that the goal was beyond Canadian reach, except indirectly through the United Nations, and by partial disengagement from collective defence. The rust-out of Canadian forces during the 1970s can be seen as a means of reducing the degree to which Canadian foreign policy was controlled by the demands of collective defence.

Post–Cold War perspective

The pessimist's view is that, despite their best efforts, post-war Canadian politicians and the Department of External/Foreign Affairs have been conducting a rearguard action against American control, which has become a reality.[42] In retrospect, the demands of imperial defence appear less demanding than are those of continental defence. Canadian commitments to continental defence are virtually automatic, and there is no question of Canada having the sort of influence, either formally or informally, over the formation of American foreign policy which the British offered in the 1920s. In the 1990s the Canadian Armed Forces have begun to participate in operations which appear to be inconsistent with the historical restraints. The transformation of the Canadian fleet into Task Groups of technically advanced ships managed through data links as single forces composed of surface, sub-surface and air units, has facilitated co-operation with similarly organised United States formations. Canadian naval units are deployed to serve with United States battle groups on foreign operations, and, because of recent technical developments, the degree of transnational integration is substantially greater than was possible hitherto. In the future it is not difficult to foresee that weapons may be fired from Canadian warships by a computer located on board an American one. The 1999 air war against Milosevic's Yugoslavia, made possible by the structural integration of NATO air forces (always more integrated than either ground or naval forces), authorised by a complex diplomatic structure, and commanded by institutions of collective defence, is the bittersweet fruit of this system of compromises.

While the pessimist fears that Canada has become an automatic accomplice to American foreign policy, the optimist, on the other hand, is entitled to observe that the alliance relationship with the United States is less demanding than it would have been had it not been, de facto if not de jure, a part of the multi-lateral NATO system, and that the Canadian government is not incapable of influencing Washington, at least when its objectives find some support within the United States. Engagement with American military forces, in order to meet the technical requirements for joint action and in order to establish mutual trust, makes it possible for Canada to co-operate with the United States when it seems appropriate, and also makes a decision to withdraw from an interventionist action a meaningful statement of divergence.

Consultation, in such fora as the NATO Council where unanimity is the rule, but where smaller nations recognise the need to stay on board to meet their general security needs, is the substitute for transnational policy formulation. The technical integration of the Canadian Navy into American battle groups, and their occasional command by Canadian officers, addresses the Canadian 'Dieppe' neurosis—the entirely 'rational' fear of Canadian forces becoming cannon fodder for the generals and admirals of the dominant ally of the day.

Enlightened ad-hocery, in the present day as it was in the imperial age, places the responsibility for leadership primarily in the hands of the greatest powers, but has the very great advantage that it is unlikely a consensus will be found for what were once known as 'imperial adventures'. The smaller powers retain a right to vote with their feet. For them to exercise that right, however, there must be a potential for them to participate if they approve of the cause, which they can do only if their forces are equipped, trained, and experienced for transnational cooperation. There will always be concern about whether Canada, and the other smaller actors in the world drama, can continue to ride the American tiger without ending up inside, but was not that the concern of Dominion leaders in the first half of the century, fearing the 'centralising proclivities' of Whitehall?

The struggle to develop a system of imperial naval defence created a pattern of international behaviour which is now manifest in the system of transnational defence. I also suggest that contemporary experience should give historians a degree of perspective in their study of imperial defence, leading them away from the nationalist blinkers, which too frequently narrow the view.

5 Maritime forces and expeditionary strategies: we are all Corbettians now

Peter Hore

In London it is customary for the Royal United Services Institute to invite the service chiefs of the Navy, Army and Air Force, when they leave office and retire from active duty, to give a valedictory speech at one of the institute's open, lunchtime meetings. The chief, no matter of what coloured cloth, will use the occasion to reflect on his—we are not yet in a position to say her—30 and more years' service: the changes that have taken place and the deeds that he has accomplished, usually with special reference to the battles that have been won in Whitehall, the new equipment which he has brought into service and the morale of his people, who will be the best in the world.

Admiral Sir Jock Slater—two traditions

On 29 September 1998, Admiral Sir Jock Slater, the retiring First Sea Lord and Chief of Naval Staff, broke with the customary style of speech for these occasions. It was an important speech which I hope and expect that the students and indeed historians of strategy will note as being seismic, one which caught the grand strategic rhythms of our time. It is such an important speech that I have no qualms in drawing extensively upon it. Talking about the 'Maritime Contribution To Joint Operations', Jock Slater said:

> I want to speak in some detail about the practicalities of the maritime contribution [to joint operations]. But before I do I would like to set the

scene by reviewing historically the Navy's joint credentials and reflecting a little further on the strategic dynamics we face today . . . As First Sea Lord I am the inheritor of two separate traditions which, although they have been as enduring as the application of naval power, have been placed into particularly sharp focus by the history of the Royal Navy since 1815—an arbitrary date, but one with an obvious significance which will not be lost on this audience. The first tradition is unreconstructed navalism, a view which contends that the twin principles of the decisive fleet engagement and command of the sea represent the proper application of maritime power, particularly British maritime power during a period which started with naval pre-eminence and is still today characterised by naval prominence . . .

As an aside, I wanted the First Sea Lord to use the word 'preponderance', thereby signalling the connection with his reading of Colin Gray's edition of Charles Callwell's *Military Operations and Maritime Preponderance*. 'This is a tradition', continued the First Sea Lord,

> which its advocates would argue saw its consummation on the 21st October 1805 [Nelson's victory at Trafalgar], and while such singular victories have eluded the Royal Navy in the twentieth century, it is a tradition which has been carried on by the American victories in the Pacific campaign in the Second World War . . .[1]

Horatio Nelson and Alfred T. Mahan

The principal witnesses that advocates of this first tradition would call to assist them are Nelson and Mahan. They might add that when fleets have met without decisive result—and the obvious example is Jutland—this was the result of local, tactical factors and offers no general compromise of the central tenet of decisive, annihilating victory. Had the 'bloody ships' in Beatty's phrase behaved properly, normal historical service would have been maintained in 1916, the German High Seas Fleet destroyed and the British Grand Fleet permitted to go about its everyday business of the unchallenged exercise of command of the sea. It is a tradition which draws on a history of battles which were not only decisive but also annihilating— including not only Trafalgar but also Navarino, Tsushima and Midway. It is, of course, a view not unique to Britain. It is a view which perhaps reached its zenith in America in the late 1940s, when it was described by Secretary for War Stimpson as:

> the peculiar psychology of the [United States] Navy department, which frequently seemed to retire from the realm of logic into a dim religious

British battle cruisers steam into action at the tactically indecisive Battle of Jutland, 31 May 1916. HMAS *Australia* missed the battle after a collision in fog; she nevertheless played an active part in the overall British strategy of blockade against Germany. (HMAS *Creswell*)

world in which Neptune was God, Mahan the prophet and the United States Navy the only true church . . .[2]

To Mahan the prophet, Nelson was the embodiment of this powerful religion. And ever since, the sayings of Mahan or the deeds of Nelson have been summoned as examples of what war at sea is about. What actually happened or what was actually written hardly matters in this context, since it is a well-established fact that neither statesmen nor warriors nor many of the public read histories. History, as Lord Esher wrote, 'is written for school-masters and arm-chair strategists'.[3]

Undoubtedly Nelson was a genius, a great leader, a skilled tactician and an inspired strategist, who set the very highest standards. Yet strangely, Nelson's successes in battle have created victims on his own side. Poor Sir Robert Calder! Calder, who in the summer of 1805 scored a significant strategic victory over the French by preventing the juncture of the French fleet under Villeneuve with the French squadron in Brest— in modern doctrine-speak he helped shape the battle-space—was sent home in disgrace on the eve of Trafalgar, and in one of the best battleships too, because John Bull thought he had not done enough: he had not sunk or taken enough ships. Sir John Jellicoe too was a victim. The Victorian interpretation of Nelson was of an authority-figure, and Victorians perceived the anxious and self-doubting control-freak Jellicoe as the next potential Nelson. It was considered a result of his hubris that the strategic victory of Jutland was not also an annihilating victory on the scale of Trafalgar.

Sir Julian Corbett

'But', and this is the First Sea Lord speaking again,

> I am also the inheritor of a second tradition which has run in parallel with the first, whose main spokesmen are Corbett and Richmond and which sees the application of Maritime Power as inextricably linked with operations on the land. This is a view which is joint rather than navalist and one which sees the coveted fleet engagement as relevant only in so far as its effects can be measured in the prosecution of a land campaign. As an illustration let me remind you of Corbett's revisionary view of Trafalgar. The battle coincided with Napoleon's masterpiece[s at Ulm and] at Austerlitz. [Trafalgar], Corbett claimed, did little more than conflict an existing strategic situation; Ulm and Austerlitz destroyed the only viable continental coalition, and established French hegemony in Europe.
>
> Yet the same period showed a definitive example of the use of maritime force to complement land operations. The Peninsula campaign commenced with the amphibious withdrawal of Sir John Moore's Army at Corunna and its re-insertion under Wellington through the port of Lisbon. It was a campaign sustained by maritime power and one which used frequent and imaginative tactical manoeuvre from the sea. To the advocates of this second tradition the cameo of the Peninsula shows all the features which Liddell Hart would later characterise as the British way in warfare: limited expeditionary operations in a minor theatre sustained from the sea and accompanied by the generous subsidy of local allies. Indeed, there is sophistication about our conduct of grand and military strategy in the Napoleonic era that repays study today . . .

These two traditions, eventually those of Mahan and Corbett, cohabited uneasily for most of the nineteenth century and came perilously close to divorce in the twentieth century. It is extraordinary to think that while Corbett was penning the words which would remind the world that

> men live upon the land and not upon the sea, [that] great issues between nations at war have always been decided—except in the rarest of cases—

Although Australia had sent separate military and naval contingents to both the Boer War and the Boxer Rebellion, its tradition of combined operations really began in September 1914 when the Commonwealth sent the Australian Naval and Military Expeditionary Force to seize German New Guinea. The Victorian and South Australian contingents of the ANMEF are seen here on parade before embarkation. (AWM: 305442)

either by what your army can do against your enemy's territory and national life or else by the fear of what the fleet makes it possible for your army to do . . . ,[4]

almost contemporaneously a figure of the establishment, William Laird Clowes, historian of the Royal Navy, was actually calling for a larger and better organised army so that 'calls for assistance of the Navy on shore would be fewer' and the Navy could go about its proper business.[5] Although since, by Laird Clowes' own reckoning, the Navy had not in the previous 85 years been involved in any 'purely maritime war of any importance . . . [and] not called upon to fight one considerable action in the open sea', we can only speculate what Laird Clowes and the Board of Admiralty thought that this business might be.

There is therefore this duality in the rich tradition of British naval heritage—a heritage which the Australian Navy shares to a large degree. By tradition I mean here, of course, the received tenets of Mahan and Corbett, not the actuality as it has been interpreted for us by distinguished colleagues like Professor Jon Sumida.[6] On the one hand, a simple and direct inheritance of a so-called Nelsonic tradition of seeking battle on the sea; on the other, the application of maritime force as part of an integrated, joint approach to war. The first is a glorious tradition of which we all are proud, and which we are preparing to celebrate with full effect as the bicentenary of Trafalgar approaches in 2005. I would like to suggest, however, that it is the second which establishes the precedents which will inform naval operations in the twenty-first century.

From theory into practice

Both Mahan and Corbett wrote in times of shifts and imbalance in world politics, and both were endeavouring to analyse and to predict the appropriate maritime response. We also live in what the Chinese would call interesting times, and volumes have already been written on our changed strategic circumstances. So much for the theory. How is it being applied in practice?

About three years ago I wrote that we were on an historical cusp between periods of continental and maritime pre-eminence.[7] I now judge that I underestimated the extent of the changes that were taking place. My contention now is that Western nations and others, of course, are adopting military strategies which are essentially maritime. Let me be absolutely clear what I mean by that. I do not mean that we have a naval strategy, a return to the first tradition of which I wrote above. To quote Corbett:

> Naval strategy is but that part [of strategy] which determines the movements of the fleet when maritime strategy has determined what part the fleet must play in relation to the action of the land forces . . .[8]

Rather, I believe we have a military strategy which connects directly with the second tradition I have described, one that will depend on maritime deployment and sustainment and will permit the prosecution of operations from the sea to the land. What *The Times* of London has called a 'national maritime military strategy, scrapping the old continental military strategy, based on a concentration of troops in Germany. The focus will be on developing a capability to mount expeditionary forces around the world . . .'[9]

It should not surprise us that the United States and a number of other countries have made the same discovery. In an era of the 'bonfire of the certainties' when small wars are more likely not less, in the words of Basil Liddell Hart:

> self-contained and sea-based amphibious force[s are] the best kind of fire extinguisher because of [their] flexibility, reliability, logistic simplicity and relative economy . . .[10]

The United States of America

I should now like to deal briefly with practice in America and the United States Navy (USN), including the United States Marine Corps (USMC). Essentially, the US *Maritime Strategy* enunciated in the mid-1980s was a Mahanian concept appropriate to the era of the Cold War. Today, the West, to a very large extent through the agency of the USN during the Cold War, owns the high seas, the blue water, and this simple fact is a precondition which enables us to contemplate expeditionary operations. *From the Sea* and *Forward from the Sea* were the two American White Papers which signalled a shift in the USN's operational emphasis from blue water to brown. This shift continues and I understand that the next new USN strategic White Paper, which will be called *A Maritime Strategy for the Next Century*, has won the full approval of the USMC. I also understand that Secretary of the Navy Danzig has asked the USN to address the future of legacy systems. This latter point is good news for lesser navies, such as the Royal Navy, whose concern must be to maintain interoperability with the USN while revolutionary, technical changes—which we may not be able to afford—are taking place.

It is good news for the USN too, for the United States seeks greater burden-sharing by European countries and seeks to develop and to maintain a range of credible partners for coalition operations. In this context, preservation of close doctrinal and operational relationships between the amphibious forces of the United States and the United Kingdom is a high priority, which contributes significantly to alliance cohesion. The United Kingdom's close relationship with US amphibious forces provides privileged access to their examination of how combat power, with naval, joint and combined inventories, can be effectively delivered—the US SEA DRAGON program—and themes emerging from this work already influence British thinking.

India, China and Australia

Not all these ideas are unique. It is useful to have from India a separate and independent confirmation of our thoughts, out of a stream of consciousness which is not in essence Anglo-Saxon. In *Maritime Strategy and Continental Wars*, Rear Admiral Raja Menon tells us that 'navies must begin to think bigger . . .'[11] From another entirely different viewpoint, even the monolithic and archetypically continental Chinese Peoples' Liberation Army has begun to think about the influence of navies. I am still awaiting a translation of the chapter by my colleague, Colonel Xu Weidi, of his thoughts entitled *The Maritime Military Struggle in the World Military*

Western maritime preponderance has historically allowed the unhindered dispatch of expeditionary forces from Europe and America, but in regional theatres the situation is more complex. In 1914 it was not until HMAS *Sydney*'s destruction of SMS *Emden* that the Allies could claim undisputed control of the Indian Ocean. Only then could AIF troopships sail to Europe and the Middle East without escort. (AWM: EN0401)

Trend, a book published by the National Defence University in Beijing in 1996.

Australians also seem to be experiencing the same thought processes. The refurbished amphibious vessels HMA Ships *Kanimbla* and *Manoora* are certainly suitable vehicles for an expeditionary strategy. I have also noted the arguments of Michael Evans that Australia's security interest would be well served by adopting a sea-based manoeuvre strategy and building on the development of a credible amphibious warfare force.[12] Copies of his monograph on *The Role of the Army in a Maritime Concept of Strategy*, published by the Australian Land Warfare Studies Centre, have been distributed and well received within the British Ministry of Defence.

Europe

Within Europe the utility of amphibious forces is recognised by a number of nations embarked on ambitious programs. Currently, however, the

United Kingdom is the only country with the sustainable high intensity capability and command systems of the required effectiveness to be capable both of operating alongside the United States and of a command and control role within some combined European amphibious force. This aspect of the warfighting capability of the United Kingdom and the closely associated Netherlands Amphibious Force is enhanced by the implementation of the Royal Navy's new concept of operations for the twenty-first century, the Maritime Contribution to Joint Operations (MCJO).[13] The United Kingdom is committed to the principles of the 1996 Berlin Agreement on achieving a European Security and Defence Identity (ESDI) within NATO. In the light of the Amsterdam Treaty and of evolving European competence in defence matters, the relationship with our European partners will achieve an ever greater significance. This development is exemplified by agreements such as that reached by the United Kingdom and France at St Malo in November 1998, in the round of six-monthly bilateral summit meetings.[14] Thus, the United Kingdom 'seeks to take forward the debate on how to develop an effective mechanism for the European Union to direct defence issues ...' As ESDI gathers effective and practical momentum, the United Kingdom's amphibious forces offer an organisation capable of providing operational leadership for a European force.

NATO first

Of course, not least to avoid duplication, the underlying practical military capability will remain rooted in NATO. As far as Britain is concerned the development of European amphibious relations will necessarily have to take account of obligations and trends within multilateral organisations such as NATO and the Western European Union, and of British bilateral linkages with the United States and the Netherlands. Among allied nations amphibious capabilities and aspirations differ, associated plans and programs are rarely in harmony and regional factors influence likely employment and compatibility.

As far as the Netherlands is concerned, we can assume that the Royal Netherlands Navy and Marine Corps' integration with the British amphibious forces in the shape of the UK–Netherlands Amphibious Force or UKNLAF—which in 1999 celebrated its 25th birthday—will endorse this strong, bilateral alliance. Other relationships, or the potential for such, vary widely in quality and consistency, and are influenced by issues of national interest, operational compatibility and doctrinal congruence. While there is no prospect of any other European amphibious force achieving the same degree of integration as the UKNLAF in the foreseeable future, there is, however, long-term potential to establish an interoperable, large-scale European force capable of rapid and independent action from the sea.

Northern Region

In the Northern Region there is no amphibious capability amongst the Norwegians, the Germans nor Danes (although the Germans are seeking to deploy an air defence system in support of UKNLAF, and aspire to a limited amphibious capability). The Swedes have an amphibious arm tailored to inshore operations but politically are severely constrained from working with other nations, unless in the spirit of partnership-for-peace (PfP). The French have a considerable amphibious force, although following their decision not to re-integrate within the NATO military structure, are sensitive with respect to operating too closely with other NATO nations. NATO problems apart, an increasing French interest in bilateral initiatives such as the Anglo–French declaration at St Malo, an ambitious building program, and the growing thirst, at the working level, for advice and practical assistance all indicate that France intends to develop her participation in amphibious operations. Apart from Poland, whose amphibious operational capability and political perspective have yet to be fully gauged, the Northern Region's amphibious expertise and capability reside unequivocally with the United Kingdom and the Netherlands in the form of the UKNLAF.

Southern Region

In the Southern Region, Portugal has a growing amphibious capability and would appear to welcome closer ties with other NATO amphibious forces. The Spanish, who are a significant amphibious force, have formed the Spanish–Italian Amphibious Force (SIAF).[15] Both nations appear committed to raising the level of their own operational capabilities and have ambitious plans for the expansion of their amphibious forces.[16] The regional role of France, with the exception of her involvement in the European Maritime Force (EUROMARFOR), is constrained by French politics, but there are indications that she may wish to develop closer amphibious ties. Greece and Turkey have independent and relatively primitive amphibious capabilities and, given regional sensitivities, neither is active in pressing for closer links with other amphibious forces (although they are prospective members of EUROMARFOR).

Conclusion

This chapter began with the dichotomy between the received traditions of the British Navy, traditions which are shared with the RAN and are mirrored in other navies. On the one hand there is received wisdom about what Nelson did and Mahan wrote, and there is—or rather was—the US *Maritime Strategy* of the Cold War. On the other hand we have Corbett ('men live upon the land and not upon the sea') and the pronounced shifts that have taken place since the end of the Cold War, away from fixed dispositions on the plains of Germany towards expeditionary strategies. These shifts are taking place in many countries simultaneously, but are particularly pronounced in Europe, where there are several initiatives concerning amphibious forces and the potential for more. Britain has the most capable European amphibious and expeditionary forces, with longstanding links to the Netherlands Marine Corps, and the capacity to operate alongside the USMC. These twin relationships must not be jeopardised, but Britain also has the capacity to lead within Europe the further development of Europe's sea-based expeditionary forces. The development of a separate European defence identity must, however, give precedence to NATO.

6 Strategic culture and the Australian way of warfare: perspectives
Michael Evans

This chapter seeks to identify the existence and characteristics of Australian strategic culture and to analyse the related concept of a way of warfare. Four areas are examined. First, a snapshot is provided of the comparative research into the idea of strategic culture and the notion of a way in warfare along with an assessment of the difference between the two concepts. Second, there is a focus on research into Australian strategic culture concentrating on the degree of continuity and change during the twentieth century. Third, various approaches to analysing an Australian way of warfare, from the Anzac/Digger legend to more recent attempts to develop a way of warfighting at the operational level of war in the modern Australian Defence Force (ADF), are assessed. It is suggested that a way of warfare should be seen as a sub-set of strategic culture—a military operational manifestation of a society's values and deepest beliefs about how it should defend itself.

Fourth, perspectives from both strategic culture and a way of warfighting are applied to Australia's recent attempt to develop a maritime concept of strategy for the twenty-first century. The chapter argues that the development of a maritime concept of strategy is complicated by the existence of contending continentalist and navalist traditions in Australian strategic practice. These opposing traditions represent a division that must be overcome if the ADF is to maximise all of its capabilities and combat power to meet the demands of future conflict.

The concept of strategic culture and its relationship to a way in warfare

What is meant by the term strategic culture? The concept of strategic culture first emerged in the 1970s as an attempt by scholars to understand the American calamity in Vietnam. Another aim was to provide an alternative to the arid technological determinism that had gripped much of Cold War strategic studies. The basic assumption of strategic culture is that there exists in a nation-state a distinctive and lasting set of beliefs, values and habits regarding the threat and use of force, which have their roots in such fundamental influences as geographical setting, history, ideology and political culture.[1]

Such factors act as a transmission belt between a society's experiences and its strategic decision-making. Strategic cultures are not rigid but, because they rest upon distinctive burdens of historical and institutional experience, change is usually slow. The definition of strategic culture devised by the British political scientist Ken Booth is instructive:

> The concept of strategic culture refers to a nation's traditions, values, attitudes, patterns of behaviour, habits, symbols, achievements and particular ways of adapting to the environment and solving problems with respect to the threat and use of force.[2]

One needs to be careful, however, not to attribute any determinism to this definition. The Royal Air Force (RAF) Chief of Staff Sir John Slessor's view in the 1950s that the Russians could be relied upon to be cautious in matters of strategy, because chess rather than poker was their national game, is a good example of the dangers of ethnocentrism.[3] Obviously Slessor had never heard of the game of Russian roulette.

Anglo-American scholars have completed the most important work on strategic culture.[4] Colin Gray and Anita Arms have, for example, identified various core features influencing American strategic culture. These features include a geography of isolation, an ideology of individualism, a political idea of Americanism, a rhetoric of moralism, faith in technology, and a belief in the use of massive force increasingly expressed through a preference for air power.[5] Recently, the study of strategic culture has expanded to cover various Asia–Pacific states including Japan, China and Indonesia. Asian scholars such as Muthiah Alagappa have attempted to broaden the Western idea of strategic culture into a notion of security practice—a concept that accommodates characteristics which are believed to be particularly important in Asia—especially the relationship between internal and international security and the challenge of developing an Asian tradition of multilateral security.[6]

Strategic culture is, of course, linked conceptually not only to political culture, but to an older school of scholarship that has analysed the historical roots of national ways in warfare.[7] The language of strategic culture may be modern but the ideas it seeks to illuminate tend to be well known to many historians.[8] As the British military historian Sir Michael Howard has put it, 'the military system of a nation is not an independent section of the social system but an aspect of it in its totality'.[9] This raises an interesting question: what is the difference between a strategic culture and a way in warfare? Are they compatible themes? This question is of more than rhetorical importance because there can be a temptation to use the two terms loosely without concern for any methodological differences between the two concepts.[10]

While there is a close relationship between the modern notion of strategic culture and the older idea of a way of warfare, they do differ in methodology and in scope. The idea of a strategic culture is a broader and more recent social scientific construct than the notion of a way of warfare as developed by military historians. As the American strategic analyst Carnes Lord has observed, strategic culture tends to represent a holistic pattern of beliefs and attitudes within a society relating to the theory of strategy and defence. It is concerned with how to use military force in statecraft.[11]

In contrast, the idea of a way in warfare is more restrictive in scope; it is usually concerned with the operational and organisational aspects of military strategy and operations as gleaned from historical evidence. In short it is about how to fight. A way of warfare can be defined as a set of attitudes and beliefs held within a military establishment concerning the political objective of war and the most effective strategy and operational method of achieving it. This definition concentrates on the military practice of a nation's armed forces. For this reason, the idea of a way of warfare is, in a modern sense, probably best viewed as a sub-set of strategic culture.[12]

A good example of warfighting as a sub-set of strategic culture can be found in the 1993 edition of the United States Army's FM 100-5 *Operations*. In this manual there is a clear attempt to translate perceived American national values into the idiom of military operations. A section entitled 'The American Way of War' states:

> The people expect the military to accomplish its missions in compliance with national values. The American people expect decisive victory and abhor unnecessary casualties. They prefer quick resolution of conflicts and reserve the right to reconsider their support should any of these conditions not be met ... In the end, the people will pass judgment on the appropriateness of the conduct and use of military operations. Their values and expectations must be met.[13]

The notion of a way of warfare has stimulated some interesting military history. Liddell Hart's famous study *The British Way in Warfare* in the early 1930s and Russell Weigley's well-known book *The American Way of War* in the early 1970s are perhaps the best-known examples.[14] Liddell Hart's claim that the strategy of indirect approach represented a distinct British practice of war began the modern debate between maritime strategy and the continental commitment in British strategic thought that continues to this day.[15] Similarly, Russell F. Weigley's theory of an American way of war based on what he termed 'the strategy of power' using decisive force was a major contribution to understanding the nature of American military practice.[16]

In the late 1980s, the American classical scholar Victor Davis Hanson sought to expand the way of warfare debate to include the notion of a generic Western way of war.[17] Hanson suggested that there was a distinctive Western way of war derived from the ancient Greeks and based on pitched battle. Great encounter battles from Cannae to Normandy could be traced in spirit to the phalanxes of Hellenic hoplites on the fields at Marathon and Delion.[18]

In the 1990s Hanson's ideas have influenced such writers as John Keegan and Lawrence Freedman. In his 1993 book *A History of Warfare*, Keegan drew on Hanson's ideas in an attempt to demolish the idea of a Western way of warfare, which he believed had been codified in Clausewitz's doctrine of decisive battle.[19] Clausewitz's ideas on force were contrasted unfavourably with Sun Tzu's axiom that the supreme art of war is to subdue an enemy without fighting. Keegan called for a new Western way of warfighting using principles of intellectual restraint and cultural ritual that he associates with Eastern military traditions.[20] More recently, Lawrence Freedman has argued that the Western way of war in the information age should aim to maximise the new techniques of the perceived Revolution in Military Affairs (RMA) to achieve swift, decisive force-on-force victory with minimum casualties.[21]

Australian strategic culture

To date, research into Australian strategic culture has been mainly the work of a group of scholars from what might be described as the school of 'New Left Australian isolationism'. These scholars view Australian strategic culture as being based on 'discourses of danger and dread frontiers'.[22] The New Left school argues that Australian strategic culture is relatively unchanged in the twentieth century and reflects the geopolitical isolation of a small Anglo–Celtic nation occupying a huge continent on the edge of Asia.[23] Graeme Cheeseman argues that cultural isolation, unfavourable demography and vast geography have moulded a rigid strategic culture centred on the twin pillars of national fear of Asia and the need for dependence on great allies, first Britain then the United States.[24] These factors have meant that Australian strategic culture reflects a style of thinking based on xenophobia, threat-obsession and military subordination in coalitions.[25]

The problem with this New Left profile of Australian strategic culture is twofold. First, it affords no independent rationale to a mode of Australian strategic thinking that has historically been conditioned less by the constant of geography and more by the variables of diplomacy.[26] For most of its history Australia has confronted two great paradoxes: the paradox of geographical proximity to, but cultural distance from, Asia and the paradox of geographical distance from, but cultural intimacy with, the Anglo-Saxon heartlands. This strategic dilemma of a small nation caught between Eastern geography and Western history is too easily portrayed as xenophobia when it was, as Prime Minister Joseph Cook put it in 1914, a 'problem of highest statesmanship'.[27] In June 1988, the Minister for Defence, Kim Beazley, put it well when he said that Australia with one per cent of the earth's population was condemned to defend twelve per cent of the earth's surface and to do this successfully it required nimble statecraft.[28]

Second, the New Left strategic cultural model tends to ignore the changes in Australian political culture and strategic thinking which have occurred over the last 25 years. These changes are well summarised in Paul Kelly's 1992 study of Australian politics and economics, *The End of Certainty*, arguably the most significant analysis of Australian political culture since the work of Sir Keith Hancock in 1930.[29] Kelly's work is very useful in illuminating various connections and continuities between Australian political culture and strategic culture. Kelly argues that twentieth-century Australian political culture can be divided into two eras: the era of the Australian Settlement that lasted from Federation in 1901 to the end of the Vietnam War in 1972; and the era of internationalism and globalisation which started with the Whitlam–Fraser era in the 1970s and is continuing into the twenty-first century.[30]

What Kelly calls the 'era of the Australian Settlement' was the product of Federation in 1901 when Australia became a modern nation. Australia was founded as a New Britannia based on Benthamite utilitarian beliefs. The Settlement era was distinguished by faith in social egalitarianism manifested through policies of industry protection, wage arbitration and state paternalism.[31] According to Kelly, these policies were developed in the context of the ideology of White Australia, which formed the bedrock both for Australian nationalism, and for the theory of British imperial defence, which flourished as guarantors of Australia's security. The pillars

The arrival of the RAN Fleet Unit caused an outpouring of nationalist sentiment and the first real consciousness of Australia's maturity. A scene from the full-length movie *Sea Dogs of Australia*, previewed in December 1913, which featured German spies, an heroic RAN lieutenant, and a climactic battle between HMAS *Australia* and an enemy cruiser outside Sydney Heads.
(*Screen and Sound*)

of the Australian Settlement were reflected in Australian strategic culture. Defence thinking was closely aligned to diplomacy and the courtship of powerful allies, first the British and later the Americans. From the First World War to Vietnam, alliance-diplomacy and expeditionary warfare as part of international coalitions were used by successive generations to ensure Australia's security.[32]

Between the 1970s and the late 1990s, however, the pillars of the Australian Settlement were swept away. Free market economics, labour deregulation and a global information age have either destroyed or eroded protectionism, arbitration and state welfare. The ideology of White Australia has been replaced by a national policy of multiculturalism. Asia has ceased to be perceived as a region of threat and has become instead a region of economic opportunity and security engagement. As the Settlement ideology eroded, so too did the traditional foundations of Australia's strategic culture.

Five factors are worth noting. First, in the era of internationalism, the development of a more cosmopolitan and multicultural society has seen Australian strategic culture develop more independent, indigenous and conceptual elements. Second, from the 1970s until the late 1990s, reliance on expeditionary warfare ceased to be the driving force behind defence planning and the strategic focus moved more towards defending Australia from a base within Australia. Third, in the 1980s, the notion of military dependence on allies was reformulated as 'self-reliance in an alliance framework'.[33]

Fourth, Australian geography—for so long seen by many as a liability—was recast by a new generation of strategic planners as a positive asset that enabled an almost impenetrable defence-in-depth. Defence planning focused on the theory of Australia as a 'dry archipelago'.[34] This geostrategic approach balanced the former exclusive concern of strategic policy-makers with the diplomacy of alliance commitments. Fifth, the culture of Australian defence planning ceased to be threat-oriented and focused instead on military capabilities. These new features make Australian strategic culture much more complex and varied than the New Left scholars would have us believe.[35]

The Australian way of warfare

Is there such a phenomenon as a distinctive Australian way of warfare? And if so, how does it operate as a sub-set of strategic culture? This chapter suggests the notion of a special Australian martial tradition. This tradition is older than the concept of an Australian strategic culture, and has been embraced by many soldiers, politicians and writers. As Jeffrey Grey has noted, the idea of an Australian way in warfare has often been connected to the figure of the Anzac Digger—the quintessential infantryman—as celebrated by Charles Bean in his *Official History of the First World War*.[36] However, unlike the debates over British and American ways of warfare that tend to emphasise a *style of strategy*, the emphasis in discussions about the existence of an Australian way of warfighting is often on a particular *style of fighting*—usually expeditionary infantry operations at the tactical level of war. Indeed it has been argued by Gareth Evans and Bruce Grant that one of the curiosities of Australian history is the development of martial tradition before contemplation of the essential art of self-defence.[37]

In 1966, the sociologist Sol Encel, in his paper *Militarism and the Citizen Tradition in Australia*, argued that there was a distinctly Australian way of warfare based on the Anzac infantryman.[38] Thirty years later not a great deal appeared to have changed. In 1996, in the *New Zealand Army*

Journal, a trio of Australasian military historians, Carl Bridge, Glyn Harper and Iain Spence, identified what they styled as an 'Anzac way of war'. The latter, they suggested, was based on the citizen soldier; the use of well-trained infantry; participation in coalition warfare as a junior ally; and logistical and other arms support from stronger allies.[39]

In all of this writing, the influence of Charles Bean and the Anzac/Digger fighting tradition, with its egalitarianism and mateship, has been strong.[40] Bean's influence shows few signs of waning. In 1997, for example, Major General Steven Gower, the Director of the Australian War Memorial, described the fighting Digger's 'spirit of mateship' as typifying the Australian way of warfare.[41] The difficulty with equating the Anzac/Digger fighting tradition with an Australian way of warfare is, however, fourfold. First, the Anzac tradition is more than a way of warfare; it is a metaphor for Australian nationhood and has an enduring symbolic power far beyond questions of strategy.[42] Second, as historians such as Peter Pedersen and Eric Andrews have argued, the Anzac/Digger military tradition ignores such fundamentals of modern warfare as logistics, training, leadership and strategy.[43] Third, and related to the previous point, the present ADF is a professional, long-service force dedicated to exactly such fundamentals of modern warfighting. Fourth, various Australian air force and naval writers have argued that the Anzac/Digger military tradition is an Army ideal. They believe that, given the importance of the Royal Australian Air Force (RAAF) and the RAN in the defence of Australia since the 1970s, the Anzac tradition is less relevant to contemporary Australian strategy.[44]

What has been missing from the debate over an Australian way of warfighting is a serious discussion of the impact of changes in the operational–strategic environment. The most important work in this area has been completed by David Horner but unfortunately remains unpublished.[45] The operational–strategic aspects of Australian warfighting only really began to emerge during the 1990s, when developments in joint command structures and theatre doctrine began to emerge in the ADF. In 1997, official interest in investigating the notion of an Australian way of warfare was stimulated by the formation of Headquarters Australian Theatre (HQAST)—the first joint operational theatre headquarters in the ADF's history.[46] In late 1997, HQAST published a warfighting concepts document entitled *Decisive Manoeuvre* aimed at providing the basis for the 'creation of an Australian Way of Warfighting'.[47] The aim was to try to resolve the dichotomy in Australia's military experience between tactical expertise and operational level inexperience and so develop a joint framework for campaigning.[48]

The purpose of *Decisive Manoeuvre* is to develop a twenty-first-century way of warfighting which encompasses synchronised operations

By 1918, especially after the enormous losses on land, the ill-fated Gallipoli landings had replaced the fleet unit as the symbol of Australia's coming of age. Endlessly repeated re-enactments, such as this one filmed in the 1930s (using Royal Marines) have promoted a stereotypical image of Australia's way of warfare. (Naval History Directorate)

by joint forces to attack an enemy's critical vulnerabilities and unhinge his centre of gravity.[49] This is the language of the operational art and of the information age and it demonstrates how the debate over Australian warfighting is reflecting a more mature strategic culture. ADF warfighting ideas are now focused on developing an approach to applying combat power emphasising manoeuvre warfare and logistical austerity. The core concepts of this new warfighting approach are timely force projection, tailored sustainment, co-ordinated precise engagement and effective interoperability. These concepts are being refined as the ADF gradually develops doctrine designed to dominate the modern battlespace and so achieve decision superiority in operations.[50]

In late 1998 Air Vice Marshal Peter Nicholson, Head of Strategic Policy and Plans in the Department of Defence, indicated this process of doctrinal refinement. In an address at the Chief of Army's Exercise in Brisbane, Nicholson sought to identify some of the key characteristics of the Australian way of warfare in the twenty-first century.[51] He argued that Australia's evolving way of warfare embraced seven characteristics. First, *manoeuvre* must be emphasised in order to allow the ADF to offset its demographic weakness and conserve its human resources; second, *intelligence and surveillance* are critical in helping a small ADF to develop flexibility to offset its vast strategic geography. Third, there is a need for the *availability of strike options* for the problem of both deterrence and military response; fourth, there is a key need for an *emphasis on technology*—again because of unfavourable demography. Fifth, Australia requires *interoperability especially with alliance partners*—and this should be seen as an extension of Australia's military history and liberal-democratic political tradition; sixth, *joint operations* are essential to enable the ADF to maximise synergy and combat power; and seventh, a favourable *disposition of forces and assets* must be sought as a means of protecting the maritime approaches to Australia including the northern archipelago.[52]

Nicholson situated his ideas in the context of the emergence of information operations in general and the development of asymmetric warfare in particular.[53] One does not have to accept all of Nicholson's ideas at face value to appreciate that they do represent a serious attempt to reinvigorate the way of warfare debate. The aim is to move discussion away from a preoccupation with Anzac ideology and the tactical level of warfare towards a better appreciation of the contraction of the levels of war and the needs of joint operations. The emphasis is firmly on those elements of warfighting the ADF may need to develop in order to operate effectively in the new century.

Strategic culture, a way of warfare and a maritime concept of Australian strategy

The ADF is now committed to a maritime concept of strategy: that is, a joint approach using all arms—Army, Navy and Air Force—to maximise combat power in a littoral environment. How can perspectives drawn from ideas about strategic culture and the debate over a way of warfare assist Australia to understand the requirements of such a strategy? The notions of strategic culture and a way of warfighting are particularly useful tools in helping to illuminate how Australia has historically conceptualised war in terms of separate continentalist and navalist dimensions. In terms of both strategic culture and warfighting practice, Australia has limited experience of joint maritime operations.[54] Consequently, the ADF will have to develop a maritime strategy against the weight of a past that has never favoured such a warfighting approach.

As John Bach has pointed out, 'there has been [in Australia] a lack of what might be called a national maritime tradition'.[55] A maritime tradition is a missing element in Australia's sense of its national history and, by extension, of its strategic culture and way of warfare. This is a striking paradox in that, as an island-continent dependent on sea communications and trade, Australia should be the archetype of a maritime nation. Yet a maritime character is not imprinted on the Australian national psyche. As the leading Australian maritime historian Frank Broeze has lamented, Australians are a coastal people with a continental outlook, an island-nation with an inward focus.[56]

The land, not the sea, is the dominant feature of Australian culture. Three examples serve to demonstrate this reality. First, in terms of political philosophy, Australian Federation in 1901 was the culmination of a philosophy of continental union rather than of island-unity. Second, following Gallipoli, the experience of continental warfare in Europe from 1916 to 1918 was a powerful force in cementing the idea of Australian nationhood. Third, a sense of continental awareness infuses both Australian literature and art—from the novels of Patrick White to the paintings of Sidney Nolan. White's most internationally acclaimed novel is *Voss*, a novel of harsh landscape based on the life of the overland explorer Ludwig Leichhardt. Nolan's famous paintings of Ned Kelly capture the interior world of the bushranger, not the seafarer.[57] For most Australians, then, the sea is a moat which guards a continental culture and in this sense Australia has a naval rather than a maritime tradition. In 1987, Defence Minister Kim Beazley stated with some frustration: 'despite a host of good reasons for the contrary, Australia is not a maritime nation and its people do not sustain much of an interest in maritime strategy'.[58]

Without a maritime tradition to help unify the land–sea interface, Australian strategic culture has exhibited a longstanding divide between the conceptual opposites of continentalism and navalism. The continental–naval divide in Australian military thinking permeates twentieth-century Australian military history. The pre-1914 defence debate between such figures as Lieutenant Colonel J.W. McCay, the Minister of Defence in the Reid–McLean Government (who favoured land defence), and Captain William Creswell (who favoured the formation of an Australian navy) inaugurated the continentalist–navalist division.[59]

In the interwar years the Australian Army pursued continental defence while the RAN favoured 'blue-water' imperial defence based on the Singapore strategy. This was the context in which the fierce debates between continentalists and navalists were conducted in the 1920s and 1930s. Continentalists such as Colonels J.D. Lavarack and D.H. Wynter on one side and navalists such as the Australian Secretary for Defence Frederick Shedden and the British strategist Admiral Sir Herbert Richmond on the other struggled for intellectual supremacy.[60] The navalists prevailed and successive interwar Australian governments embraced the Singapore strategy. 'Isolated fortresses', Richmond warned in 1933, 'however large, have always fallen; that is a very plain lesson of history'.[61] Ironically for

Richmond, the isolated fortress that fell was not Australia, but that great bastion of imperial naval defence, Singapore.

The Second World War saw Australia fight a desperate maritime campaign for national survival in the South-West Pacific. But in the era of Forward Defence in the 1950s and 1960s and on into the Defence of Australia period from 1972 to 1997 the continental–naval divide in Australian military thought resurfaced rapidly.[62] By the 1980s the division had become almost institutionalised through the creation of separate environmental commands (land, air and sea) and the adoption of a vertically layered strategy of defence-in-depth deploying the RAN and RAAF in the northern sea–air gap while largely confining the Army to continental operations.[63]

In the 1990s, post-Cold War security changes and growing tensions between a defence policy of self-reliance and a foreign policy of regional engagement finally forced Australian defence planners to confront the need for a modern maritime concept of strategy. But the 1997 strategic policy document which emerged, *Australia's Strategic Policy* (ASP 97), while being more focused on a strategy of maritime offshore operations, largely failed to provide a means for integrating all aspects of Australian combat power.[64]

ASP 97 demonstrated a failure to understand the requirements for a joint maritime strategy as advocated by the great British maritime strategist Sir Julian Corbett.[65] Four flaws are worth noting. First, the 1997 review reflected a strategy–force mismatch between land forces for continental operations and naval–air platforms for defending the sea–air gap. There was no concept of an integrated sea–land–air gap existing throughout the northern archipelago.[66] Second, the authors of ASP 97 believed that the West's post-Cold War shift from oceanic to littoral warfare did not really apply to the Asia–Pacific region because, they argued, unlike in the Euro–Atlantic area, sea control remained critical in order to defend sea lines of communications (SLOCs).[67]

The corollary was that many strategic planners, until very recently, saw little use for the Australian Army in maritime operations. In this sense, the authors of ASP 97 were Mahanian navalists rather than Corbettian maritimists. Third, because ASP 97 continued to perpetuate the historic continentalist–navalist divide in Australian strategy, it proved inadequate to address the strategic consequences of the Asia–Pacific economic crisis and the political crisis in East Timor. The deployment of 4500 Australian peace enforcement troops to East Timor in 1999 put more pressure on Australia to accelerate the development of a littoral strategy. Fourth, the United States' embracing of force projection expeditionary operations aimed at mastery of the Pacific littoral means that Australia will need to adjust to new operational realities for conducting alliance warfare in its own region.[68]

The advantage of a Corbettian joint maritime approach is that it may help the ADF to begin to bury once and for all the continentalist–navalist divide in its strategic culture and way of warfare. Such an approach would promote complementary capabilities for contingencies requiring modern amphibious and airborne operations. A modern maritime strategy must be concerned with a sea–land–air interface as one battlespace which generates in turn a single spatial strategy, not a layered strategy.[69] For maritime warfare, the ADF, as a small force without aircraft carriers, requires joint capabilities—including shipboard and land-based missiles, attack helicopters, UAVs (unpiloted aerial vehicles), amphibious assault forces, specialist aircraft and additional special forces.

The ADF has to develop an integrated Maritime Operations in a Littoral Environment (MOLE) fighting philosophy based on joint strike warfare—with an ability to apply force against the shore from the sea—what Sir Julian Corbett once called 'war by contingent'.[70] It is important to note that, in this context, there is a genuine need for Australian strategy to try to accommodate what might be styled 'parallel warfare' in the form of blue water (that is, SLOC and battlespace control operations) and green water (that is, littoral warfare) requirements.

Conclusions

The American strategist Admiral Henry E. Eccles once wrote that 'the ultimate source of strategy lies in the values of the people of a nation'.[71] Study of Australian strategic culture and investigation of an Australian way of warfare illuminate the truth of these words. Perspectives gleaned from strategic culture reveal both continuity and change in Australia's view of the use of military force. They demonstrate how political culture, geography and history have influenced decision-making; they throw light on the persistence of the infantry tradition in Australian warfighting practice; and they reveal the rationale for the continentalist–navalist divide in Australian strategy.

Study of Australian strategic culture and a way of warfare also help us understand how a small, largely Anglo–Celtic society successfully fought two world wars. In the post-Cold War era, further research into strategic culture and warfighting practice may yield more useful lessons and insights. Much remains to be learned about how the Defence Force of a larger, multicultural and more diverse Australia might conceptualise the use of force for both independent campaigning and for coalition operations. Such lessons and insights may assist us to blend older geographical and historical affinities with newer political, technological and global characteristics. Finally, study of strategic culture and warfighting practice reveals how self-knowledge can become the most important form of strategic wisdom by helping us to understand how the shape of the future is conditioned by the way the past impinges on the realities of the present.

PART II

PERSPECTIVES ON IMPERIAL AND AUSTRALIAN NAVAL DEFENCE

7 Australia, the *Trent* crisis of 1861 and the strategy of imperial defence
Andrew Lambert

In the nineteenth century Australia was never attacked by a foreign power, nor was there any realistic prospect that it would be.[1] Consequently discussions of 'Imperial Defence' from the perspective of Sydney and Melbourne tended to have a strong flavour of unreality, in which the appearance of a puny Russian corvette in 1882 could be translated into a terrible threat. In truth much of the debate was about local politics and responsible government, rather than real security concerns. It should be stressed that Britain provided external security for the Empire. Furthermore between 1814 and 1914 it did so with conspicuous success: no major power attacked Britain, or any imperial territory. In a period dominated by aggressive, expansive nations willing to use force to further their aims, this was a remarkable achievement. It was rendered that much more remarkable by the very low level of real defence spending between 1815 and 1890.

This raises an important question. How was Australia defended? Focusing on one of the most serious challenges to imperial security of the era this chapter examines how the system worked, and how it evolved to reflect new political and technological conditions between 1856 and 1865.

The strategy of 'Imperial Defence'

At the end of the Napoleonic wars Britain retained a chain of small, generally insular, possessions around the world, either as bases for the Royal

Navy, notably Malta, or to deny them to potential enemies, such as Mauritius and Heligoland. The defence of Empire was a naval question: while Britain had a dominant navy she could control the use of the oceans by other nations. The security of outlying territories was based on the blockade or destruction of an enemy fleet in European waters; any threat outside European waters would necessarily be limited. The core concern of the British legislators was commercial, not territorial. In 1815 they had handed important colonies back to Holland and France, while keeping the key naval bases. Territory was only occupied to secure trade, or strategic harbours. Consequently British policy was essentially defensive, reactive and based on the avoidance of war through deterrence. Britain had demonstrated the capacity to engage larger states with powerful armies in prolonged wars of attrition, using maritime power to avoid defeat, and bolster state finances. The key issue remained stability and peace in Europe. If this was secured any threats to outlying imperial possessions would be minimal. Consequently the main British forces were stationed in European waters, and their war role would be the blockade or destruction of enemy naval forces. There was little chance of French or Russian warships reaching Sydney if their own coasts were under attack.

Down to the late 1850s the strategy of imperial defence was essentially unaltered, however much the political and economic aspects of the problem had been debated. While the three main strands of British political thought, tory, whig/liberal and radical, held different views on the level of military force to be stationed in the colonies, they agreed that British forces should not be tied down on internal security duties, consequently the size of the army deployed in the colonies fell consistently from 1815. In 1846 Earl Grey, then Secretary for War and the Colonies, launched a program to impose some logic on the system. He began by handing over the forts and barracks in New South Wales to the colony, and removing the British troops. He also concentrated the troops deployed in Canada into two major fortresses.[2] With responsible government came responsibility for internal security. External security remained a naval question, although fixed defences had an important role.

The most important single factor in the rise of British naval mastery in the eighteenth century had been the sustained application of capital to the creation and expansion of naval bases, both at home and around the Empire. Only fleets with local bases for supply, repair and concentration could maintain command of key sea areas. While bases were expensive, they proved invaluable. New bases were developed after 1815 to meet the expanding demand for naval support from the aggressive, expansionist British commercial sector. These included the Falkland Islands, Aden, Hong Kong and Sydney. Base facilities developed in Australia to meet recognised needs, rather than a central plan. Consequently there was little sense of urgency, and no attempt to co-ordinate naval and military planning. This has led existing accounts to miss the underlying logic of the results.

Colonial defence concerns

Sydney became a significant naval base in the 1830s, relying on facilities developed to support commercial shipping.[3] It provided victuals for the East Indies Squadron, and a naval stores depot.[4] The vital requirement for sustained naval operations was a graving dock. This was also the most expensive element of a naval base. While the Royal Navy formed a stores depot at Garden Island it did not build a dock. In 1845 the Colonial Legislative Council of New South Wales suggested to the Governor that a dock capable of holding warships would be of great advantage to the colony and the Empire. Despite the initial refusal of the Admiralty to offer financial support the project went ahead, and in 1847 the Admiralty reconsidered, offering a substantial sum, provided the dock could take 'a large frigate or steamer' and Royal Navy warships received priority. The Fitzroy dock was finally opened in September 1857, and the first vessel to enter was HMS *Herald*.[5] By meeting the growing commercial demand for maritime infrastructure, Sydney became capable of supporting a significant Royal Navy squadron, rather than merely acting as a forward base. This development would soon be followed by the establishment of a local squadron to protect that commerce.

The contribution of the base to the defence of Australia was obvious. It acted as a force multiplier for Royal Navy units, enabling them to refit, repair and reprovision more effectively, and more rapidly, than any rival force in the region. However useful Sydney was as a naval base, it was first and foremost a thriving commercial port, situated in a colony with responsible government. Consequently it did not become an 'Imperial Fortress', like Bermuda, where all the costs fell to the Imperial Government in London. While Bermuda was a prime strategic position, vital to the defence of British trade, and to the conduct of offensive operations in the Western Hemisphere, the islands were of little commercial value.

This point was most obvious in the provision of local defences. The development of Australian coast defences, like the coast defences of the rest of the British Empire, was concerned with the protection of ports from which warships could operate, and the concentration points of commercial shipping. They did not relate to defence against invasion. The level of coast defence reflected the degree of threat felt by the local legislature, and the level of support available from the Imperial Government. Unlike Canada, Australia could rely on sheer distance for much of her security: there was no European army within 1000 miles and the only way to attack the continent was by sea. Local defences in Australia were limited and until the Crimean War their construction had not been attended with any urgency.[6]

In 1839 Captain Charles Wilkes, USN, had created a scare when his two warships entered the harbour at night and were discovered lying at anchor close by Sydney the following morning. Nor was the concern misplaced, for Wilkes observed with some relish that he could easily have destroyed the shipping, shelled the town, and retreated in perfect safety.[7] The most obvious result of Wilkes's visit was Fort Denison in Sydney Harbour, which was begun in 1841. However, the level of alarm can be judged from the fact that the fort was only completed in 1857, after a fresh burst of activity prompted by the Crimean War.[8] While Fort Denison was obsolete before completion, the other colonies had no serious fixed defences.[9] This weakness threatened to tie any Royal Navy units in the area to local and harbour defence in the event of war, a role which would negate their mobility and strategic flexibility.

The Admiralty believed that the floating trade of the Empire should be defended by the Royal Navy, but that colonial harbours were the responsibility of the colonial authorities. The granting of responsible government to New South Wales in 1856 allowed London to expect that the colony would contribute to its own security.[10] In essence this meant that the colonies should defend their own harbours and develop facilities to support Royal Navy operations on the high seas.

The colonies and British global strategy

While the Crimean War had reminded the Australian colonies of the need for defence, the profound changes in material, tactics and strategy that it had heralded forced the British Government to revise national strategy.[11] The French challenge, based on ironclads, coastal offensives and an invasion base at Cherbourg, forced the ministers to redistribute the fleet, and reconsider the basis of imperial defence. They did so in search of security and economy. New fortification programs were adopted to secure the major dockyards against a surprise attack, and to maintain the position at Alderney, which effectively countered Cherbourg. Together with the powerful coast assault fleet built to fight Russia and the volunteer movement these measures defeated the French challenge. However, the cost forced the ministers to investigate other aspects of defence expenditure.

The attention of the Admiralty was drawn to the issue of global strategy by the Queen. Alarmed by what she had seen on a visit to Cherbourg in April 1858, she demanded that her naval advisers, the Board of

Admiralty, report on the naval tasks in the event of war with France. Rear Admiral Sir Alexander Milne, the Third Sea Lord, stressed the primacy of securing command of European waters, and taking the initiative against the French harbours. Milne reckoned the Australian station would require eight frigates and ten sloops with 5400 men for war service, but admitted the navy was simply too small to provide such a force so far from home.[12] The Fourth Sea Lord, Captain James Drummond, went further:

> Our extensive Colonies would in war prove a weakness. They *must be* considered *after our home defences* are in a measure provided for; and it becomes a question to what extent the Colonies could be independent, and provide towards their own defence, by raising men and fortifying their harbours.
>
> We should also require to consider our several coaling stations abroad, and the protection necessary to keep them available.[13]

This was the basis of Admiralty colonial defence policy. It was an approach that linked in with the defensive concerns in Australia. In 1856 Sir William Denison, Governor of New South Wales, proposed a cost-sharing arrangement for local defence. The Admiralty had no intention of sharing control over Royal Navy warships, in peace or war. Nor could naval defence be determined on a local basis; it remained a global question, which must not be hampered by local considerations. Consequently if the colonies wanted their own naval forces the Admiralty encouraged them to acquire local defence craft, and contribute towards the cost of the imperial squadron.[14] This response was circulated to the Australian colonies, leading to further correspondence.

While Denison was primarily concerned with the fixed defences of Sydney, Victoria examined fixed and floating defences for Port Phillip Bay. The wealth of the new colony, and in particular the gold shipments, encouraged a liberal expenditure that provided a 580-ton warship and powerful artillery for coast batteries. In 1858 the Governor of Victoria, Sir Henry Barkly, reported local alarm that a European war, which seemed imminent, might result in Russian or French squadrons appearing off Port Phillip. His Legislative Council had not been impressed by the Admiralty suggestion that the colonies contribute to naval defence costs,

> so long, at any rate, as the force on the station is so small as to render it impracticable for a man of war to visit its shores for years at a time, for however efficient a protection might be conferred by confining an enemy's vessels in their own ports, it would not dispel the apprehensions excited at this great distance, nor reconcile the Colonists to paying for services of which they could scarcely estimate the real value.[15]

While the Admiralty recognised that Barkly's paper raised 'important and difficult questions of state policy', these were government issues, and 'had nothing to do' with the Admiralty.[16] The following year Barkly requested a blockship, possibly armoured, and the creation of a local admiral's command. The Admiralty reply, drafted by Milne, repeated that the decision to defend Australia by naval forces was a question for the Cabinet, and would require a significantly larger squadron on station. Consequently they could not comply, and observed that the force had recently been enlarged, and established as an independent commodore's command.[17] The squadron was:

> necessary not only to provide for the defence of the Colony, but, in the event of war, to give periodical convoys to treasure ships proceeding home either by the Cape of Good Hope or Cape Horn.

However, they were prepared to send more ships, including a first-class frigate, gun vessels and gunboats, 'as soon as the home defence is sufficiently provided for'.[18] That sufficiency was never achieved. Later that year Barkly requested four first-class frigates, and three 'men of war' for the defence of Port Phillip, while South Australia feared a bombardment of Port Adelaide. Sir William Denison was more concerned by the threat from New Caledonia, advising that the French colony should be seized at the outbreak of war. The Admiralty deflected such calls, observing that it could not provide a large enough force on all stations to meet every contingency.[19]

Barkly obtained a report on the defence of Port Phillip Bay from Captain Frederick Beauchamp Seymour, RN.[20] Seymour had commanded a floating battery at the end of the Crimean War, and declared it would be impossible to tow one out to Australia. As the Admiralty would not send a blockship, he advised Barkly to obtain gunboats, which, together with heavy batteries on the Heads, would be the basis of wartime defence. Seymour had used the colonial steam warship *Victoria* to inspect the bay, and praised her officers and crew. Barkly was so pleased with the reports that he had them printed, and sent to London.[21] The Admiralty was concerned at the anomalous legal position of the *Victoria*, and advised the Colonial Office that it would be necessary to consult the Law Officers of the Crown.[22] In the interval the Colonial Office sought colonial views on the necessary regulations for local naval forces.[23]

Down to 1859 the ships detached from the China Station for service in Australian waters were small frigates, corvettes, sloops and from 1846 small steamers. Only one major warship had visited the continent, the battleship HMS *Warspite* in 1826. While a handful of small ships had been adequate on this the most distant of all stations, the discovery of gold in the early 1850s made Australian shipping a worthy target for

HMS *Galatea* during the Duke of Edinburgh's 1868 visit to Australia. (RAN)

commerce destroyers, although the Admiralty expected any attack would come in the Atlantic. To this end the formation of an enlarged and separate Australia Station in March 1859, based at Sydney, recognised the increased threat and the ability of the colonies to support such a force. The governors of Tasmania and New South Wales had requested a distinct squadron in 1858, and the Admiralty had complied.[24] The nature of the threat envisaged can be gauged by the second-class cruisers and smaller craft that comprised the squadron for the next 25 years. It would be eight years before another major warship visited Australia. In 1867–68 HMS *Galatea*, a huge wooden screw frigate, brought the Duke of Edinburgh on a Royal Tour. The local role in imperial defence was demonstrated when the *Galatea* used the Fitzroy Dock before setting out for home.[25]

The new station answered naval as well as colonial needs. In early 1859 Captain William Loring reported that acting under the Commander in Chief on the China Station weakened his authority with local governments, while 'communication is more difficult and uncertain than with Your Lordships'.[26] By June he had received word of his elevation to Commodore, independent of China; but the alarming state of affairs in Europe forced him to remain close to Sydney, for the earliest news. With such a small force at the end of such long, and uncertain communications Loring had to be cautious.[27] The following year would be dominated by the Maori land war in New Zealand. This led to constant struggle between the Governor and the naval commander to direct the tiny squadron.[28]

In early 1861 Seymour, now Commodore, visited New Caledonia. He found a small, weak colony, with a 32-gun frigate and a small steamer, 20 heavy guns, of which 18 were not mounted, and 600 troops. The three 60-gun sailing frigates, which had recently arrived, turned out to be troopships, and had not remained on the station. Seymour evidently knew his history and strategy, for he recognised that the French colony would only be a threat if the squadron it contained was superior to the local Royal Navy force, using the example of Mauritius between 1793 and 1810. Otherwise it was quite useless. He requested copies of the latest French chart, which he had seen, but not been able to acquire.[29]

Back in Sydney, Sir William Denison responded to the Colonial Office Circular on local naval forces. He did not believe any colonies 'would be willing to incur the expense of constructing and equipping armed vessels, or of maintaining them in a state of efficiency', and suggested that the *Victoria* had not been a success. He remained convinced that the best method was for the Imperial Government to provide the vessels, and the colonies to pay half the cost. There was no call for local naval forces.[30] However, the Board was certain that cost-sharing arrangements which interfered with the proper distribution of ships in peace and war would cause local friction, and hamper operations. The best solution was:

> that authority should be given to the Colony to commission and man for their defence vessels of war to protect them either against internal enemies, or against hostile attacks from abroad.

These would be 'Royal Colonial Navy of Victoria' warships, wholly owned, operated and paid for by the colony. Such a force would enable the Imperial Government to reduce the forces on station in peacetime. In wartime the local commander could take the initiative, secure in the 'knowledge that the principal ports on the station were free from the attack of a single vessel'. The Admiralty would be prepared to assist the colony to acquire vessels, either by selling surplus units, or providing plans.

> Looking to the vast demand that would be made upon the Board of Admiralty for the protection of the Colonies of Great Britain, in the event of war with a Great Naval Power, my Lords consider that the simple plan of encouraging each colony to trust in a great measure to its own means of naval defence is one which must be decided on by the Country.[31]

Under the new imperial defence strategy the Royal Navy would cover the colonies against outside threat, and more realistically secure their shipping from hostile cruisers. The colonies could be left to develop their own local defence forces. Here the Admiralty was slightly in advance of the government. In 1859 the Conservative Secretary for War set up a Departmental Committee to search for general principles underlying the defence of the colonies. The Treasury, War and Colonial Office group found no principles, and little method, just years of *ad hoc* decisions. They recommended distinguishing between imperial and colonial positions, encouraging the colonies to contribute to the cost of local defence, under the overall defence provided by 'naval superiority'.[32] The Report was published in March 1860, by a new Liberal government, prompting further discussion. Twelve months later Arthur Mills, a Liberal MP with a well-developed interest in colonial questions, moved for a select committee of the House of Commons to consider colonial military defence and costs.

Despite his personal opposition the Prime Minister, Lord Palmerston, allowed the motion to go forward, recognising the interest of Gladstone, the Chancellor of Exchequer. Gladstone was already engaged in a long-running, and ultimately unsuccessful battle with Palmerston and the First Lord of the Admiralty, the Duke of Somerset, to rein in the unprecedented level of peacetime naval expenditure required to defeat the French naval challenge. With support and ideas from the radical wing of the party, Gladstone sought economies on the distant stations to counterbalance increased expenditure at home.[33]

The Mills Committee Report recognised that the strategic pattern of imperial defence had been profoundly affected by coastal offensive warfare with ironclads, and the development of reliable global communications. Consequently, and somewhat ambiguously, it concluded that:

> the tendency of modern warfare is to strike blows at the heart of a hostile power; and that it is therefore desirable to concentrate the troops required for the defence of the United Kingdom as much as possible, and to trust mainly to naval supremacy for securing against foreign aggression the distant dependencies of the Empire.[34]

The 'defensive' cast of this summation was misleading. The Imperial Government was thinking of applying British maritime power from the centre against the 'heart of any hostile power', either to deter aggression, or to force an aggressor to disgorge captured territory. Any maritime force acting from the centre would necessarily include the concentrated military force. However, such a strategy could not be openly promulgated, for the Liberal majority in the House of Commons included a significant and vociferous radical element who wished to dispose of all colonies, and opposed any military spending that was not purely 'defensive'. One consequence was an excessive reliance on coast defence vessels, which the radicals were promoting as economic substitutes for forts.[35] Before this report could be acted upon the issues it had considered were thrown into sharp focus by an imperial crisis.

The 'Trent crisis'

Unlike Australia, Canada had been attacked by America in 1776 and 1812. On both occasions the Americans were repelled by imperial and local forces. In 1861 it seemed likely that there would be a third invasion. While the immediate impact of the 'Trent crisis' would be less dramatic, in Australia it provided a crucial focus for the development of a new imperial strategy. Existing accounts of the 'Trent crisis' concentrate on International Law, diplomacy, the deliberations of the British and American Cabinets, public opinion and the role of the dying Prince Consort.[36] The two studies that focus on the strategic balance do not explain why the United States gave way.[37] They ignore the underlying offensive/deterrent dynamic in British thinking, and the scale and proficiency of the naval forces available, focusing on the small military force sent to Canada. These troops were merely the symbol of British strength, raising the cost of any invasion and bolstering Canadian morale. The real basis of British deterrence was the long-matured and recently demonstrated power of the Royal Navy to conduct large-scale offensive operations against the best defended harbours in the world as the core of a unique maritime warfighting capability.

Around midday on 8 November 1861, the USS *San Jacinto*, commanded by Captain Charles Wilkes, USN, intercepted the British Mail Steamer RMS *Trent* in the Old Bahama Channel, north of Cuba, and forcibly removed the Confederate States' envoys Mason and Slidell.[38] Wilkes became a national hero, but wiser heads realised that Britain would respond. However, the British Government had no desire for war with America. The Empire, already global, would require an immense effort to defend, while the European situation was threatening. The French Emperor, Napoleon III, had built a powerful ironclad fleet, which he hoped would neutralise the Royal Navy, forcing Britain to acquiescence in his ambition to redraw the map of Europe.[39] This was a challenge Britain had to defeat, and by late 1861 the naval arms race had reached a critical point. Superior British resources, commitment and funding would win through, but the French challenge ensured that the defence of Canada could not take top priority in 1861. Under the circumstances it is little wonder Australia was forgotten until the crisis was almost over.

The British were not surprised by the *Trent* outrage. They had been expecting an American attack, either at sea or across the Canadian frontier,

The Royal Mail steamer *Trent* was stopped by the sloop USS *San Jacinto* on 8 November 1861. Two Confederate commissioners were removed and taken captive. The event provided a crucial focus for the development of imperial defence strategy. (*Illustrated London News*)

since the mid-1850s. When the Civil War broke out Palmerston reinforced the garrison of Canada, sending three regiments and new rifled artillery aboard the colossal steamship *Great Eastern*. His overriding aim throughout the crisis was to deter American aggression in Canada. He acted with vigour because he did not expect any trouble with France during the year.[40] The Queen shared Palmerston's perspective, and presciently warned that, while the United States would be too busy on land to attack Canada, she might 'commit acts of violence at sea'.[41] Palmerston was anxious to avoid intervening in the Civil War alongside France.[42] When Foreign Secretary Lord John Russell suggested sending two more frigates to Halifax, Palmerston agreed: 'the Yankees will be violent and threatening in proportion to our local weakness, and Civil and Pacific in proportion to our local strength'.[43] When he wanted to send more troops in September the Colonial Secretary, the Duke of Newcastle, the First Lord of the Admiralty, the Duke of Somerset, and the Secretary of State for War, George Cornewall Lewis, objected. In line with the Mills Committee, they wanted to shift imperial strategy from the large stationed forces that Palmerston favoured to a local screen and a central reinforcement. The key to this strategy would be improved communications. However, the Atlantic telegraph cable was not operational during the '*Trent*' crisis'. In later life both the British Ambassador in

Washington, Lord Lyons, and the American Ambassador in London argued that a cable would have made war more likely.[44] Without a cable the Admiralty could only provide overall direction to the Commander in Chief on the North America and West Indies Station, Rear Admiral Sir Alexander Milne. Milne's response to the 1861 crisis reflected the calm, judicious professionalism that made him a success in high office. Having been a junior naval lord from 1847 to 1859, he had an unrivalled insight into the Admiralty, a curious hybrid body, largely designed for peacetime administration, but with a requirement to provide strategic direction in war. Milne understood the Admiralty's problem.

From Washington, Lyons advised the government to demand immediate redress and the release of the envoys. He was not optimistic.[45] Milne moved his force from Halifax to Bermuda. These two fortified naval bases were the key to an effective blockade of the American coast. They were adequately protected, and contained the facilities required to sustain powerful naval forces in the Western hemisphere. When news of the *Trent* incident reached London on 27 November, the ministers agreed to demand an American apology and the release of the envoys.[46] Outside the Cabinet the pro-Northern radical leaders Richard Cobden and John Bright wrote to Senator Charles Sumner, Chairman of the Senate Foreign Relations Committee, warning him that a quarrel with Britain would end any hope of restoring the Union, and advising concession.[47] They, like many before and since, confused the alarming rhetoric of the press with the real objects of Palmerston's sophisticated and calculating political mind. The radicals saw preparations for war where Palmerston was creating an effective deterrent. Milne was ordered to remain at Bermuda and protect British shipping.[48] Privately, Somerset stressed that reinforcements would be sent before active operations began.[49] Several ships were prepared, but not commissioned, while battleships and cruisers were sent from the Mediterranean and home ports.

Unimpressed by Foreign Secretary Russell's draft instructions to Lord Lyons, Queen Victoria effectively built a 'golden bridge' for an American retreat. Her amendments advised the Americans to disavow Wilkes' action so they could release the envoys and apologise for the insult to the British flag.[50] Between 10 and 28 December Palmerston was confined to bed by a severe attack of gout. He was also profoundly affected by the death of the Prince Consort on the 14th.[51] Earlier Palmerston had reflected that with the support of France, already heavily involved in Mexico and hostile to the Federal Government, and indeed almost the whole of Europe, this was a golden opportunity to take revenge for years of American insults.

> If the Federal Government comply with the demands it will be honourable for England and humiliating for the United States. If the Federal

Government refuse compliance Great Britain is in a better state than at any former time to inflict a severe blow upon and to read a lesson to the United States which will not soon be forgotten.[52]

He had no doubt Britain would be successful: 'I feel at my ease as to all our points of attack and defence except Canada ... we shall have a great advantage by sea, and we must make the most of it'.[53] While this advantage existed Somerset was careful not to spend any money mobilising ships, simply shifting some of those currently deployed to meet the French challenge. He did not want another battle with Gladstone over the naval budget.[54]

In the absence of a British naval staff, the Hydrographer of the Navy, Captain John Washington, performed the functions of intelligence gathering, strategic analysis and war-planning. Captain Washington reported on the navigation, fortification and value of the ports in Federal hands. The prominence of the hydrographer emphasised the littoral character of contemporary naval warfare. Captain Washington considered Boston was too strong for a successful attack, but New York, while formidably defended, was so important that the risk might be warranted and Washington was vulnerable. Somerset planned to remove the Federal blockade, defeat the American Navy, occupy Chesapeake Bay, and then blockade New York. Captain Washington advised that 8 battleships, 9 frigates, 23 sloops and 20 gunboats would be required to blockade the American coast.[55] Milne would soon have enough battleships and frigates; smaller ships would be sent if required. While Somerset sent 10 000 tons of coal to Bermuda and the West Indies, he was reluctant to incur any expense in Canada. The Admirals at Rio, Esquimault, Malta, Hong Kong and eventually Commodore Seymour at Sydney were advised of the danger.

Signalling was a critical element in nineteenth-century deterrence, and Palmerston used it to leave the American Government in no doubt Britain was serious. At *The Times*, the most important daily paper, editor John Delane mounted a sustained attack on the American position, Delane reflecting a national desire to have revenge for 'the foul and incessant abuse of Americans, statesmen, orators and press' over past decades. He was also pleased to report that 'For once, the Navy has been found ready when wanted'.[56] The Americans were struck by reports of double-shift work in the dockyards.[57] This impression was critical. Having received his instructions late on 18 December, Lyons thought the Americans would only give way 'if the next news from England brings note of warlike preparations, and determination on the part of the Government and people'.[58]

Although Somerset moved forces from the Home Ports and the Mediterranean, he did not interfere with the Channel Fleet, the key to

Anglo–French relations, and ignored the Great Lakes. Captain Washington's confidential 'Memoranda on the Assistance which can be rendered to the Province of Canada by Her Majesty's Navy in the Event of War with the United States' advocated the early capture of the American forts Champlain, Niagara, and Makinac.[59] Somerset did nothing, admitting that any defensive measures on the Lakes would be very costly, and 'it is difficult to take any steps which will not involve very large expenditure whilst the control over such expenditure can never be otherwise than imperfect'. If there was to be a war he would act, but not before.[60] This lack of urgency also reflected an American communication, received on 17 December, that Wilkes' action had been unauthorised.

Before Milne received his first response to the crisis from London, on 20 December, he had planned to capture the American Gulf Coast squadrons, destroy the American fleet on the east coast, open the Southern ports, and prepare for large-scale assault operations. He required 54 ships, mostly corvettes and sloops for blockade, supported by frigates and battleships, and expected ironclads and gunboats would arrive in time to attack the major harbours. He had no doubt he could defeat the Americans, with New York as the key to victory.[61] In December, 12 steam transports left England carrying 11 000 troops, in an impressive demonstration of global mobility and strategic lift. Their arrival in midwinter provided a focus for a clear and potent demonstration of Canadian nationalism, based on loyalty to the Crown and resistance to American threats.[62] Imperial defence only worked if the Empire wanted to be defended and was prepared to take part in the defence effort.

After 17 December the heat went out of the crisis. Furthermore, Palmerston had always been more concerned with the balance of power in Europe. He was convinced Napoleon III would attack Austria and Prussia in the spring: 'if we are engaged in a war on the other side of the Atlantic he will think himself free from our interference'. Only one force stood between Napoleon and European hegemony:

> The Prussian army, though brave, is quite behind the progress which the French have made in the art of war. They still attack in columns, which would be blown to pieces by the French rifle artillery long before they could come into contact with their opponents.[63]

This would be a disaster, destroying the European equilibrium that was the foundation of British global security. Such concerns put the '*Trent* crisis' into context.

On 25 December the Lincoln Cabinet gave way. Lyons believed 'the real cause of their yielding was nothing more nor less than the military preparations made in England'. He wanted to exploit the occasion:

'[U]nless we give our friends here a good lesson this time, we shall have the same trouble with them very soon, under less advantageous circumstances'.[64] Milne agreed: '[T]he steps adopted in England will have done good, not only to bring down the pride and arrogance of the American people, but it will have shewn the necessity for keeping our colonies prepared'.[65]

The news reached London on 9 January 1862. The Queen created the legend that Prince Albert had avoided the war.[66] Those more intimately involved in the crisis, Lyons and Milne, knew better, but historians on both sides of the Atlantic have preferred the myth, largely because there was no real mobilisation, which left the forces on station looking rather thin. The most recent study argues that the Royal Navy could not have blockaded the American coast, and would have been exhausted trying.

> Perhaps the British Government was never serious about going to war over Mason and Slidell, perhaps the Americans were not the only ones who could play the game of 'brag', a version of poker.[67]

In fact Britain did not need to mobilise; she had force enough to deter. Additional strength would only have been necessary if the Americans had decided to fight.

When Anglo–American tension increased in late 1862, the Admiralty moved the new ironclads to Lisbon, where they were linked to the telegraph and only a few days from Bermuda.[68] Together with a larger Canadian garrison, improved militia and modernised defences at the imperial fortresses of Quebec and Halifax, this would suffice.

In 1861 the American administration understood British power. Since 1815 American defence spending had been dominated by coastal fortresses, but by 1861 these forts had been rendered obsolete by steamships, rifled guns and armour plate. In the nineteenth century technology shifted the strategic balance between land and sea forces to favour navies. The point had been made during the Crimean War when British fleets outmanoeuvred obsolescent Russian defence systems intended to deal with wooden sailing ships. The American Government recognised the strategic threat. In 1861 only a combination of fixed barriers, guns, mines and local defence craft could stop ironclad steamers. Naval offensive power was based on a combination of long-range fire, mortars, guns and rockets, followed up by concentrated broadsides. The Royal Navy had the resources for a sustained coastal offensive campaign. It was the recognition of the strategic power of the Royal Navy that deterred the United States in 1861, not the movement of ships and men.

The implications for Australian defence

News of the *Trent* incident only reached Australia on 14 January 1862, by which time the crisis was over. Commodore Seymour reported that the news had been sent in commercial telegraphs to Malta, which directed local agents to start charging 'war rate' insurance and redirected valuable ships like the SS *Great Britain* to return via the Cape of Good Hope, rather than Cape Horn, to avoid privateers. American agents were hurriedly trying to sell or re-register any American-owned ships. Seymour was concerned that the new American telegraph line from Washington to San Francisco would give the federal government 'a great advantage in the event of war being declared... we might therefore expect privateers to appear in these waters within sixty days of the breaking out of war'. Consequently he had ordered the two steamships in New Zealand waters to join him at Sydney. He went on to report on local fixed defences. Victoria had 30 heavy guns at Port Phillip, but not one had been mounted and there were only 350 soldiers. Sydney likewise was denuded of troops, most being in New Zealand, but the batteries were already built and armed.[69] Seymour had judged the situation well, and his actions were approved by the Board.[70]

Others were less impressed. With perverse short-sightedness, the Governor of New Zealand, Sir George Grey, was infuriated by the sudden removal of the ships, which he had counted on to bolster his prestige at a forthcoming meeting with the Maori chiefs. Seymour sent Grey's blistering official letter to the Admiralty, observing that he had acted 'according to the best to my judgement for the good of Her Majesty's service and the protection of the very valuable commerce which is being carried on between Great Britain and the Australian colonies'.[71] His orders, which were only sent out on 26 December, noted that one or more vessels would be sent from China to assist him in the only task that was worthy of notice, 'protecting British commerce'.[72] The Duke of Newcastle later rebuked Grey, noting Seymour had exercised 'a wise discretion'.[73]

News that the '*Trent* crisis' had been peacefully resolved reached Sydney on 6 March, via San Francisco. It was confirmed by the English mail on the 15th. The government of New South Wales, hitherto desperately trying to upgrade the fixed defences of Sydney, immediately stopped work, despite Seymour's warning that the city was at the mercy of a pair of steam corvettes. By contrast Victoria, which had been lagging behind before the crisis, was keeping up its efforts.[74]

Just as the crisis was ending the Admiralty had responded to the latest Victorian plea for naval defence. The Colonial Office was not convinced the course of action proposed would be in line with national or colonial policy, but requested a draft Act of Parliament to establish colonial navies for consideration. In reply the Admiralty stressed their ambition to mobilise the resources of the colonies in the event of war with 'a Great Naval Power', rather than allowing them simply to rely on the Imperial Government. The key task for the colonial forces would be the protection of ports and coastal cities from attack. These defences ought to be provided locally, and the logic also applied to the Canadian cities on the St Lawrence. Colonial naval forces would 'materially save on our expenditure', and would be sustained by self-interest and national pride. They would not remove the need for imperial forces to protect commerce, but would prevent a public outcry at every alarm of war. Ultimately,

> It would seem to be sound policy to let them learn gradually how to protect themselves and also the cost of doing it. It would not probably hasten the time when they would desire the whole burden to rest on their shoulders.[75]

The Colonial Office stressed that the possibility of an individual hostile cruiser appearing off Australian harbours could not be discounted. Local measures were believed to be in hand, and should be completed. When the crisis was over the Colonial Office pressed local authorities to take active measures for their own defence.[76] Curiously, while this circular had been inspired by Seymour's criticism of New South Wales, which had been copied to the Colonial Office, it resulted in him landing the heaviest gun of his flagship at Sydney, to meet a request inspired by the Colonial Office circular.[77]

For the next four years occasional alarms kept the issue of Australian defence alive, notably when the large steamship *Great Britain* entered Hobson's Bay firing her guns in 1863, and in 1865, when the Confederate raider CSS *Shenandoah* sailed into Melbourne.[78]

The problem for the imperial and colonial authorities was how to balance responsible government, local defence and imperial security.[79] The 1865 Colonial Naval Defence Act allowed the colonies to create their own navies but, fearful that these local naval forces might cause an international incident, they were restricted to colonial waters.[80] This met the objects of the Admiralty, which required secure and well-equipped ports from which to operate imperial squadrons. In Canada and the West Indies the key bases were in ports that lacked the commercial traffic to warrant extensive dock facilities, and therefore the charge fell wholly on the imperial budget. However, the maritime trade of Australia was growing so rapidly that adequate facilities were available for the Royal Navy.

After 1861 the development of harbour defences at Melbourne, Sydney, Newcastle, Hobart, Adelaide and Fremantle made them secure bases. The first to act was Victoria, which built a graving dock, and with imperial assistance acquired a powerful coast defence ironclad in the late 1860s, making Port Phillip Bay a secure haven.[81] These developments made the imperial squadron on station vastly more powerful than any possible threat, not from increased numbers or strength of ships, but because the British ships could rely on secure harbours, coal and other naval stores, potential recruits, vital graving docks, engineering back-up and the best communications in the region. Once the submarine telegraph cable reached Australia in 1872, British communications with the region were superior to those of any possible rival. Even before this the frequency of sailings, and sheer weight of shipping, leaving aside the mail steamers, normally gave the local commanders superior intelligence.

The Flying Squadron strategy

After 1861 British strategy shifted away from the stationed forces, both land and sea, of the previous 60 years toward the mobile, centrally controlled units that had been advocated so strongly by the Mills Committee, and urged as an economy measure by Gladstone. With suitable local facilities and good communications these stationed forces were reduced in quality, rather than the quantity necessary to meet the widespread demands placed on the navy in the area.

The triumph of Gladstone as Liberal Party leader and Prime Minister in late 1868 ensured the adoption of the detached squadron strategy he had been urging since 1859. The original idea and much of the detail had been provided by his long-time ally the quasi-radical First Secretary to the Admiralty, Captain Lord Clarence Paget. Alone among the radicals Paget had the professional standing to propose such a strategic shift, and used his position at the Board to develop this line of policy from 1859.[82] In late 1864 Gladstone renewed his call for a 'Flying Squadron' strategy. Paget and Civil Lord Hugh Childers provided financial detail.[83] Palmerston remained resolutely opposed to the concept. Paget conceded it depended on future improvements, and the Cabinet rejected Gladstone's proposal.[84]

When Gladstone took control of the Liberal Party the 'Flying Squadron' strategy was put in place with almost unseemly haste. Childers outlined the rationale in the House of Commons in 1867. When Gladstone formed his first government, in late 1868, Childers became First Lord with Seymour as his Private Secretary. Within weeks he had settled the reduction of overseas squadrons with the Foreign Secretary, entirely as an economy measure. While there were extensive cuts, Australia continued unchanged with four ships and 700–800 men.[85] This reflected the wide range of policing tasks that fell to the force, not a local strategic threat. Childers summed up his work:

> The diminution of the force permanently maintained in distant seas will enable my Lords to send a cruising squadron of frigates and corvettes to

A naval review was held in Port Phillip Bay on the occasion of the 1869 visit of the Flying Squadron. The colonial warship HMVS *Nelson* is seen in the lead. Aboard HMS *Phoebe* was Midshipman William Rooke Creswell on his first visit to Australia. (National Library of Australia)

visit the stations from time to time, and my Lords anticipate that much benefit to the naval service will be derived from this policy.[86]

Within days a 'Flying Squadron' of four frigates and two corvettes had been created under Rear Admiral Sir Geoffrey Hornby. In November 1869 they arrived at Melbourne, going on to Sydney and Hobart. Hornby's force then crossed the Tasman Sea.[87] This was the most powerful naval force yet seen in the region.

In 1878 and 1885 the possibility of war with Russia was deterred by the assembly of a power projection fleet at Spithead, not the local defences of the British Empire.[88] While the Russians feared for St Petersburg, Sydney and Melbourne were safe. In the interval only one aspect of naval strategy for the Australian station had changed: the sound policy of convoying the trade had been replaced by patrolling.[89]

Conclusions

The *Trent* crisis had demonstrated that Britain could not station forces in Canada to meet the United States Army. She had to rely on deterrence.

Her global empire could not be secured against serious attack by local defences. This was a matter of basic economics and political expediency. Britain would not pay for a high level of local defence, nor would her colonies. The only strategy that combined real power, global reach and relative economy was one based on the offensive strength of the Royal Navy. Throughout the nineteenth century the Royal Navy had the power to destroy any rival navy, securing British interests and releasing the fleet for further offensive operations, including an economic blockade, the seizure of overseas or isolated territories as diplomatic assets, and attacks on major cities. The war would be fought with a limited commitment of manpower and money; while it could not destroy a major power, it would exhaust their military and economic resources and ultimately break their political will. Sea power gave Britain the ability to attack an enemy at their weakest or most sensitive point, rather than simply countering an attack at the point it crossed the imperial frontier. A maritime striking force could be dispatched from the centre of the Empire, staging through the global chain of bases, to project power against any rival.

Because the British never wrote down their core strategic doctrine in the period 1815–1914 many historians have argued that there was no strategy. This is not correct. The British retained the strategy of the Napoleonic wars, consistently upgraded to integrate new technologies and political realities. Between 1856 and 1865 the strategy shifted from stationed forces to a centrally controlled 'expeditionary' strategy. The long-term success of British strategy is obvious. Between 1814 and 1914 no major power attacked Britain. While rival powers could identify areas of relative British weakness, the North-West frontier of India, Canada and oceanic trade, none could develop a strategy that could coerce Britain. By contrast Britain did have a strategy that could deter her rivals, and in consequence the reality of British power was written in stone, at Cherbourg, Cronstadt, New York and Wilhelmshaven.

8 New Zealand's naval defence, 1854–1914
Richard Jackson

The European settlers of New Zealand were granted responsible self-government in 1853. Although internal security was the government's major concern—the first Land War had been fought between 1845 and 1848—within a year the nation had to make its first decision on external defence: to fund earthworks to protect cannon covering Auckland's inner harbour.[1] In 1854 problems of external defence were urgent since the British Empire was at war with Russia. The Crimean War acquired a Pacific dimension when the Royal Navy pursued a Russian fleet from the Hawaiian Islands to the Kamchatka Peninsula.[2] The failure of the British to engage the Russian ships successfully underlined the vulnerability of Britain's Pacific colonies to a surprise attack from enemy cruisers. Such an attack was all too likely in an era when it took 90 days to get an urgent message from London to Auckland.

New Zealand's external defence priority was the protection of its ports and harbours, and this issue would remain the nation's principal such concern for the next 50 years. In 1854 (and for nearly a century afterwards) the *pakeha* (European) settlers could take for granted that their ultimate security was ensured by the Royal Navy. The Royal Navy had been essential to the European discovery of and subsequent founding of the new nation. British warships were a frequent presence around New Zealand's coasts, and both ships and naval landing parties played a full part in the campaigns against the Maori. Hence the new settlers could, with confidence, turn to developing the land, while turning their backs to the sea. But two major factors would constrain their government in its defence decision-making during the remainder of the nineteenth century: internal security and finance.

While relations with the Maori tribes were calm in the 1850s, by 1860 tensions were rising and the nation would engage in more than a decade of military operations. It was not until 1881 that the issue of internal security would finally come off the government's agenda.[3] There was also the problem of the economy. If the new state were to grow, it needed to borrow to invest in infrastructure. To pay for those borrowings it needed to export. Australia was the nearest market, but it too was producing many of the same products. New Zealand's economy remained fragile until new technology enabled frozen meat to be exported directly to Great Britain in the 1880s. Thus the state of the government's finances was always a factor in defence decision-making.

The New Zealand Government's first defence measure was the Militia Act of 1858, which authorised the formation of citizen militia units for land and coastal duties.[4] Naval Artillery Volunteer units were part of the new militia, and these units were the first step in the evolution of New Zealand's national maritime forces. The concept of a volunteer militia for home defence was being adopted across the Empire in the late 1850s.[5] London had made it clear that colonies were responsible for local and harbour defence. So the militia was generally responsible for manning the gun batteries which covered the main harbours. With no overland rail or road routes, most New Zealand towns were small coastal communities linked only by coastal shipping; their citizens had a direct sense of exposure to surprise attack. Hence, as well as manning artillery, the Naval Volunteers also carried out harbour patrol work and similar duties within the harbours, tasks that might otherwise be demanded of the crews of visiting warships.[6]

The first unit of 'Navals' was formed in Auckland in 1858—3 officers and 97 men who wore naval uniform, adopted naval ranks and trained according to Royal Navy drills. Eleven other units of Naval Artillery Volunteers were subsequently formed, including ones at Devonport, Thames, Petone, and Wellington. The unit in Bluff was founded by a young man, Joseph Ward, who also recommended Bluff as a naval coaling port.[7]

New Zealand's first regular armed force, a small unit of mounted soldiers, was authorised by the Colonial Defence Act of 1862.[8] But in 1867, under the Armed Constabulary Act, a small cadre force of specialists was authorised. As a result, the Permanent Militia was organised into four corps—Artillery, Infantry, Engineers and a Torpedo Corps. The Torpedo Corps were a regular 'Naval' unit of 50 men, with responsibility for instruction and maintenance of harbour mine defences. Harbour defence was a vexed question, since not only did the colony have to defend its ports against any sudden attack by an enemy raider, but it also had to provide a secure harbour for units of the Royal Navy. Auckland was not a naval base as such, but the deeper water off Sandspit (now Devonport) had been the preferred naval anchorage since 1840, while a Royal Navy stores site had been established there since 1841.[9]

In the second half of the nineteenth century weapons technology began to change. Muzzle-loading guns gave way to breech-loaders, explosive shells replaced solid shot, while submarine mines and, later, locomotive torpedoes were developed. Sail power for ships was also under threat, although the range and endurance provided by sail was not matched until the triple expansion steam engine came into widespread use after 1885.[10] Hence each time the government sought expert advice it was offered a different solution. With little continuity in planning, the story of New Zealand's harbour defences was one of 'procrastination and parsimony'.[11]

The Torpedo Corps and the 'Navals' operated the first warships acquired for New Zealand's external defence. These were four Thorneycroft spar torpedo boats. These slender, small craft were steam-powered, capable of 12 knots and armed with a 38-foot spar tipped with a guncotton charge.[12] Ordered in 1882 and arriving in 1884, the four craft were deployed to the four main ports of Auckland, Wellington, Lyttelton and Dunedin. Later, the spar torpedoes were replaced with Whitehead mobile torpedoes, which could be launched from the torpedo boats by means of dropping gear amidships. However, the narrow hull remained stable only if both torpedoes were dropped simultaneously. There was no question of flotilla tactics, since the four harbours were too far apart. Rather, each boat was a single-shot weapon, but integrated into the overall defence plan for each harbour.

The 'Navals' and the Torpedo Corps existed until after 1900, when they were merged with the Garrison Artillery. The torpedo boats, by then thoroughly outmoded, were neglected and not replaced. But while the Permanent Militia was primarily modelled on the Army, the 'Navals' had brought naval ranks and duties, Royal Navy instructors and a distinct maritime role into New Zealand's defence culture.

In the subsequent 1909 Defence Act, there was no provision for the 'Navals' or the Torpedo Corps. Instead, applying the lessons of the South African War, the focus was on a land force manned through compulsory military training.[13] But the government had not allowed its maritime responsibilities to lapse. In 1905 HMS *Sparrow* was taken over to become Training Ship *Amokura*: not a commissioned warship but a government-funded training ship to prepare young New Zealanders for either naval or merchant service.[14]

New Zealanders had been officially allowed to join the Australian Squadron of the Royal Navy since the 1887 Naval Agreement, although some wealthy families sent their sons directly to the United Kingdom. The 1887 Naval Agreement, however, is noteworthy as the turning point in New Zealand's consistent effort to have Royal Navy cruisers stationed in

New Zealand waters. The 1865 *Colonial Naval Defence Act* had enabled colonies, such as wealthy Victoria, to establish their own navies.[15] But in New Zealand, politicians such as Colonial Treasurer William Fitzherbert recognised that 'naval defence of the colonies could only be secured on the open sea by a fleet under imperial command'.

Yet there was also dissatisfaction that the Australian Squadron, based in Sydney, did not visit New Zealand more often. Indeed, the impact of the American Civil War, which caused the Commodore of the Australia Station to concentrate his ships in Sydney in case of outright conflict with the United States, at the time of the second Land War—when the Governor of New Zealand wanted Royal Navy ships in Auckland with sailors available to form naval brigades—was well remembered in Wellington.[16]

The sense of vulnerability was demonstrated in 1873 when a hoax newspaper report, about a raid on Auckland by a Russian cruiser called the *Kaskowhiski*, caused panic, with some citizens fleeing the city.[17] A later war scare in 1885, caused by the shifting balance of power in Europe and increasing European colonisation of the Pacific, gave the government the impetus to complete New Zealand's harbour defences.[18] The war scare also made Wellington receptive to the evolving imperial naval agreement.

The 1887 Imperial Conference led to the Naval Agreement. Britain, Australia and New Zealand agreed that the ships of the existing Australia Squadron would be supplemented by a new combined naval force of five cruisers and two torpedo gunboats.[19] These ships would be specially built for Australasian service and based in Sydney, forming a new Australian Auxiliary Squadron. But two ships, one from the imperial squadron and one from the new squadron, would be stationed in New Zealand waters. New Zealanders were eligible for service in the new naval squadron, and there was clearly a presumption that reserves would also be maintained to help man the three ships which would not be in full commission. The New Zealand Government agreed to pay London a subsidy of £20 000, one-sixth of the cost of the new force. The Naval Agreement was subsequently attached to Wellington's annual Appropriations Bill: New Zealand's first legislation for a sea-going naval force.[20]

This policy—of subsidising imperial naval defence to keep a cruiser presence in New Zealand waters, while enjoying access to the Royal Navy for New Zealanders—was followed by Wellington for the next 20 years. New Zealand's approach suited the Admiralty, which opposed independent colonial navies and sought to maintain a centrally controlled imperial navy. But more importantly for Wellington, the policy reflected the economic and industrial realities of New Zealand, with its small population, export-dependent economy, state-funded education and transport systems, and huge demands for infrastructure development. The cruisers on station were nonetheless seen as 'our' cruisers by New Zealanders. In 1900 HMS

Mildura transported the New Zealand Governor-General to the Cook Islands when they were annexed by New Zealand.[21] 'New Zealand waters' were considered to include Fiji as well as the Cooks, which suited the expansionist attitudes then prevalent in Wellington.

The 1902 Imperial Conference modified the Naval Agreement, offering two annual naval cadetships to New Zealand and eight to Australia, and providing for Royal Naval Reserve branches in both countries. It confirmed that one British cruiser and one drill ship of the Auxiliary Squadron would be stationed in New Zealand waters, while New Zealand's subsidy would be increased to £40 000.[22] The subsidy grew to £100 000 as imperial naval defence became more pressing during the Anglo–German naval race. But the 1909 Imperial Conference was a watershed for the Dominions. The Admiralty was no longer opposed to independent navies, and the nascent Australian Navy soon emerged in its own right.

The New Zealand Prime Minister, however, was Sir Joseph Ward, founder of the Bluff Naval Volunteers and subsequently a prominent businessman who had prospered through exports and imports. He was a firm Imperialist. With the imminent creation of a distinct Australian Navy, Ward suggested that the New Zealand naval force comprise two light cruisers, three destroyers and two submarines detached from the China Station, and manned by New Zealand officers and men.[23] This proved impractical to the Admiralty, but it was compatible with the concept of a British Imperial Pacific Fleet, which was mooted about this time.

Ward, however, temporarily resolved New Zealand's naval policy by offering to fund a 'first-class battleship' for the Royal Navy. He made this offer on 22 March 1909, just before the Conference was convened and then later explained the offer to a reluctant Parliament and the New Zealand public.[24] Ward was personally convinced of the need for a centrally controlled imperial fleet, but he also saw the offer of one (and if need be, two) battleships as a tangible focus for New Zealanders, while symbolising to London New Zealand's willingness to play a role. While, in a strict sense, the battle cruiser HMS *New Zealand* was simply another unit of the Royal Navy, there is no doubt that the ship was viewed with special affection by New Zealanders. On a world tour in 1913, the battle cruiser spent nearly three months in New Zealand and was visited by over 360 000 people—over one-third of the population. For the surrender of the German Fleet in 1918, *New Zealand* embarked five soldiers from the New Zealand Division and a New Zealand newspaper reporter.[25] The link was renewed when *New Zealand* was chosen as Admiral Jellicoe's flagship for his 1919 tour of the Dominions to report on their naval defence.

Funding a Dreadnought, however, was essentially a diversion in terms of the development of New Zealand's naval forces. Ward's government fell in 1912 and the Reform Party implemented a more nationalistic approach.

The battle cruiser HMS *New Zealand*. (RAN)

The new Minister of Defence, Colonel James Allen, advocated a local naval capability together with close co-operation with Australia.[26] After what were described as 'difficult' negotiations with the Admiralty, agreement was reached on the loan of a Royal Navy cruiser for training, to prepare New Zealanders to man a planned force of modern, New Zealand-owned cruisers. The necessary legislation, the New Zealand Naval Defence Act 1913, was passed by Parliament and on 15 July 1914 the old cruiser HMS *Philomel* was commissioned as a New Zealand warship.

War of course broke out in Europe the following month and, as a Dominion, New Zealand was naturally involved. While the Great War would delay the birth of the nation's own navy, it is relevant to note the strength of the naval forces in New Zealand waters at that time: HMS *Philomel*—protected cruiser; HMS *Torch*—drill ship from the former Australian Auxiliary Squadron; HMS *Pyramus* and *Psyche*—British ships but with some New Zealanders among their companies; TS *Amokura*— merchant and naval training ship.[27] Some 200 New Zealanders were also serving in the Royal Navy.

For a nation of barely one million people, New Zealand was, in 1914, pulling its weight in terms of naval defence. Wellington's naval policy had been cautious and was reliant on co-operation with the imperial power, but since taking responsibility for self-government, the New Zealand Parliament had consistently recognised the need for maritime defence. The evolution of New Zealand's naval forces reflects the constraints of a small economy, but also shows the government as being responsive to external threats. As New Zealand grew as a nation, so the government sought the means to defend its oceanic region.

9 Colonial naval forces before Federation
Bob Nicholls

The majority of pre-Federation Australian colonies possessed naval forces, and the details and histories of their ships and craft have been comprehensively covered in at least two books.[1] The acquisition of these dedicated naval forces did not occur until the 1870s and 1880s. However, when examining the naval defences of the colonies it is revealing to study first the circumstances which led to the requirement for those forces.

The problem in the century before Federation is that there were not any discernible threats—not in the formal sense that we understand them nowadays, anyway. On the other hand, a series of what one might call 'scares' confronted and perturbed the Australian colonies.

The first three-quarters of the nineteenth century saw the development of the Australian colonies from puny little settlements into a country of vast areas serving a number of thriving cities and ports, the majority of which were co-located. In those early years colonial energies were expended more on establishment and existence, without much attention paid to external menaces. This was probably just as well, as there was no credible military force available. For most of the period, the British garrison of one, sometimes two, infantry regiments, usually well under strength, was the entire military presence. The force was disposed in penny packets throughout the continent on non-soldierly duties such as surveying, guarding convicts and standing guard outside Government Houses.

Referring to the dispatch of troops of the 58th Regiment to New Zealand in the late 1840s, Governor Fitzroy gave some indication of the disposition and duties of troops under his command:

[the dispatch] will leave New South Wales with only 830 rank and file, or with sergeants and drummers 887 men, a number that will not be more than sufficient for the duties that are absolutely required to be performed by the military. The duties are ... including the dispatch of 100 men to Melbourne rendered necessary by the occasional religious riots between the lower orders of the Catholic and Protestant portion of that town, and, elsewhere, to prevent the aggressions of the blacks ...

[I]t is right that I should also mention that exclusive to the specie in the Colonial Treasury and the Military Chest, I am reliably informed that there are nearly £700,000 in specie in the different banks in Sydney; and I need not point out to your Lordship the inducement that the knowledge of this fact would be for plunder, should the mob of Sydney ever get beyond the control of the executive power.[2]

The first scare of note occurred late in 1854, when news of the outbreak of war with Russia reached Australia. In the principal colony, New South Wales, a voluntary artillery company was formed 'among the young gentlemen in the service of the Government'. An indication of the seriousness of purpose and dedication of the unit may be gathered when it is known that, according to one account, 'it was assumed that paid help would be found to clean the guns'.[3] Unfortunately, as the unit was never issued with any artillery, the question of who was going to clean it—and perhaps, as a last resort, fire it—will never be known and, with the passing of the scare, so did the Volunteer Artillery.

There was no real thought given to the raising of any local naval force, while the Royal Navy's presence was limited to a few paddle and sailing sloops on temporary detachment from the East Indies Station and usually employed on survey duties.

In the colony of Victoria, founded three years earlier, the opportunity was taken to acquire at the instigation of the newly arrived Governor, Captain Sir Charles Hotham, RN, a 'war steamer'. The order originated in a dilemma stemming from the discovery of gold in 1851. How might the bullion be protected until it could be sent safely on its way to England? Further, might not all this gold, lying in bank vaults in Melbourne, prove an irresistible temptation to a marauding buccaneer? The colonists' fears seemed well founded when the then enormous sum of £30 000 was stolen from a ship in Port Phillip Bay. This had prompted the governor of the day, La Trobe, to ask for the Royal Navy's protection. His specific concern was an attack by an American raider on the gold ships.

The Royal Navy responded by sending the next-to-useless sailing sloop *Electra*. (This deficiency did not stop Whitehall demanding part of the expense of the deployment.) However, *Electra*'s obvious shortcomings were responsible for the Victorians ordering their own armed ship. The steam sloop, named *Victoria* (it is no longer clear whether this was a result of colonial pride or after the sovereign), was—when she was eventually delivered—indeed a handsome vessel. However, she was of dubious legitimacy. According to the Admiralty's lawyers, in order to be regarded in international law as a British man-of-war, an armed vessel must be placed 'in commission' and be commanded by an officer holding a commission issued by the Crown. This was not so in *Victoria*'s case. Captain William Norman was a merchant marine officer employed by the colony of Victoria acting as the owners and operators of the ship.

On the evening of 7 September 1854 the sound of cannon fire in Hobson's Bay and the ascent of signal rockets to seaward provided the clearest indication possible that the Russians were indeed about to descend on the town and lay it to the sword. According to a newspaper account the following day:

> The Colonial Secretary, Sir Robert Nickle was called out and he and other distinguished public characters rushed hither and thither in a state bordering on frenzy. Bugles were sounding, drums were beating, and the soldiers in the barracks were hurriedly got under arms and stood ready to receive orders to proceed to the scene of the action.[4]

And the cause of all this commotion? The steamer *Great Britain* had arrived several days before and had been placed in quarantine because of smallpox on board. The ship had been released that afternoon and to celebrate the captain had let off rockets as he came up harbour to Melbourne. In accordance with nautical courtesy, other ships in the harbour had followed suit.

The next perturbation of note took place, again in Melbourne, in the early 1860s. The incident cannot, however, be labelled even a scare as it was quite unanticipated. The first real Russian naval ship to enter Hobson's Bay was the frigate *Svetlana*, which arrived quite unheralded. The batteries defending the city failed to return the visitor's gun salute because, it was later alleged in Parliament, they had no ammunition. A similar incident took place in March 1863 when the Russian corvette *Bogatyr* arrived off the port, again unannounced.

Some time later, details emerged of what had apparently been a Russian invasion plan. It had been made in anticipation of recurrence of war with the United Kingdom. If this happened, the Russian admirals in the Pacific and North Atlantic had orders to combine their squadrons, make for Australia and attack the colonies. There were to be twelve warships and two transports. The revelation that for the past year the colonies had been under the threat of invasion, although there was no supporting evidence for this dubious tale and tensions between the two countries had eased, caused uproar when it first leaked out.

It is perhaps worthwhile to note that the countries most feared in the colonies were Russia, France and the United States. The pecking order varied from time to time but, with the exception of the French primitive penal settlement in New Caledonia, no country had anything remotely resembling a base within practical distance from which to launch predatory operations against the Australian colonies.

Nevertheless, the Victorians' fears for their safety were given added emphasis when, on 25 January 1865, 'a ship of war with a few iron muzzles peeping forth from portholes' steamed, again unheralded, into Hobson's Bay and anchored off Port Melbourne. The ship, flying the flag of the Confederate States of America, was the commerce raider *Shenandoah*. The visit did not inspire confidence in the ability of the government to handle intruders. The ship's commander, Lieutenant Waddell, was able to place his ship on a slipway for refit, and embark stores and a number of new crewmembers unimpeded, despite the British Government's declaration of strict neutrality in the conflict between North and South. Refreshed, Waddell continued his rampage of the North's fishing fleets in the northern Pacific. The Victorian Government's inactivity led to a Dutch arbitration commission later finding that the British Government was responsible for Waddell's post-visit activities and fining it a total of US$3 875 000 for acts committed by *Shenandoah* and her fellow-privateer, *Alabama*.[5]

The full title of the *Colonial Naval Defence Act*, passed in London in 1865, was 'An Act to make Better Provision for the Naval Defence of the Colonies'.[6] This gave a colony the authority to raise its own naval forces for coastal defence purposes. However, the authority extended only within a colony's territorial waters, which of course were for a distance of three nautical miles. The only colony to take advantage of this legislation was Victoria. Within five years a monitor (*Cerberus*) for the defence of the Heads at the entrance to Port Phillip, where the width of the strait was too wide to be covered by the artillery in the already existing forts, had been built in the United Kingdom and delivered. London had, however, paid for her construction.

While *Cerberus* was under construction, the Victorians went ahead with the construction of a gun raft, designed and built by a Mr Douglas Elder. It can hardly be described as a sea-going naval vessel, but at least it could be towed from one sheltered water position to another.

Across the border the New South Wales Government was considering a design for a monitor. This incorporated 24 100-pounder breech-loading guns mounted round the rim of a steam-powered doughnut-shaped hull 50 metres across. Whether she were to charge into the middle of an invading fleet with all guns blazing or merely revolve on her axis firing her guns as they came to bear is not now clear, if in fact it ever was. Unfortunately for posterity in this sense, the design was not adopted.

Communications were becoming more rapid. The opening of the Suez Canal in 1868 enabled larger numbers of people, troops included, and warships to move from one part of the British Empire to another with comparative ease. As far as telegraph cables were concerned, by 1870 the Colonial Secretary was able to inform the colonial governors that any important war news— i.e. concerning the Franco–Prussian War—would be sent by cable to Ceylon, and then by steamer to Adelaide, where it would connect to the telegraph service within Australia. The continent would not be connected by direct cable for another two years—and even then at 7s 6d a word.

The British Government withdrew the army garrison from Australia in 1870. This was more a symbolic gesture than anything else since, as we have seen, the troops were quite incapable of providing anything other than a token defence force. However, the Royal Navy maintained its newly-formed Australian Squadron at a slightly improved numerical level. The squadron usually comprised a steam corvette and half a dozen small screw sloops and paddle gunvessels.

The ships deployed to the station, although based in Sydney, spent much of their time cruising the South Pacific rather than concentrating on the near-water defence of the Australian colonies. This was principally owing to colonisation and settlement of the Pacific Island territories, but also because there was no discernible threat to the continent. With the improved communications available, the view in London was that Royal Navy ships would know the position of any potentially hostile warships and could keep them under surveillance.

Another scare erupted in 1876, centring on the Balkans and involving Russia and the Ottoman Empire, with England siding with the Turks over Russian ethnic cleansing in Bulgaria. The New South Wales Premier, Henry Parkes, now took an initiative and suggested to his colleagues that they ask the imperial authorities for someone 'to give good professional advice with regard to placing them [the colonies] in a proper condition of defence'. For once, his fellow premiers agreed. The British Government thereupon appointed two soldiers, Colonel Drummond Jervois and Lieutenant Colonel Peter Scratchley, to examine the problem.[7]

The team met in Sydney in May 1877 and over the next ten months visited each Australian colony. Their initial task was to convince each colony that some form of defence was necessary. This they did by preparing a general threat assessment study applicable to the whole continent, which they then followed with what was in effect the forerunner of the modern 'Strategic Basis for Australia's Defence' paper. They then applied the conclusions of these two studies to the circumstances in each colony and concluded with specific recommendations for its defence.

Their thinking was based on Britain's worldwide naval supremacy. They also took into account the distance of the Australian colonies from any potential enemy's military bases, which meant that any full-scale invasion with a view to permanent occupation was highly improbable. The most the colonies had to fear was raids, with the object of plunder; the extortion of money after the capture of merchant ships; or bombardment, or its threat, of coastal cities. Perhaps an enemy could land bodies of troops to enforce their demands, and even temporarily occupy an undefended town or city, but the size of the force which could be carried in transports accompanying the raiding squadron would be limited to a couple of thousand men at the outside.

And all this could only be achieved after the Royal Navy had been defeated. If ships flying the White Ensign had merely been evaded, then the marauders would be in constant fear of being caught whilst besieging a city—with their men on shore and stocks of fuel and ammunition low. Even if the Royal Navy had been defeated, it would have been a local affair and retribution would inevitably follow.

Both officers were Royal Engineers and, not surprisingly, advocated building lots of forts. This followed similar measures in the United Kingdom and indeed throughout the British Empire. However, in their reports they went further by defining sea power as a first line of defence. Warships were to intercept any enemy force while still well out to sea. Then floating gun platforms, operating in concert with forts, would engage any enemy force managing to elude the Royal Navy and close the coast. The newly introduced and fashionable torpedo boats were intended to dash around in sheltered waters firing their weapons very much as a last-ditch measure. Although they did not specifically say so, Jervois and Scratchley clearly implied that the first line of defence would be provided by the Royal Navy.

The publication of these reports did not attract universal support locally.[8] Opposition was partially based on the colonists' perceptions of their relationship with the mother country. One view was that, in the event of an enemy laying siege to a port and demanding a ransom, it should be paid. Then, after the enemy's inevitable defeat, peace arrangements would include the reparation of the ransom—with any luck including interest into the bargain. Adherents of this view were presumably drawing on their history books and recalling the payment of Danegeld in earlier times, a 'subsidy to withdraw'.

Others believed that wars in which Great Britain became embroiled were no concern of theirs and finally there were those who believed that the Australian colonies were not worth attacking anyway. In the event, any question of the Australian colonies acquiring afloat naval defence forces languished in the years following the issue of the Jervois/Scratchley reports.

The defences of the colonies may have been developed in the face of perceived Russian threats—although to be fair, Russia still alternated with France and America as the bogy-man—but again there was apparently little adverse reaction to a visit by a Russian squadron to the main colonial ports in the latter part of 1881 and early 1882. Rear Admiral Aslanbegoff visited Sydney, Melbourne, Hobart Town and Glenelg (for Adelaide) in his flagship accompanied by two sloops. There appears to have been no mobilisation of the defences in any of the ports they visited. On the contrary, the visitors were feted wherever they went.

Towards the end of the visits, the Melbourne *Age* published an 'intercepted confidential dispatch' from Aslanbegoff to his headquarters in St Petersburg advising them of his ability to carry out a successful attack on Melbourne, where, once again, he had arrived completely unannounced. This sensational report was followed by others which described the Russian plans to swoop, when war broke out in April (by then scant weeks away!) on the four major capitals just visited for the purpose of looting and acquiring the gold stored in their banks. This was the age-old bogy revived with a vengeance, and might have elicited some response had it been published some weeks earlier. As it was, doubts were immediately expressed as to the authenticity of these communications and they were soon revealed as a hoax.

However, one reaction to the reports was the attempted mobilisation of the monitor *Cerberus*. This was not a resounding success as, owing to a great number of defects, she was unable to be got ready for action. The ship's boilers had definitely reached the end of their lives after 12 years in spasmodic use, and were only able to raise steam to 17 pounds per square inch (psi) as opposed to the original 30 psi achieved in trials.

The scare did have, superficially anyway, a beneficial effect on the fortunes of the Australian colonies' naval defences. Some were now prodded into ordering gunboats and torpedo craft. New South Wales did not participate, perhaps reasoning that the Royal Navy's squadron, based at Sydney, would provide any necessary protection. Thus their drive for rearmament did not stretch as far as new acquisitions. The previous year they had heard that the flagship of the squadron, the 20-year-old, wooden-hulled screw corvette HMS *Wolverine*, was up for disposal. She was not in a very good condition, which is why the current owners were anxious to get rid of her. Scenting a bargain, the New South Wales Government promptly asked for the transfer of the ship as a 'royal gift'.

Foreign warships were frequent visitors to Australian ports before Federation. This postcard depicts the Imperial German Navy's gunboat *Eber* at Farm Cove in the late 1880s. (J. Straczek)

The ship was turned over to the Colonial Government in 1882. There were only a couple of instances in which she raised steam and made the open sea. There was no question of setting sail, given the age and experience of the crew. She was indeed judged unfit to carry the by-now General Sir Peter Scratchley as far as New Guinea in 1885.

The colonies of Queensland, Victoria and South Australia ordered a total of five gunboats. These craft should properly be termed 'gunvessels'. They stemmed from a type first introduced in the Crimea 30 years before. The generic term of flat-iron gunboat referred to their resemblance to that laundry item. They were designed as a mobile platform for a comparatively large-bore breech-loading gun.

By the late 1870s and early 1880s the Royal Navy had a number in service, employed mainly on coast defence duties. It might therefore be thought that this would be the class of ship recommended by the Royal Navy and acquired by the colonial governments. However, no record exists of the Royal Navy being asked for advice, let alone offering any. Instead the three governments purchased their own craft.

Sir W.G. Armstrong's works at Elswick were the recognised suppliers of armaments to the international gentry, although perhaps the fact that

Sir William Jervois, the senior co-author of the defence reports and then Governor of South Australia, hoped to be given a directorship in the firm at the end of his appointment may have played a part in the colonial procurement decision. By the same token, Armstrong's Elswick Ordnance Company, or EOC, were the suppliers of most of the guns mounted in the Jervois-inspired forts as opposed to the British Government's rival organisation, the Royal Gun Factory (RGF) at Woolwich Arsenal. The colonial governments selected their naval acquisitions from an Armstrong's catalogue and the five ships turned up in the middle 1880s.

The Queensland Government, which had ordered two identical vessels, *Gayundah* and *Paluma*, decided that they could only afford to run one. In a deal with the Admiralty the other, unarmed, spent the next decade carrying out survey duties off the Queensland coast in an undertaking sponsored by both governments. For reasons that are no longer clear, the Victorian Government ordered two gunboats of slightly different sizes and armaments. The larger was called *Victoria* and the smaller, not surprisingly, *Albert*, although the Consort had been dead for more than two decades. The colony of South Australia went one better and ordered the deluxe version. Their ship, *Protector*, was larger than the others and approached a small cruiser in size. The role of these ships was spelled out in 'The General Scheme of Defence' of the individual colonies. They were to operate inshore. As well, a number of the newly-introduced torpedo boats were acquired from the Thames-side firm of John Thornycroft.

The concept of a colony having a Scheme of Defence stemmed from the workings of the Colonial Defence Committee (CDC) in London. The CDC was formed as part of the Cabinet Office in the 1870s. It had started off by compiling a list of the static defences and defence forces of the myriad British colonies, protectorates and dependencies. By the mid-1880s every colony was required to submit annual Schemes of Defence. These plans were commented on by the CDC and advice given about any alterations necessary.

Once the gunboats had arrived, problems emerged as the Australian colonies discovered that operating a warship was a complicated and expensive business. The complete absence of any co-operation from the Royal Navy towards their colonial cousins meant that there were no experts to mend machinery or provide maintenance facilities.

There was a minor exception in Tasmania. The Colonial Government had acquired a Thornycroft torpedo boat at the same time as the other colonies. Having acquired the craft, *TB No. 191*, it could find no one who knew how to raise steam in her. In the end, an engineer and a Torpedo Lieutenant from a visiting Royal Navy warship raised steam and took the

The Victorian Navy in 1886. Pictured are *Cerberus*, *Nelson*,
the gunboats *Victoria* and *Albert* and the torpedo boat *Childers*.
(National Library of Australia)

boat out for a run. This over, it was hoisted out of the water and into a cradle on dry land, where it seems to have remained for much of its subsequent career.

Replacement stores for the warships were also a problem, as was the provision of crews. In general, a crew consisted of a small core cadre of regulars who were employees of the colonial governments. These men were responsible for the day-to-day maintenance of the ship and her stores, armament and ammunition. They were normally retired Royal Navy men who held the same job for many years, completely isolated from the mainstream of naval developments and training.

These permanent forces were augmented by others from the naval reserve or militia—the name varied from time to time and from colony to colony. These men, either boatmen or waterfront employees, were usually paid a very modest yearly retainer and turned up for drill on a regular basis, usually at night or weekends. However, it should be remembered that most were in six-days-a-week employment and employers were less likely than now to grant unpaid—let alone paid—time off. This meant that a full crew was rarely available for seagoing exercises except during the Easter break, which had the maximum number of consecutive public holidays.

Adding to the woes of the local naval forces was the parlous state of colonial finances. Colonial ships had been ordered in a time of general boom. The early 1880s saw a great deal of expenditure on public works in general. Gunboats appear to have fallen into this category. While the good times prevailed, the unpalatable fact that warships and their crews cost a great deal of money to maintain was partially hidden. When, as was inevitable, the financial situation turned sour, savage economies became imperative and permanent crew numbers were cut, as was the amount of money provided for maintenance, fuel for cruises, provisions, and ammunition for training.

Even earlier, however, there had been problems in providing sufficient numbers of men for the crews of the ships. In the case of *Cerberus*, for example, civilian stokers and engine room personnel had to be hired (at a cost of £27 for two engineers and four stokers for the weekend). The captain of the ship even had to get permission from the colony's Treasurer before making any trip. The crews of the turrets always had to be heavily augmented by lads from the much superannuated wooden line-of-battle ship *Nelson*, which had become an industrial school or reformatory for homeless and wayward boys. (These lads were originally sent to a shore reformatory, where the intention was that they would become farm labourers. Local farmers naturally took the strongest ones, leaving the smaller and weaker boys to be sent to *Nelson*. Their ability to handle 400-pound shells in *Cerberus*'s turrets was thus open to question.)

The economic downturn of the 1890s led to the Australian naval complements as shown in Table 9.1.

It is clear that the real capability of the Australian colonies to contribute to their naval defence, no matter the threat was a remote and insubstantial one, was not very impressive, even at the peak of efficiency. The British Admiralty realised this too. Successive commodores and

Table 9.1   Australian colonies, men available for naval service, 1892

	Regular	Casual (paid)	Volunteer	Total
Victoria	236	340		576
Queensland	21	495		516
New South Wales	19	331	269	619
South Australia	17	72		89
Tasmania (Torpedo Corps)			(69)	
Total	293	1238	269	1800

Source: C. Jones, *Australian Colonial Navies.*

commanders-in-chief in the early part of the 1880s had reported on the defence of British possessions within their station, naturally including Australia.[9] Their thoughtful and detailed studies made much sense, but were generally predicated, first, on the advantages of some form of federation of the Australian colonies, and second, the willingness of those colonies, federated or not, to spend their own money on their defence. Both conditions were unrealistic.

It was not until the forceful newly arrived Commander-in-Chief of the Royal Navy's Australian Station, Admiral George Tryon (whose strong character was to lead to a famous disaster in the Mediterranean in the next decade) arrived in 1884, with instructions to make some form of arrangement with the Australian colonies, that any progress was made. The arrangements, which took two years to finalise, eventually led to the *Australasian Naval Defence Act*. This provided for a force of five third-class cruisers and two torpedo gunboats to be placed under the direct control of the British admiral but paid for in part by the Australian colonies and New Zealand.[10] The crews of the ships were to come from the Royal Navy and the arrangements would not affect the existing colonial navies in any way.

This may have resulted from the effect on the admiral of an incident in early 1885. The distinct possibility of war with Russia over the Penjdeh region, between what is now Afghanistan and India, had led Tryon to commission a couple of merchant ships as armed merchant cruisers. This was standard procedure as laid down by the Admiralty, with the ships' armament stored in overseas bases. In the case of the ships in Sydney at the time, the passenger liner *Massalia* was converted without difficulty, but the Orient Line's *Lusitania* was a different matter. The officers volunteered to join the Royal Naval Reserve but the Australian crew would only agree to join if paid colonial rates of pay, which were considerably higher than those of the Royal Navy. In the end she was given a crew of 120 Royal Navy bluejackets drawn from other ships of the squadron, but the impression left in the minds of the admiral and many British officers of the patriotism of local seafarers was not as good as it might have been.[11]

Earlier, Tryon had flirted with the idea that the best contribution the Australian colonies could make to their overall defence was by providing a reserve of trained crews for locally fitted out merchant ships armed as trade protection cruisers. The experience of 1885 led to him abandoning this idea, and instead an Auxiliary Squadron of the Australia Squadron was provided. The colonies agreed to contribute an annual sum (which, incidentally, bore scant relation to the actual cost) of running the squadron, which was to be manned by Royal Navy officers and men.

This is a convenient place to discuss the attitude of the Royal Navy's officers to their colonial counterparts. Although much research work

The men of the Cairns Naval Brigade in 1885. (RAN)

remains to be done, probably by a social historian, there are indications that there was little love lost between the Royal Navy and the colonial naval forces. A case in point was that of the commander of the Victorian naval forces who styled himself 'Officer Commanding Her Majesty's Naval Forces *in* Victoria'. The Commodore Commanding the Australian Squadron complained to the Governor and eventually a compromise was reached whereby Panter, the offending retired Royal Navy lieutenant, was forced to change his title to '*of* Victoria'. Tiffs over precedence were common, as were complaints about the uniform the colonial officers wore and its alleged resemblance to that of the Imperial Navy. In fact, although the uniforms were identical, buttons and lace were silver as opposed to gold and the executive curl was replaced by devices such as diamonds and triangles.

In New South Wales, the Admiralty instructed one admiral to boycott any public function ashore where he was not afforded his correct precedence, in this case ahead of any visiting governors of other colonies.

One exception to the lack of contact with the Royal Navy was the annual inspection of the Victorian forces by the Commodore—should his flagship happen to visit the colony at a time when the naval force could be mustered, bearing in mind that they were principally reservists with civilian jobs to hold down. But the inspection reports were always

An 1880 view of the Royal Navy's condescending attitude towards colonial naval officers. The caption reads: 'Colonial Commodore to English Middy: "After You, Sir." (*vide Plain English: "Confounded Condescension"*)'
(National Library of Australia)

addressed to the Queen's representative, the Governor, as protocol dictated, rather than to the Premier. It was as late as the mid-1890s before two officers of the Victorian naval forces were admitted into the Royal Naval Reserve—the province in those times of the British merchant service—so that they could be sent to the United Kingdom for specialist courses in gunnery and torpedoes.

The establishment of the Auxiliary Squadron had a damaging influence on relations between the Admiralty and the colonies. Despite the very modest amount of money they contributed to the ships' upkeep, the colonies tended to regard them as 'theirs', and there were frequent demands for the presence of vessels on various occasions in the colonial capitals. As well, the presence of these more modern ships, when coupled with the adverse economic climate, meant that the by-now obsolete warships had become redundant. Victoria sold both gunboats and laid up *Cerberus*.

Conclusion

To the extent that there was any defence planning in individual Australian colonies—let alone for the continent as a whole before Federation—naval forces were allotted a very minor role indeed. It is therefore reasonable to conclude that these forces were of limited utility. It is clear now that there never was a threat of any magnitude facing any part of the Australian mainland—or New Zealand, for that matter. This was also the conclusion reached at the time on more than one occasion by the CDC and the Colonial Office.[12] In fact the CDC had been moved to remark in one survey that 'There is no British territory so little liable to aggression as that of Australia'.[13]

Any formal attack by warships of any other nation was virtually unthinkable, if only because it would, correctly, be interpreted as an act of war. This leaves us with the threat of marauders or privateers, and this surely only existed in the very early period of the settlement of the continent. Even so, any such attackers would ultimately have faced retribution at the hands of an angry Royal Navy who, although they might have regarded their colonial counterparts with amused contempt, would surely have pursued any transgressor with the utmost vigour.

For there is one thing that we sometimes forget. The Australian colonies were precisely that, colonies forming part of the British Empire. Great Britain was thus ultimately responsible for their wellbeing. And that responsibility included their naval defence which had been, and would continue to be well into the twentieth century, in the hands of the Royal Navy. Yet the pre-Federation era cannot be compared with the next, ushered in by the new century, in which naval rivalry was largely to lead to the war to end all wars. By the time of the federation of the Australian colonies in 1901 the era described here had disappeared forever.

10 'A vigorous offensive': core aspects of Australian maritime defence concerns before 1914
Peter Overlack

> Australia is sea girt . . . it is vital for the very existence of the Empire that the roads for our commerce and communications should be kept clear.
>
> Vice Admiral Sir George King-Hall, 26 May 1911

In the early parliamentary debates of the new Commonwealth of Australia as many members spoke of a European as of an Asian threat. Hence the thrust of this chapter is Eurocentric, concerned primarily with defence questions arising from the presence of European powers, particularly Germany, in the Asia–Pacific region. This centred around Australia's ability to defend its lines of trade and communication, considered essential for the maintenance of the Empire upon whose naval supremacy Australia's survival was believed to depend.

While developing Australian defence concerns and policy trends also need to be viewed within the contemporary imperial framework, these have been covered in much detail elsewhere,[1] so only specific issues are highlighted here. Commentary of the day reflected an increasing divergence of opinion with Britain as to the realities of threat and the best means of naval defence for the region. My purpose is to highlight what Australians *believed* was the existing and future situation and the best means to deal with their defence requirements, and to analyse the strategic and political underpinnings of developing naval defence policy. This grew out of the nature of Australasian reactions to intrusion into what was considered a natural 'British' area of interest, of which the colonies were the self-appointed guardians.

Australians' uneasiness about their own security arose from the changing balance of power in the Asia–Pacific region and rising concerns about the vulnerability of its lines of trade and communication. The Sino–Japanese War of 1894–95 and the subsequent carving out of Japanese, German and Russian spheres of influence in China increased apprehension that Australian interests might be ignored by Britain in dealing with its global concerns. Yet the new Commonwealth Government had considerable difficulty deciding on a naval policy. While Britain had allowed substantial independence in the organisation and control of local military forces, its attitude towards naval matters was much less flexible. By the 1890s, when the Admiralty was advocating a policy of concentration and mobility, colonial navies were regarded as wasted resources, while the limitation on the movements of imperial squadrons subsidised by the colonies was seen as an unjustified restraint on freedom of action. The slogan was 'One Empire, one sea, one fleet', with London pushing the idea of colonial contributions to the 'Imperial Navy' without conditions.

Perceived threats and the growth of Australian defence consciousness

The flux of international events at the turn of the century highlights the complex relationship between economics and politics in the Pacific. While in the early years commercial interests were vocal, defence was always inseparably connected: the safety of commerce depended upon effective naval protection, and this could be provided only by an extension of Anglo–Australasian control in the near Pacific. As areas of colonial acquisition in Africa became scarcer, the Pacific became of increasing interest to the European powers. For the Australasian colonies, and after 1901 the Commonwealth, fear of foreign penetration of the self-declared Australasian sphere of influence in the Pacific dominated defence thinking. While nobody actually believed that Australia faced imminent invasion—the Royal Navy was a guarantee against that—there was an underlying apprehension about the future. Even the source of possible danger was not fixed: some thought it would come from Russian, French or German cruiser raids on ports and trade following the outbreak of a European war. Others thought it would come from Japan. Opinion was growing that the 'storm centre' of world politics was shifting to the Pacific.[2]

The menace of cruisers and armed merchantmen was raised frequently in the press and political forums. As Lord Brassey wrote in the widely-read *Nineteenth Century*, if communications between Australasia and Britain were interrupted, the consequences could be 'fatal . . . the ocean routes converging on their ports should be guarded by a fleet of sufficient strength to give security to the trade of the empire'.[3] In 1902 even Major General Sir Edward Hutton stressed the importance of naval power: while to a great extent Australia was protected by its geographical isolation, 'it is equally certain ... that Australian interests outside Australia itself are peculiarly open to foreign interference, and to possible destruction by an enemy in time of war'.[4]

With Federation achieved, the 1887 Naval Agreement and its financial obligations were taken over by the Commonwealth Government.[5] Just prior to Federation, Captain R. Muirhead Collins, Secretary of the Victorian Defence Department and later first Secretary of the new Commonwealth Defence Department, composed a memorandum emphasising the importance of an independent Australian naval force. He predicted that the Pacific would become the new Mediterranean, the scene of competing European powers against which eventuality the Commonwealth had to prepare its defences. Collins estimated that the money paid in subsidy to the Royal Navy auxiliary squadron combined with that allocated for local defence would enable the purchase of five second-class cruisers. To mollify London he added that the result would be a substantial addition to the Empire's fleet, even if not in the form the Admiralty wanted.[6]

While the Commonwealth Government adopted the scenario of a possible European threat as a rationale for its naval defence policy, this raised complex imperial problems. The American naval theorist A.T. Mahan raised the question of what the self-governing Dominions could do, not only for their own immediate security, and that of their trade,

> but for the general fabric of Imperial naval action, in the coherence of which they will find far greater assurance than in merely local effort. The prime naval considerations for them are that the English Channel Fleet should adequately protect the commerce and shores of the British Islands.

Thus the safety of the Empire's heartland would ensure that of its parts. As far as Mahan was concerned, non-professional (and even some military) minds needed to keep local and general interests 'in their true relations and proportions'. What Australia needed was not a 'fraction of an Imperial navy', but an organisation of naval force which 'constituted a firm grasp of the universal naval situation'. Australasia's role was to fortify the whole British position in the Far East.[7]

The naval writer P.A. Silburn, putting the Admiralty view, warned that an enemy 'would gladly risk a dozen of his ships to complete the destruction of Melbourne, Sydney, Brisbane, Adelaide ... It is to those very ports that the British shipping ... would naturally fly for protection'. To leave the great Dominion seaports undefended was to surrender command of the sea. But if every port were sufficiently fortified, the commerce destroyers would be helpless, cut off from coal, and easy prey for friendly cruisers. Given that the Commonwealth contributed £200 000 for the Royal Navy, which was barely sufficient to pay the interest on the cost and upkeep of two battleships, what return was she going to ask for this in time of war? Silburn stated it would be more effective if Australia's contribution were expended on harbour defences, dockyards and coaling facilities, training ships, and on personnel for the auxiliary fleet. Only then could any surplus be spent on a local navy—which should remain a unit of the Royal Navy.[8]

The 1902 Naval Agreement

The loss of control over Australian forces serving in the South African War was at the back of Prime Minister Edmund Barton's mind at the 1902 Imperial Conference.[9] Nevertheless, Barton accepted an extension of the existing naval agreement, with an increase in the annual subsidy to £200 000. Significantly, Commonwealth control over the movements of subsidised ships in wartime was ended, these now coming under the full control of the Royal Navy. In return for this concession, the Admiralty agreed to station more modern ships in Australian waters. Barton accepted this knowing that Australia could bear neither the cost of establishing its own naval force, nor of keeping it up to date.[10]

Nevertheless, there remained the strong feeling that British and Australian interests were not always likely to coincide. The *Bulletin* criticised Barton severely for what it termed the 'naval tribute'. Under the old agreement Australia paid for the services of a small and inefficient fleet, but at least in wartime it would remain in Pacific waters. Now, for more money and the possible removal of the fleet from the Pacific in wartime, there might be no defence at all when it was needed, and an enemy could bombard Australia with impunity. The arrangement was a 'broad and conspicuous hint' that Australia could not be trusted and it seemed that every time a premier went to England, there was something dreadful to explain on his return.[11]

The *Age*, although it also opposed any British attempt to centralise control of Dominion defences, was less strident. Events in South Africa had shown well enough that neither the War Office nor the Admiralty had a monopoly on wisdom. Just because the cost of establishing an Australian navy was prohibitive, this did not mean the country was tied to the old alternative of subsidising the Imperial Navy. The proposal by the then commandant of the Commonwealth Naval Forces, Captain William Rooke Creswell, had much to recommend it. The immediate purchase of a ship to £300 000 would mark a beginning, and thereafter ships could be

Captain William Rooke Creswell (1852–1933), pictured in 1900 when Naval Commandant Queensland. (AWM: PO444/214/162)

acquired gradually, with the subsidy slowly diminishing in proportion. The *Age* appreciated that the Admiralty took a dim view of such ideas, but the formation of an Australian navy would not necessarily interfere with imperial control. It would end, however, the 'present objectionable policy of taxation without representation' and provide that Australian money would be spent in protection of its own commerce.[12]

The question to be faced was how Australia could support larger imperial interests and accommodate the Admiralty, while being nagged by doubts about the effectiveness of Royal Navy protection, such doubts being fuelled by a growing nationalistic public sentiment. As the *Bulletin* pointed out in a long and angry article in November 1902, Australia's maritime problem was that all its important cities and most of its wealth were on the seaboard, and all were open to naval attack. An enemy that occupied Sydney or Melbourne for a few hours could cut the country's principal railway connections, and cable connections were just as vulnerable.

> Supposing the enemy appeared and began doing damage . . . anywhere north of Rockhampton, and from there all round the north and west and south coast to Adelaide or anywhere off Tasmania, it would be difficult for the eastern States to send assistance if the sea were wholly at the command of the enemy.[13]

The Commonwealth was currently paying for the use of a small British squadron, which was supposed also to 'wander around Maoriland, Fiji and half the South Pacific'. Australia had no control whatever over this squadron, and its operational limits were too vast to provide anything approaching reasonable security. The time had obviously come for the Commonwealth to spend this money and more on a fleet of its own, which would be where it was wanted, when it was wanted. This was not just a local issue. There was more British shipping to defend between Perth and Townsville than on most of the Empire's coasts. Also overlooked was the fact that Australia kept more gold in its banks (some £20 million) in proportion to population than almost any other country. A few armed cruisers which 'held up' Sydney and Melbourne could extort a ransom worth more than all the plunder they were likely to gain by holding possession of the trade routes to England for two years! The real difficulty of the proposal to partially relieve Britain of the burden of imperial defence lay in what Australians saw as the selfish tradition that the fleet should be wholly British-controlled.[14]

To minimise the growing local opposition, Barton and his Defence Minister, Sir John Forrest, asked for six small torpedo boat destroyers as substitutes for one of the cruisers provided for in the agreement. The Colonial Office retorted that '[t]he Australians do not seem to be able to grasp the principles of naval defence'. The proposal would only give Australia a false sense of security and could well lead to the neglect of coastal defences.[15] In Australia the agreement was seen as a stopgap measure providing naval protection until conditions—mainly financial— permitted local naval development. The speeches of parliamentarians such as Sir John Quick indicate that Creswell played a significant part in shaping this attitude.[16]

Subsequent parliamentary debate on the 1902 Naval Agreement remained heated, and the *Age* commented that the Senate would never again assent to an agreement, naval or otherwise, which emphasised the position of Australia as a dependency.[17] Shortly after the agreement was signed, Barton resigned and was succeeded as Prime Minister by Alfred Deakin with Austin Chapman as Minister for Defence. Deakin was more sympathetic to the 'local' cause and mooted reorganisation on a basis of harbour defence and ocean-going destroyers. He entered on a considerable correspondence with the Admiralty undeterred by the Committee of

Imperial Defence (CID), which reiterated that a separate Australian navy could not have a role commensurate with the cost of its creation and maintenance.[18]

One of the selling points for the agreement had been the availability of British naval power on the adjoining China Station. This was negated, however, by the removal of five battleships following the conclusion of the Anglo–Japanese Alliance in 1902. This withdrawal and other redistributions initiated by Admiral Sir John Fisher reflected financial realities and new international developments: the increasing menace of German naval strength and colonial consolidation, the development of the Anglo–French Entente, and growing Japanese naval power. Included in the 1903 rearrangement was the removal of the small coastal defence vessels, which were thought too antiquated and expensive to run. The *Bulletin* acidly pointed out that HMS *Boomerang* and HMS *Karrakatta*, which had recently been supposedly protecting Australia, and for which the Commonwealth paid £200 000 a year, were now sold for under £2000 each.[19] The *Age* was displeased that Fisher's new broom had swept away the vessels so often seen in Australian waters and presented as the embodiment of British sea power. The Australia Station was evidently 'like a paddock to which old and worn out animals were sent in ignorance of their approaching end'. This was the sort of squadron for which Australia had been paying a subsidy. The lesson drawn was that Australia had better begin to acquire some vessels of her own.[20]

The bottom line, however, was that Australia needed Britain more than the reverse, and all protestations of imperial loyalty would be ineffective in securing ships if this did not fit in with Admiralty plans. The Pacific interests of Australia and New Zealand were peripheral to the main concerns of British defence planners, whose emphasis changed markedly in the following years with the growth of the German battlefleet and the concern for defence centred on the North Sea. Yet in reality Australasian security concerns were well founded, particularly given the planned merchant warfare operations of the German East Asian Cruiser Squadron.[21] One perceptive observer noted that while British naval policy aimed at countering a concentration of enemy forces, the principal risk against which Australia had to provide was just the opposite.

> There is not the slightest doubt that any such power entering upon hostilities against the British Empire would play the double game of keeping the main line of British defences fully engaged while at the same time preying upon Colonial commerce and making descents upon Colonial ports by means of roving cruisers . . . When it is the enemy's cue to attack the nooks and corners of the Empire the part of wisdom is to provide ample defences for these places.[22]

Australian concerns in the Pacific cannot be separated from European developments. In the 1890s the German Government was under intense domestic pressure from colonial lobbies to make foreign acquisitions. The deeper reasons for German ambition are to be found in wide-ranging plans for economic and strategic penetration of the Asia–Pacific region. Now, more than ever before, the acquisition of colonial territory had more than just status value as the trappings of a world power. Colonial and naval expansion under Wilhelm II's exercise of 'world policy' invited great suspicion of Germany's motives. By the turn of the century, the German Admiralty's aim—of cutting trade and supply routes and lines of communication between Australasia and Britain in the event of a conflict—was suspected, and heightened Australasian defence concerns.[23] One is inevitably put in mind of German world-political aims. Admiral Alfred von Tirpitz stated clearly that by the twentieth century Germany would come into conflict with Britain 'in some part of the world, be it out of economic rivalry or as a consequence of colonial disputes'.[24]

Without this understanding of the internal forces at work in Germany, no proper explanation is possible of their reluctance to depart from what appeared to Australians to be unimportant remote outposts. The British Foreign Office had been persuaded by the Admiralty that only potential bases on the route to East Asia were strategically important, so the Pacific could be ignored—an error, given German commerce warfare plans for the region and the North American Pacific coast. Suspected German policy for the annexation of the Netherlands caused ongoing concern. Thereafter, 'German interests would increase in New Guinea . . . [T]he possibility of such a change of affairs, together with the increase of the German Navy, is a menace to the safety of Australia'.[25] The idea of a conflict of European powers in the region was not as hypothetical as it might seem. Mahan observed in 1902:

> The elements of future conflict in that, until now well-named Pacific, Ocean are already discernible. It seems far from impossible that the German *Drang nach der See*, to which the Emperor William has given so mighty an impulse, may tempt Germany to impose upon Holland some arrangement . . . by which the Germans would obtain a certain control of . . . the splendid Dutch colonial possessions.[26]

The *West Australian* observed that Australia was entirely dependent upon British command of the sea and, if this were lost, then Australia's position would be as perilous as that of Britain itself: 'The coast would be in the grip of the enemy's cruisers', and even if there were no bombardment, Australia would be gradually forced to accept any terms of surrender.[27] Strategic perceptions were important to Australia and New

Zealand and, given Germany's vigorous naval policy, its colonial and naval presence in the Pacific was enough to suggest expansion whenever an opportune moment might present itself.

Reaction to the 1905 CID 'Report on Colonial Defence'

In December 1904 Creswell presented an alternative policy for defence which was intended to satisfy both Australian and imperial needs. He quoted Mahan, and drew on evidence from the Russo–Japanese War to argue that the Pacific would be a new area of conflict. Australia by virtue of its geographical location was well positioned to be a major bulwark in the Eastern hemisphere. What was needed was a primary naval base, complemented by a naval force, and here Creswell advocated a strong destroyer component.[28] The limitations of the 1903 Naval Agreement, however, and the opposition of Defence Minister J.W. McCay were the reality. Pre-Federation concentration on the military defence of coastal cities against raids predominated, and McCay pointedly rejected Creswell's alternative of local naval defence.[29]

The government formed in 1905 by George Reid took the view that Australian defence efforts should concentrate on land-based military development. Reid believed that as long as the Royal Navy provided protection for Australia, the country did not need a naval force of its own. Creswell, now Commonwealth Naval Director, disagreed strongly with this view, maintaining that Australia's basic defence depended on effective sea power.[30] In October 1905, Lieutenant Colonel W.T. Bridges, the Chief of Intelligence, wrote a secret commentary on a memorandum by the Colonial Defence Committee. The latter believed that territorial aggression against Australia was impossible except on a large scale, and this could not be attempted until the Royal Navy were defeated. Given this, the question to be decided for Bridges was should the Commonwealth then make no preparation for resisting possible territorial aggression and restrict its defences to meeting raids by cruisers? The answer to this question affected the whole defence policy, 'and until it is decided no steps can be taken regarding the defence Scheme or the development of the Forces'.[31]

In mid-June 1905 a statement on defence needs by Deakin (now out of government but only a month from becoming Prime Minister again) met with universal approval and was 'everywhere the subject of animated discussion'. The Melbourne *Herald* termed it 'a great statement' on the supreme question for the Commonwealth:

> A new international situation has been established and the balance of power in the north Pacific has most materially altered . . . it is madness for

Australians to live in a fool's paradise of fancied security. Yet the man who would not sleep at night without his house insured against fire witnesses indifferently a supineness on the part of those charged with responsibility in regard to defence by which he risks seeing the coasts of Australia insulted, its shipping burned in the ports of Melbourne and Sydney by hostile cruisers.

Germany and Japan were active in the Pacific and the strength of their fleets obliged Australians to review the whole situation. As Deakin indicated, Australia was now within striking distance of sixteen foreign naval stations: 'It is even very doubtful if we are prepared to meet a dash at our weak spots delivered by two or three fast cruisers'. The backdrop for this concern was the outcome of the Russo–Japanese War, and Deakin alerted the nation to the emergence of a new power to the north. He was one with Creswell in recognising Australia's dependence on maritime commerce and the necessity of taking early action to protect coastal shipping, and he urged the immediate purchase of 'submarines, torpedo boats, and torpedo boat destroyers, the last of which would be sea-going'.[32] While Creswell declined to comment specifically, he expressed 'a sense of relief' that the matter had finally been seriously adopted by a 'statesman of Mr Deakin's eminence'. It was absolutely essential to make plain in Australia 'what is assuredly a life and death matter'.[33]

The second Deakin Government gave more support to Creswell's view. Deakin's position was that the Naval Agreement with Britain had never been popular because funds were not directed towards any specifically Australian purpose. Apart from the hotly debated issue of the subsidy to the Royal Navy, there was particular concern about the urgent need for local naval defence, with the belief that naval power must of necessity be used to defend Dominion seaborne trade.[34] The government's special adviser, Colonel J.F.G. Foxton, believed that the annual subsidy was the only practicable method of sharing the burden, 'though as a tentative and temporary arrangement only'.[35] The government suggested it could create new coaling or general naval stations in Australia, or there might be a subsidy to increase commercial steamship traffic capable of conversion to auxiliary cruisers in wartime.[36]

The Colonial Office pointed out that as the naval defence of Australia would probably take place thousands of miles away in European waters, it was against good strategy and commonsense to tie up ships on the Australia Station. This was the crux of the disagreement. Creswell's memorandum for the CID argued that Australia required a line within the defence line of the imperial fleet that would give security to naval bases, principal ports and commerce.[37] In February the *Age* had already commented that a naval policy of self-help was slowly being forced on the

Commonwealth by the inexorable logic of events. As *The Times* had made clear, a consideration which had to be paramount in the minds of British planners was the protection of Britain's food supply: 'If the routes by which foodstuffs are brought to the United Kingdom were blocked by any naval combination, even for . . . three or four weeks, there would be the beginning of an acute famine'. The massing of heavy squadrons in order to convoy fleets of merchantmen would be the essential feature of Britain's future maritime planning. The danger was that any naval combination which aimed to negate British naval supremacy and harass its maritime trade 'would at once throw into a tangled mass the whole of the naval defensive network' which Britain had attempted to weave around her distant colonial possessions. One thing was clear: Australia needed its own carefully planned local defence scheme. In the absence of such defences the coasts of the states were open to attack. Hence the Commonwealth's most urgent duty was to set its own defences in order.[38]

Britain's reliance on the Anglo–Japanese Alliance, which conveniently 'relieved the Admiralty from the necessity of attempting to re-establish our naval superiority in the Far East over any probable combination of Powers', was not well accepted by the Australian public or press. The fact that the Alliance terminated in 1915 clearly demonstrated its lack of permanence. Appropriate planning was needed in case the Japanese Fleet should thereafter act against Britain, alone or in combination with some other power. That that power might well be Germany was recognised in the CID's report. It also made clear that the Dominions could not necessarily count on immediate assistance if they came under threat. Another chilling prospect was that naval action in remote waters 'might have to be postponed until by the clearing of the situation in home waters adequate naval force could be brought to bear'. What would have alarmed and outraged Australian legislators, had they been aware of it, was the decision that if the 'temporary surrender' of local naval superiority in distant waters was 'a contingency that must in certain circumstances be contemplated', the Admiralty would potentially need to renege on the guarantee to protect British territory.[39] The CID report acknowledged that 'the most formidable combination of two naval Powers that could be arrayed against us is probably that of Germany and Japan—a combination the possibility of which cannot be left out of consideration if the Anglo–Japanese Alliance is terminated'.[40]

This report, not received until July 1906, certainly came as a shock to Australians, describing as it did a possible raid on Australia as being of 'secondary importance'. This might have been true from an imperial viewpoint, but was quite unacceptable to a Pacific Dominion pressing to be allowed to defend itself. Following from the proposals of the Australian Naval Officers' Committee, planning proceeded for a flotilla of 24 torpedo vessels, with 2000 personnel and an annual maintenance cost of £170 000. Deakin did not adopt the proposal in its entirety, mainly for financial reasons, but asked Parliament for eight of the coastal destroyers and four first-class torpedo boats, as well as sending two naval officers to Britain to obtain all necessary information to implement this program.[41]

While recognising the probability of a massive attack to neutralise British naval superiority in European waters, the report also uncannily anticipated German operational plans for Australasian waters:

> With a view to impairing our ... concentration in war, and inducing us to weaken our main fleets, the enemy may endeavour to create a widespread feeling of insecurity and alarm throughout the Empire by ... raiding our sea-borne trade and threatening distant portions of the Empire ...

It would be necessary to take a 'vigorous offensive' against such activity in order to protect trade and prevent the demoralisation which would ensue from random depredations.[42] This thinking recognised the British need for naval mobility, unhampered by Dominion considerations, and why under the Naval Agreement of 1903 the cruisers on the Australia Station were 'to ensure that all the ships of the enemy ... may be dealt with at the earliest possible moment wherever they may be found. Closely concerted offensive action ... will afford the only effective protection to Australian floating trade, whether on the high seas or in local waters'.[43] Given this, there was little liking for Creswell's submission for a separate Commonwealth navy.

1907: 'Political changes ... are unceasing'[44]

Perhaps Creswell was stating the obvious when he wrote to Deakin that the paramount defence concern had to be coastal and overseas trade. Uninterrupted sea communication was a national *sine qua non*, but its importance was not yet fully appreciated. The term 'trade arteries' was an apt description of Australian waterways and their importance for the nation's industry. Distance from foreign attack was a rapidly diminishing factor, with foreign bases being established in the Pacific and advances being made in transferring coal and oil fuel at sea. Creswell saw Australian defence in terms of the growth of naval power in countries bordering the Pacific, and of political changes affecting the possession of colonies in close proximity. It was conceivable that in the future Japan could be ranged with Germany against Britain. A foreign power which could base supplies within one and a half days' steam of Australia, where armaments could be quietly prepared for years, 'would seriously menace our existence'. Attack from main bases in the Northern Pacific was a new factor, which seriously lessened the value of the old strategic position, and made local naval development an imperative need.[45] The *Age* pointed out the necessity of 'expeditiously acquiring an Australian navy, to be composed of such vessels as . . . will best counter the mortal menace of the raiding cruiser'.[46]

The visit of the American Fleet in 1908 elicited public sentiment that the time had come for Australia to provide for her own naval defence. Given that for two decades Germany and France had been extending their presence in the Pacific, and at any time could become hostile, it was difficult to understand Britain's 'want of policy'. While those two powers had sought to secure every available position, Britain had been indifferent: 'There is an entire absence of any intelligent British activity in the Pacific'. These things came home with particular force to Australians, who could not pretend to be indifferent 'when we see Germany marching over the Pacific with an amazing stride'.[47] There was real criticism of and disaffection directed towards British naval policy, sentiments which had existed under the surface for some time. They had been expressed in Parliament by more forthright politicians but never before so widely or publicly ventilated:

> Australians feel no sort of confidence in Imperial guidance . . . for many years . . . there has never been an English Minister capable of taking comprehensive grasp of Austral and Pacific interests . . . By her weakness and indifference in the great affairs of the Pacific, she is showing to us that we have no ground for security in her management.[48]

Within a few weeks of Germany's announcement of its battleship construction program in 1909, the press voiced alarm that this would challenge British naval supremacy at worst, and destroy the Two-Power Standard at best.[49] The *Argus* highlighted Australia's vulnerable position.[50] What would be Australia's plight if approached by an enemy while local forces remained in their present state of disorganisation? The average man would be hardest hit if the British Fleet came off worst in the first engagements. Australian export trade, worth £64 million the previous year, would be paralysed. Wool could not be sold, for who would ship it? Insurance rates would rise, the traditional danger of cruiser warfare, and the risk might well exclude any cover being offered. Wheat, butter, coal, copper, tin and other commodities would not be exported. Sheep would go unshorn, farms untilled, mines unworked, and all those involved in these industries and associated transportation would become unemployed.[51]

The problem of foreign, particularly German, possessions close by was raised again. The prize was the 'future suzerainty, political and commercial, of the Southern Pacific. By supineness we may irretrievably lose our present commanding position'. The region was the 'natural sphere of influence' of Australia and New Zealand. Had Australia awakened to a serious recognition of its destiny in that vast region?[52] The term 'an Australian Navy' was increasingly being used, and its function as the first line of defence emphasised. The *Age* outlined 'certain fundamental principles': an Australian navy needed sufficient vessels to patrol the principal trade routes from Fremantle to Thursday Island; to co-operate with the fixed military defences guarding ports; and to protect the entire coast of the Commonwealth against raids. These vessels also needed local repair facilities to be independent of overseas support. To maintain personnel there had to be an infrastructure of naval militia, cadets, officer training colleges, naval scholarships, and training ships. It was also accepted that vessels and personnel had to be capable of merging with the Royal Navy in wartime.[53]

Andrew Fisher had formed a Labor Government, with George Pearce as Defence Minister, on 13 November 1908. The 1909 Imperial Conference was seen as an opportunity to press again for Australian control of naval defence. 'We cannot afford to hazard our existence ... it is well within the scope of things probable we should be invaded by a foreign foe before ... a proper system of defence [is] established'.[54] The *Sydney Morning Herald* supported whatever could be done to perfect imperial solidarity, but maintained that Australians must be prepared to protect their country themselves. Victory in the Atlantic was no guarantee for Australia, which could still be vulnerable in the Pacific. It was better to recognise this and to prepare.[55] W.M. Hughes expressed the same view in parliament, while declaring that the best way Australia could help defend the Empire was by defending itself, thus freeing imperial forces for service elsewhere: 'The Pacific is now—or will soon be—a centre no less important than the North Sea ... never were a people in such a parlous position as we are'.[56] Unless action was taken urgently, any Australian navy would still end up being 'a little thing the country would be able to carry around in its lunch bag and amuse itself with floating in a basin'.[57] The *Sydney Morning Herald* wholeheartedly agreed with Joseph Cook's assertion that 'No one can contemplate the position in the Pacific at the present time without a feeling that something ought to be done, and that soon'.[58]

The British rationale for the idea of Dominion Fleet Units has been well documented, and the 1909 Agreement met with general approval.[59] As far as the *Age* was concerned, the arrangement was 'entirely satisfactory to Australian national sentiment', and while providing the best form of defence for Australia, still constituted 'a really effective part of Imperial defence whenever and wherever Imperial interests are assailed'. It was seen as a considerable victory for Deakin that the Commonwealth would have to grant control to London in wartime. This was a considerable change of attitude on the part of the Admiralty.[60] For the *Age*, the Agreement marked Australia's 'arrival at naval maturity' and ensured the Dominions could make common measure to meet a common threat in Pacific and Asian waters.

With Britain, Australia and Canada contributing, the combination of Dominion fleets was considered an affordable force able to provide minimal protection for imperial interests in the Asia–Pacific region, and most importantly from Australia's point of view, it would be stationed permanently in the Pacific regardless of changing defence requirements elsewhere. It cannot be too greatly emphasised how important the 1909 Agreement was to Australia, and how committed the nation was to implementing it fully, particularly in light of the Admiralty's change of policy in 1914 which caused consternation, even a perception of duplicity.

Growing concerns and independent actions

The 1910 CID Report freely acknowledged that the rise of German naval power, which demanded greater concentration of British forces in home waters, had 'increased the difficulty of making the requisite naval force available ... in distant seas'. Britain could not now deal simultaneously with two first-class naval powers in different hemispheres. The matter of a regional British naval presence was thus complicated.

The situation was aggravated by concerns about the reliability of the Anglo–Japanese Alliance. In May 1909 the *Sydney Mail* had expressed the view that it would not be surprising if on its expiry the treaty gave place to a German–Japanese agreement: 'That would be Germany's game, and unless it is countered by an Anglo–American alliance, which would be the crowning diplomatic move of all, things would then be distinctly uncomfortable for Australia'.[61] Creswell's view was that while the North Sea was important, it was 'not the beginning and end of all things', and 'a German–Japanese alliance would be our death-knell'.[62] In August 1910 the *Sydney Morning Herald* also raised the specific prospect of a German–Japanese alliance after 1915. Australia could not afford to forget that such a threat might one day express itself in the most unmistakable way.

> A great deal changes in ten years ... The advantages of an understanding between Germany and Japan would obviously be great enough on each side to make it well worth working for. So far as Germany is concerned, it would solve the problems of the British fleet, which would immediately have to be redistributed on a new strategic scheme ... this would place Germany in such an excellent position that Japan might very well consider herself immune from attack and able to take the offensive in the Pacific.

It was uncertain how far Australia could rely on the United States for support, and the nation was brought face to face with the fact that in such a set of circumstances it would be left to its own devices. With the existing defence resources 'we should have a very hard, if not impossible, task in trying to hold our continent'. In the shuffling of alliances anything was possible, and Australia's most urgent need was effective defence.[63] Yet nothing seemed to be happening to ease Australia's long-term concerns. By the end of 1912 the *Sydney Morning Herald* bemoaned the lack of a coherent policy under which the disparate naval forces of the Empire could be utilised most effectively.[64]

In the dark: the reversal of Admiralty policy

Dominion feeling was aggravated by the attitude of the new First Lord of the Admiralty, Winston Churchill, as expressed in his speech on the 1914 naval estimates, which, as Defence Minister E.D. Millen put it, reassessed the whole imperial naval position in the Pacific. Australian concern centred on several of Churchill's key points:

- that a battle cruiser was not a necessary part of a Fleet Unit;
- that the presence of such warships in the Pacific was not necessary to British interests;
- the substitution of the scheme for a powerful joint imperial Pacific fleet by 'ineffective isolated units';
- an interpretation of the Anglo–Japanese Alliance unacceptable to Australia; and
- the replacement of a definite co-operative imperial policy for Pacific defence by an 'unco-ordinated, ephemeral scheme possessing neither permanence, nor clear aim and function'.

This indicated 'so startling a change from the opinion and policy in conformity with which Australia has addressed herself to naval defence', a policy predicated on the 1909 Agreement under which the battle cruiser—in fact three—was regarded as an essential component for the protection of British interests in the entire Pacific, a policy since supported by Admiral Sir Reginald Henderson's report of 1911.[65] Given that the Anglo–Japanese Alliance had existed in 1909 and 1911, it was 'difficult to see how it in any way disposes of the arguments advanced in the Admiralty memorandum [1909]'. How was it that action taken on Admiralty advice in 1909 was now stated by the Admiralty to be based on entirely wrong premises? Australia was entitled to an explanation reconciling the 1909 position with Churchill's statements. There was no guarantee of

Australians often believed that British preoccupation with the squabbles of the old world would leave them vulnerable. Norman Lindsay depicted the Japanese as a vulture ready to swoop in this cartoon published in the *Bulletin* on 5 December 1912. Caption reads: 'THE FIGHT OF THE SHEPHERDS (*Being an Australian view of the European situation*) The Vulture: "I think my chance is coming shortly." ' (National Library of Australia)

security in the Anglo–Japanese Alliance: 'The pages of history are strewn with the wreckage of fruitless alliances'.[66]

In Millen's view, Churchill had now rendered the RAN 'an isolated force, the very circumstance which [he] himself condemns'. Australia's first duty was to place its fleet and associated organisation on a thoroughly sound foundation. It was doubtful if the number of vessels was indeed sufficient to provide that foundation without which in time of war the fleet would be 'worse than useless'.[67] The *National Review* wondered why Australian proposals for an Imperial Defence Conference to consider the problems of Pacific defence were received in London 'with apparently so little realisation of the earnestness of the Government in the matter, and so inadequate an appreciation of the issues at stake'. The writer tartly noted that it was time the Colonial Office's methods in dealing with vital imperial issues received a thorough reorganisation. The non-fulfilment of the 1909 Agreement 'removes the whole foundation on which the Commonwealth agreed to establish a local Australian Navy—namely co-operation with other Imperial forces in the Pacific'. Despite Henderson's plan, Australia had received no indication of the needs which were to be met in the Pacific and what part London would play in meeting them.[68]

The *Age* pointedly stated that Churchill's policy left the Australian Navy completely isolated. Churchill's proposed Imperial Squadron which was to perambulate about the Empire was not regarded seriously in Australia, since it met neither the needs of Pacific nor European defence.[69] This was a formidable indictment of Admiralty policy, and its arguments were strengthened by the members of the Australian Round Table 'think tank'.[70] Australia would proceed with the organisation of its naval forces undeterred by Churchill's statements.

Australians soon realised that any defensive measures would have to be initiated by themselves. The lack of encouragement emanating from London seemed to imply that the Colonial Office had 'no real appreciation of Australia's position as the dominating power in the southern seas'. Germany controlled six island groups in the Pacific, New Guinea and Samoa providing considerable strategic advantages, and it had designs on the Dutch Indies. Under these circumstances any temptation by London to pursue a policy of *laissez faire* as far as Australian interests were concerned was unacceptable.[71]

A report by Australia's Naval Adviser to the High Commissioner in London (Captain Haworth-Booth) indicates that the danger posed by fast German armed merchant vessels was well recognised. The Admiralty accepted that these could not be eliminated by any number of cruisers maintained on distant stations. It was estimated that there were about 40 such German vessels, of which four were regularly trading between Europe and Australia. The initiative to mobilise them would probably be taken simultaneously in different parts of the world, and special efforts would be directed towards the destruction of British shipping on the main trade routes, the co-ordination of which would be assisted by wireless telegraphy (W/T). It was also possible that under existing conditions, some British vessels intended to act as armed merchantmen might be sunk or captured long before they reached the base where their armament was stored. Thus after 1912 the Admiralty made special efforts to persuade the major shipping companies to carry up to four 4.7-inch guns, ammunition and W/T on their larger vessels in peacetime.

> It is obvious that the adoption of such a system would be a real and definite safeguard against the menace of German policy ... It is of paramount importance to the Empire that trade in supplies of food stuffs and raw materials shall continue in war time ... arming a few merchantmen after the outbreak of hostilities won't secure it.

Since this change of policy was only in its initial stages, it was considered highly desirable that the Commonwealth take over the Royal Navy stores in Sydney and in addition also adopt the arming policy outlined. It was considered that eight vessels so armed would be secure from anything other than a warship and 'contribute greatly to the maintenance of trade in wartime'.[72]

Four aspects of the Australian naval defence problem were pointed out by the *Sydney Morning Herald* in 1913: the need for immediate defence of Australian shores; the necessity for co-operation between Australia and New Zealand for the protection of mutual interests; the desirability of joint action between Australia, New Zealand and Canada with regard to the Pacific; and the relationship between the Australian Fleet Unit and the Imperial Navy. While the new force had to be considered 'always as part of a mighty system'—for only in this way could Australia's limited resources be best utilised to protect the isolated continent against stronger powers—there was also the necessity for frequent inter-imperial consultation.[73] The German and Japanese naval threats continued to be highlighted. In particular there was not the slightest evidence that Germany had any intention of modifying its determination to secure command of the oceans, and '[w]ith Germany building ship after ship and Japan accumulating armament in the Pacific there is more than hopeful words needed from those who direct the policies and thus control the destinies of British states'.[74]

The situation in 1914

A secret report on coastal defences written early in 1914 by the Inspector-General, General Ian Hamilton, outlined briefly what was available for defence, and what was further required. Hamilton made detailed assessments of the defences of Thursday Island, Newcastle, Sydney, Port Phillip, Adelaide, Albany, and Hobart. His view was that given a sufficient land force, coastal defence existed for only three purposes: to protect naval works and shipping against direct attack, to prevent distant bombardment, and to deny enemy ships the use of roadsteads at points of strategic importance.[75] He considered that Australian ports, mostly having narrow entrances, winding channels, rapid currents and commanding gun positions, were more easily defended than others in the world. His general conclusion was that coastal defences were maintained in an efficient condition, and sufficient equipment and ammunition was available or on order. However, while complete arrangements existed for the treatment of neutral and enemy merchant vessels in wartime, work was needed on the necessary command and communications procedures, which were not in all cases complete and up to date.[76]

On the outbreak of hostilities in August 1914 the naval position in the Pacific was weaker than Churchill had argued it would be. The main

British vessels were pre-Dreadnought cruisers with a range and armament insufficient for the region, and certainly inferior to the strength projected at the 1909 conference. Of those planned forces, only the Australian Fleet Unit was in existence and ready for action. It could be argued that the Admiralty took account of *Australia*'s presence in its dispositions, and would have made provision for Pacific defence otherwise. However, in view of the general fear in British naval circles that the margin of superiority in the North Sea and Mediterranean was so thin, and given Churchill's statements that more powerful vessels like *New Zealand* would be held in Europe where they could counter newer German ships, in reality it was unlikely that anything comparable to *Australia* would have been dispatched. The main reason for the tardiness of Australian war preparations was the uncertainty of imperial naval policy in the Pacific. As far as Australia was concerned, the framework rested on co-operation between the Dominions and Britain in the creation of a Pacific Fleet—a firm agreement which had been reached in 1909, and on which basis plans were made. In contrast, the Admiralty's understanding was in terms of a general, flexible policy for the Pacific, subject to alteration if needs be.

In Australia the war situation was seen as uncertain, despite initial successes in occupying German Pacific colonial territory. In October 1914 Defence Minister Millen stated that the nation was unprepared for the realities of war. All preparation had been made for the repulsion of 'some raiding party' and none for service abroad, with the result that there had been a great deal of extemporisation: 'There was not a single man, officer, uniform, cartridge, or gun earmarked for anything but service within Australia'.[77] Creswell, from the beginning, saw one overriding strategic aim in the Pacific: the destruction of the German East Asia Cruiser Squadron. The Australian Fleet Unit had to be free to concentrate on bringing it to battle. Conversely the main concern of the squadron's commander, Max Graf von Spee, was to avoid the Japanese battleships and *Australia*.[78] In the light of German commerce warfare aims, Creswell was right to have so long urged the protection of local maritime trade routes.

In 1920 Creswell observed that: 'True strategy calls for centres of creative or producing Naval power at distant points in the Empire rather than perpetuating the grave disadvantages of depending on one central point situated possibly half the world's circumference from where it might be needed'.[79] It was in an unavoidable dispersal of forces, caused by imperial commitments, that Britain's weakness and Australia's danger lay, and this was always the driving force behind Australian defence preparations. There was a strong Australian conviction that the 'seas are one' approach was, like the naval subsidy, a thing of the past. What was needed now was a regional or Pacific approach to naval defence.

11 'The view from Port Phillip Heads': Alfred Deakin and the move towards an Australian navy

Colin Jones

Imagine if you will that it is the year 1905, and that you are talking to the Prime Minister of Australia, Alfred Deakin, coming down Port Phillip Bay on the beautiful paddle steamer *Hygeia* to your holiday home at Point Lonsdale. Perhaps you are discussing philosophical matters for, unlike some political leaders, Deakin is an intellectual, but as you pass Swan Island you can see the fort with its battery of 5-inch guns, and the columns of smoke as the torpedo boats and minelayers are getting under way. From the South Channel, a big ship is turning seawards to begin a voyage to the other side of the world, so on the approach to Queenscliff jetty, talk turns to naval defence.

Deakin is critical of the current naval subsidy arrangements, because 'No Commonwealth patriotism is aroused, while we merely supply funds that disappear in the general direction of the Admiralty'.[1] Yes, we must have the worldwide protection of the Royal Navy, but 'At present we are without any visible evidence of our participation in the Naval Force towards which we contribute' and 'the squadron is rarely seen in most of our ports'.[2] What we need, he says, are our own Australian destroyers and torpedo boats, so that we can project our defences offshore. The present disinterest of Australians in naval defence is because the people do not have any sense of ownership. As for our own naval forces, 'However well trained and organized, the efficiency of the Naval Forces must depend upon the efficiency of the ships belonging to them. Unfortunately, there are no modern vessels in the Naval Forces'.[3] Looking at the list of

Australasia's naval forces (see Table 11.1), I am sure you would have been agreeing with him.

Table 11.1   Australasian floating defences, 1905

		Tonnage	Type	Year
Victoria[a]				
	Cerberus	3344	monitor	1870
	Vulcan	125	minelayer	1889
	Countess of Hopetoun	82	torpedo boat	1891
	Childers	61	torpedo boat	1883
	Mars, Picket	45	picket boats	1891
	Gordon	12	torpedo boat	1886
	Nepean, Lonsdale	10	torpedo boat	1884
New Zealand				
	Sparrow	805	gunboat	1889
	Janie Seddon, Lady Roberts	144	minelayers	1901
	Ellen Ballance	25	minelayer	1884
South Australia				
	Protector	960	cruiser	1884
		10	torpedo boat	1884
Queensland				
	Gayundah, Paluma	360	gunboats	1884
	Midge	12	torpedo boat	1888
	Mosquito	10	torpedo boat	1884
New South Wales				
	Miner	161	minelayer	1900
	Ohm	33	minelayer	1893

Note: a. In addition the Customs cruiser *Lady Loch* would be manned by naval cadets for the Easter cruise.

The first thing to say is that the majority of these vessels were no longer young. Only about nine would survive if a criterion of age were being used. Also, of the 21 vessels, seven were in fact owned by the Army, and they were among the most modern. It is important to remember that the naval and military defences on the coastline were at that time intimately connected. Fixed defences were for the protection of naval bases and 'to defend and give confidence to great mercantile ports and the shipping which enters them'.[4] But they were a passive defence and their horizon was exactly that. If the enemy came, they were designed to catch him like a rat in a trap, but what if he lurked offshore and his cruisers

The Queensland gunboats *Gayundah* and *Paluma* on the builder's slipways at Elswick on Tyne in September 1884. They are still without their guns, but the scrollwork on their sterns is impressive. (Tyne & Wear Museums)

intercepted the shipping in the approaches to our ports? That was the job of the navy. And what if the British Admiralty had priorities for its ships in parts of the world far away from Australia? 'Far-called, our navies melt away', Kipling had written in 1897.[5] So what then? As the Admiralty admitted, fortress artillery would be useless:

> For beyond the range of its batteries, ports could be sealed to traffic by the most insignificant enemy, while a fleet of any considerable dimensions could cause the sea trade to be annihilated.[6]

Although at the beginning of the twentieth century there were fifteen fortified ports in Australia and New Zealand, by far the most important defence works were the Sydney and Port Phillip fortresses. Sydney had three 9.2-inch and twelve 6-inch breech-loading (BL) guns as well as four 6-inch quick-firing (QF), to list just the largest modern guns. Port Phillip, for comparison, had two 10-inch, four 9.2-inch, three 8-inch and eight 6-inch BL. The forts and the minefields worked together as a defensive system. If an enemy ship wished to enter Sydney Harbour or Port Phillip, it would be engaged by the forts, and any attempt to run past them at high speed would be countered by the minefield. Likewise, any attempt to sweep the mines would prove futile in the face of the light quick-firing fortress guns and electric lights. One has only to think of the failures at the Dardanelles in 1915 to realise how effective this scheme was.

There were two basic kinds of mine, electro-contact (EC) and electro-observation (EO) mines, the latter usually the larger. The size and placement depended on the depth of water and the nature of the channel, but they had to be placed accurately so that the observer in the shore station knew exactly when they were to fire them as a ship passed over. EC mines would explode when a ship touched the trigger mechanism, and were for use in shallow water against light draught vessels. In Sydney, the mines were on either side of the Sow and Pigs shoal; at Port Phillip, in the South Channel by South Channel Fort and the West Channel, by Swan Island. You can still see the remnants of the electric cables in the beach at Swan Island. EC mines were efficient and economical, although they restricted a channel and were vulnerable to counter-mining. EO mines did not hinder traffic and were difficult to sweep and counter-mine, but they had to be large and they relied heavily on the skill of the observer in the shore station. The men of the submarine mining arm were well trained. They had to be or they might blow themselves up. The most recent tragedy of this kind had taken place in Sydney in 1891. The Victorian corps could lay, test and remove a field of sixteen EC mines in less than five hours. The whole mine defence of Sydney (119 mines) could be laid out in 43 hours, and in Newcastle (24 mines) in twelve hours. The new minelayers, the *Miner* in New South Wales and the *Janie Seddon* and *Lady Roberts* in Wellington and Auckland respectively, were the best and

Submarine miners at work at Sydney's Chowder Bay Depot in 1893.
(National Library of Australia)

most efficient of their type. In addition, there were the remnants of the colonial forces, older but far from entirely useless. In particular, we should include the Victorian first-class torpedo boat *Countess of Hopetoun* and the minelayer *Vulcan*.

It is important to realise the general smallness of the Australian forces, both military and naval, and the huge importance of part-time service. There was also the way the forces were structured, resulting from a relative dispersal of population across a very large rural area. Rifle clubs were tremendously popular, and they had the support of the military. There were also cadet corps, both naval and military. These, one might say, were the forces of a free people.

Table 11.2   Australian military and naval manpower, 1906

		Army	*Navy*
New South Wales	permanent	504	3
	militia	4921	309
	volunteers	2212	
Victoria	permanent	406	108
	militia	4759	162
	volunteers	981	
Queensland	permanent	262	38
	militia	2581	317
	volunteers	168	
South Australia	permanent	60	22
	militia	1303	119
	volunteers	599	
Tasmania	permanent	42	
	militia	888	
	volunteers	714	
Western Australia	permanent	62	
	militia	800	
	volunteers	659	

Source: Defence Dept, *CPP*, 1906.

Overwhelmingly, interest in defence in Australia centred on the army rather than the navy. But the small size of the permanent forces was striking—just 1356 army, including a small headquarters staff, and 171 navy. New Zealand at the same time boasted a permanent army of just 332, scattered between its four major cities. Many of the forces were under establishment, but none more so than the navy. The manpower of the Victorian Navy was no less than 19 per cent below establishment. At the same time the Western Australian Army was 17 per cent below, the New Zealand Army 16 per cent below, the Tasmanian Army 12 per cent below, the Queensland Army 11 per cent below and the Queensland Navy 10 per cent below.

Not a single light horseman or infantryman was on the permanent payroll, and the major permanent unit in numbers was the garrison artillery, followed at a considerable distance by the army administrators, instructors and such like, the navy, the army ordnance department and the field artillery. It was much the same in New Zealand. The major investment, whether in manpower or in capital, was in the harbour-defence forts. Significance might be measured in numbers, but it is also worth pointing out that 63 per cent of the permanent naval cadre were in the federal capital, Melbourne, and influence on the spot on a personal level was also important.

A crucial change in the balance of defence priorities came when the War Office in Britain withdrew support for minelaying in 1905.[7] Its minelayers, the last of which had been launched in 1904, were mostly discarded by 1907. The Royal Navy was strong and, as they saw it, the development of submarines in particular allowed a defence to be mobile, replacing the extensive passive minefields at most imperial fortresses. It is worth noting that, not for the last time, the resultant change in Australia was not because of a change in the local environment, but rather a following of imperial prejudices. There had been a vigorous battle between the War Office and the Admiralty on the subject of coastal defences, but the usefulness of the army's submarine mining piers, workshops and barracks in Britain for the basing of submarines had been too great a temptation. The navy had won.

In Australia the forts were to be rearmed with the new 6-inch Mk VII QF gun and in 1906 it was recommended that, except at Sydney and Port Phillip, mine defences should be abandoned. In particular, 'The submarine mining service has always been a very technical one'[8] and it had been very difficult to assure sufficient efficiency at ports other than Melbourne and Sydney. Submarine mining ended in New Zealand in 1907. It was also envisaged that the fortress defences of some places such as Townsville and Albany should not be maintained. The same report was absolutely against the development of a local Australian navy.

Yet there was a new element in the argument. At the same time, the Royal Navy was putting into service a new type of destroyer which could handle the stresses of rough weather at sea, and thus reliably project a defensive posture well offshore. This was the 'River' class, of which the boats of the first two flotillas were launched in 1903 and were in service in 1904. Compared with previous torpedo craft they had 'so many advantages that a comparison seems hardly necessary'.[9] In particular, their high forecastles made them less wet, their actual speed at sea was not so different from that of the older boats, and they would not break in half and sink, as HMS *Cobra* had done in 1901.

The time also coincided with the Japanese victory over Russia: to put it in blunt terms, the triumph of an Asian navy and army over a European. There was no question about this. It had been a demonstration of just what could be done. In the case of the Port Arthur fortress, the Australian Army, for one, took comfort in the fact that 'its reduction was left almost entirely to the land forces, and care was taken not to expose capital ships to the fire of the coast defences'.[10] It may be worth observing that the First Sea Lord, Admiral Sir John Fisher, saw Singapore as the strategic key that locked up Australia's part of the world. Certainly, Britain and Japan had been allies since 1902, but when Japanese troops took Port Arthur, they suggested that, for their sons, Singapore would be a pushover.

In 1903 the Imperial Defence Committee had laid down what was rather a motherhood statement, that 'The British fleets guarantee Australia against invasion in force' and that, although there was no guarantee against commerce raiders, 'the losses they would inflict would not be of more than secondary importance'.[11] It was an idea which sat uneasily with many Australians concerned with defence matters. The floating trade of the Commonwealth, they estimated, was worth £170 million. Some estimated this to be greater than that of Spain and Portugal, or Japan.

At the same time, the strategic priorities of the Royal Navy were being overhauled under Admiral Fisher. He was contemptuous of ships on foreign stations 'that could neither fight an enemy nor escape him',[12] and in December 1904 no less than 154 ships were struck off the effective list. Ninety were put up for immediate sale. By the middle of 1905 a major change in strategic orientation had been achieved. France and Japan were friends, Russia had been crushed. The real enemy would be Germany, and what was seen to be needed was a serious concentration of force in European waters.

In fact it was a time in which the old verities of strategy and defensive hardware were being challenged. Certainly it would be unsettling, but such times are also those in which changes are possible.

It is necessary now to turn to a man whose influence would be crucial. Captain William Creswell had entered the South Australian Naval Forces in 1885. He had commanded its small cruiser, the *Protector*, from 1893, and in 1900 he became the senior officer of the Queensland Marine Defence Force. From 1904 to 1907 Creswell was commander of the Victorian Navy, and in a position to exert maximum influence on the federal policy-makers in Melbourne. In his view, there had to be an Australian navy. In an effort to improve the efficiency and experience of the existing force, he sent the torpedo boats on a cruise to Tasmania in February 1905. The *Countess of Hopetoun* and *Childers* were showing what could be

The Victorian torpedo boat *Countess of Hopetoun* presides over a yachting regatta at Geelong. The forward torpedo tube can be clearly seen. (A. Woodley)

achieved by the smallest of seagoing craft. Indeed, the *Childers* immediately revealed a weakness in her design with the stresses caused by the two torpedo tubes side by side in the bow, and on her return had to be rebuilt. Nevertheless, the cruise was repeated in the two following years.

Bass Strait, as the old sailors would say, is like a box. You do not need elaborate navigation because you are scarcely ever out of sight of land. It is also a focus for shipping, and was significantly busier then than it is now. What has not changed is its weather. Creswell would say that Port Phillip was like the English Channel, and Bass Strait the Bay of Biscay, and one needs ships that can cope with it, ships 'designed for maintaining high speed in rough waters'.[13] Similar oceanic conditions, he said, affected the approaches to most Australian ports, and in addition the long distances involved required a good steaming range.

Creswell was a master of publicity. His torpedo boats in particular were the subject of illustrated newspaper articles and a series of lantern slides, and one can imagine the audiences of those days being told of the capabilities of these small Australian warships as they saw images of their best torpedo boat speeding through the water with smoke pouring from her funnel and firing torpedoes. They would certainly be assured that better things were possible. Creswell also sent the *Protector*, *Gayundah* and *Paluma* on training cruises. Thus in 1906, for example, the *Protector* sailed from Adelaide and visited Portland, Melbourne, Sydney and Hobart, the *Gayundah* and *Paluma* sailed from Brisbane and visited Bundaberg,

Cairns and Townsville and Rockhampton and Maryborough respectively, and the *Countess of Hopetoun* sailed from Melbourne and visited Launceston. The local naval militia went aboard for continuous training and the local people took pride in this. It is not too much to say that today's navy needs skilful publicity just as much as Creswell, and not only for recruiting. A navy which is invisible, however valuable it may be, will not have public support. That is a modern view from Port Phillip Heads.

In other Dominions there were similar moves. Canada did not yet have a navy. It had rejected the idea when it was first floated in the late 1860s to cope with Fenian raids, but its fishery protection cruisers were the basis of a disciplined seagoing force. The newest and best of these, the *Canada*, a vessel of 557 tons, sailed to the West Indies in 1905 for the express purpose of training a Canadian Naval Militia. In New Zealand, the Royal Navy's former gunboat *Sparrow* had been obtained as a training ship for both naval and mercantile service. Following her transfer from the defence to the marine department in 1907, she commenced the first of a series of training voyages in that year.

It was usually agreed that Australia should take control of the defence of ports and dockyards, and the protection of coastal trade. Given this, the future for Australia lay in torpedo craft and larger vessels. Destroyers in particular were needed. As Creswell saw it, they would provide a scouting service outside the range of the forts in daylight, and an attacking force against enemy warships at night. Any attacker would have to consider his chances of meeting the business end of a torpedo if he came too close to Australian shores. A raider could never afford damage. A force of local destroyers would be a valuable auxiliary to the British fleet and its most effective substitute if it were away. The destroyer was also the sort of vessel which could easily be built and maintained locally.

The British squadron on the Australia station in mid-1905, a first-class armoured cruiser and a second-class cruiser, six third-class cruisers and a survey vessel, was supported by a subsidy from Australia and New Zealand. The subsidy agreement also specified the force structure, which had, at this stage, not fully matured. It was an easy option and a cheap one compared with the raising of a full-time naval force and the purchase and maintenance of significant warships such as cruisers. In 1903 the Australian subsidy increased from £105 000 to £175 000, and in 1905 to £200 000 per annum, to which might be added another £300 000 spent on fixed defences, garrison troops and the Commonwealth Naval Forces. The Admiralty had wanted a subsidy of £400 000, but had been argued down.[14] New Zealand contributed £40 000. The 1903 agreement, which was to run for ten years, also provided for the raising of a Royal Naval Reserve of 25 officers and 700 seamen and stokers. Three of the cruisers were to be partly manned for drill purposes and, as far as possible, by Australians and New Zealanders. Some 408 Australians and 110 New Zealanders were serving in the squadron in 1906.

The cruisers were the *Pioneer*, *Psyche* and *Pyramus*, all of which were on station by December 1905. They were newish ships of 2200 tons, with a main armament of eight 4-inch guns, some torpedoes and light guns, and a speed of 20 knots. You would scarcely call them cruisers nowadays. Indeed, even in contemporary terms they were little more than escort vessels. A navy-smitten Lofty Batt remembered his first acquaintance with one of them in 1906:

> The narrow-gutted 'Hooker', belonging to his Majesty the King, that I was looking at could throw a faint shadow only when beam on, the King must have been horribly short of cash when he bought the 'Pioneer'.[15]

The opinion of the admiral in Sydney would be expected to carry significant weight in the young nation's counsels, not to mention the general policy of the Admiralty and the Colonial Office in London. The admiral saw himself as wielding a force against the enemy wherever he might be found, and was consistently against the building of a force to challenge the enemy locally whenever he might come. In Britain the perspective was the opposite and Australians could hardly be unaware of the contrast. It was a time when Australian nationalism was high in the wake of the achievement of Federation, and the opportunity was available for the creation of a true Australian navy. But it was never going to be easy. James McCay, Minister for Defence, was still thinking in terms of harbour defence. He was a notable citizen soldier, a major in the 4th Battalion, Victorian Rifles, and noted for his practical attitudes, hence his opinion is not surprising. Australia was remote, its population and financial base were small, and its harbours should be secured before any thoughts were given to projecting force offshore. This backyard kind of thinking was to be overtaken by actions such as the withdrawal of support for minelaying.

Captain Creswell, Director of Naval Forces, had been faced with a series of ephemeral defence ministers, all of whom would have passed from the portfolio before their naval and military education were complete. Labor's Anderson Dawson had lasted less than four months. McCay was to last just eleven months. In every case, arguments had to be mounted over again from first principles. Colonel Edward Hutton, who had been employed to bring a proper professional Australian Army into existence, was always quarrelling with his ministers. His 1903 reform proposals had been attacked in parliament as militaristic, imperialistic and extravagant. The Admiralty also tended to deprecate anything in the nature of a French-style 'Defence Mobile',[16] yet the proposed force was exactly that, and a significant advance on the soon-to-be-abandoned minefields.

Creswell must sometimes have felt disheartened, but he was a fighter. He replied to McCay that 'A sea defence that would adequately protect our Coastal trade would also cover our ports, and render impossible any landing of an enemy on our shores'.[17] He went on to stress the importance of active co-operation with the Royal Navy, and the ability of his proposed torpedo forces to lurk in a large number of east coast rivers, or in Bass Strait. Creswell also had an imperial argument:

> Sea commerce is vulnerable at the points of arrival, of departure, and wherever there is convergence of trade routes. There is comparative safety on the open sea or the ocean. It is of little use guarding the approaches to the United Kingdom, the narrow seas, if the expected commerce can be snapped up at this end immediately it leaves port. There is no measure of what has been called local Naval Defence that is of such Imperial importance.[18]

Creswell presented a dogged defence of his position, arguing with whomever he could find with influence and who needed convincing. Time, he knew, was not on his side, as his ships and his officer corps were all showing their age, to the extent that 'this Service is practically on the verge of collapse'.[19] What he wanted were an extra 456 permanent personnel and 466 militia, a modest proposal on the surface, but in fact an increase which would more or less double the existing effective naval force. The imperial authorities, of course, were unsympathetic.

Creswell spent much of the first half of 1906 on a visit to England, where his reception was mixed, but he got a good reception from Sir John Fisher and it would seem that he absorbed some of Fisher's ideas. Meeting the fiery and enthusiastic Fisher, who would not? Thus, when he returned to Australia, he could report that his previous opinions about torpedo forces had been strengthened:

> The Navy may be withdrawn to other seas.
> To make up for this, we should gradually create sea power in Australia. There could not under our present conditions be a better means of initiating such a policy than a torpedo defence as proposed.[20]

Following on from this, Creswell and his committee of naval officers came forward with a detailed plan, elaborated in the formal submission to Thomas Playford, the latest Minister for Defence, dated 12 September 1906. It canvassed all conceivable arguments and concluded by proposing a fleet of destroyers based around the coast at the five major capitals. As with the old colonial navies, not all of the vessels would be kept in commission, but they would be activated on a regular basis for training of naval reservists. Apart from the destroyers, Port Phillip would have the services of the two existing first-class torpedo boats—ageing but efficient; and Moreton Bay would be provided with a division of new torpedo boats. There was, in fact, more than just a touch of Jackie Fisher in the size and composition of the force and the type of vessel specified. The progression of design is also of interest, from the little *Childers* to the big destroyers:[21]

- **Three first-class ocean-going destroyers** (1300 tons, 325 ft × 31 ft × 10 ft 9in, 33 knots). These vessels match the initial specification that Fisher put forward for a super-destroyer of the sort which became HMS *Swift*. It had proved difficult to meet and the actual vessel was larger, at some 2200 tons. The proposed armament for such a vessel, however, was meagre. *Swift* emerged in 1909 with four 4-inch guns and two 18-inch torpedoes. Range was 1500 miles at 17 knots.
- **One second-class ocean-going destroyer** (800 tons, 272 ft × 26 ft × 9 ft, 30 knots). This vessel matches the specification which Fisher put forward for the destroyers of the 'Tribal' class. The actual displacement for a boat of this size (HMS *Saracen* of 1908) was 980 tons. Armament was three 12-pounders and two 18-inch torpedoes, later increased to five 12-pounders or two 4-inch. Radius of action was 2000 miles at 15 knots.
- **Sixteen coastal destroyers** (*Teviot* class of 1903) (550 tons, 225 ft × 23 ft 6 in × 9 ft 6 in, 26 knots). Armament in 1906 was three 12-pounders and two 18-inch torpedoes. Radius of action was 1700 miles at 11 knots. Although Creswell classified them as coastal destroyers, they were stronger than previous vessels, and built specifically to keep the sea. Six of them demonstrated this by a voyage to Hong Kong and back in 1906, escorted by two cruisers which towed them at times. They were, however, lacking in speed for good fleet work.
- **Four first-class torpedo boats** (*TPB 98* type of 1900) (157 tons, 160 ft × 16 ft 6 in × 5 ft, 25 knots). Armament was three 3-pounders and three 18-inch torpedoes.
- *Countess of Hopetoun* (1891) (80 tons, 130 ft x 13 ft 6 in x 5 ft 7 in, 24 knots). Armament was three 1-pounders and seven 14-inch torpedoes.
- *Childers* (1883) (61 tons, 113 ft x 12 ft 6 in x 5 ft 6 in, 19 knots). Armament was two 1-pounders, two 15-inch and four 14-inch torpedoes.

To return briefly to the political environment, there had been a change of government, but without new elections, on 5 July 1905 and Alfred Deakin had replaced George Reid as Prime Minister. The Federal

Parliament was divided between Deakin's Protectionist (Liberal) Party, the Labor Party, and a coalition of Anti-Socialist parties. Depending on the issues, and some such as the tariff were viewed as very important, there was a constant shifting of party groupings. In the circumstances, defence was not an issue on which governments rose or fell. In modern parlance, it could be put on the back burner. Deakin adopted Creswell's proposals officially on 26 September 1906, but took a cautious point of view. He did not go all the way, but announced an initial three-year program, which would then be reviewed in the light of developments. Initially there would be eight 'River' class destroyers and four torpedo boats, to be completed by 1909. Indeed, the destroyers as they emerged were not just copies of a standard British type, but were to be specially designed for Australia. Subsequent development would look to a broader sphere.

The scheme received guarded support from the Admiralty in 1907, but although the requisite money had been set aside things were allowed to slide until another change of government on 13 November 1908. Thus it was that the first three destroyers were not ordered until 5 February 1909. But it was an important step, and four initial vessels were envisaged, followed by two of a larger type, designed to cope with the rougher waters of southern Australia. As we know, these boats were never built, but it is to be hoped that they were envisaged as having a longer range than the actual 'Tribal' class, which were always tied to their ports in the English Channel during the Great War for lack of endurance. To return for a moment to the first-class ocean-going destroyer, the *Swift* was praised for its abilities as a scout, as it was large enough to keep the sea in bad weather and carry a wireless set. It was, however, always considered too large for torpedo work. Also, its very existence implied the presence somewhere in support of a strong force of large warships. Whether vessels of this type would really have suited Australian requirements is, in fact, a nice speculation. There is one small curiosity to add. Late in 1907 it was stated that the Armstrong Whitworth company was preparing to establish a shipbuilding yard in Victoria and that it was expected to build torpedo craft.[22] Could this be one reason why the order was delayed?

I shall leave it to others to chronicle the emergence of the eventual Australian fleet unit[23] but, to emphasise the change, I want you to accompany young Stan Veale from his home at Albert Park to the Williamstown Naval Depot to see the arrival of the *Parramatta* and *Yarra* on Saturday afternoon 10 December 1910, the first new Australian naval vessels for almost two decades. He was proud to be part of a guard of honour composed entirely of the Australian Naval Cadet Corps for inspection by the Governor-General and the Governor of Victoria. The two destroyers had been met at the heads by the *Courier* with an official party of 1150 people, then the *Lady Loch* with over 200, and were followed up the bay by the two torpedo boats. There was tremendous excitement as they circled by St Kilda through a guard of honour of yachts, the beginning of a real Australian navy. Stan Veale wrote:

> We were greatly impressed by the feeling of suppressed power that these destroyers seemed to have; the constant hum of the fans in their funnels, and the smell of their oil fuel, which was something new to us. We'd never smelt oil fuel in ships before.[24]

He was also very proud of Engineer Sub-Lieutenant 'Sparker' Creswell, who had newly installed some modern radio gear in the Williamstown Depot. Captain Tickell, commanding the *Parramatta*, was modest in his reply to the official speeches, and in particular that of the Governor-General, who confessed his preference for a real Australian navy rather than a subsidy sent to Britain.[25]

So finally, you should stand again beside Alfred Deakin on Point Lonsdale looking out to the blue choppy waters of Bass Strait. This is our territory, he is thinking, and this is where all large British merchant ships make their first landfall. If the enemy ever sends his cruisers, they will certainly come here. We must ensure that, whatever happens, our home waters are safe for our own shipping and for the shipping of the world, and we must do this in a way which best suits us as a nation. Perhaps it was as well that Australia already had a strand of colonial naval tradition going back as far as 1860, and exemplified still by the quiet bulk of the old monitor *Cerberus* alongside the Gellibrand Pier at Williamstown. The horrified Canadians, who did not have this tradition, were told as late as 1911 that their warships were forbidden to cruise more than three miles out to sea. It rather stopped them in their tracks. For Australia, it would be different.

12 'A sea of troubles': the Great White Fleet's 1908 war plans for Australia and New Zealand

James R. Reckner

> When the [American] fleet entered the Pacific we remarked that the centre of gravity of seapower had changed. What the future of the Pacific is to be only the future can disclose. It may not be an American lake. It may not be a Japanese sea. But whatever its fate, the coming of the fleet . . . is another noteworthy stride towards it . . . It is likely enough that America may become our first line of defence against Asia. But whether so or no, the ties now formed will remain, and we hope that time will only serve to strengthen them on both sides.
>
> *Sydney Morning Herald* editorial, 10 August 1908

For virtually our entire lives, the United States and Great Britain have enjoyed what we have called a 'special relationship'. In an historical context, though, that relationship is a relatively recent development, despite British historian Stephen Howarth's description of a 'remarkable rapprochement' between the two nations after the Spanish–American War of 1898.[1] The officers who commanded the United States Navy (USN) during the era of Theodore Roosevelt enjoyed no such relationship, though there were noted Anglophiles, the most prominent of whom were Captain Alfred Thayer Mahan and William S. Sims, who was only a lieutenant at the end of the century.

War Plan RED

The reality at the beginning of the twentieth century was that the United States remained outside the powerful alliance systems of Europe. Great Britain remained potentially hostile. Thus, despite incipient feelings of friendship, American planners had to consider the possibility of war. In the US system of assigning colours to designate individual nations, the United Kingdom was assigned the code name RED. Interestingly, War Plan RED continued until the Washington Arms Limitation Treaties in 1922, when the principal cause for American concern, the Anglo–Japanese Alliance, was terminated.[2] Even then, it was revised a final time in 1930.[3]

Concern about a possible British descent upon the east coast of the United States actually influenced the design of the earliest US battleships, and it remained a continuing theme in Plan RED. The US Naval War College (NWC) class of 1894, for example, reported that the navy should deal with any superior naval force on the US Atlantic coast (the Royal Navy was the threat here considered; the German threat arose later) by 'effectively using bays, sounds, and interior waterways for engagements with the enemy'. Therefore, they emphasised that American battleships should 'draw less water' than foreign battleships. These findings, reaffirmed by the NWC classes of 1895 and 1896, represented the most advanced American thought on the subject.[4] The college recommended in 1894 that future battleships be built with 'an extreme deep-load draft' of no more than 23 feet, a recommendation the Secretary of the Navy included in his annual report of that year.[5]

Indeed, the NWC summer classes regularly worked on 'Strategic Situation No. 10', a war with RED in which the British were assumed to attack the United States somewhere between Delaware Bay and the New England coast. In the 1895 exercise, RED won; in 1896 and 1897, the games were judged a draw. War games after the war with Spain concluded with BLUE (US) victories in 1899, 1900, 1903, 1904 and 1906.[6]

The 1900 NWC problem examined in detail the US Navy's options should the Royal Navy attack the US east coast. The class rejected 'going to sea with our fleet' in the event of British attack, 'because history has proved it to be an unbefitting role for the inferior Navy'. Such a policy, they reported, 'would be fatal'. They concluded that the main plan should be to use 'Nantucket and Vineyard Sounds as a base of operations and port of sortie' against RED, with the possibility of 'retiring into New York' in the event of 'unforeseen circumstances'.[7] This scenario was played out in the North Atlantic Station's 1901 summer exercises, during which fleet Marines landed 5-inch gun batteries on islands at the mouth of Long Island Sound, and the fleet conducted operations throughout the sound, simulating RED attacks upon coastal bases.

This coastal mindset led to the construction of a series of shallow-draft, low-freeboard battleships. Neither of these features adversely affected a ship designed to fight in 'bays, sounds, and interior waterways'; however, shallow draft and low freeboard presented serious limitations for a fleet meant to fight in blue water.

Indeed, the first modern American battleship, USS *Indiana*, which was commissioned in November 1895, and sister ships *Massachusetts* and *Oregon*, suffered predictable problems. A British observer in 1899 noted that although the *Indiana* had been fitted with bilge keels and her commanding officer appeared to be 'perfectly satisfied with the stability and seaworthiness of the ship', nevertheless, 'she heeled several degrees in smooth water when her turret guns [were] trained on the beam'. In fact, the observer concluded, the *Indiana* represented the ' "coast-defence" phase of American naval construction'.[8] Little did the unidentified British observer, or the American reporter, know that this 'coast-defence phase' had been dictated by American concerns about British intentions. These design problems were repeated in the next three classes of battleships.

The same 1900 War College problem that led to the summer exercises in Long Island Sound included several other American problem areas. What about the Philippines, for example? Here, the NWC concluded: 'An attempt to hold Manila against the RED Fleet with the material and ships available, would, in all probability, result in the fall of Manila and the capture and destruction of the BLUE or Allied fleet'.[9] They also examined the American situation in Hawaii, and concluded that the existing naval base in downtown Honolulu was indefensible, as 'the city and all roads leading to it can be commanded by the fire of a hostile fleet in the offing'. The NWC recommended that no supplies should be stored there, and further suggested that a good location for the navy would be 'at Pearl City on Pearl River lochs', that is, the future Pearl Harbor.[10]

Thus, even before the Anglo–Japanese Alliance of 1902, the Royal Navy played a significant role in American war planning. Given subsequent developments, historians have quite naturally concentrated upon the development of War Plan BLACK (Germany) and even more upon War Plan ORANGE (Japan). However, naval officers of the day struggled to establish a framework for possible future operations in a global environment in which Great Britain and its Dominions could not be excluded as potential enemies.

For American naval officers in the decade following the war with Spain, concerns about BLACK, ORANGE, WHITE (France), and RED literally coloured their world view. The 1907 NWC assessment of the German situation unwittingly provided an interesting insight into US naval planners' perception of the American position:

> Germany's isolation has lately become complete . . . We are likewise isolated, both by our traditional policy [of entering into no treaty arrangements] and from the fact that there is no real friendship anywhere for us.[11]

Thus, when the Atlantic battleship fleet entered the Pacific in 1908, the officers naturally perceived a sea of troubles, against which proper prior planning was only prudent.

The conclusion of the Anglo–Japanese Alliance in 1902 added yet another complicating facet to the strategic scene for the US Navy. Nevertheless, for the next couple of years there were no apparent areas of discord in American relations with Japan. However, the Russo–Japanese War of 1904–05 significantly altered the strategic balance in Asiatic waters. While President Theodore Roosevelt had hoped the belligerents would fight each other to exhaustion, thereby reducing each other's military strength,[12] in fact the Japanese were singularly successful in destroying Russian naval strength in the Pacific. The post-war situation thus became more threatening to United States interests in Asia. The 1905 renewal of the Anglo–Japanese Alliance, with a new clause which required the signatories to provide each other with full military assistance in the event either signatory became involved in a war with any other power, further complicated the situation.[13]

Although future events would soon obscure the fact, in July of 1905 there were no apparent major conflicts of interest between Japan and the United States. Thus, when Secretary of War William H. Taft visited Japan, he initialled an 'exchange of views' with Japanese Premier Marquis Katsura Taro in which Katsura assured Taft that Japan did not 'harbor any aggressive designs' in the Philippines and Taft expressed the opinion that Japanese suzerainty over Korea was the logical result of their victory in the Russo–Japanese War.[14]

The unity of interests expressed in the Taft–Katsura discussions of 1905 was short-lived. As Japan extended its influence into Manchuria concern grew amongst American businessmen and diplomats in the Orient that the 'open door' in Manchuria was being closed to American commercial interests. Further, problems relating to immigration of Japanese labourers continued to bedevil relations. Then, in October 1906, the San Francisco School Board enacted a regulation requiring all Japanese students to attend a segregated school set aside for 'Mongolians'. Through the 'Gentlemen's Agreement', Roosevelt achieved a compromise in which the Japanese Government promised to restrict the flow of labourers immigrating to the United States and the San Francisco School Board agreed to remove its objectionable regulation.[15]

The Japanese Government initially failed to abide by the Gentlemen's Agreement and monthly figures for Japanese immigration showed no significant decrease. Anti-Japanese tensions flared into violence, with rioting in San Francisco and other west coast cities in May of 1907. These riots were exploited by the 'Yellow Press' in America and, playing on racial fears, were coupled with irresponsible speculation concerning the possibility of war with Japan. This was the essence of the 'War Scare of 1907'. Although easy to dismiss in retrospect, the war scare was a reality in the eyes of many Americans, and the precipitate decline in Japanese–American relations stirred concern, particularly on the US west coast, where residents felt particularly vulnerable.

Responding to this, Theodore Roosevelt requested a report from the Joint Board of the Army and Navy concerning their plans 'in case of trouble arising between the United States and Japan'.[16] The Joint Board provided a full set of measures for the President's consideration, which they recommended be carried out in the event of imminent hostilities with Japan, including a recommendation that the full United States battleship fleet be 'assembled and despatched to the Orient as soon as possible'.[17] Roosevelt reviewed these plans at a meeting on 27 June 1907 and ordered immediate implementation of the plan to assemble and send the battleship fleet to the Pacific, emphasising that the movement should 'partake of the character of a practice march' and that it 'would have a strong tendency to maintain peace'.[18] Thus the President ordered the world cruise that brought the Atlantic battleship fleet to New Zealand and Australia.

The cruise, which began on 16 December 1907 and involved sixteen first-class battleships and supporting auxiliaries, also offered an opportunity for officers of the fleet to observe and report on ports infrequently visited.[19] An intelligence team led by Marine Corps Major (later Major General) Dion Williams, the fleet intelligence officer and an expert on base defences, developed reports on Rio de Janeiro, Punta Arenas, Chile, and Callao, Peru. There was a certain naivety amongst the junior officers assigned this duty. Midshipman Lewis Maxfield commented about his intelligence-gathering assignment in a letter to his mother: 'Please don't tell anyone that officers were detailed to do such things, because some people might think it wasn't a courteous thing to do'.[20]

By the time the fleet left the US west coast, the initial fleet commander-in-chief had been relieved by Rear Admiral Charles S. Sperry, a former President of the NWC.[21] Sperry discounted the possibility of war with Japan, and probably thus reflected the NWC thinking on the topic. In the summer of 1907, the NWC had studied the Japanese problem and concluded that for the Japanese a war with the United States 'would be most unwelcome'.[22] Nevertheless, they feared that the 'serious race antagonisms existing might bring on such a war. This is the real danger'. In a similar vein, Sperry wrote in February 1907: '[I]t seems impossible that any responsible Japanese statesman should contemplate a rupture with this country'.[23]

After the successful fleet visit to Japan, Sperry confided in family correspondence that when Rear Admiral Richard Wainwright (commanding the 2nd Division of Sperry's fleet) was on the General Board (October 1904 – June 1907), he had been 'stubbornly confident that a row with Japan was imminent'.[24] Rear Admiral Robley D. Evans, Sperry's predecessor in command of the fleet, 'was another war fiend', Sperry suspected, because staff officers Sperry retained from Evans's staff 'could not believe the fleet would go home'.[25] Sperry reported he had little patience for war scares: 'I said in exasperation one day that such talk only made me question their [his staff officers'] intelligence'.[26]

What we can extract from this correspondence, at the least, is an inference that the initial fleet commander-in-chief and his staff anticipated a war with Japan, as did some other senior officers with the fleet. And although he later denied such concerns, Rear Admiral Sperry, as commander-in-chief, ordered that plans be developed for the defence of Hawaii and war plans compiled for the capture of New Zealand and Australian ports. The New Zealand and Australian plans, to be examined later in this chapter, stemmed from the premise that they were plans for use '[i]n case of a war between the United States and Great Britain *or a war involving these countries*' (emphasis added).[27] This peculiar wording, seemingly, implies the planners had in mind a war with Japan in which compliance with the provisions of the Anglo–Japanese Alliance brought Great Britain into the war on Japan's side.

Americans tended to discount the possibility that should Great Britain have to choose between Japan and the United States in a future conflict, those oft-invoked Anglo–American racial, cultural, and economic ties, not to mention strategic considerations vis-a-vis Germany, would be disregarded in favour of treaty commitments with Japan. Nevertheless, the formal British commitment to aid Japan still stood, and statements of loyalty to their ally remained fairly prominent in the British press:

> Our position . . . is that we are bound absolutely by our Treaty with Japan. That alone governs us. We ourselves never disguised some of the difficulties which we thought were created by that Treaty; but we are none the less bound by it, and shall loyally abide by it.[28]

Hawaii Defence Plan

Congress allocated $3.2 million of fiscal year 1908 funds for the development of the naval base at Pearl Harbor. Therefore, when the fleet arrived in Hawaii, a special board of fleet officers, headed by Rear Admiral Seaton

Schroeder, was appointed to investigate and report on the site and all fleet officers were ordered to make a trip there to view the site and examine proposed plans.[29] Among the junior officers of the fleet who probably got their first view of Pearl Harbor at that time were Ensign Harold R. Stark, who as Chief of Naval Operations on 7 December 1941 would bear much of the responsibility for the fleet's unpreparedness for the Japanese attack. Also present were Midshipmen William F. Halsey, Jr, and Raymond A. Spruance, who rose to prominence commanding the Third and Fifth Fleets, respectively, in the Pacific in World War II.

The details of the plan for the defence of the Hawaiian Islands need not overly concern us here. However, the plan's initial assumptions are worth considering:

> It is probable that an attack upon these islands would come from Asiatic waters, since the only power which could attack the United States from the American side of the Pacific would be Great Britain and that country already has a base of operations close at hand in British Columbia.

Thus, the team saw three possible scenarios involving an attack by Japan:

- when the US battlefleet was in the Atlantic;
- when the US battlefleet was on the US West Coast; and
- when the US battlefleet was in the Philippines.[30]

The first situation would require the sustained defence of the islands against a much superior naval force until the fleet could be dispatched from the US east coast to Hawaii—or to the Philippines. Additionally, the islands would have to be protected from 'attacks by a possible combination of a large number of Japanese subjects in the islands'. (This was a recurring theme—and fear—which proved entirely unfounded in 1941–42.)

In the second situation, attack while the battlefleet was on the US west coast, the team envisioned the battlefleet being dispatched to the Philippines via Hawaii, thus protecting the islands from everything except a possible attack by a raiding force of fast cruisers (that generation's equivalent of a raid by aircraft carriers).

The final scenario, attack while the battlefleet was in the Philippines, was deemed unlikely. Nevertheless, 'it would still be advisable to place the [Hawaiian] islands in a state of defense sufficient to protect them from capture or damage by a raiding force of fast cruisers or from serious damage at the hands of Japanese subjects on the islands'.[31]

As the American fleet circumnavigated South America, Washington received a wide range of invitations for the fleet to visit ports in Australia,

New Zealand, Asia, Africa and Europe. Ultimately, the government accepted invitations to visit Auckland, New Zealand, and Sydney, Melbourne and Albany in Australia.[32]

The fleet's visit to New Zealand and Australia came at a time when Australians had begun seriously to question the Royal Navy's commitment to the defence of Australia. The appointment of Admiral Sir John Fisher (later Admiral of the Fleet Lord Fisher of Kilverstone) as First Sea Lord in 1904 set the stage for a bold rationalisation of the composition and disposition of the British fleet. There followed a massive scrapping of units with marginal combat capabilities while Fisher unswervingly pursued a policy of concentration of capital ships in the Narrow Seas in confrontation with Germany.

The extent of the British withdrawal from the Pacific did not become general knowledge until Rear Admiral Alfred Thayer Mahan in December 1907 revealed that by May 1908, 86 per cent of the Royal Navy's battleship strength would be concentrated in or near home waters.[33] All of this made sense for Great Britain; however, it played somewhat differently in the Antipodes. The *New Zealand Herald* observed:

> Asiatic naval superiority in the Pacific endangers us, no matter though it be the superiority of a temporary ally; American naval superiority in the Pacific does not endanger us, however much we might prefer to be navally superior ourselves.[34]

Commenting on the need to concentrate the Royal Navy's forces in home waters, the *Auckland Weekly News* noted, 'This has largely brought about the much-debated alliance with Japan and inclines us to extreme friendship for America'.[35]

These sentiments were not unknown on the other side of the Pacific. Before making his decision to send the fleet to Australia and New Zealand, President Roosevelt sought the advice of his naval aide, Commander William S. Sims. 'Some day', Roosevelt told the aide, 'the question of the Pacific will be a dominant one, and it will be necessary to know the sentiment of Australia and New Zealand. I want to know what you think would be the probable reception given our fleet if it were to visit those countries'. 'The officers and men will barely escape with their lives from the hospitality of the people', Sims, a noted Anglophile, replied.[36]

For very different reasons, Australian Prime Minister Alfred Deakin, New Zealand Prime Minister Sir Joseph Ward, and President Theodore Roosevelt were in agreement in their desire that the American fleet visit Australasia. Roosevelt had implied that the Australasian visits might act as a possible medium for the extension of American protection, Monroe Doctrine style, to Australia and New Zealand: 'It is true', he told Oscar

WELCOME TO OUR AMERICAN COMRADES

In the Great White Fleet Australians saw positive evidence of an American bid for Pacific naval supremacy, something they felt Britain had too easily surrendered to Japan. So intense was the local interest that over half a million Sydneysiders gathered to view the spectacle of the fleet's arrival, far more than had gathered to celebrate Federation. (National Library of Australia)

King Davis in an interview for the *New York Times*, 'the invitation to the fleet to go to New Zealand and Australia was to show England—I cannot say a "renegade" mother country—that those colonies are white man's country—and that is why the fleet was sent there'.[37] Prime Minister Deakin clearly sought to use the fleet visit as a vehicle to further his own plans for establishment of an independent Australian navy.[38] New Zealand Prime Minister Sir Joseph Ward, however, sought to use the fleet visit to reassert New Zealand's continued dedication to the concept of imperial defence.[39] He was prepared, though, to use the visit to further his more modest objective of attaining 'dominion participation in imperial policy-making'.[40]

Underlining all calculations concerning the fleet visit were the contradictory aspects of the Anglo–Japanese Alliance. The alliance had enabled the Royal Navy to redeploy its major naval forces from the Pacific, yet Australians and New Zealanders harboured strong racial fears concerning the mother country's ally, Japan. Even before Russia had suffered any of the crushing defeats which ultimately befell her in the Russo–Japanese War, the popular press had begun considering the results of a Japanese victory, and had concluded that such a victory would unleash an expansionist drive by millions of Japanese towards the sparsely populated and ill-defended English-speaking Dominions in the Antipodes. The New Zealand *Weekly Graphic*, for example, produced a full-page cover illustration of the Pacific in which Maritime Russia, Korea, Manchuria and China had already been painted brown by a Japanese military man who was now facing south towards Australia and New Zealand. The caption read: 'Painting the World Brown. Will Our Turn Come?'.[41]

Following Admiral Mahan's December 1907 *Scientific American* article reporting the withdrawal of British naval power from the Pacific, the debate over the defence of Australia and New Zealand quite understandably was renewed. Concern over Japanese intentions was greatly heightened by the apparently conflicting commitment of the mother country's alliance with the perceived enemy. Many Australians' fears found expression in a war novel published at the beginning of 1908. *The World's Awakening* described a hypothetical world war in 1920, which stemmed from a Japanese fleet visit to Sydney during which the Japanese sailors ashore become involved in a riot and the Japanese cruisers shell the Sydney crowds. Britain seeks to negotiate, but Japan's chief demand is 'unrestricted immigration of the Japanese into Australia and full voting rights for Australian Asiatics'. At this point the British refuse, the Japanese destroy the diminutive British fleet in Asian waters, and, in a twist eerily prophetic of events 30 years later, the British Prime Minister, 'whose pathetic belief in arbitration as a panacea for all ills, meets a real shock' when Germany, in 'unholy alliance' with Japan, invades England.[42] Sydney's vulnerability to shelling by an offshore fleet was noted also in the American war plan.[43]

The World's Awakening and similar emotionally-charged works, which played on the racial fears of the people, were but a reflection of popular concern over the military and naval weakness of Australia and New Zealand. The British fleet had gone and, according to the military correspondent of the London *Times*, 'it is uncertain whether we shall be able' ever to maintain a fleet in Asia again'.[44]

New Zealanders shared these fears, as reflected by the Wellington *Evening Post*:

> We are reminded that 'only the Anglo–Japanese Alliance enabled the Motherland safely to withdraw her battleships from the Far East'. But in our view that reminder begs the question of whether Japan's progress involves a threat to Australasia. And if there is such an involvement, then plainly Australasia would be safer if the battleships remained in the Far East, instead of being supplanted by a treaty.[45]

It was in this context of the threat posed by Japan and the uncertainties of the Anglo–Japanese Alliance that the people of Australia and New

Zealand so fervently embraced the American fleet visit. As one New Zealand 'poet' put it:

> The grey fleet falters and plays with Time
> While the Yellow ships presume,
> But the ships that are as white as the frosted rime
> Are making the East give room.[46]

The same Anglo–Japanese Alliance which caused Australians and New Zealanders concern also caused thought amongst the officers of the Atlantic battleship fleet. Should war come between Japan and the United States, as so many officers thought it most certainly would, then, in accordance with the treaty as revised in 1905, Great Britain would be required to offer full military support to her ally. In this circumstance, Australia and New Zealand would become hostile territories for the USA. Thus, while the Americans were welcomed and feted in Australia and New Zealand, they gathered information for possible future use. However, in the process they also came to know and appreciate Australians and New Zealanders. This beginning of a new friendship, I would suggest, made less likely the possibility of a future conflict. As Ensign Caswell Saufley, one of the battleship officers, observed from Auckland,

> Union Jack and Stars and Stripes were intertwined upon everything. Toasts, songs, poems on this theme were written expressly for the occasion, in the commemoration of which I did and said things which I had, a few years back, as little dreamed of, as any of the Pharaoh's bricklayers did of Solomon's Temple. I had never before thought of drinking a toast to His Majesty, or of singing 'God Save the King'. These things I have done with as much zest as the veriest red coat in British service.[47]

Auckland War Plan

The basic thesis of the 'Naval War Plan for the Attack of the Harbor and City of Auckland, New Zealand' was that in the event of war between the United States and Great Britain, the issue of naval supremacy in the Pacific would arise. In such a case, Australia and New Zealand might become a theatre of operations, and the harbour of Auckland 'would be a strategic center of operations in the southwestern portion of the Pacific'.[48] Operations would thus begin with an attack upon some New Zealand port. Ultimately, the capture of Auckland would permit a refitting and reinforcing of the fleet preparatory to an advance on Sydney.[49]

The intelligence team concluded, quite correctly, that the coast of the North Island of New Zealand offered many sites that could be occupied as advance bases for the assault on Auckland. The following were suggested, with distances from Auckland (in miles) for East Coast locations, and from the Manukau Harbour for West Coast locations.

East Coast		West Coast	
Coromandel Harbour	46	Whaingaroa Harbour	61
Firth of Thames	48	Kaipara Harbour	58
Tauranga Harbor	150	Hokianga River	140
Whangarei Bay	82	Kawhia Bay	82
Whangaparaoa Bay	26		
Bay of Islands	172		

None of these ports, it was noted, were fortified, 'and any of them could probably be occupied with little or no opposition provided the attack was sudden'. Additionally, New Zealand would have difficulty concentrating its forces quickly, 'and in all probability these forces would be held concentrated at the important ports of Auckland, Wellington, Christchurch and Dunedin'.[50]

Waitemata Harbour, the main harbour of Auckland, was deemed 'easy of defense' but it was noted that defence batteries did not then exist, an aspect 'which was bitterly commented upon by the British and New Zealand military officers with whom our Intelligence Officers talked at Auckland'. The report concluded that if the main harbour's defences were ever improved, Auckland would still have a weak point in the fact that 'Manukau Harbor, on the western side of the island and directly opposite Auckland Harbor, affords a ready means for attacking the city from the rear'. Protection from such an attack would require the establishment of a second set of defences.

The planners considered the most likely action a frontal approach to Waitemata Harbour, particularly in light of the modest defensive batteries currently available.[51] It noted that local plans included the establishment of a minefield of three lines of mines along a line between the peak of Rangitoto Island and the Fort at Takapuna, but noted that mines were in short supply and largely of obsolete types, and the entire supply available in New Zealand probably would permit no more than two lines of mines at this one location. This minefield would be covered by guns on North Head, Mount Victoria and Takapuna Point; however, it was suggested that an attacker might mount guns on the western slope of Rangitoto Island, from which they could attack Auckland's fortifications. None of these measures, however, 'would prevent an invading force from anchoring its

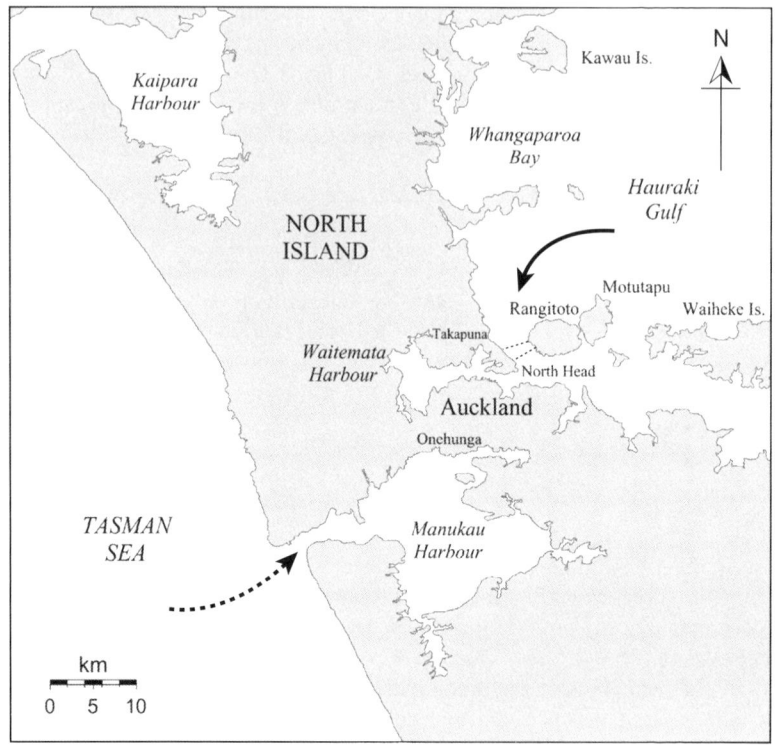

Map 12.1 Attack plan for Auckland

ships farther to the north in the Rangitoto Channel and landing an attacking force to the north of Takapuna'.

The planners also focused on Manukau Harbour, which they described as the 'back door' to the city of Auckland. They reported there were no fortifications there, though it seemed 'improbable' that it would 'be long left in its present defenseless state'. Here is their description of the envisioned operation:

> If an entrance could be forced into the anchorage north of South Head, there would be little difficulty in landing an army on the shores between this point and Onehunga, under the protection of the guns of the cruisers and gunboats of the invaders.
>
> Gunboats could ascend the channel as far as the port of Onehunga, and under the fire from these ships, the invading force could capture the natural line defined by Mount Albert, Three Kings, One Tree Hill and Mount

Wellington; and from this position the invading force would be in excellent position for the advance to capture the city of Auckland from the rear.[52]

Even if the principal attack were mounted in Waitemata Harbour, it was deemed 'advisable' to combine that attack 'with an attack from the rear by way of the Manukau Harbor'.

The study also examined New Zealand's land forces and provided a generally good assessment of them. Table 12.1 provides a short listing of the forces, as understood by the American naval officers.

Table 12.1   The Defence Force of New Zealand, 1908

Headquarters Staff	9
District Staffs	52
Permanent Forces, RNZ Artillery	265
RNZ Engineers	96
Garrison Artillery Volunteers	950
Field Artillery	461
Submarine and Field Engineers	470
Mounted Rifles	4500
Infantry	6881
Field Hospital 7 Bearer Corps	211
Defence Cadets	3100
Rifle Clubs	3500
Garrison Bands	142
Active Unattached Officers	110
Total	20 747
Distribution	
Auckland	3500
Wellington	6800
Nelson	2000
Canterbury	3300
Otago	4800

Source: 'Naval War Plan for the Attack of Auckland, New Zealand'.

The bulk of these forces were volunteers who, it was felt, were 'about up to the general average of the National Guardsmen in the United States, though not so well fitted out with field equipage and transportation'. Further, they were 'so widely scattered over so much territory that in the event of a sudden descent of an attacking force ... it would be impracticable to assemble them at the one point of chief attack'. Thus, the entire force would never have to be dealt with at once.

Sydney War Plan

After the capture of Auckland and the refitting and reinforcement of the fleet there, operations would shift to Australia, where Sydney was seen as the principal goal: A 'fortified base and coaling station for the British Navy, its attack and capture . . . would be a severe blow to British Naval supremacy in these waters' and would afford the invader the 'most desirable base for further operations both on land and at sea in and about Australia'.

Sydney posed major problems for the intelligence team. The harbour was 'comparatively strong and the entry readily mined'. And unlike in New Zealand, a significant land force was available for its defence. Therefore, the team recommended that 'no operations having in view the investment and capture of the port of Sydney should be undertaken until command of the sea is assured', as it would otherwise be impracticable to transport the necessarily large number of troops across the Pacific from the US west coast to Australia.

As for the harbour itself, the team reported that Port Jackson with its high headlands 'rising precipitously from the sea' afforded 'excellent sites for advanced battery positions'. Further, there were 'many advantageous positions for batteries back of the entrance and directly commanding it'. The principal disadvantages for the defenders included the fact that the city was 'practically directly upon the open sea coast, the center of the business portion of the city being but three miles from the open sea front'. This meant that 'a fleet could lie off the entrance to the harbor and shell the whole city at effective ranges'.

Botany Bay, just ten miles south of the entrance to Port Jackson, attracted attention as a possible avenue of attack. 'The occupation of Botany Bay by an enemy would afford a ready means of attack upon Sydney and its defenses from the right and rear, and would render Sydney untenable'. However, they concluded, this position was so important 'it would have to be fortified and held as strongly as Port Jackson, to insure the defense of the latter place'.

Looking further afield, the intelligence team assessed Bate Bay, further to the southward of Botany Bay and Broken Bay and the Hawksbury River to the north of Port Jackson. These locations, the team reported, were 'so near Sydney as to afford excellent close bases for the attack by land of that place [and] would probably have to be fortified and held in force to prevent their capture and occupation as advance bases by an enemy attempting the investment and capture of Port Jackson and Sydney'.

As to how to go about the attack on Sydney, the planners reported that if Botany Bay were 'not well fortified at the entrance it would be the ideal point at which to begin the attack', as once it was in enemy hands Sydney could easily be approached and 'it would only be a question of the invaders

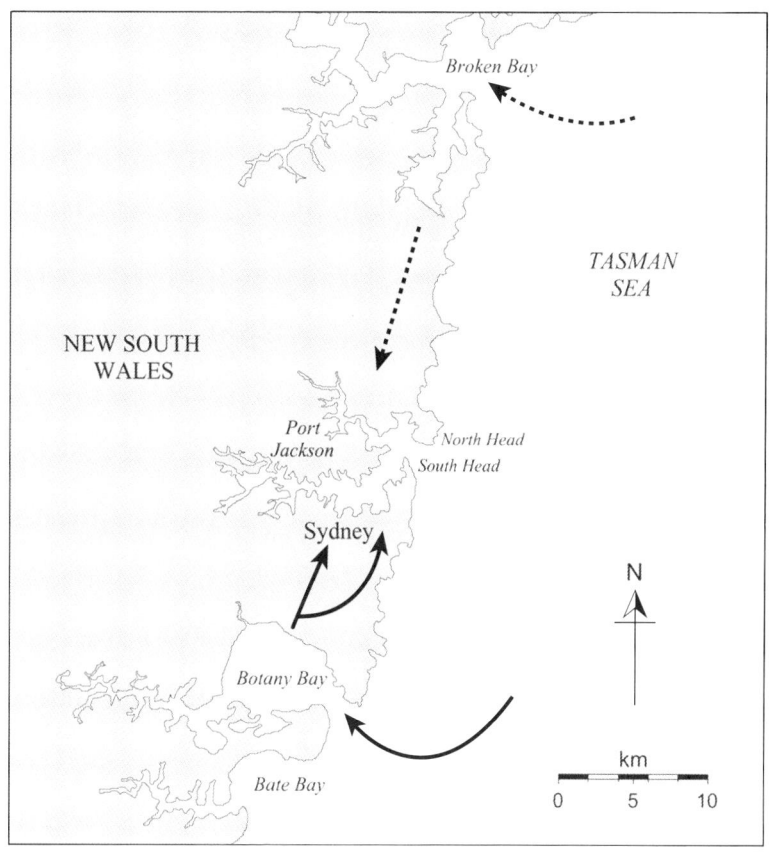

Map 12.2   Attack plan for Sydney

having a sufficient force to overcome the opposition on land of the Defense Forces of Sydney, as the permanent fortifications of Port Jackson would be of no use against a land force advancing from this direction'.

The team observed that 'there are many good defensible positions along the crests and ridges between Botany Bay and Sydney and Port Jackson, but as the country is mostly open and the ridges appear in succession through the rolling country, such positions could always be met by equally good lines on the parallel ridges and the positions could be turned by the right or left ... aided by the fire of the ships'.

The second option, Broken Bay, was considered, but, according to the intelligence team, 'such an attack would scarcely be advisable owing to the difficult ground lying between Broken Bay and Port Jackson'.

In this hilly and rough country the defenders on land would have the great advantage over the attacking force due to the nature of the ground, the defiles where defensive positions could be taken which would prove very difficult for an advancing force to turn.[53]

Broken Bay, Sydney military authorities reported, was unfortified, but it was also reported that 'in case of war the entrance would be mined and these mines protected by the erection of temporary works and field pieces on shore'.

An interesting aspect of the report is that throughout it are reflections of respect for, even admiration of, the Australian people and their military forces:

> The men of the country make good soldiers, probably better than the home Briton, and shooting clubs and the drilling of the school boys all over the country tend to foster a military spirit among the inhabitants.

Some 6500 New South Wales troops were on review in conjunction with the US Fleet visit to Sydney, where American officers reported they 'marched fairly well and were fairly well set up, while their equipage and rifles were in excellent condition'.

> From personal inspection of the troops thus mobilised and the statements of British and other officers who have inspected these troops, it may be safely stated that the Permanent Force of Australia is up to the standard of the Regular British Army; that the Militia are probably up to the standard of the better class of the National Guard in the United States, and that the Volunteers are superior in drill and set up to the U.S. Volunteers of the late Spanish War.[54]

The plan contained a detailed eight-page summary of the permanent defences of Port Jackson. The intelligence officers concluded that the defences on the South Head 'could be attacked from the rear by a force advancing from the southward as practically none of the guns bear on the land side, and there are no fortifications for the protection of the land side from attack'. This eventuality was to be covered by mobile troops of the Defence Forces. However, they reported, the guns on North Head could be brought to bear; therefore, any attack on the South Head would have to be co-ordinated with an attack on North Head.

While there were a fair number of guns already mounted to protect Sydney Harbour, the intelligence team reported that 'the force to man them is at present ridiculously small, and the great reliance placed by the Australians upon volunteers for this purpose is interesting'. The intelligence team estimated it would take at least 1500 men to man the guns and minefields, and that the 'whole defense force of New South Wales would be none too large to act as a mobile force for the defense of these batteries' from attack or destruction 'by a raiding force of an energetic enemy that might attack even without first destroying the British Fleet'.

> An examination of their defenses and the forces provided for these defenses only acentuate [sic] the firm reliance placed by all British subjects on the British Navy.[55]

But what of the Royal Navy forces on the Australia Station? At the time, that presence was limited to but three cruisers, only one of which had any military significance. Reporting on this in a private letter, Lieutenant Commander Ridley McLean, USN, a gunnery expert stationed on the fleet flagship USS *Connecticut*, reported:

> These vessels were, with the exception of the *Powerful* small and unimportant, and though frequent conversations were held with the officers, the comparative inattention given to Gunnery on the Australian Station rendered the information available of no value and of little interest. Among the British Officers this is known as the Society Station and by tacit consent little work is done.[56]

McLean also discerned strains between British officers in Australian and New Zealand waters and the inhabitants of those countries:

> It may be stated that the feeling between the British Officers on this station and the Australians and New Zealanders is not the best, the latter in many cases regarding the officers as snobbish, while they in turn evince a feeling of suppressed disdain toward the general class of the inhabitants. This feature was very frequently remarked upon, particularly by the middle classes . . . they often mentioned the democratic qualities in American officers in comparison with the aristocratic airs of the officers of the Royal Navy.[57]

What we see here, even in a private assessment of the Royal Navy, is a discovery of common ties with the Australian people. It also occurred at the personal level, in genteel society with the officers and in much more earthy ways with the enlisted force during the fleet visits to New Zealand and Australia. Nearly 200 American sailors overstayed leave in Melbourne in September 1908, and about half of them were never recovered. I assume they went on to live profitable lives in Australia and have often wished for the opportunity to track some of them or their descendants down, just to discover what happened to them subsequently. Perhaps some energetic graduate student will do that some day.

Melbourne Plan

War plans notwithstanding, the American Fleet visit to Sydney was marked at every step with the most remarkable displays of hospitality. Indeed, so great was the welcome that it actually became physically demanding on the officers who were required to attend the welter of official functions. Sims's advice to President Roosevelt at the time the Australian invitations had been accepted—that the men of the fleet would 'barely escape with their lives from the hospitality of the people'—proved true at Sydney. As one future four-star admiral recorded, 'We have at last escaped from the hospitalities of Sydney only to be swallowed up in those of Melbourne'.[58] And once again, in Melbourne, the intelligence team went to work.

The team noted that after the capture of a base port in New Zealand, Sydney would be the logical next step. However, if for any reason it were not advisable to attack Sydney first, Port Phillip and Melbourne 'would for many reasons be a logical point of attack'.[59] As with Sydney, the

Rehearsal for an American victory parade? USN bluejackets march through Sydney on 20 August 1908, the day after the fleet's arrival. Pitt Street had been renamed 'American Avenue' for the occasion, but local sensitivities precluded the visitors from carrying ammunition for their weapons.
(US Naval Historical Center: NH 77295)

planners here confronted a city with 'comparatively strong' defences and a defence force which they estimated would be strong enough to defend the port 'against a landing force of less than 15,000 effective troops backed by a strong fleet'. Therefore, they proposed no operations until command of the sea were secure enough to transport an army of at least 25 000 men across the Pacific. Further, such operations would presuppose the occupation of some base closer to Melbourne than existing American facilities in Hawaii and the Philippines. Thus the first step was considered to be the capture of a port in New Zealand.

The entrance to Port Phillip presented problems: the channel was not straight, the land on both sides was sufficiently high to provide excellent sites for batteries, and the water was mineable, so it was practicable to defend the entrance. However, 'once the entrance to Port Phillip is gained the attack of the city of Melbourne and its adjacent towns ... would be an easy matter'.

Surveying the surrounding areas, the intelligence team settled on Port Western as the best avenue of attack against Melbourne from the rear of the defences of Port Phillip. There was some concern about a proposed scheme to mine the entrance to Port Western; if it proved to be mined and fortified at the time of the attack, the team recommended

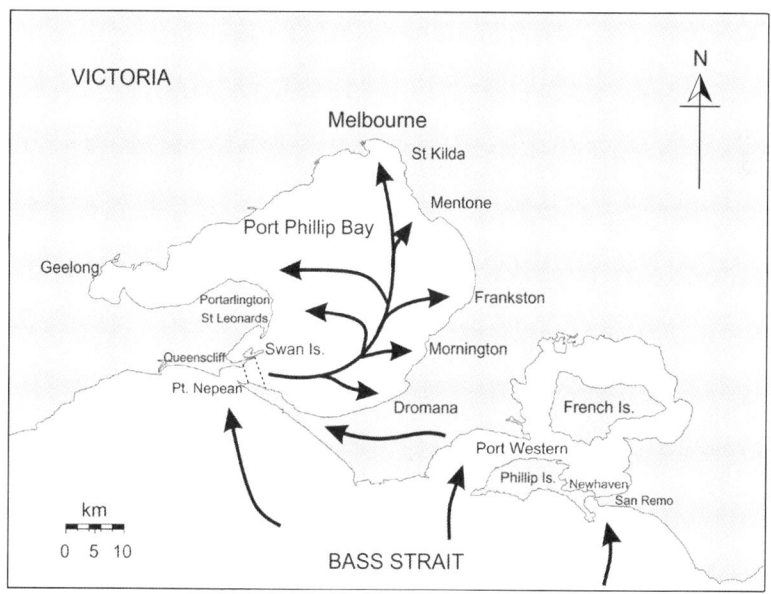

Map 12.3   Attack plan for Melbourne

it would be best to land at San Remo and New Haven, at the eastern entrance to Port Western, and from there capture Phillip Island and thence clear up the entrance to Port Western, which would leave this road to the attack upon the defenses of Port Phillip open and also give a base upon which to advance upon Melbourne.

Capture of Port Nepean would allow mine-clearing operations and subsequent entrance of the fleet into Port Phillip.

The intelligence team carefully noted the fortifications at Queenscliff and Swan Island, Nepean Point, the Crow's Nest and Quarantine Station. They commented at some length about the possibility of mining and the probable disposition of mines at the harbour entrance. Concerning the guns in the various fortifications, it was noted that '[a]fter the attacking force of ships is once inside of Port Phillip the fire of the forts at the entrance would be of little or no avail against it'. Once within Port Phillip, 'forces would be landed at some of the small towns having jetties and piers'. The towns mentioned included Dromana, Mornington, Frankston, Mentone, Sandringham, Brighton, St Kilda, South Melbourne, Williamstown, Geelong, Drysdale, Portarlington, St Leonards and Queenscliff.

Concerning the overall defences of Melbourne, the report concluded: 'The greatest weakness in the defenses of Melbourne is the fact that the entrance to Port Western is not defended'. And it was upon this weakness that they built their plan.

Western Australia War Plans

The officers of the fleet also drew up plans for attacking King George Sound and Albany in Western Australia,[60] and also Perth and Fremantle.[61] Though the problem was relatively simple due to the almost total lack of defensive forces and fortifications, the reports were extensive and thorough, comprising some 32 and 25 pages, respectively.

The thesis with the Albany plan was that if, in a war with Great Britain, operations extended into the Southwest Pacific, and the situation should for any reason require an advance from the westward across the Indian Ocean, or from the north through the Netherlands East Indies, 'the United States fleet might find it advisable to establish a base in Western Australia, and in this case King George Sound would offer a favorable point of attack'.[62] From there, the fleet might continue operations eastward towards Adelaide, Melbourne and/or Sydney. Additionally, as the Perth Plan indicated, after taking King George Sound, it was likely units of the fleet would have extended operations to Perth and Fremantle, 350 miles to the northward.

Summary and conclusion

It is worthwhile noting that each of the reports referred to in this chapter was quite extensive. They examined and recorded in detail all aspects of the locations covered: rail networks and connections; shipping lines and frequency of sailings; shipyard facilities; coal availability; the layout of the cities; even the nature of the sewage system; the state of electrification; hospitals and medical care; finance; hotels and other facilities; and detailed listings of the military forces available.

But what should we make of these plans? Were they serious? Or were they simply exercises to keep the junior officers busy? There are obvious, glaring weaknesses in the plans. I will point to just one or two. I am certain that Australian historians, with much more intimate knowledge of the terrain and Australian conditions in 1908, will find many more.

One thing seems overwhelmingly obvious: nowhere in the plans was there any consideration of the likely reaction of the Royal Navy, aside from the minor units on the Australian Station. Perhaps such an attack would have triggered the British descent on the US Atlantic coast which had been the underlying fear of the Naval War College planners throughout the decade before the fleet cruise. Although the Royal Navy was increasingly constrained by the need to counter the threatening German High Seas Fleet, it is difficult to believe they would not have reacted to American operations in the Antipodes.

On another plane, there is almost no consideration of the logistical complications involved in conducting combat operations thousands of miles from the nearest American base. The US Navy had not yet solved the problems of the fleet train and of refuelling at sea. Those things would wait at least another decade or two before they were resolved, as would the concepts of modern amphibious operations.

There is no indication, either, about how Great Britain's Pacific ally, Japan, would react. Just as the Royal Navy was committed to support the Imperial Japanese Navy, so also were the Japanese committed to come to the aid of the British. Thus, the Japanese, who were at this time much feared in Australia and New Zealand, might have come to the aid of the beleaguered Commonwealth and Dominion.

Finally, I should note that War Plan RED through its many versions and war games always involved RED aggression and BLUE defensive measures. Thus the war plans described here did not fall within the general framework of the RED exercises conducted by the Naval War College. Further, they were never apparently updated or revised. After approval by the fleet commander-in-chief, they were submitted to the Department of the Navy and then, apparently, spent the next nine decades in storage.

On the positive side, however, the information-gathering process at the heart of developing these plans did much to acquaint a generation of US naval officers with the actual situation in New Zealand and Australia. The fleet visits and the remarkable hospitality displayed by the people of Australia and New Zealand became the basis for a long-term friendly relationship between the three countries which survived two world wars, Korea and Vietnam.

Such intelligence-gathering, particularly during calls to infrequently visited ports, is a routine aspect of naval visits by all nations' navies. The development of these war plans during visits in which the guests were hosted so magnificently says much about the true nature of international relations. It was after all a British statesman, Lord Palmerston, who reminded us that nations have no permanent friends, only permanent interests.

In 1942, Auckland, as the 1908 plan suggested, did become 'a strategic center of operations' in the Southwest Pacific, but with a single enemy: Japan. No American surface warship ever bombarded an Australian port, as suggested in the Sydney war plan. Notwithstanding some submarine attacks, the Japanese did not achieve this either. But it is interesting to know that HMNZS *Black Prince* actually did in 1954, when several rounds from its 133-mm guns 'exploded' in a small town near Jervis Bay.[63]

The only American invasions of Australia and New Zealand have been peaceful ones, at the invitation of those governments, during World War II. The spirit of co-operation which developed in those years led to several decades of friendly operations for which I am eternally grateful. One such operation, DEEP FREEZE, brought me to New Zealand in 1959, a visit which eventually led to my marriage to a Kiwi lass.

In my early years in the US Navy, it was always a sailor's dream to make a port call in Australia. In preparing this chapter, I wondered whether that sentiment still prevailed. Leafing through the May 1999 edition of the *US Naval Institute Proceedings*, I was delighted to find that it does. A Master Chief Petty Officer is quoted as saying, 'Every sailor hopes for Australia'.[64] May it ever be that way.

13 A.W. Jose in the politics and strategy of naval defence, 1903–1909

Ross Lamont

No consideration of the history of Australian naval defence strategy can afford to overlook the contributions of D.C. Sissons and N. Meaney.[1] In their view the outcome of the Russo–Japanese War, and in particular the Battle of Tsushima in May 1905, represented a defining moment for both the evolution of Australia's defence and foreign policies and the growth of an independent nationalist spirit. 'After Japan's defeat of Russia ... Australia ... introduced compulsory military service, acquired a navy and looked to the United States for support against Japan.'[2] This basically monocausal interpretation has gained overtones of orthodoxy, perhaps of myth.[3] From which a short, but arguable, step has Australians before 1909 thinking of an Australian navy as a defence against Japanese assault.

By contrast, other writers, in particular J.A. La Nauze and R. Norris, offered a less dramatic but more complex explanation of the emergence of both Australia's defence structure and her nationalism.[4] The latter, in concluding his analysis of the defence policies of the Prime Minister who dominated Australian policy-making from 1905 to 1910, wrote, 'Thus Deakin's campaign from 1905 owed little to the war or strategy ... his sponsorship of national defence just as the war ended was largely a coincidence ... For Deakin the truly vital issues were not directly strategical, but political and constitutional.'[5]

While acknowledging the value of the Sissons–Meaney demonstration of increased Australian concern about enhanced Japanese power after 1905, this chapter inclines strongly to the alternative view. It suggests that an already established fear of Japan was not the most important factor contributing to the evolution of Australian sentiments and policies. It further intimates that although the war heightened fears for Australia's ability to maintain the unifying White Australia policy, these fears did not translate, apart from one failed parliamentary bill, into anything other than official rhetoric and inquiry. Nor did the war provoke any serious Australian thinking as to the strategic use of any likely Australian naval forces: the naval defence policies proposed or adopted did not address the problem of countering a coercive invasion either in the short or long term.

The analysis is based largely on the papers and publications of Arthur Wilberforce Jose, who returned to his adopted home of Australia as the correspondent of the London daily newspaper, *The Times*, just as the Russo–Japanese War began.[6]

In the closing years of his life, reflecting on his career as *The Times*'s Australian correspondent, Jose indicated that the main subjects of his reports from 1904 to 1915 were 'compulsory arbitration, immigration restriction and especially the maintenance of the White Australia'.[7] This apparent neglect of defence, whether by sea or land, is belied by Jose's considerable personal involvement in military or military-related activities. He was a lieutenant in the Australian Intelligence Corps; he served on the Executive Committee of the Australian National Defence League almost from its foundation; he was also a member of the United Service Institution of New South Wales.[8]

It is less surprising then that, even before his return to Australia in 1904, he had recognised naval defence as an issue of significance in Commonwealth politics. In August 1903, after the parliamentary debate on the Naval Agreement Bill, he forecast that 'none of its other virtues will save the present Commonwealth Ministry if its increase of the naval subsidy happens to occupy a prominent place in the mind of the voters'.[9] Four months later the election was held and the Deakin ministry lost seats, to the Labor Party in particular. Understandably, Jose suggested that the 1903 Naval Agreement had been one factor in that loss.[10] On his return to Australia he diligently gathered opinions on the Naval Agreement and after two years came to the conclusion that 'the policy which it embodies is misunderstood by most Australians, and repudiated by the majority of the few who understand it. It is, indeed, one of the most dangerous weapons now in the hands of the small but always active anti-Imperial section.'[11]

The 1903 Australian Naval Agreement has been derided, but many of the advantages and disadvantages attendant upon its negotiation, signature and legislative passage have lacked sufficient appreciation. First and foremost it was a continuation of the general pledge that the Royal Navy would secure Australia against all forms of attack. Australia acknowledged this by agreeing to subsidise the British naval estimates with a sum larger than that contributed to the costs of the former auxiliary squadron. The agreement also anticipated the ultimate creation of an Australian navy of some kind: provision was made for the naval training of Australian men on board Royal Navy ships. Finally, just before the parliamentary debate on the agreement there came the Defence Minister's announcement indicating that 'our present naval forces, permanent or militia, are not to be wholly dispensed with after all'.[12] This decision was an affirmation that there was already and would continue to be an Australian naval force.

On the other hand the agreement had the effect of reducing incentives for Australians to start thinking about their strategic responsibilities. These matters could be left to British experts. The major issue of planning a naval defence against invasion was seen to be outside the scope of Australian naval policy. Thus the various Australian naval forces suggested or considered by Captain W.R. Creswell and the leading politicians conformed to the ineluctable circumstances—they had to be affordable, result in a body of Australian naval personnel trained in the navy of the global British community and minimally interfere with the Royal Navy's strategic responsibility for Australia's territorial integrity.[13] The modest size of the force advocated by those wanting a distinctive Australian squadron down to 1909 thereby confirmed Australian strategic dependence on the Naval Agreement with Britain.

The above criteria informed Jose's understanding of Australian desiderata, which he reported to London in May 1906. Having acknowledged both the unpopularity of the agreement in Australia and Admiralty dissatisfaction with it, he outlined consideration of its modification or replacement. He believed the Federal Government's thinking was for a two-part scheme—'Contributions to the general defence of the Empire, harmonizing with Admiralty practice at home . . .' on the one hand and 'A scheme for local coast-defence based on Captain Creswell's report . . .' on the other. What was in question was the mode, not the principle, of sharing in imperial defence. He declined to enter upon questions of strategy, suggesting that the new doctrine of 'one Empire, one Navy' and commitment to decisive battle were discounted in Australia. The concentration of its population on its littoral and its incomplete land communications required special attention to defence of interstate trade and coastal harbours. '[A] successful cruiser-raid on Sydney or Melbourne, while the Australian squadron was away working out the most scientific strategies in the Japan Sea, say, would go further towards breaking up the Empire than the most successful battle would towards saving it.'[14] Until 1909 this determination to have a local coast defence against any enemy was seen as both minuscule qualification of official Admiralty strategy and the strategic maximum for all proposals for an Australian navy.

Missing, however, from Jose's May 1906 analysis of Australian thinking on naval defence matters, his first article on Australian defence, was any indication of a new, especial concern with Japan. In the considerable bulk of Jose's letters and writings there is no reference to either the great Japanese naval victory in the Korea Strait in May 1905 or to the events of the Russo–Japanese War. For him 1905 did not mark a strategical watershed or turning point for naval development.

Defence was first mentioned in July 1905 when Jose reproduced the new Deakin ministry's program for the remainder of its term. This included 'defence as specially deserving of reconsideration, particularly in view of recent developments'; and indicated that the ministry intended 'at a later date to make proposals of an important character'.[15] In October he reported privately both the first public meeting of the Australian National Defence League and broader Australian dissatisfaction with the Admiralty's apparent failure to fulfil their side of the Naval Agreement.[16] A month later he showed that Parliament would not consider defence until 1906.[17]

There was good reason for the ministry's delay, which Jose then learned. In October 1905 Leo Amery, *The Times*'s colonial editor, had asked the Australian correspondent to find out if it was true that, firstly, the Australian Government were trying to alter the 1903 Naval Agreement and, secondly, whether they were seeking to use the subsidy of £200 000 in some other way.[18] This was a spectacularly abbreviated but accurate summary of Deakin's somewhat wordy official letter of 28 August, which possibly had been leaked to Amery.[19]

Jose's initial response to Amery's request was to suppose that there was misunderstanding. He was not aware that the matter had any importance but, setting himself to learn what was involved, sent Amery's letter to Deakin. The Prime Minister advised Jose of what had been happening with naval policy. He requested this information should be sent to Amery but not by cable.[20] Jose obliged, but sent Amery no further report.[21] In January 1906 he routinely wrote that Parliament would await the result of Deakin's initiatives, particularly the request for a report by the Committee of Imperial Defence on Australian defence generally.[22] The next naval reference was a brief mention in March of Australian worry about a 'new German naval station in New Britain' and the possibility of a French one in the New Hebrides.[23]

Amery then requested a complete article on the naval subsidy and on Creswell's report favouring an Australian navy. At the same time he cautioned Jose that, while he personally supported the 'Colonies building their own navies and *administering* them under the Admiralty', *The Times* was strongly opposed to any change in the present position and especially to any Australian navy.[24] Jose took a month to contact Creswell and other

Alfred Deakin (1856–1919), three times Australian Prime Minister (1903–04, 1905–08, 1909–10) and a key figure in the establishment of the Royal Australian Navy. (National Archives of Australia)

defence people.[25] The finished articles were sent off in early May, seven weeks after the receipt of Amery's request.

The slow passage of time and Jose's casual reporting of naval defence reflected no sense of urgency concerning Australia's security. Jose's first serious consideration of Australian naval matters came two and a quarter years after his return to Australia and almost one year after the close of the war in the Pacific. In all this there was no mention of Japan, no report of new imperatives for defence policy, no perception of an altered strategic environment, nor any sense of crisis.

Jose's failure to report strategic deterioration in 1905 will be questioned by those who see Deakin's interview published in the Melbourne *Herald* of 12 June as both a reaction to Japan's victory and a turning point in Australian defence policy. A careful analysis of Deakin's interview suggests, however, that he was not concerned with Japan alone. He stressed not the victory of one power but the global phenomenon of navalism.[26] Instead of Japan having become the focus of real concern he offered Australians a choice of sixteen, or three, potential enemies. He wished to awaken Australians to their defence responsibilities in an arming world.

Japan's recent success was mentioned, but for Deakin a Russian victory would have brought the same message. Consistent with the minimalist and non-specific strategy of those who thought of increased Australian defence spending, he concluded:

> But the very least with which we can be content is such an expenditure and such defence forces as will afford us reasonable guarantees of safety to our ports, our cities and our coasts.[27]

Deakin's comments on his interview are free of any strategic insight: there is no suggestion of a changed defence environment. His speech to the Imperial Federation League of Victoria two days after the *Herald* interview 'urged unity of Imperial defence and ... Imperial alliance in some form'. He lamented generally that his recent 'condemnation of the inadequacy of our defences and particularly of the absence of protection of our ports and harbours' had fallen on deaf ears, being regarded by 'our anti-Socialists and Socialists alike ... as far-off secondary issues'.[28]

A second purpose behind Deakin's June 1905 interview could have been political. If Jose's view is correct that the unpopularity of the Naval Agreement had contributed to the ministry's lost votes in the 1903 election then, before the next, Deakin had to act on naval defence. Following consultation with Creswell and the other naval commandants his ministry set about reviving and organising the naval forces. Before he resigned as Prime Minister in April 1904 destroyer and submarine costs were requested.[29] The successor administration, the first Commonwealth Labor Cabinet, led by J.C. Watson, continued this policy, believing mistakenly that they were initiating it. In Parliament Watson expressed personal disapproval of the Naval Agreement, foreshadowed the eventual elimination of the obsolete colonial naval units and indicated an intention to begin the training of Australian naval forces in modern vessels, in the first instance hiring destroyers but looking to build at least one per year. The Admiralty was approached, but unsuccessfully.[30] It seems probable then that, even before the outbreak of the Russo–Japanese War, the December 1903 electors had set the course to an Australian navy. Writing seven weeks before his electoral reverse, Deakin claimed that 'the tide of popular sentiment had carried [the Naval Agreement] triumphantly through'.[31] By August 1905 his view had altered: 'the present Naval Agreement is not, and never has been, popular'.[32]

Reid's ministry followed Watson's but, with limited parliamentary support, was able to achieve little. The period of political instability or inaction from April 1904 ended when Deakin returned as Prime Minister in July 1905, by which time the next elections were less than eighteen months away.[33] The remarks in the interview of June 1905 showed that

Deakin was close to the position adopted by the Watson Government. Deakin's observations made it easier to neutralise any electoral advantage Labor had gained from its defence policy, while keeping open the way to informal alliance, with Labor supporting his prime ministership—as happened until November 1908.

It is possible, therefore, that Deakin's *Herald* interview was motivated more by political calculation than strategic perception. If the move towards a more modern Australian navy had to wait upon politics rather than strategy, it is relevant to note here that the clarification of the political situation in Australia came less than two months after the great Japanese victory. That is to say, the near coincidence of two quite unconnected events can explain any differences of interpretation as to whether strategic or political factors determined the evolution of Australia's navy. A political interpretation is consistent, moreover, with both a lack of urgency and a wish to 'reconsider' the question of an Australian navy. It further helps us to understand the absence of significant strategic thought in Australia after Tsushima. This persistence of past imperatives would also explain Jose's relaxed reporting of defence before May 1906.

Division had been an understandable and ever-present factor in the evolution of Australian naval policy. Even before Federation there were those who looked for an Australian navy and those who did not: a few idealists hoped for no naval defence. But it is not the differences between those for and against an Australian navy that Jose reveals to us. His exposure was of differences among those working for an identifiable Australian naval force.

In the longer view the most serious difference was probably that between Creswell and the other naval officers serving Australia on the one hand, and its political leadership, Deakin in particular, on the other.[34] For closely related to this issue of division is that of lack of direction. Deakin chose to place the responsibility for shaping national naval policy almost entirely on his own shoulders: 'he has absolutely forbidden any other Minister to touch on the subject at all'.[35] For one who admitted to little expertise in this field, whether of strategic theory, marine technology, naval weaponry or logistics, this was an extraordinary political choice. Some of his initiatives seem to have ignored the need to seek advice or to have set it aside when it came from Australian naval personnel.

Under circumstances of self-imposed isolation, Deakin's course was understandably erratic. In August 1905 his proposal was that the Admiralty should support a subsidy of fast mail ships which during wartime could be converted to merchant cruisers. These would not only provide a weekly mail service but also give Australians maritime experience.[36] Then,

'The Peace Rainbow: The Threatening Eastern Storm'. A cartoon published in Melbourne *Punch* on 3 September 1908 during the visit by the Great White Fleet. (National Library of Australia)

after the blunt rebuff from the Committee of Imperial Defence the Prime Minister in September 1906 opted, along Creswellian lines, for 'four first-class torpedo boats and eight vessels of the Teviot class' by the end of three years.[37] After his return from the 1907 Imperial Conference he abandoned a purely destroyer force and in December of that year decided on nine C-class submarines and six torpedo destroyers.[38] During the visit of the American Fleet in August he talked of something quite different, 'that from our own shores some day a fleet will go out not unworthy to be compared in quality, if not in numbers, with the magnificent fleet now in Australia'.[39] When the Dreadnought offer was made in March 1909 he at first rejected it and supported the Labor Government's policy of building destroyers instead. Within a few days he was backing the Dreadnought proposal, thereby separating himself from the government's policy.[40]

Another weakness in Deakin's management of naval policy was apparent impatience. He approached the Admiralty in August 1905 with his mail boat suggestion but, before giving their Lordships time to reply, sent off a request to have the Committee of Imperial Defence consider Australian defence *in toto*.[41] Also brought to this account is the casual way in which Creswell was sent to England in 1906 without clearcut official backing. None of these steps suggests any deep sense of serious emergency or the need for care. Instead they point to Deakin's uncertainty as to what he really wanted to achieve in naval policy. Without firm or clear leadership, division within the movement for an Australian navy was inevitable.

Jose first gave a hint of this division in November 1906:

> [t]he news from home about the reduction in the naval building estimates . . . is giving several leading politicians out here seriously to think, for it strengthens the cry of certain extremists who want to get in the end a substantial local navy, and the leading men I refer to are above all things anxious to keep the new squadron strictly subsidiary. The question of expense will keep it that for a bit; but it's a pity to give the Separatists, a single argument more than you can help, now or ever.[42]

If there was real anxiety about Japan, a rejection of a substantial local navy is baffling. Further fragmentation was found in the November 1907 issue of *The Call*:

> But just when all difficulties seemed overcome, division has arisen in the ranks of the victors. Frightened by the expense of a really efficient scheme, some of the most ardent supporters of Australian self-defence are putting forward a dilatory makeshift plan; 'Borrow an old battleship,' they say, 'and use it for training a large number of Naval Reserve men.' After doing this for ten years, they suppose that we shall have accumulated a strong *personnel* ready to man any boats we may then be in a position to build.

In his article Jose set out to demolish this proposal to delay the acquisition of Australian ships. He believed that those advocating a 'big reserve' were simply trying to block all ways to naval progress. There would be no point in a reserve without an already established 'fighting line whose losses must be supplied'. A fighting line came first; especially if the reserves were to have incentive during training. More specialised training for naval men was now the order of the day: 'it should be a principle for us, too, to train our naval forces in the duties and, as much as possible, on the ships we shall expect them to use in war time'.[43]

A much more serious 'fork' in the road to an Australian navy appeared the following month. On 13 December 1907 Deakin announced the government's new defence proposals. These reverted to the idea of training Australians in borrowed old P-class cruisers, the idea which Jose had just condemned. Worse, in Jose's view, some of the destroyers and torpedo boats of September 1906 had been replaced by submarines. Deakin's parliamentary speech was no more than the announcement of a proposed policy. The introduction of a bill giving it effect would wait until September 1908. It included no provision for any serious overseas attack upon Australia. Indeed in his speech Deakin stated: 'A large invasion is not expected, but we must be prepared for sudden raids'. The traditional pre-1905 strategic doctrine had not been modified.[44]

Deakin's announcement of submarines to be acquired over a period of three years left Jose stunned. He saw the 'submarine' idea as a retrograde step, a return to working outwards from securing harbour defence first and coastal trade defence second. Blue-water capacity was not even mentioned. This return to the ideas of the Deakin ministries of 1903 and 1904 denies any intervening strategic revolution. Writing to London, Jose declared:

> The naval half of the Deakin scheme however, has been very differently received: it would hardly be an exaggeration to call it stillborn, and it certainly has no chance of living. It is, perhaps, the one thing the Prime Minister has conceived that pleases no one but himself.[45]

Jose protested against the submarine proposal in letters to Deakin. First, he argued, in their then state of development they were unsuitable for Australian waters beyond harbours, and second, they required the most advanced specialist trained crews, 'service in them trains for nothing else'.[46] Given that the Royal Navy had no submarine crews to spare, Jose believed that in recommending a force requiring expert personnel the Admiralty had trapped Deakin into supporting a scheme which would delay indefinitely the creation of an Australian navy. It was

> urgently necessary that we should at as early a date as possible suffice for our own coastal defence: not merely for the defence of two or more harbours already mainly defensible by land fortifications and minefields, but for the foreknowledge, interruption, and possibly prevention of raids and landings on any part of our coast. Submarines won't help us there, any more than obsolescent cruisers will. Sea-going torpedo destroyers are the smallest boats that will be in any way useful to *us* . . .

He continued by claiming that Deakin's naval scheme of December 1907 would meet with 'very strong, probably with fatal, opposition . . . any attempt to make [the submarines], or the out-of-date cruisers, a substitute for a real local squadron is pretty sure to lose your scheme and, possibly, your Ministry'.[47]

But the most significant and powerful division in the movement towards an Australian navy came in March 1909 with the Dreadnought offer. If this was no more than a very material gesture of Australian imperial sentiment it need not detain us. But Jose's interpretation was quite different, believing the offer of a Dreadnought for work in the North Sea to be a move to stop the emergence of an Australian navy.

The immediate reaction to the Dreadnought proposal in Sydney was confused. Jose identified four or five groups, the general public who were wholeheartedly behind the offer as a dramatic patriotic gesture, those who saw it as an anti-local squadron opportunity, those who wanted to increase the annual subsidy, those who wanted both the Dreadnought gift and a continuation with the local squadron and finally those who wanted to put the special offer aside altogether and who believed 'with Fisher and Deakin—that every penny Australia can be induced to spare should be put into her at present absolutely inadequate defences of her own coast, and reckons that a better relief to England's overstrained finances than any sudden proffer of a single ship'.[48]

The first thing that might be said is that offering a battleship for use in the North Sea was an unusual gesture if an independently-minded Australia was concerned at the prospect of attack by Japan. Rather did it reflect Australian belief that its defence depended on the Royal Navy. The second point is that there does seem to have been a powerful upsurge of popular sentiment. Up until then naval defence issues exercised only a handful of Australians. The support in March 1909 for the mother country in its growing difficulty of maintaining British naval power in European waters was much more widely based. The enthusiasm shown during the visit of the American Fleet is also well known, but neither gesture suggests a popular concern with a Japanese threat. It might be remembered that similar enthusiasm, in poor weather conditions moreover, was shown when a Japanese squadron visited the east coast of Australia one year after the battle of Tsushima.[49]

The third and a more important thing to notice is that the local reaction eventually settled into a groove which Jose saw as dangerous for both the movement towards an Australian navy and for the country as a whole, especially in its relations with the United Kingdom. As indicated, the initial reaction to the Dreadnought offer amongst the elite was complex, with many, including both Andrew Fisher, the Prime Minister, and Alfred Deakin being against it. Jose reported on 23 March, 'Heney of the [*Sydney Morning*] *Herald* said to me yesterday afternoon, you can't get the important men to touch it'. Six days later, however, he wrote, 'the movement is now mainly in the hands of anti-local-squadronites'.[50] The situation became even more serious when Deakin changed his opinion and decided on 1 April to support the Dreadnought offer. The survival of the United Kingdom was more important than any possible worry about the Pacific. Jose saw that the 'question of Australia's contribution to the defence of the Empire' could become submerged in party politics. On 28 April, therefore, he wrote to both Fisher and Deakin, now opposed on the Dreadnought issue, recommending the postponement of 'all active defence legislation until the advice of the Admiralty or the Imperial Committee of Defence' had been taken.[51] We do not know what effect this letter might have had. It is the case, however, that on the following day Fisher cabled London requesting a conference.

Although this Australian request for a conference, and the coincident invitation to one from the British Government, avoided political damage in Australia, the question remains as to why Australia had become or threatened to become divided over this issue. According to Jose those mainly opposed to an Australian navy were the Sydney merchants and socialites, those large landowners who only marginally worked their Australian lands and any remaining ultra-Imperialists.[52]

For the Dreadnought offer had posed the question of how the ship would be funded.[53] In turn this raised dramatically the question of Commonwealth finance. This is a convoluted issue for present purposes but it is fairly safe to state that for the first decade of its existence the Federal Government had no scope for more than the most fundamental administrative expenditure. That there was insufficient revenue for expensive national policies such as defence followed from the continued financial superiority of the states' treasuries for the first 10 years after Federation. And in Jose's view state politics and press were largely controlled by the capital city merchants or the large landowners.

But if there was an urgent threat to Australia's security then there was an imperative need to reform Commonwealth–state financial relations. This did not happen. Here is another argument from silence, one that seems compelling. The failure to effect significant change in the Commonwealth's revenue base seriously undermines the historiographical argument that Australia's attitude to defence matters changed significantly after the great Japanese naval victory. There were many other increasingly important national projects, most of which were also not adopted at that time. To defence must be added the establishment of a working old age pension scheme and the establishment of the Federal Post Office, the implementation of a national immigration policy, the taking over of the Northern Territory, the setting up of the High Commissionership in London, and the building of the Federal capital and two transcontinental railways.[54] Some of these, moreover, had defence implications.

Before the Dreadnought offer there was an unexpected development. In the issue of *The Call* for February 1909 Jose published a short essay which considered a future Australian navy's place in imperial defence. This would be a navy different from but additional to the local coastal defence squadron: it would be a navy with undoubted blue-water capability. Jose, as an ardent supporter of Creswell even to the point of disagreement with Prime Minister Deakin, had never before entered upon this ground. His new and radical concept was of imperial, not Australian, defence based upon oceanic fleets, each one being paid for and controlled by those British Dominions which bordered a particular ocean. Imperial interests in the Pacific would be defended by a fleet contributed by Australia, Western Canada (New Zealand was not mentioned) and to some extent Britain herself, especially after the opening of the Panama Canal. Britain would maintain the Empire's power in the North Sea, the Mediterranean and the Atlantic Ocean. In this Atlantic role Eastern Canada and, possibly, the West Indies would have some share. 'India and South Africa, with an Australian contribution to represent West Australian interest, would look after the Indian Ocean'.[55]

Although this was a rejection of the doctrine that 'the sea is one: the navy must be one', it is doubtful if the thought processes were really based upon the concept of separate oceans. Rather were they determined by different enemies. Here was an outline of a strategy to counter Japanese aggression:

> Can we contemplate a war in the Pacific, say, in defence of White Australia, while the home islands remained at peace and the Atlantic fleet went its ordinary rounds? Is not this perilously close to separation and colonial independence? It would be if the Pacific fleet engaged belonged to a single colony ... The Pacific navy of our dreams is not Australian or Canadian; it belongs to the Pacific States of the Empire, which can control it in unison because the interests in whose defence they would like to use it are largely identical—a thing which you cannot say safely about the interests of, say, Britain and Australia ... we doubt whether the voter of the home islands ... does share, or even understand, the White Australia sentiment, which is the nearest thing we have to a national religion. In Vancouver, in Durban, that sentiment *is* shared; the control of the navy which must defend it may be safely shared also.[56]

Current naval policy was not the article's concern: it speculated about a navy 'twenty years hence'. Its avoidance of the key issue of command of the combined fleets was a weakness. It lacked any notion of fleet units or their tactical use. The principle of separate oceanic fleets acting imperially and financed by combinations of British Dominions, however, might have stimulated some Admiralty thinking before their July 1909 proposals to 're-establish a large British fleet in the Pacific'.[57]

How might we account for this dramatic shift in the scope of Jose's strategic thinking? There are several possible influences. In the first place the article itself stressed that its ideas had been occasioned by a reading of Bean's book *With the Flagship in the South*, which contained a dream of a co-operative Britannic imperial fleet in the Pacific Ocean. So Jose did not claim to be the originator of the radical 'oceanic' strategy. Later he asserted that this 'far wider and more Imperial idea had already been put forward among Australian enthusiasts'.[58]

A second possible contribution to the radical departure from the official strategy can be found in growing appreciation of the challenge to Britain's naval supremacy. We saw a first hint of this in November 1906.[59] Two years later the Governor of New South Wales, Admiral Sir H. Rawson, warned that

> there would be more difficulty every year in getting from the British Parliament enough money to build the Dreadnoughts which the Empire must have for its safety. Consequently, said R., the colonies had better wake up at once to the absolute necessity of providing for self-defence, as in case of war they might find themselves isolated and Britain unable to spare them any sort of naval protection.

Jose's letter further revealed that the editor of *The Standard* believed that it was 'certain that we shall be fighting Germany within seven years—it is to be hoped, before the Japanese alliance is at an end. That is the limit we have for Australian preparation.'[60]

Concern at Britain's ability to maintain her naval supremacy could be openly stated in Australia too. Colonel H. Foster had published articles on the defence of Australia in the Melbourne *Argus* of October 1908. These and Creswell's attempted refutation were published as a Commonwealth Parliamentary Paper by the Fisher Government in the December following. Foster's view was that Australia's naval defence was completely secured by the Royal Navy: Creswell stressed the dilemma Britain would face in maintaining her naval supremacy simultaneously in two oceans, if the Anglo–Japanese alliance lapsed in 1915.[61]

Growing awareness of a British feeling of unease about maintaining naval supremacy was confirmed in letters Jose received from his immediate superior on the editorial staff, no longer Amery but Mr E.W.M. Grigg. One of these, containing a troubled analysis of contemporary thinking in Britain about naval matters, would have reached Jose in the first week of January 1909, the month before his article in *The Call* appeared.[62]

Although we have in the above instances possible stimuli to Jose's article, there can be little doubt that in his mind the much more fundamental impetus, not only to appropriate strategic thought but to the question of what kind of Australian navy there should be, came from the policy of *The Times* itself. Jose frequently referred to the hints given in the newspaper's leading articles between September 1907 and September 1908 that if Australia drove her pursuit of a White Australia as far as a serious quarrel with Japan, then she should not count on being defended by the Royal Navy.[63] That is to say that the fundamental strategic principle securing Australia from invasion was in doubt, not only from a British need to limit expenditure but from the possibility of fundamental policy difference.

This phase in *The Times*'s policy began when Amery took an enforced holiday; and lasted until Grigg returned from Australia to take charge of the 'Foreign and Imperial' section. During these twelve months a succession of leading articles in the newspaper treated with ill-concealed sarcasm virtually everything suggested or done by Australia, not only defence, but, for example, immigration, an imperial tariff and Deakin's 'New Protection'. This period also saw continuation of *The Times*'s failure to print almost all Jose's articles following those on naval defence of May 1906. Jose protested vigorously against this derision of Australian policies.[64] How seriously we should take this eccentric phase in the paper's policy is difficult to decide.[65]

We have reached what Jose argued was the real turning point in the road towards an Australian navy. Somewhat later he wrote:

> There was a time, some years ago, when a *Times* leader made us jump by telling us that White Australia depended on the British fleet, and that the fleet would probably not be available if White Australia meant war: and that, not the American fleet, was the beginning of the active local-squadron movement.[66]

Before such a threat to the traditional basis of Australia's security there was no need for Australians to think profoundly about the strategic purpose of a navy. Significantly it is from late 1907 that one finds in Jose's correspondence much more frequently expectations of having to face Japan alone and with a force very different from Creswell's proposed coastal and interstate trade defence squadron. On the last day of 1907 Jose told Valentine Chirol, the Foreign Editor of *The Times*, 'the mass of people here look on Japan as the future enemy'.[67]

The corollary of a sizeable navy is found in a letter written one week earlier:

> [A]s Sir H. Campbell-Bannerman told the Imperial Conference, the navy and foreign policy hang together: Australia has a foreign policy of her own—the defensive White Australia policy—in which it seems possible that the mother country will not altogether agree. If in the future there should be such disagreement, Australians acknowledge that the responsibility of supporting their own policy will rest with them; therefore they must have their own squadrons to defend their own coast. And what they want now is

The Japanese armoured cruiser *Nissin* in Sydney Harbour during World War I.
(J. Straczek)

a scheme from which those squadrons may germinate. Mr Deakin has not given them such a scheme.[68]

Nor was there any need, before this hint of an Australia abandoned by Britain, to look for alternative sources for her security. But an early indication of an Australian wish to have allies other than the mother country herself, in particular the USA, is found in January 1908.[69] This followed by a few days Deakin's request that the world cruise of the American fleet should include Australia. It is not likely that Jose knew of that invitation.

It is at this time, moreover, that the political rhetoric and unfolding of differing proposals about Australian defence is replaced by some action, however limited. At long last Deakin came off the rhetorical fence. In December 1907, qualifying some of his 1906 defiance of the Committee of Imperial Defence, he announced the government's defence proposals and introduced the first defence bill in September 1908—this more than three years after Tsushima; but only one year after the first of *The Times* leaders critical of Australia's policies.

With the resignation of Deakin's ministry, his defence bill failed. The successor Labor administration hastened to act, ordering destroyers in February 1909. This Creswellian step showed that Jose's more advanced strategic thinking had not affected official decision-making. This official Australian rejection of a strategy to face Japan was not confined to Labor ministries. At the subsequent Imperial Naval and Military Defence Conference in July and August 1909 the Australian representatives, Colonel J. Foxton and Creswell, faced with the Admiralty's breathtaking proposal of a fleet unit, clung stubbornly, but unavailingly, to the more modest local coast defence squadron idea.[70]

From 1903 to 1909 White Australians accepted the responsibility of nationhood in an increasingly navalist world by addressing, along with other policies, the question of naval defence. In these years dependence on the Royal Navy for the preservation of Australia's territorial integrity was not seriously questioned. Advocates of an Australian navy rarely considered more than a coastal trade defence squadron. The idea of a subsidiary, embryonic force did not secure, however, national support. Disagreement as to the form of an Australian navy and the failure to develop a relevant naval strategy strongly suggest that the Russo–Japanese War had not concentrated Australian minds. Consequently, legislation for a local squadron, when introduced in late 1908, was governed by pre-1904 political ideas.

The Australian fleet unit agreed in 1909, however, bore practically no resemblance to almost all of the ideas previously debated in Australia. With definite potential to participate in a strategy of deterring Japan, this fleet resulted from a fortuitous, eccentric and ultimately evanescent development in imperial policy. In 1909 Admiralty concern at Japan's rising power coincided with Australian fears of that nation. The outcome, thereby, was not the attainment of an independent Australian navy. Instead Australia acquired a fleet unit subject more to imperial consideration and strategic requirements than to Australian.[71]

14 Sir John Fisher, the fleet unit concept, and the creation of the Royal Australian Navy

Nicholas Lambert

However much the Commonwealth of Australia might have wanted a navy in the early years of the twentieth century, they could not have one without the prior approval of the British Government. Support of the British Government in this matter, moreover, depended almost entirely upon the attitude of the Board of Admiralty.

The British Admiralty and Australian naval power

Historians of the Royal Australian Navy have traditionally portrayed every Board of Admiralty as unequivocally hostile to the creation of an independent Commonwealth navy. Documentary evidence, however, shows that these beliefs require considerable qualification.[1] During the 1870s and 1880s, for example, the Admiralty had made several important concessions to the Victorian and New South Wales naval defence forces and had provided officers, instructors, warships and ordnance at virtually cost price, or even below cost price in some cases. British naval leaders at that time believed, moreover, that the terms of the 1887 Australian Naval Agreement had been generous and that everything possible had been done—some argued the Admiralty had conceded too much—to accommodate Australian maritime aspirations. That being said, however, not one British admiral took the Australian naval forces seriously or expected them to make any useful contribution to imperial defence.

The Admiralty recognised that independent colonial navies as envisaged, or as could be afforded, by the Australian colonies would inevitably remain very small forces comprised probably of semi-obsolescent ships manned by reservists. Such forces might be useful for cementing imperial solidarity but in terms of imperial defence an Australian colonial navy could offer nothing of real value. The Admiralty's fear was that these 'tuppenny halfpenny navies', as they were often called, would in time of war be a potential source of weakness and, in the event of a disaster, embarrassment. There was always the background fear that in the event of a war a hostile armed merchant cruiser might engage and sink a colonial gunboat and thereafter claim that they had sunk a British imperial warship. For this reason the Admiralty refused to encourage any links between the Royal Navy and the Australian colonial navies, much to the latter's resentment. This did not stop the colonists from trying; there are numerous letters of complaint in the Admiralty archives that the Australians tried to identify themselves as part of the Royal Navy, for instance by dressing in British naval uniforms.

Many historical narratives have insisted that at the beginning of the twentieth century the Admiralty remained wedded to the nineteenth-century strategic notion of 'one ocean—one navy', and that the board were determined to maintain centralised direction and deployment of all naval forces throughout the Empire. Leaving aside for the moment the validity of this criticism, few have thought worthy of comment that in 1909 there occurred a reversal in the Admiralty's position. At the 1909 Imperial Conference the British naval representatives not only proposed the formation of an Australian navy, but called for the handing over of effective control of the entire Australia Station to Melbourne, threw the British imperial dockyard facilities in Sydney into the bargain, and offered an initial subsidy of up to a quarter of a million pounds per annum. This was far more than even the most extreme Australian navalists had ever imagined possible. The price, the Admiralty spokesmen concluded, was relatively modest. All Australia had to do was buy one fleet unit, comprised of a battle cruiser, three smaller cruisers, six destroyers and three submarines.

This was a remarkable turnaround: or apparently a remarkable turnaround. My recent volume of documents, *Australia's Naval Inheritance*, has shown that between 1904 and 1908 the Admiralty had already been conceding quite a lot of ground to Australian opinion. In fact as early as 1905 the Admiralty had advised the Committee of Imperial Defence (CID) no longer to oppose the formation of an independent Australian navy. On that occasion the Colonial Office and the Foreign Office had disagreed and as a result the official British Government position had remained unchanged. But in February 1907 the Admiralty had unilaterally resolved actively to encourage Australia to build its own navy and later, at the opening of the Colonial Conference in April, openly declared that Britain would allow the formation of all independent colonial defence forces. Henceforth, the board advocated that all self-governing Dominions should build a flotilla comprised of destroyers and submarines, and promised that control would remain vested with Dominion authorities.

More meaningful, however, was the Admiralty's offer in 1908 to allow Australian naval personnel to be completely interchangeable with those of the Royal Navy, after Australia's Prime Minister, Alfred Deakin, wrung this concession out of the Admiralty. Having seen the inefficiencies of the Victorian Naval Forces in the 1880s and 1890s, Deakin understood that any force divorced from the imperial navy just could not remain militarily effective unless it could achieve a continual interchange of personnel and ideas with the Royal Navy. For most of the period 1905–07 the Admiralty's civil servants, who would have had to administer such an exchange which was bound to involve difficulties, objected to Deakin's request for such a scheme to be set up. But in 1908 the Admiralty overruled their objections, apparently thereby giving Australia, and Deakin in particular, all that was necessary and for which he had asked.

The 1909 naval scare

So why did this sudden change occur? The usual context for understanding has been the 1909 naval scare. On 16 March 1909 Reginald McKenna, First Lord of the Admiralty, stood up in Parliament and announced that Germany had accelerated the construction of Dreadnought battleships and also now had the capacity to outbuild the Royal Navy in the construction of large armoured warships. As a precautionary measure McKenna advised the House of Commons that it would be necessary to lay down at least four capital ships in 1909 and possibly an additional four, making eight in all. This was quite an increase over the previous years. In 1908 there had only been two capital ships laid down, while in 1907 there had only been one. More seriously, McKenna was proposing a considerable increase in the naval estimates at a time when the governing Liberal Party wanted to achieve an overall reduction in naval expenditure and to divert the money saved towards the embryonic welfare state. The opposition Conservative Party sought to exploit the consequent rift within the government by demanding that the Admiralty be given at once all eight ships—knowing full well that the Exchequer could not possibly afford to pay for them without either postponing the introduction of already promised social reforms or raising the rate of taxation.

New Zealand, it is often argued, was the first to detect the undercurrent of crisis within the mother country and the Dominion proceeded to offer to fund the building of one or possibly two battleships as a gesture of imperial solidarity and to ensure that the Royal Navy remained supreme at sea. Australia and Canada, meanwhile, offered less tangible promises of assistance at sea contained in promises to develop their local naval resources. When Alfred Deakin returned to power in June 1909, the Australian contribution to imperial defence was expanded into the offer of 'a "Dreadnought" or such addition to its Naval strength as may be determined after consultation with London'.[2] The traditional understanding is that these offers of aid prompted the Admiralty or British Government to hold a conference to discuss these proposals. The problem with this perception is that although the 1909 naval scare was an important factor, it was not the only factor.

An examination of CID documents shows that actually as early as the end of 1908 there had been discussions over the possible implications of what to do when the Anglo–Japanese Naval Alliance, that had been renewed in 1905, came to an end in 1915. The Admiralty opposed the continuation of the relationship because they believed the Japanese were more interested in stealing the Royal Navy's latest doctrines and technologies, and obtaining whatever else they could for commercial advantage. The Foreign Office and Colonial Office were likewise arguing that there were decidedly expansionist tendencies in Japan, and they too expressed concern at the apparent weakness of Britain's strength east of Suez relative to that of the Imperial Japanese Navy. The CID proceeded to endorse the Admiralty's recommendation to return a fleet of armoured ships to the Pacific well before that date and, as an afterthought, agreed to consider this reinforcement in the light of desires expressed by various Dominions to establish their own navies. The invitation was issued at the end of April 1909 and in late 1909 the delegates began to arrive in London.[3]

Despite clear instructions from the CID to consult with the Dominions, the majority of Admiralty officials remained doubtful that their offers of assistance would ever materialise, and even if they did, questioned whether they would really be useful. Majority naval opinion continued to believe that the cost of establishing a navy was simply far too great. Officers also took onboard the underlying warnings of the Australian and Canadian Governors-General that, although offers had been made, it would be difficult to get the colonials to place their cash on the table. A modern capital ship cost two million pounds—a sum that represented more than the annual defence expenditure of all the self-governing Dominions combined.

The sceptics were quickly proved to have been quite right to caution that neither Australia, Canada nor New Zealand could or would actually provide this amount. In fact, the Dreadnought proposals translated into offers to pay the interest on loans raised on the London Stock Market, and since no Dominion had the capacity to raise such a large amount of money at an acceptable rate of interest it had to be done by London. Nevertheless, the Admiralty generally accepted that for reasons of imperial solidarity they would talk to the Dominions and perhaps accept their offers.

Admiral Sir John Fisher

Admiral Sir John Fisher regarded the offers by the Dominions in a quite different light. In 1909 he held the office of First Sea Lord, and, ex officio, the post of senior naval adviser to the CID. Not everybody accepted his radical views on naval warfare, but despite the progressive weakening of his authority—mainly as a result of his disagreements over the direction of naval policy with Admiral Beresford and others—he remained the dominant force inside both the Admiralty and the CID.[4]

Fisher came to power in October 1904 with a radically different vision of how to fight wars at sea. He revised completely the existing understanding of how one applied naval force. Traditionally the Royal Navy was centred upon the battleship fleet. The purpose of the battlefleet was

Admiral of the Fleet Sir John Fisher, 1st Baron of Kilverstone (1841–1920). Fisher was First Sea Lord of the Board of Admiralty 1904–1910 and 1914–15 and the architect of a profound British military technological revolution. He sought to create a new model fleet at significantly reduced cost which was still capable of protecting Britain's global imperial interests. (RAN)

seen as twofold. First, it was a tool of diplomacy and second, a force of strategic deterrence. Many believed that, in war or peace, Britain's possession of the strongest battlefleet would normally be sufficient to ensure the preservation of her interests. Fisher, however, rejected this idea and along with it the simplistic Mahanian operational strategy[5] of concentrating the battlefleet and seeking a decisive battle.[6] Furthermore, he did not agree that what happened at the centre of the Empire was all that really mattered, and that what happened at the periphery was irrelevant in comparison. Instead of a grand strategy based upon the battlefleet, Fisher proposed two things.

First of all, he put forward a theory of flotilla defence for security of the home islands from invasion.[7] He argued that instead of relying on the battleships to deter invasion of the British Isles, the enemy invasion convoys could be deterred from putting to sea by the threat of attack from torpedo craft. Fisher wanted to invest the narrow seas—that is, the Channel, the North Sea and the Mediterranean—with a mosquito fleet comprised of submarines and torpedo boats. He conceded that French, German and Italian submarines and torpedo craft would pose an equally effective deterrent to British expeditionary forces, but argued that was not a problem as Britain had no desire to invade the European mainland, and so would be satisfied with a state of 'mutual sea denial'. Fisher demonstrated that flotilla defence would be cheaper not only in financial and personnel terms, but perhaps more importantly it would also unshackle the armoured cruiser squadrons from home defence duties and thus allow them to be used for their primary function, which was imperial defence.

The second major element of Fisher's notion of naval warfare was the 'battle cruiser theory'.[8] The battle cruiser was conceived as a multi-purpose 'armoured warship' with the capability of performing the missions previously performed by either battleships or armoured cruisers. They were fast, all-big-gun warships, which sacrificed armour protection for immense range and high speed. Believing that battleships were no longer required for home defence in large numbers, Fisher wanted the Royal Navy to divert all funds allocated to battleship construction to be spent instead on the building of his 'fusion' armoured warships. He envisaged battle cruisers being formed into flying squadrons that could protect the ocean trade routes from enemy corsairs or reinforce the outer marches of the Empire when necessary. If necessary, they could also be used to support the flotilla against an enemy battlefleet.

There were two other key components to Fisher's theory. One of these might be called 'advanced tactical theory'. Fisher did not believe that the navy's armoured warships should all be grouped together into a single fleet and deployed in a single line of battle. Instead he wanted to organise them in small battlegroups comprised of one, possibly two, battle cruisers, and accompanied by several high-speed scouts, 'Swifts', or 'satellites' as he sometimes called them. (The term 'light cruiser' was not adopted by the Royal Navy to describe such warships until 1912.) These battle units would operate either independently or semi-independently, engaging enemy forces at will.

The other key component that Fisher developed, much more quietly this time, was the control and exploitation of all communications across the globe and the systematic gathering and exploitation of intelligence. Basically he argued that instead of organising the imperial defence navy into independent station fleets scattered across the world, each operating within its own sphere and attempting to secure the imperial communications within its assigned area, the battle cruiser forces would be located at central geographical locations and vectored towards potential threats.

Fisher's ideas did not just exist in theory. He did in fact attempt to implement them during his administration, but unfortunately achieved only limited success because the majority of serving naval officers did not endorse them. Admiral Charles Beresford, the senior fleet commander from 1907 to 1909, rejected the notion of flotilla defence. It is often argued that Beresford's and Fisher's dispute was one of personal animosity. It was not, but they could not argue in public about what they were really disagreeing over for reasons of national security. Beresford had no wish to rely on flotilla defence for the protection of the United Kingdom from invasion, the adoption of distant blockade, or the relegation of the main battlefleet, the Channel Fleet, to a supporting role.

Notwithstanding Fisher's inability to secure the endorsement of the commander-in-chief, when he initially proposed his battle cruiser theory Fisher found considerable support among influential middle-ranking officers already serving at the Admiralty such as rear admirals Prince Louis of Battenberg and William May. At this point it was still believed that the enemies in the next war were going to be France and Russia. Over the previous decade each of these nations had developed a very large force of armoured cruisers. Moreover, they had developed a doctrine which called for systematic commerce warfare across the globe. This was a major threat to British security. The Royal Navy's relative strength in armoured cruisers was weak, and Fisher and his predecessors took the threat very seriously. Under the 1905 construction program it was agreed to lay down just one battleship, the prototype Dreadnought, and four battle cruisers— although the latter were soon reduced to three as a concession to the government's desire to cut overall naval expenditure. The destruction of the Russian Fleet at Tsushima, the solidifying of the Anglo–French Entente, and growing concern in diplomatic circles at German aggressiveness changed Admiralty perceptions of the international situation, and the degree of support for Fisher's battle cruiser theory started to ebb.

SIR JOHN FISHER AND THE FLEET UNIT CONCEPT

The cruiser HMS (later HMAS) *Pioneer* at Hobart before World War I. Despite Fisher's dislike of ships which could neither fight nor flee, vessels of this type remained on colonial stations where, as he had predicted, they proved inferior to German cruisers. SMS *Königsberg* sank *Pioneer*'s sister ship, HMS *Pegasus*, off East Africa in September 1914. (D. Robertson)

The Australian fleet unit

Fisher did not give up and, as Jon Sumida has shown in his book *In Defence of Naval Supremacy*, he made more than one attempt to implement his ideas. Fisher always remained convinced that the Admiralty would eventually agree to replace the entire British battlefleet with battle cruisers. One of these battles was going on in 1909 immediately prior to the preparations for the forthcoming Imperial Conference. Fisher had been arguing very strongly that the eight ships promised by the government that year should be laid down as battle cruisers.[9] Unfortunately for Fisher, in April 1909 the majority of the Sea Lords remained unconvinced over the wisdom of this proposal. They nevertheless agreed to a compromise by which Britain would lay down four battleships and four battle cruisers. But Fisher's influence with the board rapidly waned during the early summer of 1909, and the building schedule was watered down in the end to six battleships and two battle cruisers.

Again Fisher refused to bow to majority opinion. At the end of June 1909, he suddenly came up with the proposition that the capital ships offered by Australia and New Zealand should be built as battle cruisers. Furthermore, that these battle cruisers should form the nucleus of a new independent Australian navy, and possibly also Canadian, Indian and South African navies. The model he proposed for these fleets was his tactical unit, comprised of one battle cruiser plus several fast scout cruisers. Recognising the weakness of his position within the Admiralty at this time, however, Fisher attempted to sidestep his opponents inside Whitehall by pleading that the creation of an Australian navy was a colonial matter which ought to be considered by the CID. By this manoeuvre the First Sea Lord had hoped to gain no more than a fresh hearing for his ideas; but to his undoubted surprise the civilian members of the CID not only agreed to hear the case but, after listening to the testimony of retired Admiral of the Fleet Sir Arthur Wilson, they immediately endorsed the fleet unit concept without bothering to consult any other members of the Admiralty. Wilson, regarded almost universally throughout the fleet as the pre-eminent fleet commander of his generation, was an extremely conservative officer who had never been a partisan of Fisher's ideas. His sudden enthusiasm for the fleet unit concept remains hard to explain.

Fisher, in conjunction with his newfound ally, subsequently repackaged the 'fleet' or 'battle' unit theory (by adding on a local defence flotilla comprised of six destroyers and three submarines) and presented it to the Australians as the ideal force structure for a new Australian navy. To everybody present at the Imperial Conference it appeared extremely logical and met all Australian concerns. Not only did it provide a proper framework for the establishment of a semi-independent navy, but at the same time it also provided officers and men with a coherent career structure. The Admiralty had argued for a very long time that if the colonies wanted to build an independent or semi-independent naval force then it was essential to provide men with the promise of a lifetime career in the service, warning that if this consideration was ignored then the service would not be able to attract and retain the first-class talent it needed. The idea of a tactical unit superimposed over a career structure worked remarkably well. The proportion of officers to ratings, as well as senior to junior personnel, was approximately right when one had a coherent grouping of large, medium and small-sized ships. Because the various fleet units were basically identical in terms of material and tactical doctrine, moreover, it was believed that the interchange of personnel between navies would be practical. This was something which Alfred Deakin had so rightly seen as essential to the long-term prosperity and health of an Australian navy.

Although the fleet unit was expensive, more expensive than any Australian politician had anticipated, it was by no means unaffordable,

SIR JOHN FISHER AND THE FLEET UNIT CONCEPT

HMS *Invincible*, one of the first battle cruisers, working up to full speed at the Battle of the Falklands in 1914. Fisher had dispatched a tactical unit centred on two battle cruisers to the South Atlantic: a practical demonstration of his ideas. It brought Vice Admiral Graf Von Spee's German Squadron to action and destroyed it relatively swiftly with no British ships lost. (HMAS *Creswell*)

especially when one allowed for the considerable amount of real estate the Admiralty was prepared to include, and the British offer of a subsidy of a quarter of a million pounds per year. The latter figure, after all, represented approximately one-third of the annual running costs. Fisher's fleet unit also offered Australia a navy more than capable of fulfilling the maritime aspirations of the Australian people. Although not invulnerable, the fleet unit possessed the speed, mobility and firepower to retain tactical initiative and therefore would not be the source of weakness and potential embarrassment so feared by the Admiralty. It was indeed powerful enough to defeat any conceivable force likely to appear in local waters. This was quite remarkable and rightly regarded as a very attractive proposition by many Australian politicians. The Royal Navy was effectively offering to provide Australians with virtually their own independent strategic deterrent.

Conclusions

The traditional view of the creation of the Royal Australian Navy is that it is of peripheral importance to pre-1914 naval history, simply because it is believed that the Royal Navy was organised primarily for North Sea conflict, and hence that the 'Grand Fleet' was the focus of all Britain's naval effort.[10]

However, recent research shows that the concept of a 'Grand Fleet of Battle' was a decidedly *ad hoc* creation, only in fact conceived in 1910.[11] Subsequent attempts to make the system work in 1910–13 convinced the majority of flag officers that it was not a viable tactical system and in 1913 plans were drawn up to adopt one more closely akin to the fleet unit concept. The instigators of these plans were waiting merely for the officers who held current command, David Beatty in the case of the battle cruisers, Sir George Warrender and Sir George Callaghan in the battleships, to vacate their posts at the end of 1914, or early 1915. More fundamentally, if one recognises that the Admiralty, and particularly Jacky Fisher, possessed a more imperial outlook than previously supposed, then the creation of the Royal Australian Navy can no longer be regarded as being of peripheral importance. In fact it is of central importance because the Australian fleet unit was effectively the test bed for the Royal Navy's newest warship types, as well as the latest (albeit controversial) tactical ideas and doctrine. It also served to test the practicality of smaller nations participating in a system of 'collective security' to protect their interests, rather than sheltering under the defence umbrella provided by the strongest nation. Ultimately, it could be argued that the RAN was conceived as the exemplar of the new model navy intended to protect the British Empire into the twentieth century.

15 'Defend the north': Commander Thring, Captain Hughes-Onslow and the beginnings of Australian naval strategic thought
David Stevens

Often viewed as a mere adjunct of an imperial navy, the early RAN still has a reputation for being the most politically and strategically conservative of the Australian services. Because its senior staff was mostly composed of British officers, it seemed to follow logically that they were firmly linked to British interests and therefore encouraged a certain institutional remoteness from Australian affairs.[1] This impression, while misguided, owes much to the interwar period when, starved of funds, the RAN was rapidly reduced to virtual strategic impotence. What most historians have failed to appreciate, however, is the lively debate that took place in Navy Office during the brief period between the formation of the RAN and the beginning of World War I. The initiators of this debate recognised Australia's need to embrace an alternative maritime strategy—one that took into account the unique circumstances prevailing in the Pacific and that, if necessary, could function independently of imperial needs.

Commander Hugh Thring

The central figure behind much of this debate was an ex-Royal Navy officer, Commander (later Captain) W.H.C.S. Thring. Hugh Thring was born in Wiltshire in 1873 and, at the age of 13, entered the cadet training ship HMS *Britannia*.[2] He passed out as a midshipman in 1886. After heading the examination lists he served as a gunnery lieutenant in the Channel, Pacific, and China Squadrons and the Mediterranean Fleet. By 1903, he had been promoted commander and, in 1908, became flag commander and Chief Intelligence Officer to Admiral Lord Charles Beresford, when the latter commanded the Channel Fleet. Unfortunately, Thring's career thereafter became a casualty of the bitter rivalry between Beresford and the First Sea Lord,[3] Admiral Sir John Fisher. Disappointed by his diminished prospects, Thring chose early retirement in 1911.

Described by a contemporary observer as a 'clever, silent well-informed man',[4] the Royal Navy's loss was the RAN's gain. Propitiously the Australian naval liaison officer in London had been seeking a suitable officer to act as assistant to the First Naval Member, Rear Admiral William Creswell. Thring accepted the appointment and left England with his new wife at the end of January 1913. He brought with him a high level of theoretical knowledge in naval strategy, extensive staff and sea-going experience and a recent background in intelligence.

Thring arrived in Melbourne at a time when local confidence in imperial defence plans was showing definite signs of decay. As earlier chapters have indicated, Australians were well aware that Whitehall considered them the 'Outer Empire'. Nevertheless, the Imperial Conferences of 1909 and 1911 had raised local expectations that naval forces maintained in the Pacific would be adequate to defeat or at least hold an enemy in check 'until the main decision had been obtained in the decisive theatre'.[5] Australian support for the acquisition of a 'fleet unit', therefore, had much to do with its role as part of an Imperial Pacific Fleet, and this had been a point of view consistently promoted by Admiral Sir George King-Hall from his position as CinC of the Australia Station. Although Australia had made a firm start on its new navy, support for the other fleet units had yet to materialise. As 1912 wore on, Australians became accustomed to see references in the British press to the 'world-wide needs of the Empire', in which the North Sea and sometimes the Mediterranean were mentioned, but never the Pacific.[6]

Notwithstanding the closed discussions taking place within the Admiralty and the Committee of Imperial Defence, from an Australian perspective the problem was obvious. The Commonwealth was far from the centre of the Empire and, while the people of Great Britain faced an immediate threat in Europe, they were not directly exposed to the Japanese menace. Hence, they did not appreciate that the traditional balance in the Far East had changed and that a first-class naval power had arisen in the Pacific. Most important, Japan was an Asiatic power, one which had recently defeated Russia, and now sought equal international rights for its citizens and an outlet for its growing population. These interests clashed

Captain Thring and his wife outside Buckingham Palace in 1920. For his wartime service at Navy Office in Melbourne, Thring was awarded both the CBE and Japan's Order of the Rising Sun, 3rd Class. (M.W. Thring)

directly with Australian national policies and, despite persistent Admiralty claims to the contrary, made the 1911 Anglo–Japanese Treaty a somewhat unreliable safeguard in local eyes.[7]

Imperial authorities were at least partly responsible for this lack of confidence. Having presented their proposal for a 'Pacific Fleet' at the 1909 Conference, the Admiralty had failed to maintain the momentum once Sir John Fisher retired as First Sea Lord in 1910. The British Government had since treated the conference conclusions as a flexible statement of policy rather than as a firm agreement and Australia received little or no advance warning of changes. The Admiralty, meanwhile, not only neglected to divulge the grand strategic objective of British forces in the Pacific but also failed to finalise the status and relationship of the RAN within an imperial navy.[8] There was no evidence in Australia to show that any general naval strategy existed and, in 1913, even Admiral King-Hall had to admit to Senator E.D. Millen, the Australian Defence Minister, that the Admiralty's Pacific policy was unknown.[9]

For both dominion and imperial authorities the situation was less than ideal. The Australian fleet was soon to become the strongest British squadron in the East but, with no progress towards a Pacific fleet or theatre command, the Admiralty's war plans directed that Australia's battle cruiser and light cruisers be parcelled out between the China and East Indies squadrons.[10] Without the core elements of the fleet unit, the vessels that remained in local waters would hardly be the self-contained deterrent first envisaged by Admiral Fisher. More dangerous for the Commonwealth was the open-ended intention to pass control of its fleet to the Admiralty for the duration of hostilities. The government would no doubt give its consent in the event of a German war, but what would happen should Japan threaten Australia while the Empire was still engaged in Europe? Without a well-understood war plan, or machinery to regain control, the government might easily find it politically impossible to release the RAN for service elsewhere.

Captain Hughes-Onslow

These were some of the problems as described to Thring by Captain Constantine Hughes-Onslow, the Second Naval Member of the Australian Commonwealth Naval Board (ACNB). A highly-strung and aggressive officer, Hughes-Onslow was called 'Crusty' by his contemporaries and, when recalled from the Royal Navy's retired list to accept the appointment, freely admitted that he had never even heard of the Australian navy.[11] As Second Naval Member he was responsible for personnel and stores matters, but he had a long record of active service and, in 1908, the Royal Naval War College thought enough of his skills and impartiality to assign him the task of investigating competing developments in gunnery fire control systems.[12] Certainly, on arrival in Australia in October 1912, Hughes-Onslow had no doubts over his competence to contribute more generally to the RAN's development plan.

Since 1911 this development had been based on the scheme devised by a previous British visitor, Admiral Sir Reginald Henderson.[13] An able dockyard administrator, Henderson had not held a flag command at sea and had never served in the Admiralty, but he did come to Australia with the backing of the still effusive Admiral Fisher.[14] Henderson's subsequent report advocated a progressive expansion of the RAN extending over a generation. By 1933, he estimated it should comprise eight battle cruisers, ten light cruisers, eighteen destroyers, and twelve submarines. Henderson created a vision for the RAN far grander than even Fisher had suggested, but its strategic rationale was somewhat lacking. He had simply based the future fleet's required strength on the expected growth rate of local population and sea trade.

Hughes-Onlsow overstated his case when he later claimed that the RAN was being 'created for the purposes of its creation rather than for any use in war', but there was also a strong element of political expediency in the Henderson plan. Acting on Creswell's suggestions, the admiral had recommended a profusion of bases and sub-bases around the coast, with at least two in each of the newly federated states. In Henderson's view the RAN's primary object was to support the rest of the Empire in retaining command of the sea, and this accorded with the Admiralty's belief that the RAN was destined to become a division of an imperial fleet rather than a truly national and independent navy.

What Hughes-Onslow had realised, however, was that Australia's security was never likely to be the first object of an imperial maritime strategy controlled from Whitehall. A far better solution he felt would be for the Naval Board to raise its own war staff and take the lead in the Empire's Pacific and Indian Ocean strategic planning from Melbourne. This would allow not just the RAN to operate under Australian control, but also all imperial forces in the Far East. Yet, while Hughes-Onslow decried the lack of local war preparations, Creswell had no desire to increase his burden.[15] At 61 years of age he was increasingly feeling overworked[16] and, so long as imperial authorities retained the responsibility for the Empire's defence, Creswell declared the Board was free

> to devote its time and energies more to the work for which it was appointed and which it has immediately at hand—the providing [of] Australia with the strongest and most efficient sea force with all the services necessary to its maintenance and expansion.[17]

Hughes-Onslow soon found himself at odds with most of his fellow board members and felt the character of its 'naval' element to be sadly lacking. The president of the board, Senator Pearce, he dismissed as 'a politician' with no service knowledge; Creswell's acquaintance with a modern navy 'was of a somewhat attenuated order'; while the professional knowledge of the finance member, Staff Paymaster Eldon Manisty, 'was of a purely clerical nature'.[18] Hughes-Onslow was in tune only with the Third Naval Member, Engineer Captain William Clarkson, and this may have been due to Clarkson's own ongoing feud with Creswell.[19]

Hughes-Onslow developed a particular dislike of Manisty, whom he felt wielded despotic powers as Naval Secretary, with little or no practical experience or understanding of the service. Manisty could not be ignored, however. His previous appointment had been as secretary to Admiral Henderson and sections of the Australian press had since christened him 'The Navy Builder', a man whose reputed genius was in translating the Henderson ideas into executive action.[20] Henderson had stressed the necessity of maintaining *'continuity of policy'*[21] and, on arrival in Navy Office, Hughes-Onslow found Henderson's *Recommendations* commonly referred

The Australian Commonwealth Naval Board in 1913. Back row (from left): Staff Paymaster Manisty, RN; Engineer Captain Clarkson, RAN. Front row: Rear Admiral Creswell, RAN; Senator Pearce; Captain Hughes-Onslow, RN.
(RAN)

to as 'the Bible', with any suggestions of modification regarded as almost blasphemous.

The tour

Not surprisingly, there were many matters of difference between Manisty and Hughes-Onslow. Relations had already soured when, in April 1913, Creswell ordered the Second Naval Member to prepare a report on the future of Thursday Island as a fortified naval base. Creswell sent the newly arrived Commander Thring along to familiarise himself with northern Australia, while the Chief of the General Staff, Brigadier General J.M. Gordon, accompanied the two naval men to provide advice on the military aspects. Creswell may have hoped that the break away from Melbourne would help to reduce tensions, but the voyage also provided time for Thring and Hughes-Onslow to consolidate their thoughts.

The tour of Northern Australia reached as far as Darwin, and was an enlightening experience for the three officers. Like the vast majority of

Australians, they were familiar only with the temperate and relatively well-populated south-east of the continent. For the first time, they were confronted with the vastness of the northern environment and the immense distances between coastal ports. No one, they realised, could form any proper idea of the intricacies of the reefs or the emptiness and difficult nature of the interior without having seen it for themselves.[22] 'It would be impossible', Hughes-Onslow continued, 'to produce a strategical report of any value without a visit to the great Northern Territories of the Mainland and Papua'.[23]

The proposed Thursday Island base was part of the Henderson plan, but the touring party soon agreed that the site was inappropriate and that any scheme to defend Australia based on small units scattered around the coast would be hopeless. Deciding that their mission was futile without a general Commonwealth war strategy, they determined to expand the scope of their study. Thereafter they consulted widely with local authorities on matters topographic and hydrographic, and on the personnel and *matériel* resources that existed or might be provided in time of war. Each of the three officers contributed his own expertise to the subsequent discussion, but all agreed that it was Thring who came up with the general idea of an 'advanced line' or 'forward policy' that became the central theme of their strategic plan.

Assumptions

The plan was based on four major assumptions. The first was that Australia faced attack from the north. Previously all naval thoughts and activities had been confined to the south, where hostile raiders might readily plunder the centres of population and commerce. But, as Thring pointed out, Australia's sea frontier ran from Singapore, through Java, Timor, Papua, and the Solomons, to Fiji. As was still echoed by Australia's strategic policy in the latter part of the century, any threat against the nation had to be projected from or through this northern archipelago.[24] Even should New Zealand be the enemy's first objective the threat must still come from the north and Australia would be obliged to respond. Hence, the defence of both Dominions was inseparable.

Still, Australia must always be the enemy's ultimate objective and for geostrategic reasons as much as the value of conquest. The possession by a nation of highly strategic points, Thring argued, was even more provocative than territories sought after for their intrinsic wealth.[25] In his opinion, Australia held the highroad to the Pacific:

> A strong power in Australia . . . can keep that road open, or close it, at will. It could control the sea borne commerce of Asia, the most densely

populated portion of the Globe. A strong sea power in Asia would hold India, the Malay Peninsula, the Islands and China largely in its power.[26]

For Thring, the control of Eastern Asia by an Oriental power appeared a natural event. Japan's expansion had already begun and a descent on Australia's north would provide strategic command of all Asiatic trade and territories. Such a move, Thring believed, made far more sense than the American fear that the Japanese would invade the west coast of the United States. Furthermore, and of vital interest to all Australians, the north of the continent was the key to the defence of the Commonwealth's southern heartland. Should an enemy fleet become established in the north it could stop all Australia's coastal and oceanic trade and extort terms at leisure. This made it unnecessary to conquer the whole of the country and made the enterprise even more attractive to the adversary.

The plan's second assumption was that, notwithstanding its membership of the Empire, the Commonwealth could not afford to rely solely on external help. Like ancient Rome, Britain had withdrawn its legions from distant possessions to defend the Empire's centre. Already preoccupied by the German threat, the Royal Navy was, in Admiral King-Hall's words, 'practically confined to the vicinity of home waters'.[27] To further reduce the risk of interference Japan had only to wait until a European war had begun (as indeed was the case in 1941). Thereafter, even should the 'Armageddon of the North Sea' have been fought and won, it must be some time before the British Fleet would be in a material condition to assist. Hughes-Onslow had spent many hours at the Naval War College and, as he later reminded Creswell, 'in nearly every War Game played . . . where England and Germany are engaged . . . Britain emerges from it terribly crippled, her ships seriously mauled and quite unable to send a large fleet out to the East'.[28]

With no force capable of meeting the Japanese battlefleet on equal terms, the enemy would readily clear the seas of all remaining imperial warships and establish control of Australia's maritime communications. While this control held, there would be no military assistance from England or India and the Japanese could deal with both Australia and New Zealand in detail. Faced with a long and hard campaign to regain the Empire's extremities, Britain might find it more attractive just to accept Japanese control of Australasia.

The plan's third assumption was that existing defence policy was inadequate to meet the Japanese threat. That Australians understood the danger was evidenced by the inception of the RAN and the 1909 Defence Bill, which had introduced compulsory military training. Indeed, by 1911–12 Australia's naval and military estimates amounted to 21 shillings per head of population, some four times greater than only one or two years earlier.[29]

Nevertheless, Thring felt the prevailing plan to mobilise in the south and leave the north defenceless was inviting defeat and humiliation. Equally dangerous was the perception that Australia could be defended by either purely military or naval operations. Again, it was Hughes-Onslow who warned: 'The idea that, in the event of a serious war, there could be any separate strategies for the sister services of the Commonwealth is a phantasm of suicidal tendency'.[30]

However, although Australia's existing defence plans made it practically certain that the Japanese would attempt a descent, this did not mean that the situation was hopeless.[31] The Commonwealth had six or seven years to prepare, and the plan's fourth assumption was that comprehensive preparations would not only save the country from disaster should war occur, but might render that war unlikely.[32] Australia's strategic aim must be to deter an adversary, but this was not provided by a misleading dependence on overseas assistance. Hence, all preparations must maximise self-reliance, invoking the direction of all aspects of national power in a comprehensive strategic policy:

> Such strenuous and vital operations as would be necessary to frustrate the attack of a formidable enemy advancing from the North *would require not only the heartiest co-operation between the whole of the armed forces of the Commonwealth, but every Department of Government*, and the further back that co-operation starts and the more heartily it is entered into the more likely are we to succeed in defeating our prospective enemy [emphasis in original].[33]

From these assumptions Thring, Hughes-Onslow and Gordon developed their alternative maritime strategy. Although it was based on war with Japan—the most powerful of Australia's potential enemies—its authors expected it to hold good in a range of contingencies and no matter whether the ultimate enemy were Germany, France, Holland, the United States or even a revived and reorganised China.[34]

The strategy

They made no acknowledgement, but the ideas put forward by Hughes-Onslow and Thring displayed many similarities with the contemporary work of Sir Julian Corbett, and specifically his maxim that even in maritime operations the defensive was the stronger form of war.[35] Most important, for those who still believe that all Royal Navy officers had an obsession for the decisive fleet action, both Hughes-Onslow and Thring saw that the traditional naval policy of blockade and vigorous offensive had neither sense nor place in the Pacific.[36] By 1920, Japan would possess 27 battleships, together with all their subsidiary forces. Clearly Australia had not the resources to build and man a fleet able to meet Japan on the high seas. Here Corbett seems to have provided the solution, for in his definition maritime strategy 'determined what part the fleet must play in relation to the action of the land forces'.[37] It seems clear that this understanding provided the underlying rationale for the scheme developed by Thring and Hughes-Onslow.

In fact, Corbett's belief that, against invasion, the enemy's army and not his fleet must be the primary defence objective immediately reduced Australia's problem to manageable proportions.[38] Although the whole of the Japanese battlefleet could be brought to bear against the Commonwealth, Japan could only bring as many troops as it could transport at one time, perhaps no more than 80 000 men.[39] In 1913, Australia's military authorities expected to muster as many as 100 000 men for the Commonwealth's defence, and a large proportion of these would be available as a mobile expeditionary force.[40] Hence, the essential aim of any local defence strategy was to concentrate this force at the enemy's landing point. To do this Australia needed to know as much as possible about its likely adversary—to have what today we would term 'the knowledge edge'—and then impose on that adversary Australia's own conditions of warfare.

The plan was later derided by Creswell as the 'Thring Line', and described as 'nearly as futile as building a wall to catch a bird',[41] but Thring was not planning a barrier. His two 'strategic lines' as he called them were for surveillance; flexible tripwires that would alert the Commonwealth's defence forces to take action.[42] Both lines began at Torres Strait, one projecting north-west to Singapore while the other extended east to Fiji, and in peacetime they would be pushed out a further 500 miles beyond. Behind these lines Thring planned a well-organised, layered defence that made use of emerging technology and strategic geography to extract maximum effectiveness from the Commonwealth's relatively small defence forces. Wireless telegraphy (W/T) both ashore and afloat provided the command system that held the scheme together, relaying news of the enemy's advance, while allowing Australia to maintain the initiative. Each layer supported the next, and every commander would be fully aware of, and deeply imbued with, the general ideas. Consequently, when definite instructions or information were lacking a commander would still have an adequate guide to his actions.[43] Mobility was the key and Hughes-Onslow was very clear about training priorities:

> [A]*ll our Naval activities should be pushed to the North with the utmost vigour*, so that our Officers may in peace time be acquainted, as far as

possible, with the amazing intricacies of the reefs and dangers that are so thickly strewn in the waters they would have to navigate in war time [emphasis in original].[44]

The outer layer consisted of a network of coastwatchers equipped with portable W/T sets and positioned adjacent to each of the straits through the northern archipelago. In conjunction with a comprehensive intelligence system, the coastwatchers would give first warning of the enemy's approach. As noted above, a highly mobile land force would provide the last layer but, between these two extremities, maritime operations on, over, and under the sea would ensure that the enemy was kept off balance. The RAN's ships were far too valuable to be thrown away, so the initial naval role was reconnaissance, avoiding action except in favourable circumstances. By tracking and reporting the enemy's movements, cutting up his troop convoy where possible, and forcing him to attack in one of two or three definite spots, the navy could best assist the army to defeat the invader on Australian territory.

How Thring and Hughes-Onslow intended to achieve these results again showed a link with Corbett's understanding that 'command of the sea ... means nothing but the control of maritime communications'.[45] The Japanese might hold command of the sea but, in any future expedition against Australia, their critical vulnerability would continue to be their extended lines of communications. The slow passage of the troop convoys and their reliance on coaling stations made it certain that the enemy would seek to annihilate any naval force established on his flank. Hence, once the enemy's intentions were confirmed the Australian Navy would seek refuge in one of two fortified harbours and thereafter act as a 'Fleet in being'.[46]

Thring envisaged one harbour on each of Australia's strategic lines, with the Torres Strait acting as a gate. This gate would open to allow Australian forces to reinforce one or the other base but, once passage was denied to the enemy, would ensure that he was left only one possible objective. Having found Darwin an unsuitable site for the western base, Thring and Hughes-Onslow determined that the nearby Bynoe Harbour was far better provided. The eastern base, 'Base A', they did not attempt to investigate, but felt it should be situated at the south-east end of Papua. Because Australia's own maritime communications would either be under threat or untenable, both bases would be supported by internal communications. Bynoe Harbour would require a rail link to the Queensland system and 'Base A' a road through to Port Moresby. Desert and jungle respectively would make both supply routes virtually invulnerable.

Force structure

Australia's capability priorities followed naturally once an appropriate strategy had been determined but, even in 1913, no one worked from a blank sheet of paper. The RAN had no need for battleships, as these were both prohibitively expensive and useful only against a battlefleet. However, the soon to arrive 'fleet unit', Thring pointed out, 'formed a very convenient basis on which to build'.[47] The battle cruiser, using its high speed and heavy armament, would push through the enemy's cruiser screen to determine the makeup and direction of the troop convoy. The light cruisers would pass on the news. Destroyer flotillas would concentrate at favourable points and harass the enemy, facilitating the escape of the cruisers during the first phase and thereafter defending the fortified harbours and keeping the enemy's blockading fleet at bay.

Although they were still unproven in war, Thring also intended to make extensive use of two other weapons provided by modern science, and which he felt were 'excellently adapted for defensive warfare'.[48] The first was the submarine, a craft that Corbett likewise felt might become 'a new card which, when skilfully played in combination with defensive fleet operations, may lend fresh importance to the "Fleet in being"'.[49] Since destroyers operated most effectively at night, Thring expected the RAN's submarines to take over their role as torpedo craft during the day, perhaps replacing them completely as submarine capabilities improved and local manufacture began. The second new weapon was the 'water-plane', something that Corbett had yet to incorporate into his views, but which Thring intended to use both as the eyes for the submarines and as another means to attack the enemy's transports. With its units acting together in accordance with the agreed plan, the RAN alone 'would make an attack by Japan an extremely hazardous operation'.[50]

Thring argued that, with only minor augmentation, two fleet units would provide the minimum requisite strength for each advanced base, while the Torres Strait guard force would need a further strong division of at least eight large submarines or destroyers. Using their stealth and extensive local knowledge, the torpedo craft could hide or find refuge at will, making use of short cuts through the reefs to appear where least expected. They would operate as something of a maritime guerrilla force and, by incorporating a tanker and depot ship into the flotilla, could make do without a fixed base.

The two strategic bases on the other hand required full fortifications and garrisons. Thring felt that 'Base A' could be manned by native troops led by European officers, but Bynoe Harbour would rely on the Australian military. This did not, however, mean stationing European troops permanently in the north in adverse climatic conditions. Once established, the rail line would allow the base to be provisioned and garrisoned within a week, which was well within the expected warning time. The mobile expeditionary force would likewise travel by train and, on arrival, would be guided to the enemy landing-site by Aboriginal scouts. Making full and effective use of indigenous skills was vital to Thring's plans and, displaying an attitude well ahead of his time, he continued: 'From the Defence point of view therefore the disappearance of the natives is a matter of serious moment'.[51]

Navy Office discussions

Thring and Hughes-Onslow were back in Melbourne by the end of May 1913 and had their conjoint but separate reports ready for the Naval Board by the first week of July. The reports had a similar foundation, but Thring had concentrated on Australian self-reliance and only briefly noted that if New Zealand joined in the scheme with a base in the Solomons, then it would greatly strengthen his line of defence. Hughes-Onslow, however, viewed the plan as the basis of security for all British interests in the Pacific and Indian Oceans and therefore envisaged a combined force closer in strength and makeup to the original 1909 plan for a Pacific Fleet.

The Second Naval Member faced immediate opposition from Manisty. Work had already begun on the Henderson base in Cockburn Sound and the Naval Secretary saw Thring's plan for advanced bases as a threat to the Henderson scheme in general, and the Western Australian base in particular. In a matter of days Manisty had produced his own paper on an appropriate naval policy. This favoured trading space for time by a concentration of naval forces in the southern half of Australia, which would then become the focal point for a reconquest of the ceded territories. Some 20 fleet units gathered together at Cockburn Sound could, Manisty felt, protect India and dominate the Pacific. Hughes-Onslow was less than happy to have an officer of the accountancy branch dictate strategy and was scathing in his criticism of Manisty's ideas. A specific complaint was that, while Manisty expected to gather non-existent fleets from around the world some time after war had broken out, the Thring plan envisaged a fleet in existence before the outbreak of war and constantly prepared to take action.[52]

The Naval Board met to consider the competing plans on 17 July 1913. Not surprisingly no definite strategy emerged from the discussions, but the members did manage to reach an understanding on several aspects. They agreed that the threat must come from the north and considered that 1921 and the end of the Anglo–Japanese Alliance would be the beginning of the danger period for Australia. They also agreed that the participants in any scheme of Pacific defence should include all British dependencies in the eastern hemisphere, Canada and South Africa. This, they hoped, would allow a permanent combined fleet at least 70 per cent of the strength of the strongest potential enemy. They left for later consideration the position of appropriate bases, but the minutes noted that those necessary for the effective working of the fleet 'should be provided', with the cost divided between the participants.[53] As a practical step the Naval Board endorsed the idea of discussion of all these issues at the next Imperial Conference. However, the cable eventually sent by the Governor-General to the Secretary of State for the Colonies made no mention of the board's thinking. Rather, it merely indicated that the Commonwealth wished to discuss questions arising out of the 1909 Conference and naval policy generally.[54] Unfortunately, the next Imperial Conference was deferred, first until 1914 and then until war's end, by which time Australian and imperial circumstances were vastly different.

Meanwhile, Hughes-Onslow chafed at the delay and, together with Clarkson, the Third Naval Member, decried the board's lack of energy and determination to lead. The strong criticism stung Creswell and a series of increasingly angry minutes passed around Navy Office either finding fault with or defending the various plans. Creswell eventually conceded that the Thring plan was a sane and practicable possibility for the future, but he saw it only as an extension of the Henderson scheme, believing that to try to hold the Thring line with only the forces proposed was out of the question. Creswell found the costs particularly frightening. The RAN's works budget was only £180 000 in 1913 and he estimated that the two proposed bases would cost at least £6 million to establish plus annual maintenance costs of not less than half a million pounds. Creswell maintained that Australia's greatest danger continued to be cruiser attacks on commerce in southern waters and that, even should the Japanese attempt a major invasion in the north, their preponderance would allow them to easily envelop and contain the RAN. The inevitable result would be the loss of the Thring bases and most of the fleet, while the vital parts of the Commonwealth would still be open to attack.[55]

The claims and counter-claims continued into September 1913 and, before any more could be achieved, the developing crisis between Creswell and Manisty on the one side and Hughes-Onslow and Clarkson on the other reached boiling point. Several observers had noticed that the Second Naval Member was becoming increasingly erratic and excitable and, with the board's members no longer on speaking terms, the Defence Minister was forced to step in.[56] In late October Hughes-Onslow was relieved of his duties and, on 19 November, dismissed from the board. Manisty's victory was shortlived, for he followed Hughes-Onslow out of Australian service within months.

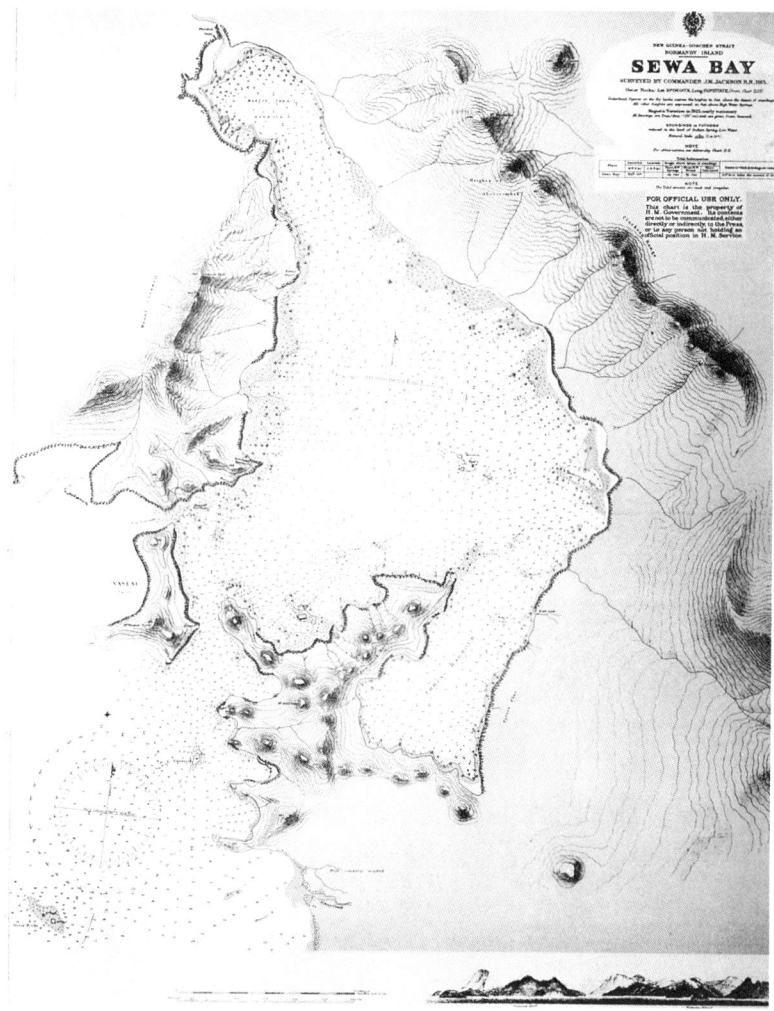

Sewa Bay with Thring Harbour in the lower right portion. (United Kingdom Hydrographic Office)

This was not, however, the end of the Thring plan. The commander published a modified version in the Royal Navy's professional journal, the *Naval Review*, in 1914, and he continued to develop his ideas during the war while working as Creswell's Director of War Staff.[57] These later versions of the plan maintained Hughes-Onslow's emphasis on a regional approach to Pacific defence, but also Thring's reliance on forward basing.

Consequently, when Lord Jellicoe arrived in 1919 to review Australia's naval defence he did not have to develop his Pacific plans from scratch. Most interesting, perhaps, was Jellicoe's intention to establish two major fleet bases in Bynoe Harbour and Papua.[58] The site for the latter was Sewa Bay on Normanby Island, which had been surveyed in 1915 at the direction of the ACNB. The officer conducting the survey, Commander J.M. Jackson, RN, had evidently been well briefed on the task, and the protocol to be used when naming features. The bay was overlooked by Mount Creswell in the west, and Clarkson Range in the east and scattered around were the names of various other Australian naval personalities. Noticeably absent were the names of Hughes-Onslow and Manisty, but the key feature, the site of the submarine jetty, aerodrome and naval base itself, was Thring Harbour.[59]

Conclusion

There is no question that Australia's enormous size, isolation, small population and limited financial resources have convinced many people that the nation's security cannot be accomplished without the close co-operation of major allies. That this reliance has inhibited the development of independent strategic thought seems to have been taken for granted. This is not the whole story, however, and the work of Thring and Hughes-Onslow illustrates that, even in 1913, Australian strategic planning was far more complex than a simple subservience to imperial defence.

There were clearly flaws in the Thring–Hughes-Onslow plan for advanced fortified bases. To modern eyes the Japanese development of a sophisticated fleet air arm in the following decades is perhaps the most obvious. Nevertheless, in 1913 the case studies available in Melbourne were not Taranto, Pearl Harbor and Darwin, but the long and difficult Japanese siege of Port Arthur.[60] The Thring plan must therefore be judged in the context of its times. Without doubt, raising the necessary funds, ordering the additional ships and providing the extra crews would have posed substantial, probably unassailable, difficulties. But any failings should not detract from the scheme's place as the first attempt by local planners to examine comprehensively the potential wartime functions of an independent Australian navy and that service's relationship to other aspects of national power. Moreover, in view of the enduring imperatives of Australian strategic planning, we should not be surprised that many of its features echo those enunciated in recent strategic policy guidance. The combination of deterrence and decisive response continues to underpin Australian security planning, while the use of high technology to provide a capability enhancement, the interdiction of shipping in Australia's maritime approaches by sub-surface, surface and air assets and, of course, the final reliance placed on troops on the ground still maintain their contemporary relevance.

16 Divergent paths: problems of command and strategy in Anglo–Australasian naval operations in the Asia–Pacific (August–November 1914)
Geoffrey McGinley

The exercise of maritime power against the German forces in the Asia–Pacific region during 1914 was a major aspect of British strategy in the opening months of World War I.[1] The Naval Staff Monograph states that 'the German East Asiatic Squadron exercised an influence in the first months of the war only second to that of the High Sea Fleet'.[2] Indeed the repercussions of Admiral Craddock's defeat at Coronel, the Royal Navy's first in a hundred years, were felt all the way back to the Grand Fleet's operations area in the North Sea. This chapter will investigate those long months before Coronel from August to November 1914 and consider exactly what importance was placed upon hunting down the German East Asiatic Squadron, and how the hunt fitted into wider Anglo–Australian strategy.

A navy ready for war?

The Australian Navy which went to war in 1914 was a modern and powerful, albeit small, blue-water force. It represented the choice made at the 1909 Imperial Conference between the alternatives of a small navy for local defence of Australian cities and ports (proposed by Rear Admiral William Creswell) and the blue-water force favoured by the Royal Navy.

Unlike the new Australian Fleet, which was superior to the German Pacific Squadron in all aspects, the British force on the China Station, under the command of Vice Admiral T. Jerram, had been drastically reduced from the level promised in the agreement of 1909 and was barely the Germans' equivalent. Besides the outdated battleship *Triumph*, it was centred on the two middle-aged armoured cruisers *Minotaur* and *Hampshire* and the two new light cruisers *Newcastle* and *Yarmouth*. The German East Asiatic Squadron, commanded by Vice Admiral Count Maximilian von Spee, was composed of the armoured cruisers *Scharnhorst* and *Gneisenau*. At the outbreak of war, the light cruisers *Emden* and *Nürnberg* were in the western Pacific, while *Leipzig* was to operate off the west coast of America.

British strategic plans for the region were based on broad generalisations about seeking out and engaging the enemy, and showed a fundamental misunderstanding of the Pacific. In particular the position of the Germans and their strategic options were poorly understood. The British expected the Germans to operate off northern China from their base at Tsingtao, or perhaps from the Dutch East Indies in alliance with (or tacit compliance of) the Netherlands.[3] Accordingly, the war plans called for a concentration in northern Chinese waters to allow 'a prompt attack upon the enemy's ships'.[4] In contrast, German naval plans envisioned a sea-denial strategy. The East Asiatic Squadron would act as a raiding force, abandoning its base at Tsingtao and using concealed anchorages and afloat logistic support to avoid superior British forces and threaten trade in the entirety of the Indian and Pacific Oceans.[5] With British war plans avoiding any satisfactory consideration of hunting down the Germans, of the role of the Japanese Navy, of the need to concentrate imperial troops in Europe, or of the importance of the German Pacific possessions, the outbreak of war would see British strategists having to adapt to unforeseen circumstances.

The Admiralty war orders for the RAN saw division of the available forces with the flagship *Australia* slated to join the China Squadron while the modern light cruisers *Sydney* and *Melbourne* and the older *Encounter* would provide defence of Australasian waters.[6] The ACNB, however, recognised what should have been obvious, that these orders would only be effective 'against Germany when the German ships are in the north of China'. The board felt it essential that any armoured enemy ships in Australasian waters be brought to action before the battle cruiser left the station. Modified war orders along these lines were finally issued by the Admiralty three months before the outbreak of war.[7]

Although the ACNB had identified the risk of leaving Australia undefended, it neither provided nor sought from the Admiralty detailed operational plans. It was never specified exactly how *Australia* would bring the enemy armoured ships to action, how it would be decided that enemy ships were in Australasian waters, or indeed where the boundaries of Australian waters lay. Most significantly, it was never explained *who* would decide whether *Australia* was to defend northern Australian waters or join the China Squadron.

Such confusion was to typify the naval command arrangements in 1914. The war orders stated that the ACNB was to be 'in relation to the Admiralty, in the same position as a Commander in Chief on Shore and the Australian seagoing fleet in the same position as a squadron of the Royal Navy'.[8] This statement appears to imply that the ACNB would act as the operational commander under the Admiralty for the Australia Station and all British and Dominion ships on it. Yet this made the Australian Minister for Defence, chairman of the Naval Board, the de facto CinC Australia Station, responsible for implementing British political and military decisions while still being responsible to the Australian Government. The situation was further confused when the Admiralty claimed for itself the ability to pass orders directly to Rear Admiral Sir G.E. Patey, Rear Admiral Commanding the Australian Fleet (RAC) and to the commanding officers of individual ships.[9] Additionally any co-ordination between Patey and the ACNB would be most delicate as Rear Admiral Creswell, the professional head of the board, was junior to his subordinate Patey. As opposed to Jose's claim in the official history, personal tact and imperial enthusiasm would not be sufficient to remedy these failings in the command structure of British maritime power in the Pacific.[10]

Opening movements

The opening movements of British and Australian forces in the Pacific were confused and unco-ordinated. Initial reactions in Australia during the last days of July were hampered by distance from Britain and the slow passage of information via the Secretary of State for the Colonies and the Governor-General. Working on the assumption that there were no enemy warships in regional waters the Defence Minister, Senator Edward Millen, was prepared to dispatch *Australia* to China via Albany consistent with the war orders. But he specifically kept her under Australian orders at this stage.[11] On 2 August the Naval Intelligence Branch, on the basis of intercepted W/T messages and a sighting from a small steamer, reported that *Scharnhorst*, at least, was off New Guinea.[12] The ACNB had little idea how to react to this apparent direct threat to Australian security, and contacted Patey for advice as to whether to inform the Admiralty and as to their strategic options.[13]

Patey's response demonstrated a strong sense of independence from the Admiralty. Aboard his flagship, which was preparing for war at

The German East Asiatic Squadron off the coast of Chile in 1914. The photograph was taken from SMS *Dresden* several weeks after the Battle of Coronel. Next ahead is *Nürnberg*, then *Leipzig*, *Gneisenau* and *Scharnhorst*.
(AWM: H15963)

Sydney, he initially discounted the intelligence. Possibly as a result of discussions with Millen and Creswell, however, he advised on the morning of 3 August that *Australia* should remain on the Australia Station. He believed this fundamental change to British strategy was necessary, not for local defence of Australian or regional waters, nor of the exposed light cruisers of the Australian Navy, but owing to the risk of leaving the antiquated New Zealand 'P' class cruisers isolated. His intention was to concentrate the fleet off Thursday Island, with the option of sending *Australia* onwards to China if the threat subsided. Patey made clear that this was an Australian decision, and recommended 'informing' the Admiralty and other station commanders rather than requesting permission or consulting with them.[14] The ACNB, however, sought Admiralty approval. On the night of 4 August this approval was still many hours away and they acted on their own authority to ensure that Australasian waters were not left vulnerable.[15]

During the early days of August the Admiralty was busy with mobilising the Grand Fleet and preparing for possible battle in the North Sea. This minimised consideration of Pacific issues. Their only significant regional action was to order the China Squadron to Hong Kong, away from its planned concentration off Tsingtao. The logic behind this has never been explained. Its effect, however, was to render the main tenet of British strategy for the Pacific—engaging the enemy off Tsingtao, his supposed centre of gravity—abandoned in the critical opening stages of the war. As a direct result, *Emden*, twelve colliers and other supply ships were guaranteed an easy escape into the Pacific.[16]

There is no record in the Admiralty papers of relevant intelligence summaries or consideration of the possibility that the German Squadron was not at Tsingtao. The only consideration of Pacific affairs was on 2 August after New Zealand, in an unexpected gesture of imperial loyalty, made the provisional offer to Britain of a small expeditionary force.[17] The Director of the Operations Division (DOD), Rear Admiral Arthur Leveson, suggested that such a force could indeed serve a 'useful purpose if sent to capture Samoa'. He argued that this would deprive Germany of a harbour and W/T station and thus 'serve to protect trade in the South Pacific'.[18] The Chief of the War Staff (COS), Vice Admiral Sturdee, agreed that this was indeed 'a quite feasible operation'. He believed 'the knowledge that they are ready may disturb policy and deflect cruisers from interfering with our trade'.[19]

The logic behind this projected mission was, however, questionable. Samoa was of limited strategic value, particularly in the language of decisive naval battle, when hunting for heavy German ships off northern China. Nor was it a particularly valuable base for the Germans when compared to any number of unsettled Pacific islands. Samoa lacked significant coal and food stockpiles, had only minimal repair or port facilities, and was a climatically dangerous and unprotected harbour from January to March. Its only other possible significance was as a W/T station. Indeed such a mission had been discounted in pre-war strategic planning.[20] Sturdee's initial enthusiasm for the mission seemed rather to lie in providing some use for the isolated naval and military forces in New Zealand and in encouraging the 'imperial ideal'.[21] That Sturdee was more enthused by the possibility of simply involving the New Zealand forces than by intrinsic naval priorities is apparent in the failure to consider other more flexible and efficient options. These might include bombardment[22] or raids to destroy the W/T stations and stores. In this sense, the 'imperial idea' served as an obstacle to strategic thought.

The decision to occupy all the German colonial possessions

British strategic planing diverged even further from dominion concerns on 5 August. On that day Captain Herbert Richmond, Assistant DOD, recorded in his diary that Winston Churchill, the First Lord of the Admiralty, had said, 'Now we have our war. The next thing to do is to decide how we shall carry it out.' To Richmond this was a shocking confession of the utter lack of war preparations by the Admiralty. He suggested that expeditions be sent immediately against the German colonial possessions. This would remove their bases of supply and communication, and act as a first step in a campaign of colonial occupation. Richmond felt this was 'largely a colonial war' and that such action would hasten victory. On the same day Richmond submitted a detailed minute to the First Sea Lord, Prince Louis of Battenberg, outlining his ideas.[23] Captain Hankey, Secretary of the Committee of Imperial Defence, also requested and received permission from the Prime Minister to establish a Joint Naval and Military Committee to consider expeditions against all German colonies.

This subcommittee met immediately and, with the objective of removing enemy W/T and cable communications, recommended to Cabinet that Yap and German New Guinea should be occupied by Australia, and Samoa and Nauru by New Zealand. Other British missions should be dispatched to the German possessions in Africa. The subcommittee's recommendations, however, are astonishing in their brevity and simplicity. It had been tasked with submitting to Cabinet a list of 'expeditions which might have a definite effect on the ... war' and then, once they were approved, with working out details.[24] The submission was obviously rushed, but their instructions left no scope to consider in depth the current military and naval strategic situation, especially the implications of the recently received Australian intelligence on the German armoured cruisers. Additionally, the major justification of the expeditions, the removing of communication facilities, suggests that no consideration was given to the wider strategic logic of the expeditions or other possible means of achieving the objectives.[25] The confusion of aims is further evident in the Cabinet's response, which Churchill described as being predicated on the need to remove bases for the German cruisers and to provide diplomatic 'hostages for the ... eventual liberation of Belgium'.[26]

The chairman of the subcommittee, Admiral Jackson, began planning for the missions on 7 August. Yet Jackson's justification for them reflects no continuity in decision-making. It was rather a loose synthesis of earlier discussions on the value of certain Pacific islands. Samoa was now to be occupied 'to prevent it being used as a base of operations by the armed [not the larger armoured] German ships against our trade or as a centre of W/T communication in the Pacific'. The expedition to Rabaul was aimed at removing the W/T station there and providing a base for occupation of wider German New Guinea, Nauru and Yap.[27]

Jackson believed that the light cruiser forces in local waters would be sufficient against the threat of armed merchant cruisers. He made no explicit mention of the movements of *Australia* or of local concerns about

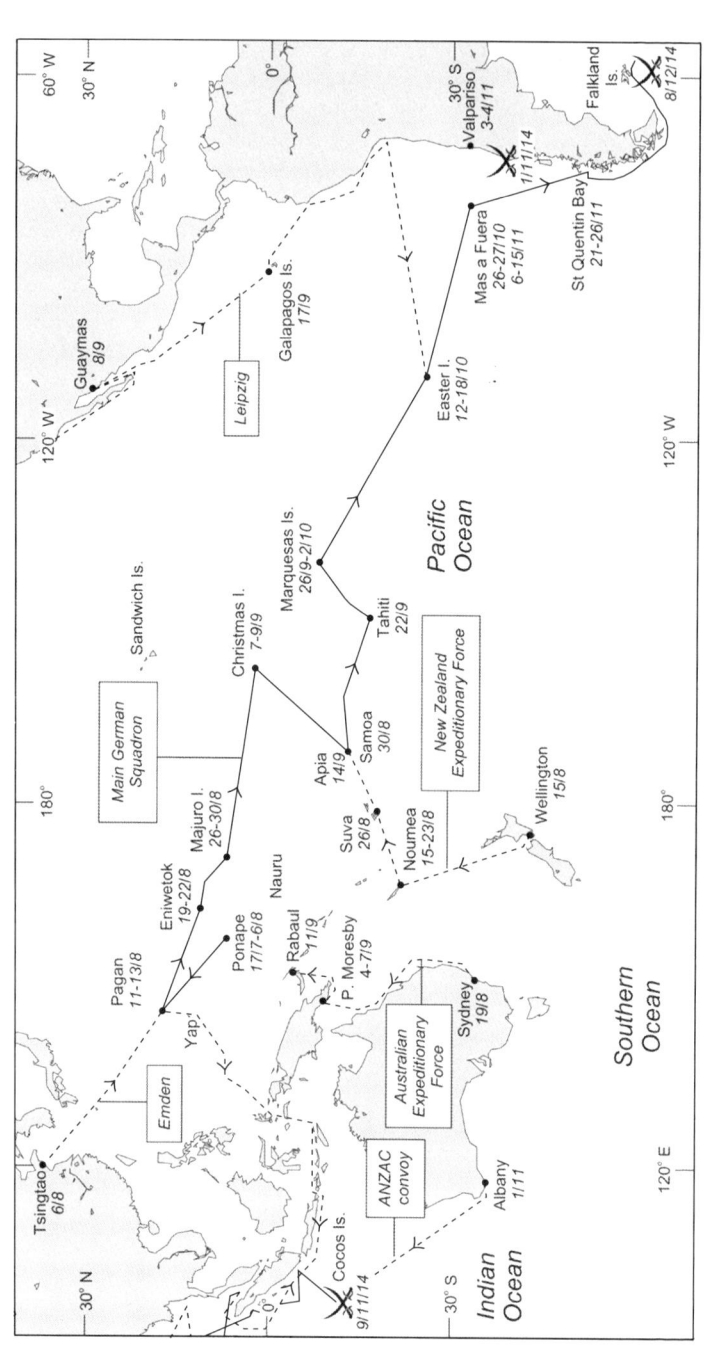

Map 16.1 The movements of the German East Asiatic Squadron, July–December 1914

regional security. Jackson assumed that the German East Asiatic Squadron was probably off north China and soon to be 'accounted for'. He did, however, make the qualification that 'the departure of this [New Zealand] expedition must be governed by the naval situation in the Pacific'.[28] The orders for *Australia*, as developed by the ACNB, remained unquestioned and the only Admiralty gloss was simply to 'get . . . in touch with German ships'.[29] The significance of *Australia*'s orders, and the impact they had on the requisite level of escort for the expeditions, was entirely missed.

Dominion reactions

New Zealand was strongly committed to the overseas expeditions, with its parliament ratifying the offer of troops within an hour of the declaration of war. A force of 1413 men was ready to depart four days later.[30] Jackson concluded, in response to New Zealand concerns over the safety of the expedition, that it faced minimal danger. He proposed that the escort of the light cruisers of the New Zealand station would be sufficient.[31] Sturdee concurred, and went on to say that the Australian and China squadrons were 'covering the *Gneisenau* and *Scharnhorst*'.[32] We may wonder about the exact nature of the protection Sturdee believed could be provided by Patey from a distance of 2000–2500 miles. Clearly the Admiralty failed to comprehend the Australian reports on the location of the Germans or the distances involved. A telegram was therefore sent from the Admiralty to Jerram and Patey on 9 August explaining that, in two days, an expedition would sail from New Zealand for Samoa and that they were to guard against interference.[33]

The British also asked the Australian Government on 6 August if it were prepared to seize the W/T stations at Rabaul in German New Guinea, Yap in the Marshall Islands, and Nauru. With German forces apparently so close, Australia was understandably cautious. Millen supported the idea in principle but felt it was 'manifestly undesirable to divert any of the warships from their present mission for the purpose indicated'.[34] But what was the 'purpose indicated' as understood by Australia? The request of 6 August spoke of the expedition's objective simply as the removal of enemy W/T stations. Yet the telegram continued by stating that all territories 'at the conclusion of war [will] be at the disposal of imperial Government for purposes of an ultimate settlement'.[35] This seemed to imply a further diplomatic goal. This telegram gave no reason to divert the fleet from searching for Spee, nor did it even recognise that this might be necessary. Britain's failure to convince Australia is evident not only in Millen's reluctance, but in Patey's comment to the ACNB that the 'W/T stations must be neglected for the present'.[36]

The Australian authorities, however, proved unable to provide a credible alternative or convincing argument against the large and cumbersome expedition. Millen requested that the ACNB consider sending it in an armed merchantman, without fleet escort.[37] The board's response was negative, stating that a force of 500 men would be available to seize Rabaul if 'supported by the fleet'. To confirm that the local defences had not been increased would require a further fleet reconnaissance. The board concluded that 'a ship armed with 4.7" guns would be equal to the actual task of seizing the W/T station without Fleet support'.[38] The minister would have been best advised listening to Commander Thring, who stated 'that the armed merchantman could carry out the purpose indicated as soon as the more powerful cruisers of the enemy are accounted for'.[39]

Despite Millen's total lack of support for the mission, no effort was made to explain Australia's position to Britain. Instead, on 10 August, the Governor-General sent notice that a force of 1500 troops was being raised.[40] In this first example of the ACNB working under the Admiralty, one thing is clear: the Australian authorities were reluctant to question the Admiralty's judgement, notwithstanding grounds for concern. As opposed to the independence of thought and action shown in deploying *Australia* northward, during the previous week, the Admiralty's influence then served to stifle dominion initiative and independent action.

Fleet movements

Patey had deployed northwards in *Australia*, and met *Sydney* and the destroyers before raiding the harbour at Rabaul on 11 and 12 August. He found neither German ships nor a W/T station. After a survey of the surrounding waters, the squadron withdrew to Rossel Lagoon and Port Moresby, with 'the ships being very short of coal and oil' arriving a few days later.[41]

Despite failing to engage the Germans, the initial movements of the Australian fleet were far from wasted. Patey had not held high hopes for the raid on Rabaul and hoped that at best it might act as a lure and draw in the German heavy ships on the following morning. He knew that the range of his ships and the 'immense distance[s]' implied by operations in the Pacific made 'the problem of keeping the ships supplied with coal and oil . . . a *most* difficult one' [emphasis in original]. His operational flexibility was thus restricted to the single raid on Rabaul.[42] Despite these difficulties Patey was able to conclude that the enemy warships had probably retreated northward or eastward, possibly towards Nauru, with the object of taking on coal, then probably proceeding towards South America, perhaps calling at Samoa on the way.[43]

Patey was partially correct, the Germans were indeed heading for South America, and would call at Samoa. But, possibly due to inexperience, Australian naval intelligence had mistaken the Germans' position. They had actually started the war at Ponape, 1500 nautical miles to the north of their reported position, before joining *Emden* and the supply ships which had escaped from Tsingtao. Spee was unable to stay off the Chinese coast owing to Japanese threats to join the war, while the co-operation of the Dutch to the south seemed too uncertain, so the squadron sailed on 13 August, heading eastward through the Marshall Islands towards South America, while *Emden* was dispatched with one collier to the Indian Ocean.

While the Australian Squadron raided Rabaul and the Admiralty prepared plans to occupy the German territories, the China Squadron had, after concentrating at Hong Kong, proceeded to Yap in hope of finding the German Squadron there. Jerram, finding nothing, bombarded and destroyed the German W/T station. Although aware of the Australian intelligence suggesting the location of the German Squadron, he was only prepared to leave northern Chinese waters on learning that Japan would declare war on 12 August and thus accept responsibility for this area.[44]

Thus far the failure of pre-war planning had meant that operations in the Pacific lacked co-ordination, with the Australian and British responses to circumstances travelling down divergent paths. The Australians, wanting to ensure regional security against the German armoured cruisers, had no idea how to achieve it. Britain wanted command of the sea in the Pacific after achieving diplomatic objectives. The Admiralty did not grasp the significance of deploying *Australia* northward, and failed to contact the operational commanders as to the viability and value of the expeditions. With the haphazard decision-making process in London, this meant that the place of the expeditions in wider Pacific strategy was never really understood or communicated, either in Britain or abroad. This did not bode well for future operations.

Opportunity or mistake? The Samoan expedition

This lack of co-ordination would have its first impact on ship movements in mid-August. On the evening of 12 August Patey received a commendable if somewhat unusual telegram from the Senior Naval Officer New Zealand. It was outside any established chain of command, having been sent on behalf of the Governor forwarding a question from the New Zealand Government. Patey was asked whether he considered it safe for the expedition to leave for Samoa, and the 'earliest possible information when you can account for large German Cruisers, as New Zealand Government are informed you have received direction from the Admiralty to cover expedition'.[45] New Zealand also wished to know, in the event that other ships were not available, whether *Australia* could act as escort. This was the first Patey had heard of such an expedition. Not surprisingly, he replied that it should not proceed 'without strong escort' and that the Senior Naval Officer New Zealand should get in touch with the Naval Board.[46]

With no external guidance beyond the second-hand New Zealand interpretation, Patey decided on his own authority to escort the expedition. He trusted that this was the Admiralty's wish, and also felt that this was a chance to bring the enemy ships to action. On the evening of 13 August, Patey contacted the Naval Board requesting approval to escort the Samoan expedition with *Australia*, *Sydney* and *Melbourne*.[47]

This decision remains one of the most controversial of the campaign. Lieutenant (later Commander) W.H.F. Warren, DSO, RAN, commanding officer of *Parramatta*, thought that the squadron's 'first & most important duty to destroy the German fleet was put subservient to the occupying of islands with troops'. Warren also felt that if 'we had had a fast collier with us [and] proceeded at once to the Marshall [and] Caroline Islands, there is no doubt that we would have run [the enemy] to earth'.[48] To his mind the squadron was being distracted from its primary task at a critical juncture.

Historians have stated their views on Patey's decision. The Naval Staff Monograph claims that both 'the Admiralty and Admiral Patey agreed that the *Australia* should be diverted from her task of searching for the enemy' so as to be available to escort the Samoan expedition. In this version, both Jerram and Patey thought it pointless 'to proceed into the spaces of the Pacific in order to look for an unlocated enemy'.[49] Jose, by contrast, argues in the Australian official history that Patey deployed with the aim of being in a position to bring Spee to action on his way east to South America, and had no intention of returning for the German New Guinea expedition.[50] Corbett, in the British official history, claims unconvincingly that the Admiralty feared Patey might be distracted 'from the paramount duty of seeking out the enemy's ships and dealing with their centres of intelligence'.[51] These conflicting accounts need to be reconciled, and this will highlight key aspects of the operations in the Pacific.

There was a definite possibility of meeting the *Scharnhorst* and *Gneisenau* at the Marshall Islands as they passed through between 26 and 30 August en route to South America. Although an approximation is difficult, if Patey had gone north, leaving Port Moresby on 17 August, travelling via Nauru (a distance of 2200 nm) to destroy the W/T station as required by the Admiralty at the standard 12 knots, calculations would place him arriving at Jaluit on or about 26 August. Yet while this would put the Australian Fleet (Patey would probably have sailed with *Australia*, *Sydney* and *Melbourne*) in the vicinity of the enemy, Patey would still have had to pinpoint the German ships and force them to action. Short-range W/T intercepts might give some indication of the ships' position, especially since the German Squadron included various cumbersome and unwieldy supply ships. Attention to the limited number of focal points such as harbours, population centres and W/T stations might also have assisted Patey. While Spee's orders were only to engage 'equal or inferior forces', a process made easier by the 'reckless and constant' use of W/T by the British ships, his later actions, both at Samoa and off South America, indicate his willingness to fight.[52] Once contact had been achieved, Spee would have found it difficult to outrun the faster and longer-ranged *Australia* and faced probable defeat.

As opposed to the feasibility of a patrol to the north, logistics would have greatly limited Patey's operational flexibility. The theoretical cruising range of *Australia* was about 6300 nm and that of the light cruisers 4500 nm. The round trip to Jaluit from German New Guinea would have used two-thirds of the light cruisers' fuel, leaving a margin of 1500 nm at cruising speed for scouting operations, or a mere 400 nm at 22 knots. *Australia*, with her relatively larger fuel bunkers and efficiency at higher speed, did not have these limitations. Even so, for Patey to avoid being stranded to the north, he would have needed a rendezvous with a collier after, and preferably before, battle. Yet the RAN, despite desperate calls for a collier before the war, remained dependent on slow merchant colliers, the availability of which was still haphazard.[53] Moreover, to include a collier with a speed of about 10 knots into the squadron reduced its speed, while the use of prearranged rendezvous left fuel supplies vulnerable to the lightest of enemy ships, while simultaneously restricting Patey's flexibility.

The squadron, however, had an even greater constraint on its battle effectiveness and range—the quality of its coal. Despite Patey's previously expressed concerns, the squadron was forced to use the poor quality southern (Australian) coal as opposed to the higher grade Westport coal from New Zealand. This drastically reduced the actual range and speed of the ships from the theoretical figures already given. Calculations from the ships' log books place *Australia*'s actual range in these conditions at about 4500 nm, while that of the light cruisers was a dismal 3000 nm.[54] A one-way deployment from German New Guinea would use half the available fuel, while one from Rossel Lagoon would use two-thirds. This suggests that coaling would be required before seeking out the Germans. *Australia*'s ability to force battle thanks to her greater design speed would be in jeopardy, given that the German cruisers had quality coal.

The issue of why Patey proposed to support the expedition to Samoa has long needed re-examination. It was far from pointless for Patey to deploy into the Pacific. Although there were undeniable difficulties, his decision to head for Samoa is only partly attributable to them. Escorting the expedition meant that the Australian Squadron was moving towards, rather than away from, the quality Westport coal, thus potentially solving its logistic difficulty. Also, in the light of the limited intelligence available, it seemed to offer a reasonable chance of finding the Germans. Upon reading a draft of Jose's official history, Patey declared that his primary intention in going east was in the hope that

> I might have had an opportunity of bringing Admiral von Spee to action, as I felt sure he would be in the vicinity, and I thought that, once I had got so far to the east, I might have been left free to deal with the German Squadron in my own way.[55]

It seems unlikely that such a movement eastward was Patey's first preference, with a patrol to the northward offering—then and in retrospect—significant potential for success. Instead it was the combination of poor logistical arrangements and confusion within the command structure which resulted in his deciding to escort the Samoan expedition. What is apparent is that while operational command of the Australian Squadron remained Patey's responsibility, he could react to changing circumstances in quick order.

Churchill's navy: London takes charge

On 12 August, the Admiralty, under strong diplomatic pressure from New Zealand, decided independently of Patey and for entirely different reasons that the admiral should escort the Samoan expedition. As Patey complained to Creswell, however, 'the Admiralty made a mistake in trying to run the New Zealand expedition without consulting me'.[56] The timings provided were unrealistic, no consideration was made of his fuel state, and the escort proposed for the Australian expedition was far too light. Furthermore, the Admiralty was to prove unable or unwilling to consider local modifications of their plan. They would not postpone the New Zealand expedition by three days as proposed by the ACNB to allow the Australian expedition to Rabaul, which was now ready for departure, to proceed first under the escort of *Australia*.[57] This poor co-ordination meant that when Patey had escorted the Samoan expedition, he would have either to abandon his plan to operate off Samoa and spend a further two weeks retracing his steps to escort the Rabaul expedition, or allow the Australian troops to proceed with an unacceptably light escort.

This episode is symptomatic of a larger problem of British naval command in 1914, when the operational level of warfare became entangled with the strategic and largely ceased to exist. The information revolution of the early 1900s (long-range W/T combined with older cable links) meant that communications between Britain and ships in the Pacific was now possible within hours. This did little, however, to clear the fog of war or allow for co-ordination on diplomatic, strategic and operational issues. Instead it allowed the Admiralty to assume the role of the operational commander, with the task of Patey becoming little more than that of tactical leadership by a senior naval officer afloat. It has been argued that such reliance on signalling is both cause and evidence of doctrinal deficiencies while being destructive of initiative and independent action and thought.[58] Patey, faced with detailed instructions from the Admiralty, was continually unwilling to question these orders, their underlying (normally tacit) priorities, or to express his own opinion.

The failures in command and control arrangements for the Pacific were evident within the Admiralty itself. Churchill would regularly interfere with operational orders which at the very least were the task of Battenberg and his staff, if not the local commanders. Not only did this create confusion; it limited the time available for top-level strategic discourse and consideration. As John Hattendorf has written, the lack of proper staff procedures confused the situation for subordinates, who complained that they were unsure of their priorities and of whether they were correctly interpreting what was wanted. Battenberg, for example, a man unfairly dubbed 'I Concur', was forced to acquiesce in Churchill's Pacific strategy while having little understanding of its nature.[59]

On 20 August Churchill, as part of a wider plan to expedite the military concentration in Europe, had outlined the priorities for the Indian and Pacific Oceans. These were first the escort of the Australian and New Zealand forces to Europe, second the escort of the Pacific expeditionary forces, and finally the hunt for Spee.[60] Three days later, however, Battenberg order Jerram to proceed with 'the destruction of the *Scharnhorst* and *Gneisenau*' as his and Patey's task of 'the first importance'.[61] The Naval Staff Monograph implies that this demonstrates a focus on the German armoured cruisers.[62] In fact Churchill intervened, demanding instead that the China Squadron relieve the Australian ships scheduled to escort the New Guinea expedition, so that they might be available to escort the ANZAC convoy as soon as possible. He saw this as an object so 'important that nothing except [the] *certain* prospect of fighting enemy ships should delay it'.[63]

Local commanders in the Pacific, not being informed of Churchill's strategic priorities, and confused by Battenberg's invocation to seek out the enemy, continued to think of their first priority in terms of destroying the enemy fleet.[64] Jerram responded to Battenberg's instructions by recommending a patrol of the Dutch East Indies by the China Squadron. He thought that there was no need for extra forces to the north of Australia, and that his first priority should be to counter the possibility of the Germans being on the trade route. Although he never felt able to tell the Admiralty, he saw little relevance in the expeditions to Samoa and German New Guinea, or in defending northern Australia. He did, however, propose that, to guard against the Germans making for America, the Australian Fleet examine the Marshall Islands after the Samoan expedition (due for completion in the first days of September).[65]

Battenberg and Churchill agreed that the China Squadron should clear the Dutch East Indies, so that no attack on the troop transports could be made from there. Possibly smarting from his recent chastisement by Churchill, Battenberg did not consider altering (as suggested by Jerram) the orders issued on 20 August—for *Australia* and *Melbourne* to return from Samoa to escort the expeditions to occupy Rabaul, Anguar, Nauru and Yap.[66] Patey was still unconvinced of the value of these expeditions, and in his private correspondence observed that the Germans were 'amongst some of the more distant Pacific islands or they may be on their way across to America'.[67] But he made no suggestion of deferring these tasks in favour of a more active hunting for the Germans. One may assume that Patey, regardless of his own opinion, simply felt unable to question or advise on the strategic direction provided by the Admiralty.

Australia and *Melbourne* eventually sailed from New Guinea on 17 August and met the New Zealand force, including its light escort of three 'P' class cruisers, at Noumea. Samoa surrendered without a fight on 30 August with no sign of a German vessel. After landing the troops and supplies and standing out to sea overnight, the force dispersed the next day. *Australia* returned to escort the New Guinea expedition, while *Melbourne* headed for Nauru to destroy the W/T station there. Meanwhile *Sydney*, the destroyers and the submarines *AE1* and *AE2* had been escorting the 1500-strong Australian Expeditionary Force (AEF) embarked in *Berrima* northwards from Sydney.

The imperial framework: the ANZAC convoy and the dominion concerns

Admiralty efforts to ensure the safe transport of the Australian and New Zealand troops were to dominate British dispositions in the Indian and Pacific Oceans from September 1914 onwards. As early as 2 September it had been brought to the attention of Churchill, Sturdee and Jackson that if the Germans were not accounted for in Eastern waters by mid-September, it would be necessary to detach some of the China Squadron as escort from Fremantle to Colombo.[68] The following day Patey was instructed to detach *Sydney* and *Melbourne* to escort the convoy departing Sydney on 22 September. This

The submarine *AE1*, the destroyer *Yarra* and the battle cruiser *Australia* during the operations to capture German New Guinea in 1914. *AE1* went missing in the area shortly afterwards. (RAN)

message was not, however, received until 9 September, and before the ships could be detached German New Guinea had to be occupied. The occupying force rendezvoused with *Australia* on 9 September before landing troops at Rabaul two days later, with the German Governor surrendering the territory on 15 September. Concerns for the troop convoy continued to arise within the Admiralty, and by 11 September orders were dispatched for *Australia* to join *Sydney* and *Melbourne* as escort, while the China Squadron, including *Minotaur* and *Hampshire*, would act as covering force to the north. Exactly why such a heavy escort (virtually the entire British Pacific force) was felt necessary is unclear.

Jerram reported on 12 September that he had found nothing to suggest that the Germans were in the Indian Ocean, and that the Dutch were observing strict neutrality. He offered his view that it was very likely the Germans would next be heard of off the American coast.[69] Yet the Admiralty demonstrated a lack of preparedness for such a sudden change of circumstances. They seemed at a loss for a plan to use the China Squadron, while the entirety of the Australian Squadron including *Australia* remained scheduled to escort the ANZAC troop convoy.

The Admiralty's inability or unwillingness to consider issues beyond the escort for the troop convoys was finally to be challenged by German action in mid-September. On 14 September it was reported that *Emden* had been active in the Bay of Bengal, while two days later the Governor of New Zealand reported that *Scharnhorst* and *Gneisenau* had appeared off Samoa on the same day as *Emden* was reported, but had left without firing a shot. Sailing from Majuro on 29 August, Spee had made for the Christmas Islands, arriving on 7 September, before meeting *Nürnberg*, which had visited Honolulu for supplies and news before raiding the cable station at Fanning Island. Having learnt from *Nürnberg* of the occupation of Samoa, Spee decided to attack the harbour there in the hope of surprising *Australia*. Finding only the New Zealand troops, he had left and turned towards Tahiti and America. Meanwhile *Emden* was causing havoc in the Indian Ocean, after a passage via Anguar and the Dutch East Indies.

The Admiralty quickly signalled Patey, now heading south to escort the ANZAC convoy, to reverse course to Rabaul. He returned with *Australia* and *Sydney* on 19 September to protect the Australian troops and light vessels there. On arrival Patey dispatched *Sydney* to destroy the W/T station at Anguar, while proceeding with the French cruiser *Montcalm*, *Encounter* and *Berrima* to accept the surrender of the small colonial outpost of Friedrich Wilhelmshafen.[70] At this point Patey recorded in his operational report (a report that could not reach the Admiralty for several months) 'that it would be better to defer occupying any more of the islands until the German Squadron had been accounted for'.[71]

This was easier said than done, especially with erroneous reports still placing the German Squadron in the Marshall Islands. The situation was starkly clarified on 3 October, when Patey heard that Papeete in the Tahiti Islands, almost due east of Samoa, had been bombarded and the French gunboat *Zelee* destroyed (on 22 September) by *Scharnhorst* and *Gneisenau*. Patey immediately began moves to head eastward to establish a base at Suva, with the main elements of his force arriving on 12 October. The German movement eastward across the Pacific should now have been obvious, particularly when on 5 October Patey was informed by Suva of an intercept indicating that *Scharnhorst* was on her way from the Marquesas Islands even further to the east.[72]

Patey, however, spent the next month at Suva 'like a dog tethered to his kennel'.[73] He made dashes into neighbouring waters but was pulled back before any results could be obtained. It is difficult to determine why this 'attitude of weak and defensive expectancy' (something warned against by Churchill before the war) was adopted to defend trade out of Fiji.[74] The Naval Staff Monograph suggests, unsupported by external evidence, that the Admiralty orders were largely a response to alarm in Australia and New Zealand over unchecked German activities.[75] Possibly, the focus on the hunt for *Emden* in the Indian Ocean, which was causing Churchill much political discomfort, meant that the Pacific was forgotten. Certainly Patey's second and last modern light cruiser—*Sydney*—was detached by Churchill to join the hunt for *Emden*, while Patey was refused permission to mount a patrol to the Marquesas.[76] Richmond described in his diaries an Admiralty environment without awareness of the possible effect of (what was to him) a blindingly obvious German move to the east upon the South American and South Atlantic situation.[77]

Meanwhile the provision of sufficient escort for the ANZAC convoy became a point of contention between the Admiralty and the Dominions. Australian and New Zealand confidence in the Admiralty was suffering from its apparent failings thus far. Both countries were dubious of the British proposal for the troopships to proceed individually from their ports of origin to Albany before concentration for escort westward. The issue was brought to a head by the appearance of Spee off Samoa and of *Emden* in the Indian Ocean, while persistent and inaccurate rumours meant that Admiralty assurances went unheeded. Both countries refused to allow the ships to sail on 22 September. Corbett attributes this decision to the immaturity of the Australian Government in particular and to its lack of knowledge of 'the inscrutable lore of the sea'.[78] While the dominion concerns were probably exaggerated, Britain had continually failed to explain how this mysterious lore operated and how it would keep the troops safe. A more consultative and communicative approach, which presented orders and requests in their wider context, was needed to more effectively manage the diplomatic relationships.

Once Spee appeared off Papeete, Australia again became keen for the ships to sail unescorted to the concentration point. New Zealand, however, remained dogmatic and their ships did not sail from Wellington until 16 October under the escort of *Minotaur*, *Ibuki*, *Pyramus* and *Philomel*, arriving at Albany, where the Australian transports were concentrating, on 28 October. The full convoy, with *Sydney* and *Melbourne* as escorts, finally sailed on 1 November. On the morning of 9 November, while the convoy was passing the Cocos Islands, an emergency message was intercepted from the island that it was under attack. In turn, *Sydney* was detached and defeated *Emden*.[79]

The Admiralty's failure to counter the German East Asiatic Squadron effectively was to have disastrous effect when, on 1 November 1914, Admiral Cradock's critically weak squadron was destroyed with great loss of life at the battle of Coronel. While *Australia* was finally dispatched eastward in the massive over-reaction which ensued (including the dispatch of three battle cruisers from the home fleet), Spee's squadron was surprised and sunk at the Falkland Islands before the Australian flagship could arrive.

Conclusion

The course of the naval war in the Asia–Pacific in 1914 reveals a critical lack of leadership within the Australian and British high commands. The Australian Commonwealth Naval Board lacked the skills, knowledge, experience and status to act effectively to secure Australian general interests. The Admiralty lacked the organisational structure and probably the intellectual capacity to manage the campaign. With simplistic pre-war planning, the strategic direction and entire concept of operations had to be quickly improvised. Not only did this cause confusion and faulty guidance, but also a lack of common understanding with, and *modus operandi* for, the operational commanders. As is common in such situations, the Admiralty attempted to micro-manage the operational details in an attempt to overcome these failings. This in turn stifled initiative, effective communication and quick, informed and decisive action. This also meant that the Admiralty could not stand back and appreciate the wider picture and trends of the campaign, such as the diminishing (if any) value of the German Pacific possessions or the increasingly obvious move eastward by Spee prior to his victory at Coronel.

Yet, as Colin Gray observes, strategy need not be elegant: one simply needs to win,[80] and in 1914 the Allies won the naval war in the Asia–Pacific. Not only did they eventually sink the German East Asiatic Squadron, they completed the imperial troop concentration (of which the ANZAC convoy was only one part) without the loss of a single man. Additionally, the occupation of the German Pacific possessions was successfully achieved (to whatever gain) and the trade routes were secured without excessive or long-term disruption. This was due in no small measure to the overall superiority of the Royal Navy, and to its ability to supply and reinforce distant squadrons when the need became serious. Spee's squadron, in contrast, was in Churchill's words a 'cut flower in a vase; fair to see, yet bound to die', isolated from its parent navy and beyond lines of communication, supply and reinforcement.[81]

Spee was therefore correct in believing that the longer his squadron avoided battle and remained in existence the longer he could exert an influence on events. But his mere presence within the vast expanses of the Pacific was insufficient to significantly constrain and disrupt British imperial priorities and trade. In 1914 as now, within the vastness of the Pacific it was the interface between land and sea (including sea routes and coastal waters) which proved pivotal. While he avoided such key British maritime interfaces, Spee drifted into irrelevance. Conversely, when he appeared off Samoa, and *Emden* in the Bay of Bengal, the resulting disquiet echoed around the British Empire. Here lay Spee's dilemma. The actions most likely to bring success were also the most likely to undermine the prospect of remaining a fleet in being.

British strategy was irrevocably tied to this interface between land and sea. Its rationale lay in the ability to move forces between ports, cities and areas at the edge of this maritime interface. The German East Asiatic Squadron, moreover, was tied to the Pacific islands to obtain food, information and extremely brief respites for its crews and—most importantly—sheltered waters in which to coal. British commanders did not (and did not need to) talk of the pointless patrolling of wide expanses of ocean. Instead they concentrated upon patrolling and destroying key installations at these Pacific islands without necessarily occupying them. The Australian fleet was effective in 1914, not because it provided close defence of Australian ports and local waters, but because its range, firepower and operational reach, when combined with that of the Royal Navy, were sufficient to deter the Germans from challenging its strength in the broader maritime interfaces which were vital to Australia. This, as much as the lesson of coherent command and control structures, is not only history but surely wisdom for today.

17 A strategy for the lower deck of the early Royal Australian Navy
Kathryn Spurling

As the Royal Australian Navy evolved during the decade following Federation, so too did the strategy for manning the fleet. Not surprisingly, but perhaps rather naively, this strategy assumed that Australian-born volunteers would accept a preponderance of Royal Navy officers and ratings, and Royal Navy discipline, conditions of service and attitudes. This chapter will offer an insight into the individuals who, and forces which, moulded that strategy. It will also examine the suitability of the policy implemented.

The Commonwealth Naval Forces

In 1902 William Rooke Creswell proposed the formation of a federal force out of the colonial navies. His was one of the first Australian voices to proclaim:

> Sea defence is of vital importance to island peoples, there can be no sea defence without seamen. If our shipping and sea trade is manned by foreigners who have no interest in defending us we shall have neither seamen nor sea defence.[1]

Creswell was adamant that Australians should be recruited and trained to man effectively warships deployed by the Royal Navy east of the Suez.[2] As a former naval commandant of both South Australia and Queensland, he held a high opinion of Australian-born sailors. When the South Australian ship *Protector* sailed for China in 1900 and service with imperial ships in the Boxer rebellion, Captain Creswell was in command and believed that his ship 'commissioned and manned in Australia was efficient for active service'.[3] Creswell was not surprised when a visiting officer had 'marvelled' how hard the ship's company worked, and Creswell wrote: 'I knew them, and their desire to make themselves and their ship as fit as possible for active service'.[4] When the Admiral of the Imperial Fleet, Sir Edward Seymour, asked him what additional assistance with coaling the crew of *Protector* needed, Creswell replied that none was required. The admiral retorted to his flag officer: 'Ho, going to teach us how to coal, is he? Better send a committee of officers to see how he does it'. *Protector*'s men justified Creswell's belief in them and the following day completed the coaling in half the time allowed for the exercise by imperial authorities. Creswell described with obvious pride: 'As we swung clear, the flagship made the commendatory signal, "Very well done" '.

Creswell's faith in Australian volunteers was not shared by his Royal Navy peers. Officers who had served in the Australian squadron had continually struggled with high desertion rates amongst Royal Navy seamen in Australian ports. The causes for desertions were complex, but Australian society and the 'great emotional attraction of a free and easy society for men accustomed to English conditions and naval discipline' was held largely to blame. British officers believed there existed in Australian society a resistance to 'the established order', the basis of which resistance was considered to be 'the Irish element'.[5]

The entry of Australian-born seamen and stokers into warships of the Australian squadron did cause friction. A problem arose over wages because Australian Ordinary Seamen were better paid than British Petty Officers. But there were cultural nuances too. Australian ratings were seen as having a less respectful disposition than British ratings. This may have been an accurate assessment if the attitude displayed by colonial seaman 'Lofty' Batt was shared by his companions. Batt described an inspection by Admiral Sir Richard Poore onboard HMS *Challenger*:

> Dicky Poore was bred in the old navy tradition when men amounted to less than a coil of rope ... to him, Colonial Matelots did not amount to much, they didn't give a damn about standing smartly to attention and saluting every brass button that came along, and he didn't like that.[6]

For Australians respect was not an automatic right of commissioned personnel, but needed to be earned. This was unappreciated by British officers and reinforced the commonly held poor opinion of their colonial charges. Australian ratings were seen as having a bad influence on Royal Navy ratings. By 1907 the Admiralty admitted it wished to discourage the recruitment of colonial seamen because, apart from their being 'much more expensive', they 'can never be trained so efficiently as the men enlisted at home'.[7] Within the first decade of the twentieth century the total naval personnel in the Australian squadron averaged 4000. The Australian-born component was restricted to less than 20 per cent.[8]

The Australian colonies united under one flag in 1901, but it was 1904 before the Colonial Naval Forces came under Commonwealth regulations and 1907 before they were disbanded and their members united in a naval militia, the Commonwealth Naval Forces. The union was an uneasy one. There were incidents that arose from the perception of favouritism towards one colony's naval force over another.[9] Just as the act of Federation did not immediately extinguish colonial rivalries, neither did it immediately extinguish rivalries between colonial navies.

Following his appointment as Director of the Naval Forces, Creswell recommended that a navigation school be established and a boy seaman entry scheme commenced as soon as possible. British authorities were unimpressed. Vice Admiral Sir Arthur Fanshawe, Commander-in-Chief of the Australia Station between 1902 and 1905, publicly disapproved of Creswell's announcements. Fanshawe, in his communication with the Admiralty, had spoken of Creswell in cautionary tones, as one 'not in sympathy' with the imperial naval cause. He had also voiced concern that the careers of imperial naval personnel could be affected 'by the entry of Colonial men'.[10]

Naval personnel continued to serve on ancient vessels. Some, such as the drill ships *Pyramus* and *Psyche*, although relatively modern, were small and narrow-gutted. Of them it was said that a man standing by the port bulwarks could easily be seasick over the starboard side.[11] When Sub-Lieutenant Henry Feakes reported to assume duties in the ex-colonial ironclad *Cerberus* he was met by an elderly rating who escorted him below 'through the dingy gloom' with an oil lantern. *Cerberus* had last sailed down Port Phillip Bay in 1906, and Feakes was clearly unimpressed by his vessel's condition, of which he wrote:

> Not since an armoured belt had been clamped around her ample waist upwards of 40 years before had God's fresh air, or germ-destroying sunshine, penetrated into the vitals of the old ship. Forty years of potted air, and bilge! The smelly oil lamp did the rest.[12]

His seaman guide had spent 36 years on the ironclad.

The 1909 Naval Agreement specified that Australian training and discipline should be uniform with that of the Royal Navy to enable the interchangeability of officers and men. Nicholas Lambert has written that 'the British Admiralty consistently refused to help the Dominions "play the game" by any rules except their own'.[13] No deviation from the agreement was deemed acceptable, and the Admiralty informed Australian authorities that it would supply suitable men to act as instructors. Royal Navy officers would be loaned to administer the service.[14]

The history of the Royal Navy was long, and specific traditions as to the treatment of the men of the lower deck deeply entrenched. Historians offer a harsh portrayal of the lives of the men of the Royal Navy lower deck and of the deep divisions between them and their officers. Royal Navy commissions were conferred on individuals largely through family connections and this naval patronage accounted for the 'social comprehensiveness of the officer corps'.[15] By the time of Australia's Federation the conditions of service for ratings had improved little since the early nineteenth century and the Royal Navy 'was frozen into rigid classes' with 'the gulf between quarter deck and lower deck ... wider than it had ever been'.[16] Anthony Carew has referred to the Royal Navy as one suffering from 'general stagnation', a service 'hidebound by tradition and it was often the less glorious side of tradition that most affected the lower deck'.[17] These traditions were now to be imposed on the men of the RAN.

Within the halls of the Australian Parliament the game of musical chairs continued and the country had its eighth government in ten years. Largely through the enthusiasm of the new Defence Minister, Senator George Foster Pearce, an 'independent navy' again became a priority. Pearce's administration passed Australia's first Naval Defence Act in 1910, which set out the legal status and administration of the Commonwealth Naval Forces, established a Commonwealth Naval Board and an Australian Naval College.

But naval forces were divided into the Permanent Naval Force and the Citizen Naval Force. The Citizen Naval Force was in turn divided into Naval Reserve Force and Naval Volunteer Reserve Force and the Naval Reserve Force was broken into the Commonwealth Naval Reserve (M) and the Commonwealth Naval Reserve (O). Such divisions did little to encourage unity.

A contingent of ratings travelled to the United Kingdom for gunnery, signals, torpedo and engine-room training before joining the first two ships built for the Australian Navy, the destroyers *Parramatta* and *Yarra*. The colonial seamen, known locally as the 'Wallabies', completed their courses at Portsmouth Royal Naval Barracks with impressive grades.

Not all ratings reacted favourably when informed they were to be transferred to Commonwealth jurisdiction. The last British Commander-in-Chief, Vice Admiral Sir George King-Hall, was of the opinion that men enrolled under the 1903 Naval Agreement could be sent to England to man Australian ships. The Crown Solicitor disagreed. Two stokers who declined were returned to Australia and dismissed 'Unfit for the defence force of the Commonwealth'.[18]

In March 1911, Admiral Sir Reginald Henderson, RN, submitted his *Recommendations* for the Australian Navy. On 10 July, King George V granted the new naval force the right to be known as the Royal Australian Navy. Admiral King-Hall found himself supporting the concept of an independent and strong Commonwealth Naval Force, which would foster 'the spirit of Australian Nationality'. The opinion being expressed by their representative in Australia did not please the Admiralty. King-Hall wrote in his diary in February 1912: 'Long telegram from Admiralty, do not approve of Commonwealth proposals'. Admiral King-Hall's support for the Australian Navy did not encompass the issue of command. On this he agreed with his superiors, that Australians should not yet hold places of authority in their own navy. Captain Gaunt, born in Australia but serving in command of HMS *Challenger*, had thought that he might be the one to be commodore of the new Australian unit.[19] King-Hall, however,

> told him that I did not think so . . . He being an Australian was too much in with the politicians and people and that an Admiral was required ready to stand up against them, especially in the incipient stages of the RAN . . .[20]

Raising a ship's company

Admiral Henderson's plan envisaged that Australia would eventually need to recruit 13 832 officers and men, with 4384 required in the first five years.[21] The Naval Board was finding the implementation of a strategy to man the fleet more complicated than the traditional order of priority would suggest. Traditional naval thinking regarded lower deck policy as the least important issue. The cruisers HMA Ships *Sydney*, *Melbourne* and *Brisbane* had been ordered with swiftness, yet arrangements to prepare men to crew them proceeded slowly. In 1911 a site on the shores of Westernport Bay, Victoria, was purchased for a naval training base which would include gunnery and torpedo schools.[22] Building progress was slow. Owing to the limited accommodation available at Williamstown Depot, recruiting could not commence until the middle of 1912.[23]

At the commencement of the first RAN recruiting campaign, copies of a booklet, 'How to join the Royal Australian Navy', were distributed. Those who wished to join as normal entry had to be 'Smart active youths and young men between the ages of 17 and 25 years, of very good character'.[24] Initial enlistment was for five or seven years. Candidates were required to pass a medical examination and English and arithmetic tests.

The ships being built for the RAN incorporated the new technology of the twentieth century and required a new breed of rating. Gone were the days when a member of the lower deck 'wore a pigtail and as long as he could swear, fight and drink his rum neat' was fit to man one of His Majesty's ships.[25] Being merely 'strong and able-bodied' no longer sufficed; ratings needed to be literate and capable of undertaking technical training. At least 20 per cent of volunteers accepted were men with trades.

Admission to the majority of seamen categories was open only to those recruited under the Boy Seamen entry scheme. The Commonwealth converted a 317-foot sailing ship moored permanently in Sydney Harbour into the Boys' Training Ship, HMAS *Tingira*. Naval recruiters warned that 'Only boys of very good character and physique'[26] between 14 and 16 years need apply. By October 1913, 300 boys had joined *Tingira*[27] and authorities believed the steady stream would continue. The newspaper the *Sydney Morning Herald* agreed, suggesting that a career in the Australian Navy was 'full of promise'.[28]

Mortimer Froude, born on 7 July 1897, a rivet boy from Mort's Dock, is believed to have been the first boy to enter the training ship. Froude would be killed in HMS *Defence* at the Battle of Jutland.[29] Leslie Brooks was another of the early enlistees. Born at Kalamunda, outside Perth, the son of a farmer, Leslie Brooks had decided on a naval career after seeing the visiting American fleet at Fremantle in September 1908. Brooks would serve in the RAN through two world wars, and die at age 96.[30] Robert E. Wilson joined at 14 for reasons he offered as:

> to travel, the spirit of adventure . . . cruising around various countries, meeting different races, observing their ways of living, seeing some of the historical places we were told about at school.[31]

The model for Australian boy seamen training was that established in the Royal Navy in 1854. The Royal Navy treated its young recruits with 'extraordinary conservatism'.[32] This was the model replicated to train boy seamen from a different national culture, a hemisphere away, in a different era. Furthermore, by 1905 the Royal Navy had moved its boys ashore to a 'stone frigate'.[33] The RAN, preparing to take receipt of technologically advanced warships, was training its youngest recruits on a sailing hulk.

The training regime was demanding, with a strong emphasis on discipline and physical exertion. Boy Wilson recalled that on Wednesday mornings boys

> were at the whim of the old man, sometimes it was away all boats, pull around Rose Bay, another time it would be a morning's sailing, in cutters and whalers. Other times it was a route march, with field guns, to the sand

Boy trainees aboard HMAS *Tingira*. (RAN)

dunes of North Bondi . . . We were able to come to terms with these outings, because we knew we had the afternoon off.[34]

Weeks of seamanship instruction were replaced by gunnery training. For many boys the highlight of the week was the silent movie shown in *Tingira*'s canteen. The only distraction from the evening's entertainment was the sound from the piano played by the canteen manager. He could only play one song and through westerns, dramas or comedies the strains of 'I'm Forever Blowing Bubbles' continued with monotony.[35] After 12 months in *Tingira*, boy seamen were drafted into the fleet. One officer wrote of the young Australians, 'they are physically a splendid lot of boys, healthy, hard as nails and as nimble as kittens'.[36]

Admiral Henderson had initially recommended the loan of 1623 Royal Navy officers and men whilst recruiting only 800 Australians. Those who doubted the willingness of Australian youth to take up the challenge of a naval career were proven incorrect. By March 1913 the training establishments were filled to capacity. But there was a breakdown in the training schedule of new recruits, as the Admiralty was not releasing sufficient instructors to train the incoming enlistees.[37] To restrict further applications the age of entry was raised. By 1913 some 3400 officers and men made up the RAN, 1740 being members of the Royal Navy. The commissioning crews of *Melbourne* and *Sydney* were 400 strong, yet onboard *Melbourne* there were only 190 Australian ratings whilst within *Sydney*'s ship's company there were only 146.[38] It is difficult to answer the question 'Could fewer Royal Naval personnel have been accepted at this time?', particularly given the shortage of experienced ratings in Australia. But this ratio of personnel was vital to the potential of the RAN to become a cohesive service and an integral part of Australian society.

When *Parramatta* and *Yarra* arrived home the ships' companies were astounded by the depth of public interest in the Australian Navy. At the official welcome held at the Sydney Cricket Ground, 15 000 citizens waved and cheered as RAN personnel marched. A large fireworks display filled the sky as the patriotic official speeches were concluded. Yet barely had the bunting and banners been removed when rumours circulated suggesting that all was not contentment in the new force.

Matters of political concern

Senator Thomas Chataway announced in the Australian Parliament that 'something rotten' was happening in the fleet. Politicians voiced their concern over the adoption by the RAN of the Royal Navy code of discipline. Senator Arthur Rae declared that such a disciplinary code would lead to unnecessary tyranny and unfairness on the part of Royal Navy officers in the management of Australians. Senator Allan McDougall, declared:

> It is hard to bring Australians down to what men have to stand in the navy of the Old Land and other navies. It is hard to break the spirit of the Australians. But let him know that he is in exactly the same position as the best on the vessel though holding a humbler position in life, let him know that one man is as good as another, and you will find that the Australian will be ever ready to take his place in the front fighting line, not only on the land, but at sea.[39]

McDougall's words were prophetic. He had touched on the essence of the Australian naval rating. Nonetheless he did not appreciate the strength of the naval culture imposed upon Australian volunteers.

Unrest amongst the men of the RAN became a regular feature in the Australian printed media. The issue of deferred pay was seen as a major

Portrait of the crew of HMAS *Yarra* in 1913. The manning of the RAN's first two destroyers required virtually the entire strength of the Commonwealth Naval Forces at the time. The two sub-lieutenants in the centre row still wear the triangular insignia of the CNF on their jacket sleeves. (AWM: P1244/02/01)

concern. Deferred pay was included in the gross salary figure but was withheld until completion of service. Naval administrators said that no man would lose his deferred pay unless he were discharged due to 'very severe misconduct'. Sailors were not convinced and the future would prove them correct. There would be many instances when ratings discharged on grounds other than 'very severe misconduct' would find the navy retained all or part of their pension money.

Another persistent allegation was that non-Australian ratings were being shown preference over those trained in Australia in the matter of promotion. The promises made to Australian volunteers in the first recruiting booklet were not fulfilled. The deteriorating morale among Australian volunteers resulted in the Minister for Defence conceding that 34 men from *Yarra* and twelve men from *Parramatta* had requested discharges after their return home to Australia, but this, he had concluded, was due to misplaced anxiety and apprehension concerning their prospects.

Clearly the minister's assurances had little effect because James Mathews, the member for Melbourne Ports, thereafter received 107 separate rating complaints.[40] These included concerns over wages. Ratings believed senior naval officers had uncontested power to adjust their own salaries while ratings had no sympathetic representation. The member for Corio, Alfred Ozanne, believed an even more basic issue lay at the centre of much of the men's discontent, namely food. He had discovered the diet of the men in *Yarra* and *Parramatta* consisted of a breakfast of porridge and bread and butter, a lunch of roast meat and potatoes with no other vegetables, and pudding only twice a week, and a supper of bread and butter and tea.

The RAN had implemented a general messing system in the larger ships. An allowance was paid to the Paymaster Officer for each rating on his ship. Not all paymasters were competent and in some instances the victualling allowance was spent unwisely and food became scarce. Ships travelling in company could easily have victualling of entirely different quality. Successful messing of the men of the RAN also depended on the integrity of senior naval administrators. Complaints from the ship's company of *Sydney* were raised in Parliament during October 1913. It was alleged that although the allowance was 1s 4d per day per man only 4d per man per day had been spent during the ship's voyage to Australia from England. This left naval administrators with a saving of £200, whilst the men of *Sydney* had been fed foul meat and contaminated tinned sardines.

Those in charge of the RAN chose not to address the conditions of service of the men. They chose instead to treat the consequence rather than the cause, to attempt to resolve unrest with increased disciplinary measures and resort to subterfuge in an attempt to diminish the visibility of the problem. Men transferred from the colonial naval force were seen as the ringleaders and King-Hall wrote that the decision had been made 'to get rid of those men at once', and not let them poison the minds 'of new volunteers'. This pattern of response would be repeated by ensuing generations of naval administrators and would contribute to continued unrest within the lower deck of the RAN for many more decades.

The problems of naval men were also obscured in the Australian Parliament as disagreement of a different kind dominated naval debate. By 1913 friction within the Naval Board, particularly between the Finance Member, Staff Paymaster H.W. Eldon Manisty, and the Second Naval Member, Captain Constantine Hughes-Onslow, was disrupting naval administration. Manisty had been the instigator of the method of general messing. Hughes-Onslow argued that not only was there no effective barrier against dishonesty and fraud but that the victualling of the men was dependent on the 'caprice [sic] nature of the Accountant Officer'. Moreover, there was also friction between Admiral Creswell, who was now First Naval Member, and the Third Naval Member, Engineer Captain Clarkson. Naval Board antipathy was discussed in Parliament fifteen times in three months. By November 1913 the new Liberal Government admitted the situation within the Naval Board had further deteriorated, that 'harmonious relations' were entirely absent and that the board was so marred by personal friction and hostility that members were no longer on speaking terms.[41] The government believed that the Naval Board was in a state of paralysis. Hughes-Onslow was suspended. He asserted that this was because 'I would not connive in defrauding the personnel, so as to curry favour with the Minister and enable the estimates to be cut down'.[42] The government also favoured replacing Creswell with a Royal Navy admiral. Events in Europe would delay this change until 1919. Acrimony within the Naval Board destabilised naval administration at a time when a strong united front was needed.

The flagship and its ship's company

The pride of the new Australian Navy was HMAS *Australia*. Built at John Brown shipyard, Clydebank, the battle cruiser had cost the Australian people the princely sum of £2 000 000. Examination of *Australia*'s five-inch-thick ship's book reveals enormous detail about nuts and bolts, but just three pages are given to information concerning the ship's complement. The emphasis on nuts and bolts continued the tradition of taking

Members of HMAS *Sydney*'s lower deck take a break after coaling ship.
(HMAS *Cerberus* Museum)

personnel for granted. When beginning a warship design British naval shipbuilders would first incorporate engineering, armament and other non-personnel specifications. Provision of lower deck living spaces was addressed almost as an afterthought. The ships became larger but the living spaces did not. The men on the Dreadnoughts were almost as cramped as Nelson's sailors on the *Victory*, a vessel a third of the size. A width of 14 inches was allowed each man to swing his hammock; these were slung above spaces used for meals and recreation. No attempt was made to improve ventilation to 'fetid, condensation-dripping messdecks'.[43]

The flagship's ship's company typified the mix of ratings who now wore RAN tally ribbons.[44] Illustrating the mixture were Chief Petty Officer Henry Batterham, Leading Seaman Dalmorton Rudd, his brother Stoker Leonard Rudd, Able Seamen Robert Wilson and John Hellyer, Ordinary Seamen Kenneth Patterson and William McIntosh, and Stoker Frederick Smith.

Chief Batterham was born in Southampton, England. He had served 19 years in the Royal Navy before being loaned to the RAN from April 1913. Leading Seaman Rudd was born in Sydney in 1896. His occupation on RAN entry was given as 'packer' and his religion as Roman Catholic. Able Seaman Robert Wilson was only 14 years old when he entered as a Boy Seaman 'for adventure'. Able Seaman Hellyer was born in Gosport, England, in 1882. He was recruited in England as part of the commissioning crew, signing on for a period of five years. His wife Mabel would remain at the family home in Scotland. Stoker Smith was born in Geraldton, Western Australia, in 1895, baptised in the Church of England, and worked as a farmhand before he entered the navy in 1913.

Of these ratings only Able Seaman Wilson would continue his naval service into 1920. Chief Batterham would die of scarlet fever while *Australia* undertook war service in the North Sea. Smith would be discharged when he reacted physically against a Royal Navy loan Petty Officer who, he alleged, 'has been agitating me ever since I came to the ship'. Dalmorton Rudd would be awarded a Distinguished Service Medal in 1918 for his part in the destruction of the Zeebrugge mole, but the 23-year-old, along with his brother, Patterson, and McIntosh, all aged 18, would be sentenced to lengthy imprisonment for their part in a mutiny which took place on 20 June 1919 at Fremantle, just days after the ship returned to Australia. The Admiralty directed that 'exemplary punishment must follow such grave breaches of discipline'.[45] The Australian people did not agree and the men would eventually be pardoned.

At Plymouth on 30 June 1913, Sir George Reid, the Australian High Commissioner in London, addressed the crew of *Australia* as the battle cruiser prepared to depart for the Southern Hemisphere. In the presence of the King, Reid declared that Australians were establishing their fleet not because they were 'Colonials' but because they were 'Britishers'. Applause erupted from the nearly 818-strong ship's company when Reid announced that while 53 per cent of those on board were British loan personnel, the remaining 47 per cent were Australian. In fact Reid was mistaken. Forty-seven per cent were technically members of the RAN, but nearly half of these were ex-members of the Royal Navy, recruited in Britain. In fact only 25 per cent of those on board had come from Australia and very few of these were in positions of authority.

In its report on the departure the *Evening Standard* simply referred to the RAN flagship as the 'HMS *Australia*'. A number of British naval historical texts have perpetuated this error. The Royal Navy character of the RAN meant that such a mistake was inevitable. Nonetheless, immediately after the cheers for the official party were raised, an Australian rating perched astride one of *Australia*'s 12-inch guns shouted 'Three cheers for Wallaby Land'.[46] For the Australians onboard *Australia* the RAN was part of the defence of the British Empire, but foremost in their minds was that this warship was the flagship of the navy of Australia.

Conclusion

The evolution of the Royal Australian Navy was not an easy one. Federation and the first flush of nationalism, combined with a fear of Asian neighbours and political resolve, resulted in an independent Australian navy. The early years were marred by a climate of colonial rivalries, Australian governmental instability and divided popular opinion existed over the sentiments of nationalism and imperialism. The conundrum of Australian naval policy in the years following Federation was exacerbated by the unwillingness of the British Admiralty to relinquish control of the dominion naval force.

It is feasible to suggest that the men who served first in Colonial Naval Brigades, then the Commonwealth Naval Forces and then the RAN had little understanding of the international intrigue that dictated government policy or of theories of imperial defence versus local navies, or were even aware of the acrimonious debate between Australian political parties and disagreement between Australian bureaucrats and the British Admiralty. The lives of the men were very vulnerable to these factors, nonetheless.

Undoubtedly Royal Navy guidance was necessary, particularly in the incipient stages of the RAN. The naval forces of Australia needed to acquire a degree of interoperability with those of the Royal Navy. But the traditions of the Royal Navy were long established and not always suitable for twentieth-century Australian ratings. Significant numbers of Australian volunteers were attracted to the nascent RAN, but few continued after their initial enlistment. A balance needed to be reached to enable Royal Navy traditions to be blended with local needs and modern standards to achieve the most suitable conditions of service for personnel, but this balance was not achieved. Admiralty advisers believed that there was no room for the 'A' in RAN. They were unwilling or perhaps unable to moderate their attitude towards and method of handling members of the lower deck. Cultural nuances needed to be considered in the preparation of any RAN lower deck policy but they were not. Australian ratings valued their Australian identity as suggesting egalitarianism, resourcefulness, disinclination to accept authority, distrustfulness of leaders until they had proved themselves and valuing loyalty to their mates. This concept of identity clashed dramatically with the culture of the Royal Navy. The punishment records of the first decades of the RAN show that Australians had great difficulties conforming to the behavioural expectations made of them and attest that the strategy adopted to man the early RAN was not the most successful.

18 The Royal Australian Navy, the Constitution and the law—then and now
David Letts

For a lawyer, an appreciation of history is one of the fundamental tools in providing advice and presenting arguments before a court, or one's superiors for that matter. In legal parlance, reliance on history is known as the use of precedent, but the concept is similar to the practice of historians—looking to the past for assistance in dealing with contemporary, and indeed future, affairs.

This chapter will not simply list significant legal events in the history of the RAN. Nor will it include voluminous references to passages of Imperial and/or Australian legislation that has in some way had a bearing on the navy. Rather, its main purpose is to provide an appreciation of the legal and constitutional considerations that surrounded the formation of the RAN. A secondary objective is to comment on the scope and relevance of accurate and timely legal support within the present-day navy.

In discussing the second issue, comments will be made on two areas where legal advice is currently most pertinent: international law and operational activities; and assistance with the maintenance of discipline. In drawing these considerations together this chapter will attempt to link the RAN's legal past with its present. The purpose in so doing is not to justify a role for lawyers in today's navy, but rather to demonstrate that since the RAN's earliest days legal issues have been, and continue to be, an integral part of Australian naval activities. It should then become apparent that significant advantages arise from legal advice being given to the naval commander—particularly when that advice is provided by officers with an understanding and appreciation of the context (and limitations) in which the advice is sought. This perspective can be neatly summarised in a comment made by General Colin Powell, the former Chairman of the United States Joint Chiefs of Staff, regarding the participation of lawyers in Operations DESERT SHIELD and DESERT STORM, when he remarked that his 'decisions were impacted by legal considerations at every level'.[1]

The situation in relation to the Royal Australian Navy is no different. First, the very fact that Australia has a Commonwealth Navy at all is due to the operation of section 51 (vi) of the Constitution, which provides:

> The parliament shall, subject to this Constitution, have power to make laws for the peace, order and good governance of the Commonwealth with respect to:-
>
> . . .
>
> (vi) The naval and military defence of the Commonwealth and of the several States, and the control of the forces to execute and maintain the laws of the Commonwealth:[2]

Thus it can be seen that the existence of the RAN as an organ of the Commonwealth is based upon the same piece of *British* legislation that established Australia as a Federal Commonwealth. There are of course two pieces of Australian legislation that also directly impact on the RAN, namely the *Defence Act* 1903 and the *Naval Defence Act* 1910, and these will be discussed later.

Second, the navy is a large and complex organisation and there is little that occurs anywhere in the RAN that does not have some kind of legal implication. This statement is perhaps no more than an acknowledgment that the RAN, as an entity, is part of a wider Australian community, and that the impact of the law can be felt throughout the whole of that community. However, it also reflects the fact that the RAN is not immune from the effects of changes in legal ideas and processes that apply to society as a whole. One only has to observe the burgeoning area of human rights law, both domestic and international, and its consequent impact on the military, to see the validity of this comment.

Constitutional issues—Imperial and Commonwealth legislation

An outline of the legal regime that existed in Australia at the time of Federation provides the necessary context in which the formation of a reputable 'Australian Navy' should be understood. The term 'reputable' is used advisedly, for the Australian states transferred their naval forces to the Commonwealth Government on 1 March 1901. However, perhaps one of the kinder phrases that has been used to describe those forces is 'old and neglected', and it is generally agreed that they did not comprise the type of navy that would provide for any degree of self-protection in the event of a threat to Australia's security.[3]

The first point to consider is the general legal relationship that existed between Australia and Britain during the latter part of the nineteenth century.[4] This relationship obviously had its genesis in the establishment of a series of British colonies in Australia during the latter part of the eighteenth century and the early nineteenth century. Initially, the laws that applied in these colonies were those made by the Parliament at Westminster, as Captain Phillip 'had impliedly transported the laws of the Kingdom . . .'[5] when he founded the colony of New South Wales in 1788. This position did not alter for the next 40 to 50 years, but thereafter increasing interest in obtaining greater legislative autonomy began to emerge among the settlers in New South Wales.

In 1824, the Imperial Government appointed the first colonial Legislative Council, comprising five prominent local citizens, although the council's power was limited to advising the Governor 'in the exercise of his power to make laws and ordinances for the peace and good government of the colony'.[6] As the nineteenth century progressed, more colonies were established and further enhancements were made to the powers of the legislative councils appointed for each colony. In 1856 'the legislative councils in New South Wales, Tasmania, South Australia and Victoria were replaced by fully-fledged bi-cameral parliaments . . . [and] given full powers of responsible government subject only to their measures receiving the Royal assent'.[7]

However, the imperial authorities would only permit such self-government in a limited form, as evidenced by the operation of the *Colonial Laws Validity Act* 1865 (Imp). This Act, ostensibly passed with the purpose of confirming 'the law-making jurisdiction of all colonial representative legislatures',[8] had the additional purpose of preventing the colonies from passing legislation that was 'repugnant to any legislation enacted by the Imperial parliament'.[9] Clearly, the concept of 'Empire' and the unity of that Empire were at the forefront of the minds of the politicians and public servants in England at the time. It is also noteworthy that the final demise of the *Colonial Laws Validity Act*'s application in Australia did not occur until the Queen gave royal assent to the *Australia Act* 1986 (C'th) on 2 March 1986.

A former Chief Justice of the High Court has described 'the progression from colony to nationhood [as] being evolutionary . . .'[10] and this term perhaps best captures the way in which Australia's legal system developed—and continues to do so. The process of removing Australia's legislative manacles was assisted by the passage of the following legislation:

The Constitution Act 1900 (Imp.); the *Statute of Westminster* 1931 (Imp.) and its subsequent adoption in Australia by the *Statute of Westminster Adoption Act* 1942 (C'th); and the *Australia Act* 1986 (C'th) and corresponding legislation passed by the British Parliament and Australian state parliaments.[11]

Limitations of space in this chapter prevent a laborious examination of each of these Acts, but a comment is needed on a number of provisions in the Constitution that impacted directly upon the formation of the RAN. Section 51(vi) of the Constitution, the provision that gives the Commonwealth the power to make laws with respect to naval and military defence, has already been noted. The next sections relevant to the formation of the Commonwealth Department of Defence (of which the naval forces were obviously a part) are sections 64 and 69.

The operation of these two sections was conveniently described by the High Court in its 1997 decision in *Henderson*'s case.[12] The main issue in this case was consideration of Commonwealth constitutional immunity from the application of state laws. However, in reaching its decision the court noted that the Constitution envisaged two separate legal circumstances relating to the establishment of a Department of Defence. First, section 64 of the Constitution provides, *inter alia*, that:

> The Governor-General may appoint officers to administer such departments of State of the Commonwealth as the Governor-General in Council may establish.

It is self-evident that this provision allows the Governor-General in Council to establish departments of state of the Commonwealth, and the Department of Defence was one of the original Commonwealth departments so established, pursuant to section 64, on 1 January 1901.[13]

However, as one would expect, the Constitution also made provision for the transfer of the existing state forces to the Commonwealth. Section 69 of the Constitution provides that:

> On a date or dates to be proclaimed by the Governor-General after the establishment of the Commonwealth the following departments of the public service in each State shall become transferred to the Commonwealth:-
> Posts, telegraphs and telephones:
> Naval and military defence:
> Lighthouses, lightships, beacons and buoys:
> Quarantine.

The Governor-General proclaimed this transfer on 19 February 1901 and it took effect on 1 March 1901.[14] Thus it can be seen that within three months of Federation, the necessary legal processes for the creation of a Commonwealth Navy, and the transfer of existing naval forces, had occurred.

One other provision of the Constitution that impacts directly upon the RAN should also be highlighted. Section 68 provides that:

> The command in chief of the naval and military forces of the Commonwealth is vested in the Governor-General as the Queen's representative.

At first glance, one might expect that the width of this power enables the Governor-General, if so minded, to step into the ADF Command Centre in times of crisis and provide the Chief of the Defence Force and the service chiefs with his considered military opinion on current operations. While some governors-general may have served in the military at various stages of their careers, it can be safely assumed that whatever matters of state occupy our present Governor-General's time, the desire to assume actual command of the ADF is not one of them.

Sir Ninian Stephen discussed the operation of section 68 of the Constitution in an address to the Joint Services Staff College in June 1983.[15] In that address, Sir Ninian reviewed the history of vesting command of the forces in the Crown, and concluded that the title of commander-in-chief provided by section 68 of the Constitution was purely titular—and that this had clearly been the intention of the drafters of the Constitution. Nevertheless, Sir Ninian concluded that by virtue of the existence of section 68, there clearly exists a 'quite special relationship between the Governor-General and the armed forces of the Commonwealth'[16] and that this special relationship continues to the present day.

The formation of the RAN—legal issues

The preceding discussion represents a rather simplified analysis of a very specialised and complex area of law.[17] In the broader sense, the High Court has been quite regularly asked to decide on various matters related to the defence power provided by section 51 (vi) of the Constitution. These matters all originate in one way or another in the requirement for the naval and military forces of the Commonwealth to conduct their business in accordance with the powers granted to the Federal Government by the Constitution, and indeed for the Federal Government to limit its activities in the same way.

We should now address the legislation most relevant to establishing the Royal Australian Navy, noting that a Commonwealth Naval Force

The first new warships for the Australian Commonwealth, the destroyers *Parramatta* and *Yarra*, lie alongside at Williamstown early in 1911. The old cruiser *Protector* is on the other side of the pier and the vessel in the foreground is the *Macedon*. The Union Jack was replaced on naval vessels by the Australian national flag later in the year. (A. Woodley)

existed for ten years before the RAN was officially 'born' in 1911. This legislation continues to affect today's navy, although it has, of course, been amended on many occasions since it was first enacted.

The earlier chapters in this volume have addressed the issue of imperial defence and the consequent impact of this issue on the formation of the RAN. This was the context confronting the new Australian Parliament when it contemplated whether or not to allocate funds for a modern Australian navy. We have seen that on Federation 'the new federal government assumed full control and financial responsibility for all existing naval and military units ... [but at this time] there were no plans to create an Australian Navy'.[18] Thus, while the legal position as expressed in the Constitution clearly vested responsibility for the naval (and military) defence of the Commonwealth in the Federal Government, the practical situation was that Australia was almost totally reliant on the Royal Navy Squadron based in Sydney for such naval defence.

The first piece of Commonwealth legislation specifically dealing with matters of defence which was passed by the new Australian Parliament was the *Defence Act* 1903 (C'th), which was stated to be an 'Act to provide for the Naval and Military Defence and Protection of the Commonwealth and of the several States'.[19] The *Defence Act* applied to 'all the Naval and Military Forces of the Commonwealth, whether existing at the commencement of this Act, or raised thereafter, and to all members thereof, whether appointed or enlisted under this Act, or under any State Act'.[20] The *Defence Act* contained provisions dealing with matters affecting the Defence Force including:[21]

the administration of the Naval Forces, including the appointment of a naval officer to be the Officer Commanding the Naval Forces of the Commonwealth;
the establishment of 'an institution for the purposes of imparting education in the various branches of naval and military science . . .';[22]
the constitution of the Defence Force;
a range of offences pertaining to the Defence Force; and
courts-martial and legal procedure.

As mentioned earlier, the *Defence Act* has been substantially amended since 1903, and it no longer contains provisions dealing with all of the above subjects, but it remains the principal piece of legislation governing the Defence Force generally, and the army in particular.[23] In the navy's case, it is relevant to note that the Chief of Navy is a statutory appointment made pursuant to section 9(1)(a) of the *Defence Act*, and not under the provisions of the *Naval Defence Act* 1910 to which we now turn.

The long title of the *Naval Defence Act* states, strangely enough, that the Act is 'An Act relating to Naval Defence'. One supposes this description supports the contention that parliamentary draftsmen are not known for their imagination and flair! The *Naval Defence Act* followed a similar structure to that described above in relation to the *Defence Act*, with the following key provisions:

the creation of 'a Board of Administration for the Naval Forces, to be called the Naval Board';[24]
the establishment of naval colleges and instructional establishments for the purpose of imparting education in the various branches of naval science and in the subjects connected with the naval profession;[25]
the division of the Naval Forces into the Permanent Naval Forces and the Citizen Naval Forces;[26] and
provisions relating to the service of the Naval Forces.[27]

There are two sections in the *Naval Defence Act* that should be highlighted. Section 41 amplified the powers available under the *Defence Act*

The first and second entries to the Royal Australian Naval College parading at Divisions. Among their number were several persons who would achieve fame during World War II, including Collins, Farncomb, Getting, Feldt and Waller.
(RAN)

in respect of acquiring or building ships, vessels or boats to include the construction of docks, shipyards, foundries, machine shops and other works in connection with naval defence; and section 42 laid out the conditions for the transfer of vessels, officers and seamen between the Commonwealth Naval Forces and the Imperial Naval Forces or the naval forces of any part of the King's Dominions. These two sections of the *Naval Defence Act* finally provided the clear legislative authority necessary for the formation of the Royal Australian Navy, although the necessary funds for the creation of the RAN had been provided by the *Naval Loan Act* 1909. This circumstance continues to the present day, whereby the navy receives the funds required for its activities through the budget process, as part of the overall defence budget, and not pursuant to any provision contained in the *Naval Defence Act*.

Legal support for RAN operations

For many years after the inception of the RAN, there was no perceived need for permanent legal officers in the RAN. The need for any legal support was primarily limited to disciplinary matters and was provided by counsel briefed specifically for that purpose or, in some instances, legally qualified members of the Reserve. However, in today's navy the legal service is not immune from the requirement to support operations, nor should it be. By their very nature, RAN operations are routinely conducted in areas remote from Australia's territory, and may involve aspects of the laws of armed conflict and international law that are becoming increasingly complex.

The acceptance of the Defence Efficiency Review (DER)[28] by the Defence Minister in 1997 clearly emphasised the importance of combat operations as the primary focus of the ADF. The DER in turn resulted in the initiation of the Defence Reform Program on 1 July 1997. The accompanying rhetoric from the government and senior ADF commanders highlighted the expectation that the focus of the ADF will be directed towards the 'sharp end' of the force, and the RAN has already witnessed the impact of this policy.

RAN legal officers do not routinely deploy on board ships, although the Director of Naval Legal Services, in conjunction with the Director of Naval Officers' Postings, is exploring avenues to change this situation. Nevertheless, in conducting major exercises legal advice is already accepted as an essential component in both the planning and operational phases. Additionally, a dedicated legal officer has recently been assigned to the staff of Commodore Flotillas, as part of the maritime component of the Deployable Joint Force Headquarters.

But what, one may ask, necessitates the requirement for such legal support? Particularly when for so many years the RAN survived without dedicated legal advice on international law and operational issues. Gavan Griffith QC, a former Solicitor-General of Australia, summarised his thoughts on the general emergence of international law as follows:

> On taking office in 1984 I found a High Court just starting to move away from Barwickian disdain of offshore analogues other than the mother lode of the common law.
>
> How different is the position now. Led by the High Court, there is an emerging appreciation amongst lawyers and the public of the extent to which Australia is affected by operative principles of international law.[29]

There are three key reasons for this new emphasis on international law. The first is that international legal relations between nation-states have undergone a fundamental change since the end of World War II. This change has in turn been precipitated by two major events, namely the formation of the United Nations in 1945 and the final demise of the various colonial empires that had been established prior to the twentieth century. These two events may be summarised by reference to a growing nationalistic movement throughout the world and a willingness on the part of individual states to play a greater role in international affairs. We continue to see evidence of this in various regions of the world today—particularly Eastern Europe during the past decade.

The second reason relates to the increasing tendency of states to characterise their military actions as something other than war. There is a common misconception that war is illegal *per se*. However, one can argue that this is not so, but rather that *aggression* is illegal in accordance with Article 2(4) of the United Nations Charter and also as a matter of customary international law. The UN Charter clearly contemplates that military action may be necessary in certain circumstances, such as those described in Article 42 (peace enforcement operations) and Article 51 (self-defence). Certainly, states are more often expressing justification for their actions in terms of international law. Yugoslavia's recent action against ten NATO members in the International Court of Justice[30] is an example of this.

The final and perhaps the most obvious reason for the surge in legal advice on operational matters is that Article 82 of Additional Protocol I,[31] which Australia ratified in 1991, specifies:

> The High Contracting Parties at all times, and the Parties to the conflict in time of armed conflict, shall ensure that legal advisers are available, when necessary, to advise military commanders at the appropriate level on the application of the Conventions and this Protocol and on the appropriate instruction to be given to the armed forces on this subject.

The inclusion of Article 82 in Protocol I was not accidental. Experiences during the Vietnam War, such as the infamous My Lai massacre and the psychological treatment dispensed to American prisoners of war, highlighted a fundamental lack of understanding of the laws of war among service personnel. The desire to remedy this situation manifested itself in what is now viewed as one of the core roles of military lawyers—providing legal support (including legal training) for operations.[32]

Case studies

The realisation that naval operations are subject to binding legal constraints is not new, and while the following two examples did not involve the RAN, they do indicate some of the legal difficulties that may confront naval officers while performing their duties.

The first is one of the oldest cases dealing with the issue of self-defence in international law, *The Caroline*,[33] which arose because of the actions of British forces during the Canadian rebellion of 1837. The case involved British forces seizing the *Caroline* (an American-registered vessel) in an American port, burning the vessel and then dispatching it over Niagara Falls. The reason for this action was that the *Caroline* had been supplying Canadian forces rebelling against the British. Two American nationals were killed during the incident and the legality of the British actions was addressed when the British sought the release of one of their subjects who was being held in the United States on charges of murder and arson arising from the attack.

Almost certainly there were no international or operational lawyers advising the British forces prior to the attack on the *Caroline* in December 1837, and it is probable that the course of the military action would not have differed even if there had been! However, the action did result in an exchange of diplomatic correspondence between Britain and the United States and the emergence of a 'famous formula [that] remains influential in contemporary principles outlining the criteria for a legitimate use of force in self-defence'.[34]

> The need to use force in self-defence must be an 'instant, overwhelming necessity', leaving no choice of means, and no moment for deliberation.[35]

The second case again involved British forces, this time the Royal Navy, and is called the *Corfu Channel* case.[36] Briefly, in 1946 Albania attempted to restrict the passage of both merchant ships and warships through the Corfu Channel by requiring prior notification and permission for such passage from Albanian authorities. In May 1946 the Albanians actually fired upon two British cruisers that passed through the North Corfu Channel. The British Government immediately protested and decided to send more warships through the channel in October 1946 without giving notice or obtaining authorisation. On this latter occasion two warships struck mines and in November 1946 the RN undertook a mine clearance operation within Albanian territorial waters.

The International Court of Justice was asked to rule on two key issues:

whether the passage of the British warships in October 1946 was contrary to international law; and
whether the minesweeping actions in November 1946 constituted a breach of Albanian sovereignty.

The court ruled in favour of Britain in respect of the first question and in favour of Albania in respect of the second. It was found that the Corfu Channel forms part of a strait used for international navigation between two parts of the high seas, and that international custom recognised that in times of peace states have a right to send their warships through such straits without prior authorisation provided such passage is innocent. However, in relation to the second question, the minesweeping operations conducted by the Royal Navy were found to violate Albanian sovereignty.

These two cases illustrate the practical matter of the application of international and operational law for naval commanders. The *Caroline* is illustrative of a law of armed conflict problem, while the *Corfu Channel* case relates more to the law of the sea and international law generally. In today's navy, these two areas of the law are routinely encountered by RAN units in carrying out their operations, whether on exercise or in conflict situations. One only has to look at recent press reports dealing with RAN assistance in fishery protection duties in the Timor Sea and Great Southern Ocean, assistance to customs and immigration authorities and, of course, HMAS *Melbourne*'s 1999 deployment to the Persian Gulf in support of the United Nations sanctions against Iraq, to realise that RAN commanders must have accurate and timely legal support for all such operations.

Further to this point, the impact of the 1982 Law of the Sea Convention,[37] which entered into force on 16 November 1994, and the influence of that convention on naval operations, have yet to be fully felt. This is particularly true in the Asia–Pacific region, where the potential implications for the exercise of navigation rights through archipelagic waters, and the designation of archipelagic sea lanes in areas where the RAN routinely transits, have already proved to be a major concern for the navy.

A further point relates to the multitude of international treaties and other obligations to which Australia is a party. The range of these obligations, and the scope of their application, are issues which simply did not exist for the navy of even 20 years ago, let alone for the Royal Navy at the time of the *Caroline*. Warship 'sovereign immunity' still exists under the 1982 Law of the Sea Convention, but gone are the days when naval vessels could operate outside the bounds of such legal provisions. For example, one of the initial naval concerns with recent amendments to the London Dumping Convention[38] was that a naval vessel could have been seen to be in contravention of the convention every time it deployed a non-recoverable device, such as a sonobuoy, into the water. The potential effect of this interpretation on routine naval operations could have been devastating if one considers the number of different occasions that naval vessels routinely discharge some such object into the ocean.

All of the above issues have required significant legal advice to ensure that naval operations can continue to best advantage. While not suggesting that other interested parties, either within Australia or in the international arena, are always necessarily supportive of the RAN's concerns, the provision of advice on these issues by naval legal officers has assisted those at sea in having greater understanding of the nature and extent of their legal obligations.

Discipline

The final section of this chapter relates to the maintenance of discipline in the navy. As mentioned earlier, some form of legal support had been provided in relation to disciplinary matters from the earliest days of the Australian Navy, but interestingly this support was not always provided by a legally qualified officer—even in the case of a deputy judge advocate appointed to assist in a court-martial!

I will now outline briefly the disciplinary legislation to which members of the naval forces were initially subject, and then give an example of how the application of that legislation provided the impetus for the passage of the *Statute of Westminster Adoption Act* 1942 in the Australian Parliament. In the interests of brevity the legal arrangements which existed for the maintenance of discipline between Federation and the creation of the RAN have been simplified to a level that is somewhat misleading. Nevertheless, the history compiled by a former Director of Naval Legal Services, Captain Tom Holden, provides an excellent summary of this issue for anyone with a particular interest in it.[39]

Section 56 of the *Defence Act* 1903 provided that:

> The Naval Forces shall at all times, while on active service, be subject to the Naval Discipline Act save so far as it is inconsistent with this Act . . .

The *Defence Act* defined the reference to the *Naval Discipline Act* as being the Imperial Act and this approach was carried through into section 36 of the *Naval Defence Act* 1910 thus: 'the underlying theme was of two fleets, consisting of His Majesty's or His Majesty's Australian Ships, each sharing the same disciplinary code'.[40] This legislation was supplemented by the 'King's Regulations and Admiralty Instructions for the time being in force in relation to the King's Naval Forces . . . subject to any modifications and adaptations prescribed by the regulations . . .'[41] After the passage of an amendment to section 36 of the *Naval Defence Act* in 1912, the disciplinary regime also included the application of the *Naval Discipline (Dominion Naval Forces) Act* 1911. Already the disciplinary regime was getting rather complex, and the circumstances changed depending on whether Australia's naval forces were acting alone or with others.

Charges could be heard against a member of the navy under military law or in a civil court. Military law permitted trial by court-martial or the awarding of summary punishment in a broadly similar vein to that which exists today—although the punishments available in the past were somewhat more severe.

One of the major inconsistencies between the Imperial and Australian legislation affecting disciplinary matters can be found in the different offences for which the death penalty was provided. This issue proved crucial in 1942 when a certain Stoker Riley was murdered on board HMAS *Australia* (II), and the matter was dealt with by way of court-martial. There were considerable evidential difficulties which needed to be addressed during the trial, and an extended account of these matters is available elsewhere.[42] The trial resulted in the conviction of Acting Leading Stoker Gordon and Stoker Elias for the murder, and both sailors were awarded the death penalty, which was later remitted such that each spent eight years in prison. However, two consequences of the trial should be highlighted here.

The first point of note is that an appeal was made to the High Court challenging the validity of the sentence of the court-martial due to perceived inconsistencies between the *Imperial Naval Discipline Act* 1866 (under which the court-martial was convened) and the *Defence Act* 1903 relating to the imposition of the death penalty. The High Court ultimately held that the death sentence was lawful, which 'was clearly one of the most important factors which impelled the Government to bring in legislation adopting the *Statute of Westminster*, as it [the court-martial] figured extensively in the debates when the *Statute of Westminster Adoption Bill* was introduced into Parliament'.[43] We recall here the importance of the *Statute of Westminster* in severing Australia's legislative ties with Britain.

The second point to note is that the prosecution at the court-martial was conducted by Captain Farncomb, the commanding officer of *Australia*, in accordance with the requirements of the time. Farncomb's performance was closely scrutinised subsequently by the High Court when the case went there on appeal, and he was found to have been a very fair and most competent prosecutor. The case clearly demonstrated that a naval officer with no formal legal training was nevertheless able to adhere properly to the legal requirements of conducting a prosecution in a court-martial, although this could also be testament to Farncomb's exceptional abilities. As an aside, the practice of the accused's commanding officer prosecuting in a court-martial did not cease until the 1950s.

The application of imperial disciplinary legislation continued to apply until 1985 when the *Defence Force Discipline Act* 1982 commenced operation. This Act represented a fundamental shift in disciplinary arrangements in the RAN, since for the first time since Federation the discipline of naval personnel depended solely on a single piece of Australian legislation. It also meant that RAN disciplinary arrangements could finally move forward from reliance on imperial Acts and regulations, most of which had ceased to operate in the United Kingdom.

The introduction of the *Defence Force Discipline Act* has not been without its legal difficulties. There have been three High Court challenges to the constitutional validity of the Act in the 14 years since it commenced operation.[44] While the High Court has rejected each of these challenges each time, the decisions have not been unanimous and the court has been very clear in holding that the only types of offences that may be heard under the Act are those which can be categorised as being 'for the purpose of maintaining or enforcing service discipline'—the so-called Brennan–Toohey test from *Re Tracey*.[45]

Quite aside from challenges to the constitutional validity of the *Defence Force Discipline Act*, a number of courts-martial have also reached the High Court in recent times. The last of these was the case of *Hembury v Chief of the General Staff* where the point at issue was the order in which the members of the court-martial cast their vote.[46] The court found that misdirection from the Judge Advocate on this point was sufficient to uphold Hembury's appeal against his convictions.[47]

Conclusions

It can be seen that the effect of the law on the RAN is all-encompassing, and the potential for the actions of the military to be adjudged before the highest judicial tribunals in Australia, and the world, is real. I therefore conclude with a quote attributed to Farncomb, some years after the trial of the two stokers in 1942. By this time he had been promoted rear admiral and was in command of the Australian Fleet. One day on the flagship's quarterdeck Farncomb overheard the former counsel for the accused stokers making various uncomplimentary remarks regarding the efficacy of naval courts-martial. The admiral turned to the young officer in question, Lieutenant Rapke (later Judge of the Victorian County Court and Judge-Advocate General for the Naval Forces) and said 'the trouble with you Rapke is that you don't understand the Navy. We administer justice not the law!'[48]

19 A fleet not a navy: some thoughts on the themes
James Goldrick

The observer is struck by the recurrence of two themes within this collection of essays. The first is the extent to which the Australian experience has been marked by a conflict between two key facets of the twentieth-century development of Western maritime strategy. This conflict set the requirements for a contribution to the protection of worldwide global commerce against a preoccupation with the needs of national territorial defence. The local imperative would go so far as to include the protection of ports, harbours and coastal shipping, but never really encompassed the issues of oceanic trade protection, despite the reality that national survival, albeit in the longer term, depended equally upon the latter.

Much of this dichotomy is represented in the Australian experience by the distinctions which were drawn between imperial and local defence and the resulting debates over operational control and funding. That such debates should have occurred in a context of emerging nationalism was wholly natural, but it is difficult to avoid the impression that much of the problem in resolving these issues was one of terminology and understanding and the extent to which mutual economic imperatives were concealed by the patriotic language of Empire and imperialism. Too much attention, in other words, was devoted to the areas coloured red on the map of the world and too little to the connections which sustained their collective existence and those of the other countries with which they traded.

Jon Sumida has suggested elsewhere that Alfred Thayer Mahan was one of the first to recognise the extent to which the security of the English-speaking world would rest in the twentieth century upon alliances of mutual benefit to ensure the free passage of international maritime commerce and access to raw materials and markets.[1] One sees again and again in the contributions to this collection the progressive recurrence of this theme and an at least partial realisation of the extent to which Australia's survival and prosperity in the twentieth century would depend upon these 'alliances'. The problem in determining the real needs of Australian defence lay—and continues to lie—in the incompleteness of that understanding.

The second theme concerns the relationship between the Australian nation and its navy. Ross Lamont has previously suggested that the 1909 Conference and the decision to invest in a fleet unit as part of the Admiralty's new scheme for global maritime defence resulted in Australia acquiring a navy rather than achieving it. This is an important point and one that can be taken further. It is no exaggeration to say that the scheme resulted in Australia acquiring a *fleet*, not a *navy*. The point here is that the support provided by the Royal Navy had results more far-reaching for the long term than have been realised to date.

Whatever the problems of the young Australian Navy which resulted from the imposition of British discipline and English social attitudes, the greatest issue was not such internal difficulties but the extent of the dependence of the RAN upon so much of the Royal Navy's deep infrastructure and the effect of that dependence upon both navy and nation. There can be no doubt that this dependence was regarded as a good bargain in peacetime combat capability terms for a succession of governments unwilling to expend more than a minimum of resources upon defence. Its drawback, however, was that otherwise natural connections between the navy and the nation failed to develop, not only in terms of the expertise and capabilities required of naval and civil administrations for the development and maintenance of modern navies, but in politics and industry.

The British historian Nicholas Rodger has remarked that the financial, technological and political commitment required to outfit and deploy a fleet in the sixteenth century was of a scale comparable to that required to place a man on the moon in the twentieth.[2] Rodger's thesis was that navies represented in many ways the most complex expression possible of the efforts of the early modern state. Much of the work included in this collection, together with the research of historians such as Jon Sumida and Nicholas Lambert, indicates that such a degree of relative complexity and the extraordinary demand on the resources of the nation-state which the creation and maintenance of a navy represented held equally true in the first years of the twentieth century.[3] The experience of the present day, particularly the difficulties encountered by projects such as the *Collins* class submarine, would suggest, short of major incursions into space, that navies continue to represent a uniquely complex and challenging manifestation of state effort.

The scene at Farm Cove after the arrival of the Australian Fleet Unit on 4 October 1913. (RAN)

Analysis of the development of Australian defence policy in the twentieth century has hitherto concentrated on the slow and sometimes fitful progression away from uncritical adherence to British imperial strategy towards more independent security policies. This focus has been largely political and grand-strategic in nature, tracing the deterioration of the linkages with the United Kingdom, the experience of the world wars and the growth of the relationship with the United States. It has to be said, however, that this effort, however scholarly, must be assessed as something incomplete because there has so far been little recognition that the grafting of sophisticated military forces on to the nation-state, rather than their internal generation, created different conditions and thus different issues, relationships and problems for Australia than for many other countries.

For the nature of the relationship with Britain by which the RAN was created and sustained was such that the full consequences of the defence responsibility were never properly comprehended by either the political, industrial or financial establishments of the nation—or the population at large. Those far distant naval administrative structures, research organisations, design authorities and equipment manufacturers upon which the eyes of the Australian Parliament never set stood between it and a vastly greater demand for defence expenditure for many decades. Equally to the point, they ensured that Australian peacetime defence spending could concentrate very largely upon fighting capability and its maintenance at high degrees of efficiency in ways which would have been impossible had that capability had to be wholly generated within Australia from within the same financial allocations.

Here, however, was the deeper issue. Dependence upon Britain meant that there was no development of what could be termed a 'naval–political–industrial complex' within Australia. Notwithstanding Eisenhower's warning of 40 years ago of the dangers of such complexes, it can be argued that there is another side to the picture and that the limitations of the Australian experience meant a price to pay in terms of national development and national maturity. Navies cannot be conjured up by the easy *diktat* of authoritarian governments. The reality is that the development and long-term survival of efficient and effective navies has, since the beginning of the modern nation-state, been very largely dependent upon advanced systems of state credit, upon the support of electorates and upon the availability of sophisticated industrial and human processes.[4] A navy must be built, equipped, manned and trained. These processes, history would suggest, are more consistently and more efficiently accomplished by liberal democracies than any other form of government. It may be a truism that a true navy—one that has credible warfighting capability—can be sustained only with the consent of the governed. This is not and has never been true of armies.

Many of the problems of the RAN in relation to the nation can be judged in this light. Much of the dissatisfaction with the alien nature of the naval service which was already manifesting itself within the period covered by this volume and which would be a perennial problem in the years ahead resulted not only from the strength of British connections but from the sheer *lack* of Australian connections. And the problem had two aspects. Not only did those actors within a modern nation-state who would otherwise have been involved in the maintenance and organisation of the navy's deep infrastructure never receive real exposure to such matters, but the leaders of the RAN were not in a position to develop their own understanding of what it was they had to do to foster the growth of a truly national navy.

The drawbacks of this situation tended to be disguised in time of peace but acutely manifest in time of war. The maintenance of peacetime combat capability meant just that. What did not exist, as became clear in 1914 and to a much greater extent in 1939 and 1942, were more than the rudiments of a proper basis for indigenous naval expansion in emergency. This would gravely limit Australia's ability to provide for its maritime self-defence and for the protection of the seaborne communications upon which so much depended. Much of the criticism of Australia's mobilisation efforts in 1939–45 has concentrated upon the country's industrial capabilities. The truth is that the problems which restricted Australian efforts went much deeper than that.

It is only in the last two decades that this situation has begun to change and there has been an inevitable price to be paid. Both the RAN and the nation have had lessons to learn in the realities of making navies work. In particular, the experience of the last decade in the drive to 'self-reliance' and the assumption by the RAN of parenting responsibilities for a wide range of new platforms and systems has been something quite new to Australia. Because of this, there has been a degree of immaturity, not only in the manner in which the navy and the defence organisation have gone about meeting the challenge, but in the extent to which the sheer difficulty of the problems inherent in that process has been underestimated by government, industry and the electorate.

We can thus look at 1909 and the events which followed as the real beginning of Australian naval effort, but not the true birth of an Australian national navy. It will be many years yet before historians are in a position to set the point at which this nativity occurred—the baby may still be in the hands of the midwife. The incompleteness of the Australian naval experience should not, however, disguise the quality of the Australian contribution to the maritime defence of the Western coalitions of the twentieth century. It has been important both for the nation, as in the battle cruiser *Australia*'s deterrence of the Germans in 1914, and its alliances. That the Royal Australian Navy has, since its inception, also been something uniquely and undoubtedly Australian is something that has always been apparent to other navies, if not to less expert observers.

Furthermore, even if successive governments had proved willing to make the resource commitments required, it may well be that attempts to nationalise our naval effort earlier in the twentieth century would have created the necessary infrastructure only at the expense of readiness and efficiency. The history of smaller navies which have not maintained strong links with the great powers is not an inspiring one. Perhaps the fleet unit concept of 1909 was, despite the unseen problems which it would generate, the best answer for Australia and its naval requirements.

Notes

Introduction

1 Brochure to commemorate the arrival of the Australian Fleet, Sydney, 4 October 1913.

1 The rise of modern naval strategy c. 1580–1880

1 On the ideas of Mahan and Corbett, see the essays by Hattendorf and Hunt respectively in J.B. Hattendorf and R.S. Jordan (eds), *Maritime Strategy and the Balance of Power: Britain and America in the Twentieth Century* (London: 1989).
2 G. Parker, *The Military Revolution: Military Innovation and the Rise of the West 1500–1800*, second edn (Cambridge: 1996), ch. 3.
3 N. Rodger, *The Safeguard of the Sea: A Naval History of Britain, vol. 1, 660–1649* (London: 1997), p. 379.
4 Liddell Hart defined strategy as 'the art of distributing and applying military means to fulfill the ends of policy', B.H. Liddell Hart, *Strategy*, second revised edn (repr. New York: 1991), p. 321.
5 A.T. Mahan, *The Influence of Sea Power Upon History 1660–1783* (1890, repr. London: 1965), p. 9.
6 See also W. Murray, M. Knox and A. Bernstein (eds), *The Making of Strategy: Rulers, States, and War* (Cambridge: 1994), ch. 1.
7 C.S. Gray, *The Navy in the Post-Cold War World: The Uses and Value of Strategic Sea Power* (University Park, Pennsylvania: 1994), ch. 3.
8 On these three see D. Schurman, *The Education of a Navy: The Development of British Naval Strategic Thought 1867–1914* (London: 1965).
9 J.B. Hattendorf, *England in the War of the Spanish Succession: A*

Study of the English View and Conduct of Grand Strategy, 1702–1712 (New York: 1989).
10 N. Rodger, *The Wooden World: An Anatomy of the Georgian Navy* (London: 1986).
11 C. Gray, *The Leverage of Sea Power: The Strategic Advantage of Navies in War* (New York: 1992).
12 N. Tracy, *Attack on Maritime Trade* (London: 1991).
13 J. Corbett, *Some Principles of Maritime Strategy* (1911, repr. ed. E. Grove, London: 1988), p. 163.
14 On this period see R.B. Wernham, *The Making of Elizabethan Foreign Policy 1558–1603* (Berkeley: 1980).
15 J.D. Davies, 'A Permanent National Maritime Fighting Force, 1642–1689' in J.R. Hill (ed.), *The Oxford Illustrated History of the Royal Navy* (Oxford: 1995), pp. 75ff.
16 B. Lavery, *Nelson's Navy: The Ships, Men and Organisation 1793–1815*, revised edn (London: 1990), pp. 245ff.
17 Gray, *Leverage of Sea Power*, pp. 37–8; N. Tracy, *Nelson's Battles* (London: 1996), pp. 29ff.
18 Tracy, *Attack on Maritime Trade*, pp. 3–4, 239–40.
19 Lavery, *Nelson's Navy*, pp. 281ff.
20 Tracy, *Attack on Maritime Trade*, pp. 48–9.
21 Quoted in C. Hibbert, *Nelson: A Personal History* (London: 1994), p. 43.
22 B. Lavery, *Nelson and the Nile. The Naval War Against Bonaparte in 1798* (London: 1998), pp. 302–3.
23 Corbett, *Some Principles of Maritime Strategy*, p. 114. On Nelson's extensive strategic discussions in London before Trafalgar, see T. Pocock, *Horatio Nelson* (London: 1987), p. 307. Nelson stated that he wanted a victory of annihilation which would be useful 'in the extended scale', ibid., p. 314. For a different view, that Nelson was not strategically minded, see J.S. Breemer, 'The Burden of Trafalgar: Decisive Battle and Naval Strategic Expectations on the Eve of World War I', in G. Till (ed.), *Seapower: Theory and Practice* (London: 1994), p. 46.
24 Lavery, *Nelson's Navy*, pp. 300ff.
25 J. Jones, 'The Limitations of British Sea Power in the French Wars, 1689–1815', in J. Black and P. Woodfine (eds), *The British Navy and the Use of Naval Power in the Eighteenth Century* (Leicester: 1988), pp. 45–8.
26 Gray, *Navy in the Post-Cold War World*, p. 32.
27 See Tracy, *Attack on Maritime Trade*, p. 59.
28 J.I. Israel, *The Dutch Republic and the Hispanic World 1606–1661* (Oxford: 1982), pp. 197–8.

29 R. Harding, *Seapower and Naval Warfare 1650–1830* (Annapolis: 1999), pp. 252–3.
30 Gray, *Leverage of Sea Power*, pp. 14, 288.
31 J. Reeve, 'The Politics of War Finance in an Age of Confessional Strife: a Comparative Anglo-European View', in *Parergon: Journal of the Australian and New Zealand Association for Medieval and Early Modern Studies*, 14, 1, 1996, pp. 96–9.
32 G. Symcox, *The Crisis of French Sea-Power 1688–1697: from the* Guerre d'Escadre *to the* Guerre de Course (The Hague: 1974), conclusion.
33 Lavery, *Nelson's Navy*, p. 310.
34 Tracy, *Attack on Maritime Trade*, p. 235. American commerce war against Britain in 1812 was indecisive. The Confederate *guerre de course* in the American Civil War could not succeed against the continental industrial and financial power of the Union. See F. Uhlig, *How Navies Fight* (Annapolis: 1994), pp. 29, 402.
35 M.L. Bartlett (ed.), *Assault from the Sea: Essays on the History of Amphibious Warfare* (Annapolis: 1983), p. 346.
36 J.B. Hattendorf, 'The Struggle with France, 1690–1815', in Hill, *Oxford Illustrated History of the Royal Navy*, p. 98.
37 Quoted in Corbett, *Some Principles of Maritime Strategy*, p. 69.
38 J. Reeve, 'Britain and the World Under the Stuarts, 1603–1689', in J. Morrill (ed.), *The Oxford Illustrated History of Tudor and Stuart Britain* (Oxford: 1996), p. 431.
39 Rodger, *Safeguard of the Sea*, p. 380; Black and Woodfine, *British Navy and the Use of Naval Power*, Introduction, p. 23 et passim.
40 Hattendorf, *England in the War of the Spanish Succession*, p. 268.
41 Black and Woodfine, *British Navy and the Use of Naval Power*, Introduction, p. 9.
42 Hattendorf in Hill, *Oxford Illustrated History of the Royal Navy*, pp. 88ff, 111–12.
43 For concise accounts of nineteenth-century British naval power, see A. Lambert, 'The Shield of Empire, 1815–1895' in ibid., chap. 6, and D.K. Brown, 'Wood, Sail, and Cannonballs to Steel, Steam, and Shells, 1815–1895' in ibid., ch. 7.
44 A.T. Mahan, *The Influence of Sea Power Upon the French Revolution and Empire*, 2 vols (London: 1892), vol. ii, p. 184.
45 Hattendorf in Hill, *Oxford Illustrated History of the Royal Navy*, p. 91.
46 ibid., pp. 111–13, 115–18.
47 Gray, *Leverage of Sea Power*, p. 15.
48 Hattendorf in Hill, *Oxford Illustrated History of the Royal Navy*, p. 103.
49 P.M. Kennedy, *The Rise and Fall of British Naval Mastery* (London: 1976), passim.

50 ibid., pp. 26–8.
51 Mahan, *Influence of Sea Power Upon History*, p. 29.
52 The best biography of Nelson is Pocock, *Horatio Nelson* (New York: 1988).
53 On this issue see E.A. Cohen, 'Churchill and Coalition Strategy in World War II', in P.M. Kennedy (ed.), *Grand Strategies in War and Peace* (New Haven, 1991).
54 J. Black, 'Naval Power and British Foreign Policy in the Age of Pitt the Elder', in Black and Woodfine, *British Navy and the Use of Naval Power*, p. 102 et passim.
55 Hattendorf in Hill, *Oxford Illustrated History of the Royal Navy*, p. 110.
56 See Davies in ibid., ch. 3.
57 Corbett, *Some Principles of Maritime Strategy*, p. 107.
58 On the fallacy of a monocausal explanation of this loss of command in the form of the lack of a continental ally in this war, see Gray, *Leverage of Sea Power*, pp. 50–1, and N. Rodger, 'The Continental Commitment in the Eighteenth Century', in L. Freedman, P. Hayes and R. O'Neill (eds), *War, Strategy and International Politics: Essays in Honour of Sir Michael Howard* (Oxford: 1992). On British naval operational failures in the American War see the essays by Daniel Baugh, David Syrett and Kenneth Breen, in Black and Woodfine, *British Navy and the Use of Naval Power*, chs 7–9.
59 On the various contextual issues impinging on early modern naval strategy, see J. Reeve, 'Britain or Europe? The Context of Early Modern English History: Political and Cultural, Economic and Social, Naval and Military', in G. Burgess (ed.), *The New British History: Founding a Modern State 1603–1715* (London: 1999).
60 See F. Fernandez-Armesto, *The Spanish Armada: The Experience of War in 1588* (Oxford: 1988).
61 Rodger, 'Continental Commitment', p. 54.
62 S.E. Morison, 'Thoughts on Naval Strategy, World War II', 1968, repr. in *Naval War College Review*, Winter, 1998, p. 61. Morison also refers to the influence of Corbett's *England in the Seven Years' War* on Admiral Forrest Sherman. See also the Admiralty Memorandum by Reginald Custance of 1902, printed in N. Lambert (ed.), *Australia's Naval Inheritance: Imperial Maritime Strategy and the Australia Station 1880–1909* (Canberra: 1998), p. 104, which utilises various early modern historical examples.
63 See D. Grinnell-Milne, *The Silent Victory: September 1940* (London: 1958). Appendix B gives a summary of contemporary German military opinion on the problem of British naval forces operating against Operation SEALION.
64 See L. Freedman, *The Revolution in Strategic Affairs*, International

Institute for Strategic Studies Adelphi Paper 318 (London: 1998).
65 See D. Porch, 'The Taiwan Strait Crisis of 1996: Strategic Implications for the United States Navy', *Naval War College Review*, Summer, 1999.
66 N. Friedman, *Desert Victory: The War for Kuwait* (Annapolis: 1992), pp. 85ff.
67 H. Bull, *The Anarchical Society*, second edn (London: 1995).
68 Sir Michael Howard, video interview by Brian Bond, 1994, *Interviews with Historians*, Institute of Historical Research, London.
69 On power projection doctrine, see *Forward . . . From the Sea*, US Navy White Paper (Washington: 1994), updating the earlier *From the Sea* (1992). On the possibility of a new Mahanian age, see R.A. Fry, 'End of the continental century', *US Naval Institute Proceedings*, March, 1999, pp. 40–3; E. Rhodes, ' ". . . From the Sea" and Back Again: Naval Power in the Second American Century', *Naval War College Review*, Spring, 1999.

2 Sea power in modern strategy

1 These arguments provide the framework for my *Modern Strategy* (Oxford: Oxford University Press, 1999).
2 'Barfleur' (pseud. for Admiral Sir Reginald Custance), *Naval Policy: A Plea for the Study of War* (Edinburgh: William Blackwood and Sons, 1907), pp. vii–ix.
3 See W. Murray, 'Thinking About Revolutions in Military Affairs', *Joint Force Quarterly*, Summer 1997, pp. 69–76, and C.S. Gray, 'RMAs and the Dimensions of Strategy', *Joint Force Quarterly*, Autumn/Winter 1997–98, pp. 50–4.
4 J. Bailey, *The First World War and the Birth of the Modern Style of Warfare*, Occasional Paper No. 22 (Camberley: Strategic and Combat Studies Institute, 1996).
5 R.M. Epstein, *Napoleon's Last Victory and the Emergence of Modern War* (Lawrence: University Press of Kansas, 1994); E. Hagerman, *The American Civil War and the Origins of Modern Warfare: Ideas, Organization, and Field Command* (Bloomington: Indiana University Press, 1988).
6 I am doubtful about the integrity in the title of Lawrence Freedman, *The Revolution in Strategic Affairs*, Adelphi Paper No. 318 (London: IISS, 1998).
7 S.M. Miller, *Lord Methuen and the British Army: Failure and Redemption in South Africa* (London: Frank Cass, 1999).

8 P.M. Kennedy, *The Rise and Fall of British Naval Mastery* (New York: Charles Scribner's Sons, 1976), ch. 7.
9 A.T. Mahan, *The Influence of Sea Power upon History, 1660–1783* (London: Methuen, 1965, reprint of 1890 edition), Introductory and ch. 1.
10 H.J. Mackinder, *Democratic Ideals and Reality* (New York: W.W. Norton, 1962).
11 The period of maritime supremacy which in 1904 Mackinder dated approximately to the span of years between 1500 and 'soon after the year 1900'. ibid., p. 241.
12 J.B. Hattendorf (ed.), *The Influence of History on Mahan: The Proceedings of a Conference Marking the Centenary of Alfred Thayer Mahan's* 'The Influence of Sea Power upon History, 1660–1783' (Newport: Naval War College Press, 1991), and J. Goldrick and J.B. Hattendorf (eds), *Mahan is not Enough: The Proceedings of a Conference on the Works of Sir Julian Corbett and Admiral Sir Herbert Richmond* (Newport: Naval War College Press, 1993), provide empathetic, yet not uncritical, commentaries. D.M. Schurman, *Julian S. Corbett, 1854–1922: Historian of British Maritime Policy from Drake to Jellicoe* (London: Royal Historical Society, 1981), and B.D. Hunt, *Sailor–Scholar: Admiral Sir Herbert Richmond, 1871–1946* (Waterloo: Wilfred Laurier Press, 1982), are the standard biographies.
13 H. Richmond, *Statesmen and Sea Power* (Oxford: Oxford University Press, 1946); S.W. Roskill, *The Strategy of Sea Power* (London: Collins, 1962); C.S. Gray, *Leverage of Sea Power: The Strategic Advantage of Navies in War* (New York: Free Press, 1992).
14 Richmond, *Statesmen and Sea Power*, p. 336.
15 C. Barnett, *Engage the Enemy More Closely: The Royal Navy in the Second World War* (New York: W. W. Norton, 1991), p. 838.
16 The maritime contribution to the successive defeats of Germany is well documented and relatively uncontentious. Not so for the maritime contribution to the defeat of the USSR in the Cold War. A strategic appraisal of the US Navy in the Cold War is C.S. Gray, 'Sea Power for Containment: The U.S. Navy In The Cold War', in K. Neilson and E.J. Errington (eds), *Navies and Global Defense: Theories and Strategy* (Westport: Praeger, 1995), pp. 181–207.
17 J.S. Corbett, *Some Principles of Maritime Strategy* (Annapolis: Naval Institute Press, 1988, reprint of 1911 edition with an introduction by E. Grove), p. 15.
18 Amphibious operations today are just one category of power projection from the sea. See M.L. Bartlett (ed.), *Assault from the Sea: Essays on the History of Amphibious Warfare* (Annapolis: Naval Institute Press, 1983); M.H.H. Evans, *Amphibious Operations: The*

Projection of Sea Power Ashore (London: Brassey's, 1990); G. Till, T. Farrell, and E.J. Grove, *Amphibious Operations*, Occasional Paper No. 31 (Camberley: Strategic and Combat Studies Institute, 1997); C.S. Gray, 'Amphibious Operations', in R. Holmes (ed.), *The Oxford Companion to Military History*, forthcoming.

19 A. Toffler, *The Third Wave* (New York: Bantam, 1980); A. and H. Toffler, *War and Anti-War: Survival at the Dawn of the 21st Century* (Boston: Little, Brown, 1993).

20 E.N. Luttwak, *The Political Uses of Sea Power*, Studies in International Affairs 23 (Washington, DC, 1974); K. Booth, *Navies and Foreign Policy* (London: Croom, Helm, 1977); J. Cable, *Gunboat Diplomacy, 1919–1991* (London: Macmillan, 1994); id., *The Political Influence of Naval Force in History* (London: Macmillan, 1998).

21 Carl von Clausewitz, *On War*, trans. M. Howard and P. Paret (Princeton: Princeton University Press, 1976), p. 359.

22 A.T. Mahan, *Retrospect and Prospect: Studies in International Relations, Naval and Political* (London: Sampson, Low, Marston, 1902), pp. 151–69; id., *Naval Strategy, Compared and Contrasted with the Principles and Practice of Military Operations on Land* (Boston: Little, Brown, 1919, reprint of 1911 edn.), pp. 150, 153, 433.

23 Gray, *Leverage of Sea Power*; Cable, *Political Influence of Naval Force in History*.

24 I explore the challenges of asymmetrical strategies between maritime and continental powers in my *War, Peace, and Victory: Strategy and Statecraft for the Next Century* (New York: Simon and Schuster, 1990), ch. 2; id., *Leverage of Sea Power*, chs. 2–3; id., *The Navy in the Post-Cold War World: The Uses and Value of Strategic Sea Power* (University Park: Penn State University Press, 1994), chs. 4–6.

25 A.J. Marder, *From the Dreadnought to Scapa Flow, The Royal Navy in the Fisher Era, 1904–1919: 5, Victory and Aftermath (January 1918 – June 1919)* (London: Oxford University Press, 1970), pp. 332–3; W.P. Hughes, Jr., *Fleet Tactics: Theory and Practice* (Annapolis: Naval Institute Press, 1986), pp. 26–8.

26 M. Vlahos, 'A Crack in the Shield: The Capital Ship Concept Under Attack', *The Journal of Strategic Studies*, May 1979, pp. 7–82. R.L. O'Connell, *Sacred Vessels: The Cult of the Battleship and the Rise of the US Navy* (New York: Oxford University Press, 1991), is relevant.

27 The Lanchester 'n-square law' purports to explain mathematically why quantity, rather than quality—within reason, at least—is the key to success in naval combat. F.W. Lanchester, *Aircraft in Warfare: The Dawn of the Fourth Arm* (London: Constable, 1916), chs. 5–6. Of recent decades, the Lanchester principle, which argues for a

maximum concentration of quantity of force, has been shown by Americans, and especially Israelis, not to apply to modern air power. A.G.B. Vallance, *The Air Weapon: Doctrine of Air Power Strategy and Operational Art* (London: Macmillan, 1996), p. 31. A commentator has simplified matters thus: 'Crudely put, the n-square law states that the measure of combat power is a force's effectiveness times the square of its numerical size'. J.W.R. Lepingwell, 'The Laws of Combat? Lanchester Reexamined', *International Security*, Summer 1987, p. 92. With its elevation in significance of force size over effectiveness, the n-square law is a delight to those who approach combat, indeed war, as an exercise in the exchange of firepower and attritional subtraction of military 'units'. It can be hard to find room for the art of war, or for real strategic experience, in the pure world of the mathematical modelling of conflict.

28 E.J. Grove, *The Future of Sea Power* (Annapolis: Naval Institute Press, 1990), p. 22.

29 Mahan, *Influence of Sea Power upon History, 1660–1783*, p. 25.

30 C.E. Callwell, *Military Operations and Maritime Preponderance: Their Relations and Interdependence*, C.S. Gray (ed.) (Annapolis: Naval Institute Press, 1996 reprint of 1905 edn.), pp. 52–3.

31 N.A.M. Rodger, 'Introduction', to Rodger (ed.), *Naval Power in the Twentieth Century* (Annapolis: Naval Institute Press, 1996), p. xx.

32 J.S. Corbett, *England in the Seven Years' War: A Study in Combined Strategy* (London: Longmans, Green, 1918), i: p. 1.

33 Gray, *Leverage of Sea Power*, ch. 3.

34 C. Blair, *Silent Victory: The US Submarine War Against Japan* (Philadelphia: J.B. Lippincott, 1975); Dan van der Vat, *Stealth at Sea: The History of the Submarine* (Boston: Houghton Mifflin, 1995). A problem with citing the very successful US submarine campaign against Japan is that this historical case may be held to demonstrate either that the *guerre de course* can succeed against a first-class maritime power, or that even such a power can lose a campaign for trade protection if it behaves, as did imperial Japan, with sufficient incompetence.

35 R.A. Gabriel and D.W. Boose, *The Great Battles of Antiquity: A Strategic and Tactical Guide to Great Battles that Shaped the Development of War* (Westport: Greenwood Press, 1994), pp. 256–7.

36 'I shall conquer the sea by the power of the land'. Napoleon on 6 December 1806, quoted in J. Holland Rose, *Man and the Sea: Stages in Maritime and Human Progress* (Cambridge: W. Heffer and Sons, 1935), p. 219.

37 But Mahan's views, unlike many of the reports of his views, were nuanced and, indeed, not always consistent over a long professional

lifetime. The modern defence counsel is J.T. Sumida in his *Inventing Grand Strategy and Teaching Command: The Classic Works of Alfred Thayer Mahan Reconsidered* (Washington: Wilson Center Press, 1997).
38 Grove, 'Introduction', to Corbett, *Some Principles of Maritime Strategy*, p. xxxiv. The 1910s are much more reliably viewed from the strategic perspective of today than they were from the time when Corbett's book went to press in 1911.
39 But see the discussion of Mahan's view of commerce-raiding in Sumida, *Inventing Grand Strategy*, pp. 45–8, and 149 for references to commerce-raiding in an 'analytical index' of Mahan's writings.
40 A. Gordon, *The Rules of the Game: Jutland and British Naval Command* (London: John Murray, 1996).
41 P.S. Dull, *A Battle History of the Imperial Japanese Navy (1941– 1945)* (Annapolis: Naval Institute Press, 1978), chs. 9–11; H.P. Willmott, *The Barrier and the Javelin: Japanese and Allied Pacific Strategies, February to June 1943* (Annapolis: Naval Institute Press, 1983), Part 4.
42 A.K. Cebrowski and J.J. Garstka, 'Network-Centric Warfare: Its Origins and Future', US Naval Institute *Proceedings*, January 1998, pp. 28–35.
43 Gray, *Leverage of Sea Power*, ch. 10.
44 George Robertson, Secretary of State for Defence, *The Strategic Defence Review*, Cm 3999 (London: HMSO, July 1998).
45 The 600-ship (overall) US Navy of the mid-1980s is heading towards 305 (overall) in 2005. S. Truver, 'The US Navy in Review', US Naval Institute *Proceedings*, May 1999, p. 80.
46 For a significant high-tech vision, see Admiral W.A. Owens, *High Seas: The Naval Passage to an Uncharted World* (Annapolis: Naval Institute Press, 1995). Other technology-dominated visions include G. and M. Friedman, *The Future of War: Power, Technology, and American World Dominance in the 21st Century* (New York: Crown Publishers, 1996), and R.W. Chandler, *The New Face of War: Weapons of Mass Destruction and the Revitalization of America's Transoceanic Military Strategy* (McLean: Amcoda Press, 1998).
47 R. Kohout et al., *Looking Out to 2020: Trends Relevant to the Coast Guard*, CIM 499 (Alexandria: Center for Naval Analyses, May 1997), and Office of Naval Intelligence (ONI) and US Coast Guard Intelligence Coordination Center (CGICC), *Threats and Challenges to Maritime Security 2020* (Washington: CGICC, 1 March 1999).
48 For reasons explained in C.S. Gray, *Modern Strategy*, ch. 13, and id., 'Clausewitz Rules, OK? The Future is the Past—with GPS', *Review of International Studies*, special issue, December 1999.

49 Clausewitz, *On War*, p. 89.
50 See the excellent brief essays in 'Is Major War Obsolete? An Exchange', *Survival*, Summer 1999, pp. 139–52.
51 On which subject, see R. Peters, 'Fighting for the Future: Will America Triumph?' (Mecanicsburg: Stackpole Books, 1999), and J. Bourke, *An Intimate History of Killing: Face-to-Face Killing in Twentieth-Century Warfare* (London: Granta Books, 1999).
52 E.N. Luttwak, *Strategy: The Logic of War and Peace* (Cambridge: Harvard University Press, 1987), passim, and Clausewitz, *On War*, p. 75.

3 History and theory: the Clausewitzian ideal and its implications

1 J.S. Corbett, *Some Principles of Maritime Strategy*, introduction and notes by E.J. Grove (Annapolis: Naval Institute Press, 1988; first published 1911), p. 3.
2 ibid., p. 5.
3 ibid., p. 8.
4 ibid., pp. 9–11.
5 ibid., p. 6.
6 Carl von Clausewitz, *On War*, ed. and trans. by M. Howard and P. Paret (Princeton: Princeton University Press, 1976), book two, p. 169. For Clausewitz's recognition of the use of theory to facilitate counsel, but also for his qualification of the significance of this subject, see *On War*, 'Note of 1830', p. 71, and book eight, p. 586. For the chapter of book eight on this matter that was never written, see *On War*, book eight, p. 633.
7 See D.M. Schurman, *Education of a Navy: the development of British naval strategic thought, 1867–1914* (Chicago: University of Chicago Press, 1965), p. 165; and *Julian S. Corbett, 1854–1922: Historian of British Maritime Policy from Drake to Jellicoe* (London: Royal Historical Society, 1981), p. 51; and E. Grove in Corbett, *Some Principles of Maritime Strategy*, pp. xxv–xxvi.
8 I. Berlin, 'The Originality of Machiavelli' in *Against the Current: Essays in the History of Ideas*, H. Hardy, (ed.) (New York: Penguin, 1982; first published 1979), p. 79.
9 Clausewitz, book one, p. 87; book eight, p. 605. For present purposes, the words 'policy' and 'politics' are regarded as interchangeable. As will be seen, the main argument of this essay does not depend upon a particular rendering of either the language or meaning of Clausewitz's phrase; this work will not, therefore, engage with the philological debate over these questions.

10 A. Rapoport, 'Introduction' to Carl von Clausewitz, *On War* (Harmondsworth: Penguin, 1968), p. 13; J.L. Wallach, *The Dogma of the Battle of Annihilation: The Theories of Clausewitz and Schlieffen and Their Impact on the German Conduct of Two World Wars* (Estport: Greenwood Press, 1985), p. 12; and J. Keegan, *A History of Warfare* (New York: Alfred A. Knopf, 1994), pp. 3–24.
11 A. Gat, *The Origins of Military Thought from the Enlightenment to Clausewitz* (Oxford: Clarendon Press, 1989), pp. 215–50.
12 Carl von Clausewitz, 'Note of 10 July 1827', in *On War*, p. 69, italics in the original.
13 Carl von Clausewitz, 'Unfinished Note, Presumably Written in 1830', in *On War*, p. 70.
14 'Note of 10 July 1827', in *On War*, p. 71.
15 Clausewitz, book one, pp. 119–21; and book eight, chapters seven and eight.
16 Gat, pp. 255–63.
17 'Note of 10 July 1827', in *On War*, p. 70.
18 Gat, pp. 169–71, 252; and A. Beyerchen, 'Clausewitz, Nonlinearity, and the Unpredictability of War', *International Security*, Winter 1992–93, pp. 59–60.
19 R. Aron, *Clausewitz Philosopher of War*, translated by C. Booker and N. Stone (Englewood Cliffs: Prentice-Hall, 1985), pp. 196–213; Gat, pp. 187–9, 197, 210–12; Beyerchen, pp. 59–60; and M.I. Handel, *Masters of War: Classical Strategic Thought*, Second Revised Edition (London: Frank Cass, 1996).
20 P. Paret, 'Clausewitz as Historian', in *Understanding War: Essays on Clausewitz and the History of Military Power* (Princeton: Princeton University Press, 1992), p. 130.
21 I am indebted to George Baer, Nicholas Lambert, John Reeve and Brian Sullivan for their meticulous readings of numerous earlier redactions of the present article, and to James Goldrick, Sir Michael Howard and David Rosenberg for many years of encouragement and discussion.
22 Clausewitz, book two, p. 128, italics in the original.
23 ibid., p. 133.
24 ibid., pp. 153–4.
25 ibid., pp. 154–5.
26 ibid., p. 140.
27 ibid., p. 134.
28 ibid., p. 133.
29 ibid., p. 134.
30 ibid.
31 ibid., p. 136.

32 ibid. pp. 137–40.
33 ibid. p. 136, italics in the original. See also book one, chapter three 'On Military Genius', pp. 100–12. For the source of the concept, see Gat, pp. 175–6.
34 *On War*, p. 141, see also p. 168 (theory as a guide to a commander's education).
35 ibid., p. 146.
36 ibid.
37 Carl von Clausewitz, 'On the Genesis of his Early Manuscript on the Theory of War, Written around 1818', in *On War*, p. 63.
38 *On War*, p. 149; see also book three, chapter seven (instead of denizens of the scientific world the reader finds himself encountering only creatures of everyday life), p. 193.
39 ibid., pp. 142–3.
40 ibid. p. 156.
41 ibid. See also book one, chapter three (clashes of opinion that precede major operations are deliberately concealed because they touch political interests, or are forgotten), p. 112, and chapter seven (effects of friction cannot be measured), p. 120; book two, chapter five (the mass of influential minor circumstances and many subjective motives is unknowable), p. 164; book six, chapter eight (counterweights that weaken the elemental force of war are concealed from the rest of the world and even from the commander), p. 388; book eight, chapter four (moral factors that never come to light), p. 595.
42 ibid., p. 157.
43 ibid., p. 158. See also book eight, chapter four (particular factors can often be decisive), p. 595.
44 ibid., p. 159.
45 ibid., p. 161.
46 ibid., p. 163.
47 ibid., p. 157.
48 ibid.
49 ibid., p. 165.
50 ibid., p. 167. See also book one, chapter five (feelings act as higher judgment), p. 116, and book three, chapter one (accurate fulfilment of unspoken assumptions only become evident in final success), pp. 177–8.
51 ibid., p. 161.
52 ibid., p. 168, italics in the original.
53 ibid., p. 170.
54 ibid.
55 ibid., p. 171.
56 ibid., p. 172.

57 ibid.
58 ibid., p. 174, italics in the original.
59 Paret, 'Genesis', in *On War*, p. 24.
60 R. Parkinson, *Clausewitz: A Biography* (New York: Stein and Day, 1971).
61 *On War*, p. 122.
62 ibid., p. 185.
63 'Note of 10 July 1827', in *On War*, p. 70.
64 For a description of this approach, and a critique of its shortcomings, see P. Paret, 'Clausewitz', in Paret (ed.), *Makers of Modern Strategy from Machiavelli to the Nuclear Age* (Princeton: Princeton University Press, 1986), pp. 208–9.
65 *On War*, p. 389, italics in the original.
66 R.G. Collingwood, 'The Nature and Aims of a Philosophy of History' (1924–25), in W. Debbins, (ed.), *Essays in the Philosophy of History* (Austin: University of Texas Press, 1965), p. 34.
67 ibid., p. 43. See also W.H. Dray, *History as Re-Enactment: R.G. Collingwood's Idea of History* (Oxford: Clarendon Press, 1995), pp. 233–9.
68 R.G. Collingwood, *The Idea of History* (Oxford: Oxford University Press, 1946; paperback edition, 1956), p. 302.
69 ibid., p. 305.
70 *On War*, p. 148.
71 B. Brodie, 'The Continuing Relevance of *On War*', in *On War*, p. 45.
72 Schurman, *The Education of a Navy*, pp. 164, 169, 173, 175–7; and *Julian S. Corbett, 1854–1922*, pp. 51, 60.

4 Imperial naval defence—a model for transnationalism: a Canadian perspective

1 'Papers relating to a Conference between the Secretary of State for the Colonies and the Prime Ministers of Self-Governing Colonies', Appendix IV, Document 6 in N. Tracy (ed.), *The Collective Naval Defence of the Empire, 1900–1940* (London: Naval Records Society, 1997), p. 7.
2 Public Record Office (PRO): ADM 116/1241B, ff. 265–8, 374–5, 435–43.
3 12 January 1910, Canada, Commons, Debates, 1909–10, vol. 1, col. 1746. Quoted in, 'Admiralty Policy Vis a Vis the Dominions, Outstanding Points up to 1923', by CAPT Pound, 4 May 1923, PRO: ADM 116/3438.
4 PRO: ADM 116/3104, ff. 40–53; and Admiralty memorandum

'Co-operation of the Dominions and Colonies in a System of Imperial Naval Defence', August 1920, CID 129-C, printed February 1921, PRO: CAB 5/3, ff. 269–72.

5 'Naval Defence of the Empire—Imperial Naval Policy'—abstracted in summary of proceedings of the 1921 Imperial Conference, PRO: CAB 21/187, (UK, cd. 1474).

6 Pound, 'Admiralty Policy Vis a Vis the Dominions, Outstanding Points up to 1923', PRO: ADM 116/3438. See also, RADM H.J. Feakes, RAN to Wilson, 29 November 1927, PRO: CAB 21/315.

7 In another place I have traced the line of descent from this first effort at fisheries protection, the later development of a Canadian navy, and its commitment to the defence needs of Canada's friends and neighbours, to its effectiveness as an instrument of national policy in the 1996 'Turbot War'. The measures, which had been taken in the first half of the century to develop the concept of transnational collective defence, and its later application to the needs of the Cold War, were central to the outcome.

8 Lord Haldane, Minutes of the 109th Meeting of CID, 24 March 1911, discussing CID paper 70-C, 'The International Status of the Dominions During a War in which the United Kingdom is Engaged', PRO: ADM116/1100C, ff. 169–70.

9 W. Graham Greene, Assistant Secretary of the Admiralty, to USS Colonies, 10 February 1908, PRO: ADM 116/1100c, f. 55.

10 Admiralty Memorandum on 'The Status of Dominion Ships of War', August 1910, CID 83C, July 1912, PRO: CAB 5/2, ff. 202–5.

11 Canada, Debates of the Commons, 1900, col. 1846; and Papers relating to a Conference between the Secretary of State for the Colonies and the Prime Ministers of Self-Governing Colonies, June 30 – Aug 11 1902. GB, Commons, 1902 Vol. LXVI, p. 451. Sessional Paper Cd 1299.

12 Imperial Conference 1911, 'Memorandum of Conferences Between the British Admiralty and Representatives of the Dominions of Canada and Australia', June 1911, PRO: ADM 116/1100c, ff. 264–7.

13 Clause 23. Cd. 4948, pp. 25–6 (answer to an inquiry from Canada 5 February 1910).

14 December 1 1910, Canada, Commons Debates, session 1910–11 col. 612. J.S Ewart, *Kingdom Papers* (Ottawa: no imprint, 1912), Nos. 6, 9, 11, 15.

15 C.P. Stacey, *Mackenzie King and the Atlantic Triangle* (Toronto: Macmillan, 1976), pp. 35, 64.

16 N. Hillmer, 'Defence and Ideology: The Anglo-Canadian military

"alliance" in the 1930s', *International Journal*, Summer 1977–78, pp. 585–612.
17 Chiefs of Staff subcommittee of CID, 22 October 1930, PRO: CAB 53/3, ff. 273–6.
18 S.H. Phillips (Admiralty) to USS Dominions, 16 May 1938; Note on a discussion at the War Book Sub-Committee Meeting on 18 May 1938, on the desirability of amending the War Book to meet the case where one or more of the Dominions may delay their entry into the war, or remain neutral; Hankey to Harding, 20 May 1938; Unattributed Paper, November 1938; S.H. Phillips to USS Dominions, 1 February 1939, PRO: CAB 104/18 and 19.
19 Hankey to Harding, 9 May 1938, PRO: CAB 21/670. Quoted in J. Granatstein, *Canada's War* (Toronto: University of Toronto Press, 1975), p. 3.
20 A. Temple Patterson (ed.), *The Jellicoe Papers* (London: Navy Records Society, 1968), vol. 2, pp. 315–54.
21 In March 1921 the Cs-in-C of the China, East Indies, and Australia stations met at Penang to discuss the need for a higher organisation to co-ordinate their efforts in time of war. The oil fuel requirements to ensure fleet mobility, especially so that the main fleet could be deployed to Singapore, were outlined in an Admiralty memorandum of 24 May 1921 for CID. On 7 June 1921 the Oversea Sub-Committee of CID reported its recommendation that Singapore be developed as a base, the Treasury submitting a dissenting opinion. On 13 June the 141st meeting of CID agreed to present to the forthcoming Imperial Conference the plan to develop Singapore as British governmental policy, and on 21 June the First Lord presented a memorandum to CID on 'Reserves of Oil Fuel' which considerably elaborated on that of 24 May. [171, 173–5]
22 PRO: CAB 32/2, ff. 222–73, 415–39; E32, ADM 116/3415, pp. 23–4.
23 Parliamentary Papers, 1924, vol. XV, pp. 841–55, Cmd 2083, 25 March 1924.
24 CID 354-C, PRO: CAB 5/7, f. 180; and CAB 32/91, f. 2.
25 PRO: CAB 53/4, ff. 114–17; CAB 4/22, ff. 11; CAB 23/75, ff. 440–2.
26 MO 2220/39, PRO: ADM 1/9831.
27 'Canada and the Polish War. A Personal Note', 25 August 1939, DEA Records, vol. 54, file 319–2. Quoted in Granatstein, *Canada's War*, p. 6.
28 A.W. Preston, 'Canada and the Higher Direction of the Second World War 1939–1945', *Journal of the Royal United Services Institute*, February 1965, pp. 28–44.
29 J. Granatstein, *Ottawa Men* (Toronto: University of Toronto Press,

1982), pp. 125–33; and L. Pearson, vol. 1, pp. 170, 284.
30 W.G.D. Lund, 'The Royal Canadian Navy's Quest for Autonomy in the North West Atlantic 1941–43', in J. Boutilier (ed.), *RCN in Retrospect*, pp. 138–57; C.P. Stacey, *Arms, Men and Government* (Ottawa: Queen's Printer, 1970), pp. 307–14; and M. Milner, *North Atlantic Run* (Toronto: University of Toronto Press, 1985), pp. 58–61, 229–33.
31 'Post-war Canadian Defence Relationship with the United States: General Considerations', 23 January 1945, Canada, DEA, Report of the Advisory Committee on Post-Hostilities Problems.
32 J. Holmes, *The Shaping of Peace: Canada and the Search for World Order, 1943–57* (Toronto: University of Toronto Press, 1979), vol. 1, pp. 105–24, 154–6; vol. 4, p. 76.
33 E. Reid, *Time of Fear and Hope, The Making of the North Atlantic Treaty 1947–1949* (Toronto: McClelland and Stewart, 1977), pp. 126–32.
34 J. Eayrs, *In Defence of Canada*, vol. 4, pp. 140–3.
35 NATO Information Service, *NATO Facts and Figures* (Brussels: NATO, 1976), pp. 218–21.
36 Quoted in *Canada in World Affairs* (Toronto: Canadian Institute for International Affairs), vol. 12, p. 131.
37 J.T. Jockel, *No Boundaries Upstairs: Canada the United States and the Origins of North American Air Defence, 1945–1958* (Vancouver: University of British Columbia Press, 1987), pp. 91–117; and C.A. Cannizzo, 'NORAD–NATO Linkages', *Canadian Defence Quarterly*, April 1990, pp. 21–7.
38 P.T. Haydon, *The 1962 Cuban Missile Crisis: Canadian Involvement Reconsidered* (Toronto: The Canadian Institute for Strategic Studies. 1993), pp. 68–87.
39 J.J. Sokolsky, 'Canada and the Cold War at Sea, 1945–68', in W.A.B. Douglas (ed.), *The RCN in Transition, 1910–1985*, pp. 209–32 (especially pp. 218–20).
40 P. Stursberg, *Lester Pearson and the American Dilemma*, pp. 216–24; and L.B. Pearson, 'Canada, the United States, and Vietnam', in N. Hillmer (ed.), *Partners Nevertheless, Canadian–American Relations in the Twentieth Century* (Toronto: Copp Clark Pitman, 1989).
41 Canada, DEA, Statements and Speeches, 69/9. J.L. Granatstein and R. Bothwell, *Pirouette, Pierre Trudeau and Canadian Foreign Policy* (Toronto: University of Toronto Press, 1990), pp. 236–44.
42 Granatstein, *Ottawa Men*, pp. 275–6.

5 Maritime forces and expeditionary strategies: we are all Corbettians now

1. Admiral Sir Jock Slater, 'The Maritime Contribution to Joint Operations', *RUSI Journal*, December 1998, p. 20.
2. H.L. Stimson and McGeorge Bundy, *On Active Service in Peace and War* (New York: Harper & Row, 1948), p. 506.
3. Lord Esher to Sir Maurice Hankey (Committee of Imperial Defence), 15 March 1915, cited in D.M. Schurman, *The Education of a Navy— The Development of British Naval Strategic Thought* (London: Cassell, 1965), p. 190.
4. J.S. Corbett, *Some Principles of Maritime Strategy* (Annapolis: Naval Institute Press, 1988, reprint of 1911 edition with an introduction by E.J. Grove), p. 16.
5. W. Laird Clowes, *The Royal Navy: A History from the Earliest Times to the Death of Queen Victoria*, vol. 7 (London: Sampson Low, Marston and Company, 1903), p. vii.
6. J.T. Sumida, *Inventing Grand Strategy and Teaching Command* (Baltimore: Johns Hopkins University Press, 1997).
7. P.G. Hore, 'The Strategy of Choice', in E. Grove and P. Hore (eds), *Dimensions of Sea Power: Strategic Choice in the Modern World* (Hull: University of Hull Press, 1998), p. 13.
8. Corbett, p. 15.
9. M. Evans, 'Treasury grabs £1bn defence windfall', *The Times*, 2 July 1998, p. 1.
10. B.H. Liddel Hart, 'Marines and Strategy', *Marine Corps Gazette*, July 1960, p. 17.
11. Rear Admiral Raja Menon, *Maritime Strategy and Continental Wars* (London: Frank Cass, 1998), p. 204.
12. M. Evans, 'Maritime Power and the Australian Army', in D. Stevens (ed.), *Maritime Power in the 20th Century: The Australian Experience* (Sydney: Allen & Unwin, 1998).
13. The Royal Navy's new operational concept, the Maritime Contribution to Joint Operations (MCJO), incorporates joint and combined assets into a sea-based force package to affect the situation ashore, while using the freedom of political and military manoeuvre conferred by use of the sea. Operating from a secure sea base, MCJO employs fixed- and rotary-wing aviation for simultaneous close and deep operations, maritime-based fires, an ability to manoeuvre in contact and both precision and conventional fires.
14. The Amsterdam Treaty forwards the development of an EU Common Foreign and Security Policy (CFSP), provides for the appointment of a CFSP High Representative, implementation of a

Policy Planning and Early Warning Unit and the active pursuit of new common strategies and improvements in actual European military capability. St Malo recognised the political and military weight of both France and the UK. It focuses on moving forward the practical requirements for greater European co-operation on the CFSP objectives envisaged in the Amsterdam Treaty.

15 SIAF seeks to emulate the success of the UKNLAF. Both parties commit roughly equal force components and contribute to a permanent HQ, with command being rotational.

16 These ambitions need to be tempered with budgetary realism. The force has significant C4I and sustainability shortfalls and the very significant funding required to upgrade them is unlikely to be realised in the short term.

6 Strategic culture and the Australian way of warfare: perspectives

1 See K. Booth, *Strategy and Ethnocentrism* (New York: Holmes and Meier, 1979); J. Snyder, 'The Concept of Strategic Culture: Caveat Emptor', in C. Jacobsen (ed.), *Strategic Power: USA/USSR* (London: Macmillan, 1990); Y. Klein, 'A Theory of Strategic Culture', *Comparative Strategy*, 1991, pp. 3–25; A. Macmillan, K. Booth and R. Trood, 'Strategic Culture', in Booth and Trood (eds), *Strategic Cultures in the Asia–Pacific Region* (London: Macmillan, 1999), pp. 3–29.

2 K. Booth, 'The Concept of Strategic Culture Affirmed', in Jacobsen, *Strategic Power: USA/USSR*, p. 121.

3 J. Slessor, *The Great Deterrent* (London: Cassell, 1957), p. 156.

4 See for example A. Macmillan, 'Strategic Culture and National Ways in Warfare: The British Case', *RUSI Journal*, October 1995, pp. 33–9; A.I. Johnston, 'Thinking About Strategic Culture', *International Security*, Spring 1995, pp. 32–64; and *Cultural Realism: Strategic Culture and Grand Strategy in Chinese History* (Princeton: Princeton University Press, 1995).

5 C. Gray, 'National Style in Strategy: The American Example', *International Security*, Fall 1981; and *Explorations in Strategy* (Westport: Praeger, 1996), pp. 83–109; A.M. Arms, 'Strategic Culture: The American Mind', in T.C. Gill (ed.), *Essays on Strategy IX* (Washington: National Defense University Press), pp. 3–33.

6 M. Alagappa (ed.), *Asian Security Practice: Material and Ideational Influences* (Stanford: Stanford University Press, 1998). See also D. Ball, *Strategic Culture in the Asia–Pacific Region*, Working Paper

No. 270 (Canberra: Strategic and Defence Studies Centre, Australian National University [SDSC], April 1993); P. Kerr, *Researching Security in East Asia: From 'Strategic Culture' to 'Security Culture'*, Working Paper No. 326 (Canberra: SDSC, August 1998).
7 See F.A. Kiernan and J.F. Fairbank (eds), *Chinese Ways in Warfare* (Cambridge: Harvard University Press, 1974); S.J. Blank, L.E. Grinter, K.P. Magyar, L.B. Ware and B.E. Weathers, *Conflict, Culture and History: Regional Dimensions* (Alabama: Air University Press, January 1993); S.P. Rosen, *Societies and Military Power: India and its Armies* (Ithaca: Cornell University Press, 1996).
8 See J. Shy, 'The Cultural Approach to the History of War', *The Journal of Military History*, October 1993, pp. 13–26. See also A.B. Bozeman's fine essay, 'War and the Clash of Ideas', *Orbis: A Journal of World Affairs*, Spring 1976, pp. 61–102.
9 M. Howard, *The Franco–Prussian War: The German Invasion of France, 1870–1871* (London: Rupert Hart-Davis, 1961), p. 1.
10 For a useful discussion of this problem, see C. McInnes, *Hot War, Cold War: The British Army's Way in Warfare, 1945–95* (London: Brasseys, 1996), pp. 1–2.
11 C. Lord, 'American Strategic Culture', in F.E. Baumann and K.E. Jensen (eds), *American Defense Policy and Liberal Democracy* (Charlottesville: University Press of Virginia, 1989), p. 45.
12 As Colin Gray has argued, strategic culture incorporates the more restrictive notion of a national style, or way of warfare, Gray, *Explorations in Strategy*, p. 84. See also G. Chaliand, 'Warfare and Strategic Cultures in History', in Chaliand (ed.), *The Art of War in World History: From Antiquity to the Nuclear Age* (Berkeley: University of California Press, 1994), pp. 1–46.
13 US Army Field Manual FM 100–5, *Operations* (Washington: Government Printing Office, June 1993), pp. 1–2 – 1–3.
14 B.H. Liddell Hart, *The British Way in Warfare: Adaptability and Mobility* (London: Faber, 1932); R.F. Weigley, *The American Way of War: A History of United States Military Strategy and Policy* (New York: Macmillan, 1973).
15 M. Howard, *The Continental Commitment: The Dilemma of British Defence Policy in the Era of the Two World Wars* (Harmondsworth: Penguin, 1974 edition); 'The British Way in Warfare: A Reappraisal', in *The Causes of Wars* (London: Unwin, 1983), pp. 189–207; Field Marshal Lord Carver, 'Continental or Maritime Strategy? Past, Present and Future', *RUSI Journal*, Autumn 1989, pp. 61–9; L. Freedman, 'Alliance and the British Way in Warfare', *Review of International Studies*, 1995, pp. 145–58; Macmillan, 'Strategic Culture and National Ways in Warfare: The British Case', pp. 33–8.

16 General D.A. Starry, 'A Perspective on American Military Thought', *Military Review*, July 1989, pp. 2–11.
17 V.D. Hanson, *The Western Way of War: Infantry Battle in Classical Greece* (New York: Oxford University Press, 1989).
18 ibid., pp. 14–18.
19 J. Keegan, *A History of Warfare* (London: Hutchinson, 1993), chapter 1.
20 ibid., pp. 353; 386–92.
21 L. Freedman, *The Revolution in Strategic Affairs*, Adelphi Paper 318 (London: International Institute for Strategic Studies, April 1998).
22 See G. Cheeseman and R. Bruce (eds), *Discourses of Danger and Dread Frontiers: Australian Defence and Security Thinking After the Cold War* (Sydney: Allen & Unwin, 1996).
23 L. Strahan, 'The Dread Frontier in Australia's Defence Thinking'; G. Cheeseman, 'Back to "Forward Defence" and the Australian National Style', in Bruce and Cheeseman, *Discourses of Danger and Dread Frontiers*, pp. 150–76; 251–72.
24 G. Cheeseman, 'Australia: The White Experience of Fear and Dependence', in Booth and Trood, *Strategic Cultures in the Asia–Pacific Region*, pp. 273–98.
25 ibid. See also Cheeseman, 'Back to "Forward Defence" and the Australian National Style', pp. 265–71.
26 See M. Evans, 'From Defence to Security: Continuity and Change in Australian Strategic Thinking in the Twentieth Century', in P. Dennis and J. Grey (eds), *Serving Vital Interests: Australia's Strategic Planning in Peace and War* (Canberra: UNSW, 1996), pp. 116–40.
27 Quoted in N. Meaney, *The Search for Security in the Pacific, 1901–14* (Sydney: Sydney University Press, 1976), p. 265.
28 K.C. Beazley, 'Australia and the Asia–Pacific Region: A Strategy of Self Reliance and Alliance', 30 June 1988, *Selected Speeches 1985–1989 by the Hon. Kim C. Beazley, MP, Minister for Defence* (Canberra: Directorate of Departmental Publications, 1989), p. 233.
29 P. Kelly, *The End of Certainty: The Story of the 1980s* (Sydney: Allen & Unwin, 1992); W.K. Hancock, *Australia* (London: Ernest Benn Limited, 1930).
30 Kelly, *The End of Certainty*, pp. 1–16.
31 ibid., pp. 1–2. See also H. Collins, 'Political Ideology in Australia: The Distinctiveness of a Benthamite Society', *Daedalus*, 1985, pp. 147–69.
32 Kelly, *The End of Certainty*, pp. 1–16.
33 Commonwealth of Australia, *Review of Australia's Defence Capabilities: Report to the Minister for Defence by Mr Paul Dibb* (Canberra: Australian Government Publishing Service [AGPS], 1986); *The*

Defence of Australia 1987 (Canberra: AGPS, 1987).
34 This approach is reflected in both *The Defence of Australia 1987* and its successor, *Defending Australia* (Canberra: AGPS, 1994).
35 ibid.
36 J. Grey, *A Military History of Australia* (Melbourne: Cambridge University Press, 1990), pp. 3–5.
37 G. Evans and B. Grant, *Australia's Foreign Relations in the World of the 1990s* (Melbourne: Melbourne University Press, second edition 1995), p. 22.
38 S. Encel, *Militarism and the Citizen Tradition in Australia* (Sydney: University of New South Wales, 1966), pp. 2–9, 23–6.
39 C. Bridge, G. Harper and I. Spence, 'The Anzac Way of War', *New Zealand Army Journal*, December 1996, pp. 2–18.
40 C.E.W. Bean, *The Official History of Australia in the War of 1914–1918*, vols 1–6 (Sydney: Angus and Robertson, 1921–42); *Anzac to Amiens* (Canberra: Australian War Memorial [AWM], 1946).
41 Major General S. Gower, 'Foreword', in P. Stanley, *Tarakan: An Australian Tragedy* (Sydney: Allen & Unwin, 1997), p. vii.
42 See for instance G. Serle, 'The Digger Tradition and Australian Nationalism', *Meanjin Quarterly*, June 1965, pp. 149–58; K.S. Inglis, 'The Anzac Tradition', *Meanjin Quarterly*, March 1965, pp. 25–44; 'ANZAC and the Australian Military Tradition', *Current Affairs Bulletin*, April 1988, pp. 4–15; A. Thompson, *Anzac Memories: Living with the Legend* (Melbourne: Oxford University Press, 1994), chapter 8.
43 P.A. Pedersen, 'The AIF on the Western Front: The Role of Training and Command', in M. McKernan and M. Brown (eds), *Australia: Two Centuries of War and Peace* (Canberra: Australian War Memorial, 1988), chapter 7; E.M. Andrews, *The Anzac Illusion: Anglo–Australian Relations during World War I* (Melbourne: Cambridge University Press, 1993), chapters 4–8.
44 A. Stephens, 'Introduction', in Stephens (ed.), *Defending the Air/Sea Gap: Exploiting Advanced Technology and Disproportionate Response to Defend Australia* (Canberra: Australian Defence Studies Centre 1992), p. 2; Bob Nicholls, *Statesmen and Sailors: A History of Australian Maritime Defence* (Balmain: self-published, 1995), p. 283. Both Stephens and Nicholls believe that, in continental defence, the Australian Army is the least relevant of the three services.
45 D. Horner, 'The Australian Way of Warfighting', paper delivered at the Australian Army Command and General Staff College, Fort Queenscliff, 24 June 1996. I am grateful to Professor Horner for access to this paper.

46 Department of Defence. Circular Memorandum No. 21/97, 'Establishment of Headquarters Australian Theatre', 7 April 1997, pp. 1–2.
47 ADF, *Decisive Manoeuvre: Australian Warfighting Concepts to Guide Campaign Planning* (Sydney: HQAST, November 1997), interim edition.
48 ibid., para 1.2.
49 ibid., para 1.9.
50 ibid., paras 1.21–1.27; chapter 4.
51 Air Vice Marshal P. Nicholson, 'The Links Between Strategy and Doctrine', paper presented at the Chief of Army's Exercise, Brisbane, 20 October 1998.
52 ibid., pp. 11–14.
53 ibid., pp. 14–18.
54 Only in the Second World War in the South-West Pacific theatre could Australia be said to have embraced a maritime concept of strategy. For a discussion see S. Woodman and D. Horner, 'Land Forces in the Defence of Australia', in Horner (ed.), *Reshaping the Australian Army: Challenges for the 1990s* (Canberra: SDSC, 1991), pp. 8–99.
55 J. Bach, *A Maritime History of Australia* (Sydney: Thomas Nelson, 1976), p. 5.
56 F. Broeze, 'Maritime Australia: Integrating the Sea into Our National History', *Maritime Studies*, May/June 1995, pp. 9–16; *Island-Nation: A History of Australians and the Sea* (Sydney: Allen & Unwin, 1998), pp. 1–9.
57 For an overview of Australian cultural history see R. White, *Inventing Australia: Images and Identity 1688–1980* (Sydney: Allen & Unwin, 1981).
58 K.C. Beazley, 'The Development of Australian Maritime Strategy', 26 November 1987, *Selected Speeches 1985–1989*, p. 184.
59 J. Barrett, *Falling In: Australians and 'Boy Conscription', 1911–1915* (Sydney: Hale and Iremonger, 1979), chapter 1; Meaney, *The Search for Security in the Pacific, 1901–14*, pp. 71–2.
60 Colonel J.D. Lavarack, 'The Defence of the British Empire with Special Reference to the Far East and Australia', *Army Quarterly*, January 1933, pp. 207–17; Colonel D.H. Wynter, 'Defence of Australia and its Relation to Imperial Defence', Address to the United Services Institute, 1935, reprinted in *Army Journal*, December 1975, pp. 18–36; Admiral Sir Herbert Richmond, 'Imperial Defence', *Army Quarterly*, October 1933 and January 1934, pp. 11–30 and 'An Outline of Imperial Defence', *Army Quarterly*, April and July 1932, pp. 260–79. Shedden's contribution can be found in B. Lodge, *Lavarack: Rival General* (Sydney: Allen & Unwin, 1998), chapters 2–6.
61 Richmond, 'Imperial Defence', p. 21.

62 M. Evans, 'Unarmed Prophets: Amphibious Warfare in Australian Military Thought', *Journal of the Australian Naval Institute*, January/March 1999, pp. 10–19.
63 See M. Evans, *The Role of the Australian Army in a Maritime Concept of Strategy*, Working Paper No. 101 (Canberra: Land Warfare Studies Centre, September 1998).
64 Department of Defence. *Australia's Strategic Policy* (Canberra: Directorate of Publishing, 1997).
65 Sir Julian S. Corbett, *Some Principles of Maritime Strategy* (London: Longmans, Green and Co., 1911), pp. 11–15.
66 For a critique of ASP 97, see Evans, *The Role of the Australian Army in a Maritime Concept of Strategy*, pp. 25–8.
67 Author's discussion with RAN officers, Seapower 2000 Seminar, HMAS *Watson*, Sydney, 5 July 1999.
68 See for example Department of the Navy, *From the Sea: Preparing the Naval Service for the 21st Century* (Washington DC: Department of the Navy, September 1992); General C.C. Krulak, 'The United States Marine Corps in the Twenty-First Century', *RUSI Journal*, August 1996, pp. 22–6 and 'Operational Maneuver from the Sea: A Concept for the Projection of Naval Power Ashore', *Surface Warfare*, July/August, 1996, pp. 7–13. For a good overview of the rise of Western expeditionary warfare, see Brigadier R.A. Fry, 'The End of the Continental Century', US Naval Institute *Proceedings*, March 1999, pp. 41–3, and 'The Maritime Contribution to Joint Operations', speech to Seapower 2000 Naval Seminar, HMAS *Watson*, Sydney, 5 July 1999;
69 Rear Admiral R. Menon, *Maritime Strategy and Continental Wars* (London: Frank Cass, 1998), chapters 7–8.
70 In 1999 a MOLE concept was being developed in the ADF as part of a revived amphibious warfare capability by HQAST. An important initiative was the formation of the Army Amphibious Requirements Steering Group in July 1999.
71 Admiral H.E. Eccles, 'Strategy—Theory and Application', *Naval War College Review*, May/June 1979, p. 13.

7 Australia, the *Trent* Crisis of 1861 and the strategy of imperial defence

1 This chapter benefited greatly from a wide range of discussions in Canberra and Armidale in 1999. I offer my sincere thanks to all those Australian and New Zealand scholars who attempted to expand my limited, London-based grasp of imperial defence.

2   W.C.B. Tunstall, 'Imperial Defence 1815–1870', in *The Cambridge History of the British Empire: Volume II 1783–1870* (Cambridge: 1940), pp. 806–12.
3   J. Bach, *A Maritime History of Australia* (Sydney: Thomas Nelson, 1976), esp. chapters II and XII for dock, support facilities and local coal supplies.
4   J. Bach, *The Australia Station: A History of the Royal Navy in the South-West Pacific 1821–1913* (Kensington: UNSW Press, 1986), p. 199.
5   J. Jeremy, *Cockatoo Island: Sydney's Historic Dockyard* (Sydney: UNSW Press, 1998), pp. 7–10.
6   R.K. Peacock, *Early Coast Defences in Australia, 1787–1901*, Department of Defence MS, AWM; M. Austin, *The Army in Australia, 1840–50* (Canberra: 1979), pp. 150–73.
7   C. Jones, *Australian Colonial Navies* (Canberra: AWM, 1986), p. 13.
8   W.H. Clements, *Towers of Strength: Martello Towers World Wide* (London: 1999), p. 144.
9   Peacock, pp. 18, 205–14.
10   Bach, *Royal Navy*, p. 177.
11   A.D. Lambert, *The Crimean War: British Grand Strategy against Russia, 1853–1856* (Manchester: 1990).
12   Milne memo, April 1858, Milne MSS, National Maritime Museum (NMM): MLN 142/2.
13   Drummond memo, April 1858, NMM: MLN 142/2.
14   D.C. Gordon, *The Dominion Partnership in Imperial Defence, 1870–1914* (Baltimore: Johns Hopkins, 1965), pp. 7–9.
15   Colonial Office to Admiralty, 31 August 1858, enclosing Barkly to Lord Stanley (Secretary of State for the Colonies), 9 June 1858, PRO: ADM 1/5701.
16   Minute by Sir John Pakington, (First Lord of the Admiralty) on ibid.
17   Colonial Office to Admiralty 25 April 1859; Milne minute 28 April 1859 and draft reply 30 June 1859, PRO: ADM 1/5721.
18   Milne memo, 20 June 1859 on ibid; G.L. Macandie, *The Genesis of the Royal Australian Navy* (Sydney: Government Printer, 1949), pp. 14–15.
19   Colonial Office to Admiralty 5 May 1859 re South Australia; December 1859; 9 November 1859; Denison to Newcastle, 11 August 1859, encl. Barkly to Newcastle, 16 September 1859, PRO: ADM 1/5721.
20   Frederick Beauchamp Seymour (1821–95), created Lord Alcester after the bombardment of Alexandria in 1882. A highly capable officer of proven merit. He commanded HMS *Pelorus* on the China and Australia stations between 1857 and 1862.

21 Colonial Office to Admiralty, 18 May 1860, encl. Barkly to Newcastle, 14 February 1860, with Seymour to Barkly 5, 10 and 29 November 1859, PRO: ADM 1/5744.
22 Admiralty draft reply on ibid.
23 Colonial Office to Admiralty, 14 August 1860, PRO: ADM 1/5744.
24 Macandie, p. 14.
25 B. McKinlay, *The First Royal Tour, 1867–1868* (Adelaide: 1970); and Jeremy, p. 16.
26 Loring to Admiralty, 4 March 1859, PRO: ADM 1/5736.
27 Loring to Admiralty, 12 June 1859 and 13 August 1859, ibid.
28 Seymour to Admiralty, 6 April 1861, PRO: ADM 1/5760 is typical.
29 Seymour to Captain Paget (First Secretary to the Admiralty), Private, 9 August 1861; and Seymour to Admiralty, 17 August 1861, PRO: ADM 1/5760.
30 Colonial Office to Admiralty, 7 March 1861, encl. Denison to Colonial Office, 10 December 1860, PRO: ADM 1/5770.
31 Admiralty to Colonial Office, 26 December 1861, draft by Captain Paget, PRO: ADM 13/47.
32 Tunstall, p. 828.
33 Gladstone to Somerset, 18 December 1860, Somerset MSS, Buckinghamshire Record Office: 2A/14/13.
34 Tunstall, p. 832; Gordon, pp. 10–23.
35 A.D. Lambert, 'Politics, Technology and Policy-making: Palmerston, Gladstone and the management of the Ironclad Naval Race, 1859–1865', *The Northern Mariner*, July 1998, p. 27.
36 The standard accounts are: N.B. Ferris, *The Trent Affair: A Diplomatic Crisis* (Knoxville: 1977); G.H. Warren, *Fountain of Discontent: The Trent Affair and the Freedom of the Seas* (Boston: 1981); E.D. Adams, *Great Britain and the American Civil War*, vol. 1 (London: 1925); B. Jenkins, *Britain and the War for the Union*, vol. 1 (Montreal: 1974).
37 K. Bourne, 'British Preparations for War with the North, 1861–62', *The English Historical Review*, 1961, pp. 600–32. K. Bourne, *Great Britain and the Balance of Power in North America, 1815–1908* (London: 1968); R.A. Courtemache, *No Need of Glory: The British Navy in American Waters 1860–1864* (Annapolis: USNI Press, 1977), pp. 39–66.
38 F.C. Drake, *The Empire of the Seas: A Biography of Rear Admiral Robert Wilson Shufeldt, USN* (Honolulu: 1984), pp. 33–7. Shufeldt was the US Consul at Havana.
39 Lambert, 'Politics'.
40 Palmerston to Somerset, 26 May 1861, Add. 48,582, p. 114.
41 The Queen to Palmerston, 30 May 1861, A. Benson, and Viscount

NOTES 321

Esher, *The Letters of Queen Victoria III*, (London: 1908), p. 440.
42 Palmerston to Milner Gibson (President of the Board of Trade), 7 June 1861, Add. 48,582, p. 136.
43 Russell to Somerset, 22 June 1861, encl. in Somerset to Palmerston, 22 June 1861, GC/SO/53, Palmerston to Somerset, 23 June 1861, Add. 48,582, p. 130.
44 Lord Newton, *Lord Lyons* (London: 1913), pp. 16, 62; C.F. Adams, *Charles Francis Adams* (Boston: 1900), p. 217.
45 Newton, p. 44.
46 Palmerston Diary, 28 November, 1861, Hartley Library, Southampton University: D27.
47 Cobden to Sumner, 29 November 1861, in J. Morley, *Life of Cobden* (London: 1879), p. 856; G.M. Trevelyan, *Life of John Bright* (London: 1914), pp. 312–13.
48 Admiralty to Milne, 1 December 1861, PRO: ADM 13/7/351.
49 Somerset to Milne, 1 December 1861, NMM: MLN 116/1/C.
50 The Queen to Palmerston, 1 December 1861, RC/F 1079, the Queen to Russell, 1 December 1861, Benson and Esher, III, p. 470; T. Martin, *Life of the Prince Consort*, vol. V (London: 1880), pp. 421–2, including a facsimile of Albert's draft.
51 Palmerston Diary, December 1861. There are few entries, and hardly any mention of the *Trent* crisis.
52 Palmerston to the Queen, 5 December 1861, H.C.F. Bell, *Lord Palmerston*, vol. II (London: 1936), p. 295.
53 Palmerston to Russell, 5 December 1861, Bell, p. 295; and 6 December 1861, PRO: 30/22/21, f. 620.
54 Lambert, 'Palmerston, Gladstone . . .'.
55 'List of the Chief Ports on the Federal Coast the United States, showing the Shipping, Population, Dockyards, and Defences as far as known; also how far accessible or vulnerable to an Attack, as far as can be gathered from the Charts. With an approximate estimate of the number of vessels required to blockade the several ports and Rivers.' 15 December 1861, 'Confidential'. Copies in the Milne and Somerset Archives. Somerset's is signed, DRO: MLN 114/8.
56 Delane to William Howard Russell, 11 November 1861, *History of 'The Times'*, vol. II (London: 1939), p. 373.
57 L.S. Pasley, *Life of Admiral Sir T. S. Pasley* (London: 1900), p. 273.
58 Lyons to Russell, 19 December, 1861, Newton, pp. 52–3.
59 Washington memoranda, PRO: ADM 7/264.
60 Somerset to Palmerston, 17 December 1861, GC/SO/73.
61 Courtemache, pp. 56–60.

62 R. Winks, *Canada and the United States: The Civil War Years* (Baltimore: 1960), pp. 83–4.
63 Palmerston to Russell, 30 December 1861, in F. Wellesley, *The Paris Embassy during the Second Empire* (London: 1928), pp. 233–4.
64 Lyons to Russell, 23 and 27 December 1861, Newton, pp. 56–61.
65 Milne to Admiral Sir F. Grey (First Sea Lord), 3 January 1862, NMM: MLN 116/1.
66 Palmerston Diary, 9 January 1862; Palmerston to the Queen, 9 January 1862, G. Buckle, *The Letters of Queen Victoria*, 2nd Series I (London: 1926), pp. 7–8; the Queen to Palmerston, 10 January 1862, ibid., pp. 8–9 and RC/F 1083 and 1083A.
67 Warren, p. 139.
68 Sir F. Grey to Milne, 31 October and 29 November 1862, NMM: MLN 116.
69 Seymour to Admiralty, 24 January 1862, PRO: ADM 1/5785.
70 Minute by Paget on ibid.
71 Seymour to Admiralty 19 February 1862, PRO: ADM 1/5785.
72 Admiralty to Seymour, 26 December 1861, PRO: ADM 13/7, p. 382–4.
73 Colonial Office to Admiralty 17 May 1862, encl. Newcastle to Grey 17 May 1862, PRO: ADM 1/5797.
74 Seymour to Admiralty, 20 March 1862, extract on New South Wales sent to Colonial Office, PRO: ADM 1/5785.
75 Colonial Office to Admiralty, 16 January 1862, Admiralty minute on by Romaine, PRO: ADM 1/5797.
76 D.H. Johnson, *Volunteers at Heart: The Queensland Defence Forces 1860–1901* (St Lucia: Queensland University Press, 1975), p. 33.
77 Seymour to Admiralty, 19 May and 20 June 1862, PRO: ADM 1/785.
78 ibid., pp. 43–5.
79 Gordon, *The Dominion Partnership in Imperial Defence*, provides a detailed coverage of the period from 1860.
80 Macandie, pp. 12, 21.
81 Bach, *Royal Navy*, pp. 179–81.
82 Gladstone memorandum on Naval Policy, 18 December 1860, Somerset MSS, Buckingham Record Office: 2A/14/13. The detail and specific proposals suggest this paper was inspired or drafted by Paget.
83 Gladstone to Somerset, 13 December 1864, Add. 44,304, f. 203; Gladstone to Paget, 22 and 26 December 1864, Add. 44,408, ff. 188, 196; Paget to Gladstone, 25 December 1864, ibid., f. 192.
84 Paget memo for Gladstone, 1 January 1865, Add. 44,601, f. 1; H.G.C. Matthew (ed.), *The Gladstone Diaries*, 1–31 January 1865; Paget to

Gladstone, 9 January 1865, Add. 44,409, f. 28; Palmerston to Queen Victoria, 20 January 1865; Buckle, pp. 248–9.
85 J.F. Beeler, *British Naval Policy in the Gladstone–Disraeli Era, 1866–1880* (Stanford: 1997), pp. 35–7 and Table 1.
86 Childers draft letter to Earl Clarendon, the Foreign Secretary, 23 January 1869, in J. Hattendorf, et al. (eds), *British Naval Documents 1204–1960* (London: Navy Records Society, 1993), pp. 593–5.
87 F. Egerton, *Admiral Sir Geoffrey Phipps Hornby* (London: 1896), pp. 145–50.
88 A.D. Lambert, 'Great Britain and the Baltic, 1809–1890', in Rystad et al. (eds), *In Quest of Trade and Security: The Baltic in Great Power Politics, Part One 1500–1900* (Lund: 1994), pp. 297–334.
89 Report by Commodore John Wilson (C-in-C Australia Station), RN, 22 June 1880, in N.A. Lambert, *Australia's Naval Inheritance: Imperial Maritime Strategy and the Australian Station 1880–1909*, Papers in Australian Maritime Affairs No. 6 (Canberra: Maritime Studies Program, 1998), pp. 25–40.

8 New Zealand's naval defence, 1854–1914

1 I.C. McGibbon, *The Path to Gallipoli: Defending New Zealand 1840–1915* (Wellington: GP Books, 1991), ch. 1.
2 ibid.
3 ibid., ch. 2.
4 C. Dennistoun-Wood, *Naval Volunteers in New Zealand* (Wellington: privately published, c. 1965), p. 10.
5 J.F. Beeler, *British Naval Policy in the Gladstone–Disraeli Era 1866–1880* (Stanford: Stanford University Press, 1997), p. 19.
6 Dennistoun-Wood, p. 10.
7 M. Bassett, *Sir Joseph Ward—a political biography* (Auckland: Auckland University Press, 1993), pp. 8, 15.
8 K. De Ridder, *The History of Defence Legislation in New Zealand* (Wellington: Defence Headquarters, c. 1991), p. 2–2.
9 J.O'C. Ross, *The White Ensign in Early New Zealand* (Wellington: A.H. & A.W. Reed, 1967), p. 19.
10 J. Leather, *World Warships in Review 1860–1906* (London: MacDonald and Jane's, 1976).
11 McGibbon, ch. 2.
12 Dennistoun-Wood, p. 10.
13 G.J. Clayton, *New Zealand Army: A history from the 1840s to the 1990s* (NZ Army, 1990), pp. 78–81.

14 T.D. Taylor, *New Zealand's Naval Story* (Wellington: A.H. & A.W. Reed, 1948), p. 177.
15 B. Nicholls, *Statesmen & Sailors: Australia's Maritime Defence 1870–1920* (Balmain: self-published, 1995), p. 4.
16 McGibbon, ch. 2.
17 G. Barrett, *Russophobia in New Zealand 1838–1908* (Palmerston North: The Dunmore Press, 1981).
18 P. Overlack, 'Australia and Germany: challenge and response before 1914', in D. Stevens (ed.), *Maritime Power in the Twentieth Century: the Australian Experience* (Sydney: Allen & Unwin, 1997).
19 Nicholls, p. 19.
20 McGibbon, pp. 63–6.
21 D. Scott, *The years of the Pooh Bah, a Cook Islands History* (Rarotonga: CITC, 1991).
22 McGibbon, pp. 144–5.
23 ibid., ch. 12.
24 Bassett, p. 175.
25 Pamphlet, *Onward HMS New Zealand* (*c.* 1919).
26 D. Johnson and P. Dennerly (eds), *Half a World Away* (Auckland: Royal New Zealand Navy Museum, 1998), p. 152.
27 McDougall, p.13.

9 Colonial naval forces before Federation

1 C. Jones, *Australian Colonial Navies* (Canberra: Australian War Memorial, 1986); R. Gillett, *Australia's Colonial Navies* (Sydney: The Naval Historical Society of Australia, 1982).
2 Dispatch, Governor Fitzroy to Secretary of State for the Colonies, 30 April 1847.
3 J. Morris, *Sydney* (London: Viking, 1992), p. 75.
4 Melbourne *Morning Herald*, 8 September 1854.
5 For one account of the incident, see *The Victorian Historical Magazine*, September 1926.
6 *Colonial Naval Defence Act* 28 and 29 Vic. c. 14, s. 1865.
7 See 'Papers presented to the Colonial Conference 1887', No. 78, for background to the request, PRO: CAB 13/8A.
8 The reports were issued in the following order: New South Wales, June 1877; Victoria, July 1877; Queensland, August 1877; South Australia, December 1877; and Tasmania, February 1878. Western Australia was not visited.
9 Of which the report by Commodore John Wilson, 22 June 1880, is one example, see PRO: ADM 1/6530.

10 *The Australasian Naval Defence Act* 51 and 52 Vic c. 32. See N. Lambert, *Australia's Naval Inheritance*, Papers in Australian Maritime Affairs No. 6, (Canberra: Maritime Studies Program, 1998), Document 10, p. 73.
11 ibid., p. 6.
12 See in particular: 'Local Preparations to be Made in Anticipation of War', Colonial Defence Committee Memorandum, 1 November 1886, Paper 19M, PRO: CAB 8/1; 'Australasian Defence', 9 May 1887, No. 88, PRO: CAB 13/8A; 'Remarks by Colonial Defence Committee on Report by Captain A.W. Moore RN dated 2 June 1891', No. 320 SECRET, Queensland Archives.
13 'Remarks by Colonial Defence Committee on Major General Edwards' report', 16 May 1890, reprinted in South Australia House of Assembly, 30 September 1890, as Paper No. 145.

10 'A vigorous offensive': core aspects of Australian maritime defence concerns before 1914

1 See for example, D.C. Gordon, *The Dominion Partnership in Imperial Defence, 1870–1914* (Baltimore: Johns Hopkins Press, 1965); N. Meaney, *The Search for Security in the Pacific, 1901–1914* (Sydney: Sydney University Press, 1976).
2 *Commonwealth Parliamentary Debates* (CPD), vol. III, 1901–2, 24 July 1901, p. 2989.
3 Lord Brassey, 'Imperial Federation', *The Nineteenth Century*, September 1891, p. 488. See also the *Bulletin*, throughout November 1902; the *Age*, 17 July 1903, 27 August 1908; *Sydney Morning Herald* (SMH), 24 September 1899.
4 House of Representatives, A.36, 23 April 1902, quoted in G.L. Macandie, *The Genesis of the Royal Australian Navy* (Sydney: Government Printer, 1949), p. 83.
5 At the 1887 Inter-Colonial Conference the premiers agreed to supplement the existing squadron with an 'auxiliary squadron' of five fast third-class cruisers and two torpedo gunboats, the colonies sharing part of the cost to the amount of £126 000 yearly. The subsidised vessels could not be removed from station waters without colonial consent.
6 *Parliamentary Papers*, 1901–2 Session, vol. II, No. 27, 'Report of the Conference of Naval Officers Assembled at Melbourne to consider the Question of Naval Defence of Australia'.
7 A.T. Mahan, 'The Disposition of Navies', *National Review*, July 1902, 717–19.

8   P.A. Silburn, *The Colonies and Imperial Defence* (London: Longmans, Green, 1909), pp. 160–1, 202–3.
9   *CPD*, vol. III, 1901–2, pp. 2963, 2979.
10 *CPD*, vol. XIV, 1903, pp. 1779–81.
11 The *Bulletin*, 18 October 1902.
12 The *Age*, 13 March 1902.
13 The *Bulletin*, 22 November 1902.
14 ibid.
15 Minute by Sir Montague Ommaney, Permanent Under-Secretary, CO 418/26, Tennyson–Colonial Office, 24 April 1903.
16 See *CPD*, vol. XIV, 8, 9 July 1903, pp. 1912, 1968.
17 The *Age*, 28 August 1903.
18 *Great Britain, Parliamentary Papers* (*PP*), 1907, vol. LV, Cd. 3524, p. 49.
19 The *Bulletin*, 9 November 1905.
20 The *Age*, 21 February 1905.
21 See P. Overlack, 'German Commerce Warfare Planning for the Australian Station 1900–1914', *War & Society*, May 1996, pp. 17–48.
22 *The Times*, 2 February 1903.
23 See P. Overlack, 'Australian Defence Awareness and German Naval Planning in the Pacific, 1900–1914', *War & Society*, May 1992, pp. 37–51.
24 Tirpitz' comment to Saxon military attaché, quoted in V.R. Berghahn, 'Zu den Zielen des deutschen Flottenbaues unter Wilhelm II', *Historische Zeitschrift*, February 1970, p. 67.
25 *CPD*, vol. XIV, 15 July 1903, p. 2151.
26 *National Review*, January 1902, p. 711.
27 The *West Australian*, 11 August 1903.
28 'Remarks upon the Defence Scheme for the Commonwealth of Australia', 3 December 1904, NAA(VIC): MP 729, S1/04/5468.
29 'Memorandum on Council of Defence', 12 May 1905, NAA(VIC): MP729, S1/05/5018. McCay had experience in the South African War and had studied Australian defence; his view was that it should begin 'from within and working outwards'. *CPD*, vol. XIV, 15 July 1903, p. 2133.
30 'Australia—Naval and Military Defence, 1905–1910', memorandum of J.W. McCay, Minister of Defence, 10 May 1905, PRO: Cab. 17/48.
31 Bridges to Minister of Defence, 16 October 1905, NAA(VIC): B173, S/905/187.
32 The *Herald*, 12 June 1905.
33 ibid., 13 June 1905.

34 *Proceedings of the Royal Colonial Institute*, vol. XXXVI, 1904–5, p. 48.
35 J.F.G. Foxton, 'The Evolution and Development of an Australian Naval Policy', *Commonwealth Military Journal*, vol. 1, 1911, p. 658.
36 Deakin–Northcote, 28 August 1905, PRO: CO 418/37.
37 Foxton, p. 661.
38 The *Age*, 21 February 1905. On Britain's exposed food supply and raw materials situation, see P. Overlack, 'The Function of Commerce Warfare in an Anglo–German Conflict to 1914', *Journal of Strategic Studies*, December 1997, pp. 94–114.
39 Report of CID 25 May 1906, Confidential Memorandum 'Australia', PRO: Cab. 5/1, pp. 3–4.
40 ibid., p. 5.
41 A.W. Jose, *The Royal Australian Navy, The Official History of Australia in the War of 1914–1918*, vol. IX (Brisbane: University of Queensland Press, 1987), pp. xxvi–xxvii.
42 Report of CID 25 May 1906, Confidential Memorandum 'Australia', PRO: Cab. 5/1, p. 2.
43 ibid., pp. 2–3.
44 'Captain Creswell's Memorandum of 6th March 1907 for the Hon. A. Deakin, Prime Minister, on leaving for the Colonial Conference', in Macandie, p. 176.
45 ibid., pp. 178–9.
46 The *Age*, 27 August 1908.
47 ibid., 31 August 1908.
48 ibid.
49 See A.J. Marder, *The Anatomy of British Sea Power: British Naval Policy 1880–1905* (London: Putnam, 1940), p. 456; *From the Dreadnought to Scapa Flow: The Royal Navy in the Fisher Era, 1904–1919* (London: Oxford University Press, 1961), vol. I, p. 104.
50 *Argus*, 29 December 1909.
51 *SMH*, 29 March 1909.
52 *Argus*, 18, 29 November 1909.
53 The *Age*, 12 June 1909.
54 Deakin did not attend due to the domestic situation, and was represented by Foxton as Minister without Portfolio. As a 'subsidyite', Foxton was suspect: see the lead article in the *Age* of 11 June 1909.
55 *SMH*, 14 August 1909.
56 *CPD*, vol. LII, 1909, pp. 4462–3.
57 *Queensland Worker*, 13 February 1909.
58 *SMH*, 29 August 1909.
59 On the political background to the Fleet Unit, see Meaney, pp. 182–6.
60 The *Age*, 30 August 1909. See also Lambert, p. 56.

61 *Sydney Mail*, 26 May 1909.
62 Creswell–Jebb, 31 July 1907, 24 March 1908, Jebb Papers, 813/1/36, 42, in Meaney, p. 157.
63 *SMH*, 11 August 1910.
64 *SMH*, 6 December 1912.
65 Henderson's recommendations were accepted in their entirety by the Labor Party before its defeat in 1913, but were slightly modified by the new Liberal Government under Joseph Cook. A contemporary assessment is in *SMH*, 'The Henderson Plan', 14 March 1911.
66 'Australian Affairs', *National Review*, January 1914, p. 880.
67 Papers presented to Parliament, vol. II, 5th Parlt. 2nd Session 1914, 'Naval Defence: Memorandum by the Minister for Defence dated 13 April 1914; together with Speech of the First Lord of the Admiralty'.
68 'Australian Affairs', p. 880.
69 The *Age*, 14 April 1914.
70 See L. Foster, *High Hopes: The Men and Motives of the Australian Round Table* (Melbourne: Melbourne University Press, 1986).
71 'The Future of the South Seas', *SMH*, 28 January 1911.
72 Letter, Hawarth-Booth to Secretary, Naval Board, 21 March 1912, NAA(VIC): MP 1049, 1914/0289, The British plan was implemented in mid-1913. Yet despite this more precautionary policy, ammunition was not yet carried on board. M0823/13, Confidential, Admiralty, 10 June 1913, NAA(VIC): MP 1049, 1918/0258.
73 'Australian Defence', *SMH*, 14 January 1913.
74 *New Zealand Herald*, 29 November 1913.
75 'Report by the Inspector-General of the Overseas Forces on the Coast defences of the Commonwealth of Australia, 1914', NAA(VIC): B 197, 1855/1/17.
76 ibid.
77 *CPD*, vol. LXXV, 14 October 1914, pp. 98–9.
78 See P. Overlack, 'The Force of Circumstance: Graf Spee's Options for the East Asian Cruiser Squadron in 1914', *Journal of Military History*, October 1996, pp. 657–82.
79 NAA(VIC): MP1049, S1/17/0115A.

11 **'The view from Port Phillip Heads': Alfred Deakin and the move towards an Australian navy**

1 Deakin to Governor-General, 28 August 1905.
2 ibid.

NOTES 329

3   'Naval Defence for the year 1905', p. 5, *Commonwealth Parliamentary Papers* (*CPP*), 1906.
4   Report No. XXXI of the Joint Naval and Military Committee on Defence, London, 1900.
5   'Recessional', *Rudyard Kipling's Verse* (London: Hodder & Stoughton, 1940), p. 329.
6   *Commonwealth Year Book*, No. 1, 1908.
7   The last War Office *Manual of Submarine Mining* is dated 1904.
8   'Report of Committee of Imperial Defence', *CPP* 1906.
9   E. March, *British Destroyers* (London: Seeley Service, 1966), p. 81.
10 *Military Engineering, Defences* (London: HMSO, 1925), p. 67.
11 *Commonwealth Year Book*, No. 1, 1908.
12 W. Jameson, *The Fleet that Jack Built* (London: Rupert Hart-Davis, 1962), p. 109.
13 Creswell to Minister for Defence, 2 September 1907.
14 £500 000 in those days would be equivalent to about $35 million in 1999.
15 Lofty Batt, *Pioneers of the Royal Australian Navy* (Gosford: privately published, 1967).
16 Minute, by Prince Louis of Battenberg, 2 May 1903.
17 Macandie, *Genesis of the Royal Australian Navy* (Sydney: Government Printer, 1949), p. 121.
18 'Naval Defence for 1905', p. 12, *CPP* 1906.
19 Creswell to Minister for Defence, 22 September 1905.
20 'Report of the Director of the Naval Forces on his Visit to England', p. 14, *CPP* 1906.
21 Data is based on Macandie, *Genesis of the Royal Australian Navy*, p. 328; March, *British Destroyers*; and *Conways All the World's Fighting Ships, 1860–1905* and *1906–1921* (London: Conway, 1979 and 1985).
22 The *Daily Mail*, 7 October 1907.
23 Bob Nicholls, *Statesmen & Sailors* (Sydney: privately published, 1995).
24 R.S. Veale, 'Autobiographical recollections of a Naval Reserve Officer, 1900–1953', typescript, 1975, p. 8.
25 The *Argus*, 12 December 1910.

12   'A sea of troubles': the Great White Fleet's 1908 war plans for Australia and New Zealand

1   S. Howarth, *To Shining Sea: A History of the United States Navy, 1775–1991* (New York: Random House, 1991), p. 284.

2 C.M. Bell, 'Thinking the Unthinkable: British and American Naval Strategies for an Anglo–American War, 1918–1931', *International History Review*, November 1997, p. 7. Although they were not used until after the Theodore Roosevelt period, the nations comprising the British Empire/Commonwealth were assigned code colours in shades of RED, reflective of their British orientation—Australia: SCARLET; New Zealand: GARNET; India: RUBY; Canada: CRIMSON, etc.
3 T. Holt, 'Joint Plan Red', *Military History Quarterly*, Autumn 1988, pp. 48–55.
4 J.B. Mittendorf, B.M. Simpson, and J.R. Wadleigh, *Sailors and Scholars: The Centennial History of the US Naval War College* (Newport: Naval War College Press, 1984), pp. 42–3, citing Abstract of Course, 1894, pp. 34–7.
5 Naval Constructor D.W. Taylor, 'A Handicap on United States Battleships', *Naval Institute Proceedings*, September 1904, pp. 503–4.
6 'Summary of Strategic Situation No. 10', *Naval War College Problems and Solutions, 1907*, vol. 3, Naval War College Archives (NWCA): Record Group (RG) 12.
7 'Naval Defense of the Atlantic Coast', *Naval War College Problems and Solutions, 1900*, p. 7, NWCA: RG 12. The General Board of the Navy concurred in this assessment. See Admiral George Dewey to Secretary of the Navy John D. Long, 22 March 1901, General Board Letterbook, 1900–1907, p. 187.
8 'English Criticism of the *Indiana*', *Army & Navy Journal*, 15 April 1899, p. 780.
9 'Problem of 1900, Appendix D: Defense Plans for the Philippines Islands [sic]', p. D–1, *Naval War College Problems and Solutions, 1900*, NWCA: RG 12.
10 'Problem of 1900, Appendix E: Defense of Honolulu', p. E–1, *Naval War College Problems and Solutions, 1900*, NWCA: RG 12.
11 'Problem of 1907', pp. 101–2, *Naval War College Problems and Solutions, 1907*, NWCA: RG 12.
12 Roosevelt to Cecil Spring-Rice, 19 March 1904, in E.E. Morison, (ed.), *The Letters of Theodore Roosevelt*, vol. 4 (Cambridge: Harvard University Press, 1951–54), p. 724.
13 The most authoritative treatment of the alliance is contained in I.H. Nish, *The Anglo–Japanese Alliance: The Diplomacy of Two Island Nations 1894–1907* (London: Macmillan, 1969).
14 The Taft–Katsura Agreement has been the subject of considerable academic discussion. See, for examples, R.A. Esthus, 'The Taft–Katsura Agreement—Reality or Myth?', *Journal of Modern History*, vol. 31, 1969, pp. 46–51; R.E. Minger, 'Taft's Missions to Japan: A Study in Personal Diplomacy', *Pacific Historical Review*, vol. 30,

1961, pp. 279–94; C.E. Neu, 'Theodore Roosevelt and American Involvement in the Far East, 1901–1909', *Pacific Historical Review*, vol. 35, 1966, pp. 433–50; J. Chay, 'The Taft–Katsura Memorandum Reconsidered', *Pacific Historical Review*, vol. 37, 1968, pp. 321–6.

15 This topic has received much scholarly attention. The most significant early works are T.A. Bailey, *Theodore Roosevelt and the Japanese–American Crises: An Account of the International Complications Arising from the Race Problem on the Pacific Coast* (Stanford: Leland Stanford Jr University, 1932); and R.L. Buell, 'The Development of the Anti-Japanese Agitation in the United States', *Political Science Quarterly*, vol. 37, 1922, pp. 605–38. More recent studies have concluded that these early works exaggerated the seriousness of the crisis. For example, see C.E. Neu, *An Uncertain Friendship: Theodore Roosevelt and Japan, 1906–1909* (Cambridge: Harvard University Press, 1967), and R.A. Esthus, *Theodore Roosevelt and Japan* (Seattle: University of Washington Press, 1966).

16 Roosevelt to Acting Secretary of War Robert Shaw Oliver, 14 June 1907, Roosevelt Correspondence.

17 L. Morton, 'Military and Naval Preparations for the Defense of the Philippines during the War Scare of 1907', *Military Affairs*, vol. 13, no. 2, 1949, p. 95.

18 ibid.

19 The fleet was escorted by six destroyers in its circumnavigation of South America, but no destroyers accompanied the fleet for the Pacific crossing. For an itinerary and composition of the fleet, see US Navy, *Information Relative to the Voyage of the United States Atlantic Fleet Around the World* (Washington: Government Printing Office, 1910).

20 Louis Maxfield letters, 15 January 1908, Cathcart Family Papers, Minnesota Historical Society.

21 Sperry had been President of the NWC from November 1904 to May 1906, and returned to the NWC on special duty from September 1906 to May 1907. W.B. Cogar, *Dictionary of Admirals of the United States Navy*, vol. 2 (Annapolis: Naval Institute Press, 1989), p. 263.

22 *Naval War College Problems and Solutions, 1907*, p. 101, NWCA: RG 12.

23 Sperry to Secretary of Commerce Oscar Strauss, 4 February 1907, Sperry Papers, Library of Congress (LC): Naval Historical Foundation Collection (NHF).

24 Sperry to Edith M. Sperry (his wife), 1 November 1908, Sperry Papers, LC: NHF.

25 Sperry to C.S. Sperry, Jr, 9 January 1909, Sperry Papers, LC: NHF. Evans had completed a tour as C-in-C Asiatic Station in March 1904,

served on the General Board until March 1905, then commanded the Atlantic Fleet until May 1908. Cogar, pp. 84–5.

26 Sperry to Edith M. Sperry, 1 November 1908, Sperry Papers, LC: NHF.

27 'Naval War Plan for the Attack of Sydney, New South Wales, Australia', (hereafter, 'Sydney War Plan'), US National Archives (USNA): RG 38, Register no. 1909–670, Locker U–1-k, p. 1.

28 'The Cruise of the American Fleet to the Pacific', *Spectator*, 12 October 1907, pp. 517–18.

29 S. Schroeder, *A Half-Century of Naval Service* (New York: Appleton, 1922), p. 338. *Army & Navy Register*, 16 May 1908, pp. 9–10; 25 July 1908, p. 7; 1 August 1908, p. 5.

30 'Naval War Plan for the Defense of the Hawaiian Islands', p. 1, USNA: RG 38, Register No. 1909–667, Locker U–1-l.

31 ibid., p. 2.

32 Diplomatic correspondence for the fleet cruise is contained in the US State Department records, USNA: RG 59, Case 8258. Australian invitations: files 109, 123–4, 143–5, 160–2, 215, 241. New Zealand invitations: files 237, 254, 288, 330.

33 A.T. Mahan, 'The True Significance of the Pacific Cruise of the Battlefleet', *Scientific American*, 7 December 1907, p. 407. This article was reprinted in Mahan, *Naval Administration and Warfare: Some General Principles, with Other Essays* (London: Low & Martin, 1908), pp. 307–25. That this redeployment was effected without public notice was confirmed by the personal correspondence of Admiral Fisher. In a handwritten note by Fisher on a letter from King Edward dated 10 March 1908, Fisher recorded a conversation with the King in which the latter agreed with Fisher that war with Germany was inevitable. Fisher wanted to launch a pre-emptive strike against Germany but could not get approval. The note continued:

So all that could be done was to concentrate the whole British Naval strength in northern waters, which was done, and *done without exciting observation* until Admiral Mahan unfortunately wrote an article to say that 88[86] per cent. of England's guns were pointed at Germany [emphasis added].

A.J. Marder, (ed.) *Fear God and Dread Nought: The Correspondence of Admiral of the Fleet Lord Fisher of Kilverstone*, vol. 2 (London: Jonathan Cape, 1956), p. 168.

34 *New Zealand Herald*, 7 July 1908.

35 *Auckland Weekly News*, 30 July 1908.

36 W.S. Sims, 'Theodore Roosevelt and the Navy', *McClure's*, December 1922, p. 59.
37 R. Esthus, *Theodore Roosevelt and Japan* (Seattle: University of Washington Press, 1966), p. 262, quoting O.K. Davis, *Released for Publication*, Boston, 1925, pp. 87–8.
38 J.A. LaNauze, *Alfred Deakin: A Biography* (Melbourne: Melbourne University Press, 1965), p. 490. Modern historians as well as contemporaries emphasised that Deakin's primary motivation was his own naval plans. The invitation 'was perhaps the shrewdest of his moves' to revise the 1903 Naval Agreement and gain acceptance of an independent Australian navy. D.C. Gordon, *The Dominion Partnership in Imperial Defense, 1870–1914* (Baltimore: Johns Hopkins Press, 1965), p. 213.
39 *New Zealand Parliamentary Debates*, 30 September 1908, p. 709.
40 G.P. Taylor, 'New Zealand, the Anglo–Japanese Alliance and the 1908 Visit of the American Fleet', *Australian Journal of Politics and History*, April 1969, p. 59.
41 *Weekly Graphic*, 2 April 1904.
42 'Navarchus', *The World's Awakening* (London: Hodder & Stoughton, 1908), rev. Sydney *Bulletin*, 23 April 1908.
43 'Sydney War Plan', p. 5.
44 *Sydney Morning Herald*, 11 August 1908.
45 Wellington *Evening Post*, 23 March 1908.
46 W. Lawson, 'The White Squadron', Sydney *Bulletin*, 16 July 1908.
47 Caswell Saufley to Sallie (Rowan) Saufley, 20 August 1908, Saufley Papers, M–2867, Southern Historical Collection, University of North Carolina at Chapel Hill.
48 'Naval War Plan for the Attack of Auckland, New Zealand' (hereafter, 'Auckland War Plan'), USNA: RG 38, Register no. 1909–668, Locker U–1-k, p. 1.
49 'Sydney War Plan', p. 3
50 'Auckland War Plan', p. 3.
51 For details of the defensive batteries, calibre and location, see ibid., pp. 51–4.
52 ibid., p. 32.
53 'Sydney War Plan', p. 13.
54 ibid., p. 54.
55 ibid., p. 62.
56 LCDR Ridley McLean to William S. Sims, 20 September 1908, Sims Papers, LC: NHF. This letter subsequently was typed, and became an official report entitled, 'Naval Defense of Australia', Intelligence Division, Naval Attaché Reports, 1886–1939, USNA: RG 38, file 1908–756. McLean also was the author of the first *Bluejacket's*

Manual (1902), which continues today as the primer for enlisted service in the USN.
57 ibid.
58 H. Kent Hewitt letter, 30 August 1908. Hewitt Letters, LC: NHF.
59 'Naval War Plan for the Attack of Melbourne, Victoria, Australia', USNA: RG 38, Register No. 1909–671, Locker U–1-k, p. 1.
60 'Naval Plan for the Attack of King George Sound and Albany, West Australia' (Hereafter, 'Albany War Plan'), USNA: RG 38, Register no. 1909–674, Locker U–1-k.
61 'Naval Plan for the Attack of Perth and Fremantle, Western Australia', USNA, RG 38, Register no. 1909–672, Locker U–1-k.
62 'Albany War Plan', p. 1.
63 G. Howard, *The Navy in New Zealand: An Illustrated History* (London: Jane's Publishing Co., 1981), p. 100.
64 Master Chief Machinist's Mate Mark Butler, USS *Halyburton*, quoted in B. Peniston, 'In Pursuit of "the Real Navy"', *US Naval Institute Proceedings*, May 1999, p. 68.

13 A.W. Jose in the politics and strategy of naval defence, 1903–1909

1 D.C.S. Sissons, *Attitudes to Japan and Defence, 1890–1923*, MA thesis, University of Melbourne, 1956, chapter 2; N. Meaney, *The Search for Security in the Pacific, 1901–14* (Sydney: Sydney University Press, 1976), chapters 5, 6.
2 N. Meaney, *Fears and Phobias: E.L. Piesse and the problem of Japan 1909–39* (Canberra: National Library of Australia, 1996), p. 3.
3 G. Davison, J. Hirst and S. Macintyre (eds), *The Oxford Companion to Australian History* (Melbourne: Oxford University Press, 1998), p. 356a.
4 J.A. La Nauze, *Alfred Deakin: a Biography*, vol. 2, chapter 23—see especially pp. 517, 518; R. Norris, *The Emergent Commonwealth: Australian Federation: Expectations and Fulfilment 1889–1910* (Melbourne: Melbourne University Press, 1975), chapters 4, 5.
5 Norris, pp. 157, 158.
6 This chapter is indebted to the valuable research assistance given by Sharon and Brett Farrell.
7 A.W. Jose, *The Romantic Nineties* (Sydney: Angus & Robertson, 1933), p. 93.
8 For Jose's further involvement in naval affairs see *Australian Dictionary of Biography*, vol. 9, pp. 523–4.

9   *The Times*, 31 August 1903.
10 *The Times*, 21 December 1903.
11 Jose to *The Times*, 8 May 1906, Mitchell Library (ML): Uncatalogued Mss 266/4 (hereafter 266/4), f. 630, published, *The Times*, 30 August 1906.
12 Deakin to *Morning Post*, 14 July 1903, National Library of Australia (NLA): Deakin Papers (hereafter Ms 1540), 1540/7/374, p. 74, published, *Morning Post*, 23 September 1903.
13 Creswell became Director of Commonwealth Naval Forces in 1904.
14 Jose to Amery, 8 May 1906, ML: 266/4, f. 462; Jose to *The Times*, 8, 15 May 1906, ML: 266/4, ff. 625–37, published, *The Times*, 30 August 1906.
15 Jose to *The Times*, 27 July 1905, ML: 266/1, published, *The Times*, 4 October 1905.
16 Jose to Moberly Bell, 17 October 1905, ML: 266/4, ff. 369–73.
17 Jose to *The Times*, 21 November 1905, ML: 266/4, ff. 212–16, published, *The Times*, 6 January 1906.
18 L.S. Amery to Jose, 23 October 1905, ML: Catalogued Mss B1089 (hereafter B1089). Letters between Britain and Australia took almost exactly five weeks.
19 Deakin to Governor-General, 28 August 1905, in N. Lambert, *Australia's Naval Inheritance: Imperial Maritime Strategy and the Australia Station 1880–1909*, Papers in Australian Maritime Affairs No. 6 (Canberra: MSP, 1998), pp. 115–18.
20 Jose to Deakin, 30 November 1905, NLA: Ms 1540/15/478.
21 Jose to Amery, 1 December 1905, ML: 266/4, f. 381. Deakin's enclosure, a statement on the Naval Agreement, was not found.
22 Jose to *The Times*, 4 January 1906, ML: 266/4, ff. 232, 233, published, *The Times*, 15 February 1906.
23 Jose to *The Times*, 12 March 1906, ML: 266/4, ff. 623, 624, published, *The Times*, 21 April 1906; see Bob Nicholls, *Statesmen & Sailors Australian Maritime Defence 1870–1920* (Balmain: published by the author, 1995), p. 110 for a similar concern in August of that year.
24 Amery to Jose, 14 February 1906, ML: B1089; Amery's emphasis.
25 Jose to Amery, 2 April 1906, ML: B1089.
26 Deakin used the term 'navalism' in his 13 December 1907 speech, believing he was coining it.
27 *Commonwealth Parliamentary Papers* (*CPP*), 1905, vol. 2, pp. 315–17.
28 Deakin to *Morning Post* [20 June 1905], NLA: Ms 1540/7/374, p. 155, published *Morning Post*, 1 August 1905.

29 Nicholls, pp. 80–3, whose research shows the continuity of official initiatives and inquiry from late 1903. *Commonwealth Parliamentary Debates* (*CPD*), vol. 19 (18 May 1904), 1281a; *CPP*, 1905, vol. 2, p. 317b.
30 *CPD*, vol. 19 (18 May l904), 1280a & b. Ten months earlier, Deakin had reported Watson's policy stance in almost identical terms: see Deakin to *Morning Post*, 21 July 1903, NLA: Ms 1540/7/374, p. 75, published *Morning Post*, 26 September 1903. For the approaches to the Admiralty see Norris, p. 141, and Nicholls, pp. 83, 84.
31 Deakin to Editor, *Morning Post*, 27 October 1903, in J.A. La Nauze (ed.), *Federated Australia: selections from letters to the* Morning Post *1900–1910* (Melbourne: Melbourne University Press, 1968), p. 122.
32 Deakin to Governor-General, 28 August 1905, in Lambert, *Australia's Naval Inheritance*, p. 115.
33 From May 1905 Deakin was most conscious of pending elections, not only those due in December 1906, but also any in the near future occasioned by Reid's uncertain majority in the Parliament; see all but one of his weekly letters to the *Morning Post* between 16 May and 3 July 1905, NLA: Ms 1540/7/374.
34 Before Deakin's participation in the 1907 Imperial Conference this difference is less noticeable. The 1904 Labor ministers had a simpler view: Watson—'three very competent officers, namely, Captain Creswell, Captain Tickell, and Captain Colquhoun, ... it was thought, would have some knowledge of local conditions', *CPD*, vol. 20 (12 July 1904), p. 3128b; and the Minster for Defence, Senator Dawson—'Captain Creswell is our naval expert, and if we have a naval expert, we must, to a large extent, follow his advice', ibid., p. 3151b.
35 Jose to Amery, 8 October 1907, ML: 266/4, f. 849.
36 Deakin to Governor-General, 28 August 1905, in Lambert, *Australia's Naval Inheritance*, p. 116–17.
37 G.L. Macandie, *The Genesis of the Royal Australian Navy* (Sydney: Government Printer, 1949), p. 167.
38 Nicholls, p. 127.
39 Deakin, speech at State Banquet, cited in Jose to *The Times*, 25 August 1908, ML: 266/3, ff. 158, 159, published, *The Times*, 29 September 1908.
40 Jose to Foreign Editor, *The Times*, 23 March 1909, ML: B1090; Jose to Deakin, 2 April 1909, NLA: Ms 1540/16/601.
41 Norris, p. 143.
42 Jose to Amery, 10 November [1906], ML: 266/4, f. 869.
43 'Turbine', 'Schemes of naval defence', *The Call*, November 1907, pp. 7, 8.

44 *CPD*, vol. 42 (13 December 1907), pp. 7509–35.
45 Jose to *The Times*, 24 December 1907, ML: 266/3, f. 114.
46 Jose to Deakin, 29 January 1908, NLA: Ms 1540/15/773; Jose to Foreign Editor, *The Times*, 29 September 1908, ML: B1089.
47 Jose to Deakin, 13 January 1908, NLA: Ms 1540/15/3620–22.
48 Jose to Foreign Editor, *The Times*, 23 March 1909, ML: B1090.
49 *The Times*, 28 May 1906, see Deakin to *Morning Post*, 28 May 1906, NLA: Ms 1540/7/374, p. 201, published *Morning Post*, 17 July 1906—'Admiral Shimura . . . cannot complain of any want of cordiality. Melbourne was said to have excelled herself in hospitalities, and Sydney was determined not to shun comparison . . . Our citizens had every reason to be content with the manner in which their capital arrayed herself in order to extend a fitting greeting to the great Eastern ally of the Empire.'
50 Jose to E.W.M Grigg, 29 March 1909, ML: B1090.
51 Jose to Deakin, 28 April [1909], NLA: Ms 1540/1/3641 and Jose to Deakin, 28 April 1909, 1540/16/556, 557, which has 'I am sending a similar letter to the Prime Minister'.
52 Jose to *The Times*, 26 November 1907, ML: 266/4, ff. 951, 952; Jose to Foreign Editor, *The Times*, 6 April 1909, ML: B1090; Jose to *The Times*, 6 April 1909, ML: 266/1, published 21 May 1909.
53 Jose to Foreign Editor, *The Times*, 23 March 1909, ML: B1090.
54 Jose to Foreign Editor, *The Times*, 13 April 1909, ML: B1090.
55 'Turbine', 'An Australian navy?', *The Call*, February 1909, pp. 12–14.
56 ibid., p. 14.
57 N. Lambert, 'Economy or Empire? The fleet unit concept and the quest for collective security in the Pacific, 1909–14', in G. Kennedy and K. Neilson (eds), *Far Flung Lines: studies in imperial defence in honour of Donald Mackenzie Schurman* (London: Frank Cass, 1997), pp. 56, 64, 65 and the following chapter.
58 Jose to *The Times*, 31 March 1914, ML: 266/1, published, *The Times*, 25 May 1914.
59 Jose to Amery, 10 November [1906], ML:266/4, f. 869.
60 Jose to Deakin, 19 November 1908, NLA: Ms 1540/16/447.
61 *CPP* 1908, vol. 2, 367–77. The *Argus* opposed the idea of an Australian navy.
62 Grigg to Jose, 3 December 1908, ML: B1090. Grigg had spent much of 1907 and 1908 in Australia.
63 Jose to *The Times*, 14 January 1908, ML: 266/3, ff. 121–6.
64 Jose to V. Chirol, 11 November 1907, ML: 266/4, ff. 937–9.
65 Amery believed *The Times* 'went off the rails' on the new Australian tariff, Amery to Jose, 14 October 1907, ML: B1089; and Jose to Amery, 31 December 1907, ML: 266/3, f. 18.

66 Jose to Grigg, 2 October 1912, ML: B1090.
67 Jose to Foreign Editor, *The Times*, 31 December 1907, ML: 266/3, f. 16.
68 Jose to *The Times*, 24 December 1907, ML: 266/3, ff. 115, 116.
69 Jose to *The Times*, 14 January 1908, ML: 266/3, f. 123.
70 Lambert, 'Economy or empire?', pp. 65, 66; and *Australia's Naval Inheritance*, p. 182.
71 See N. Lambert, chapter 14. For post-1909 Australian consideration of blue-water strategy see D. Stevens, chapter 15 and I. Cowman, 'The vision splendid: Australian maritime strategy, 1911–23', in D. Stevens (ed.), *In Search of a Maritime Strategy: The maritime element in Australian defence planning since 1901*, Canberra Papers on Strategy and Defence No. 119 (Canberra: SDSC, 1997), pp. 43–66.

14 Sir John Fisher, the fleet unit concept, and the creation of the Royal Australian Navy

1 See N. Lambert, *Australia's Naval Inheritance: Imperial Maritime Strategy and the Australia Station 1880–1909*, Papers in Australia's Maritime Affairs No. 6 (Canberra: Maritime Studies Program, 1999).
2 ibid., p. 175.
3 See N. Lambert, 'Economy or Empire? The Quest for Collective Security in the Pacific, 1909–1914', in K. Neilson and G. Kennedy (eds), *Far Flung Lines: Studies in Imperial Defence* (London: Frank Cass, 1997).
4 N. Lambert, *Admiral Sir John Fisher's Naval Revolution* (Columbia: University of South Carolina Press, 1999).
5 'Mahanian' is used here as an adjective. Notwithstanding this commonly accepted view of Mahan and sea power, Jon Sumida's recent treatment has determined that many traditional assumptions about Mahan's arguments are in need of revision. See J.T. Sumida, *Inventing Grand Strategy and Teaching Command: The Classic Works of Alfred Thayer Mahan Reconsidered* (Washington: Wilson Center Press, 1997).
6 Lambert, *Fisher's Naval Revolution*.
7 See N. Lambert, 'Admiral Sir John Fisher and the concept of Flotilla Defence, 1904–1910', in the *Journal of Military History*, vol. 59, October 1995, pp. 639–60.
8 For an explanation of the 'battle cruiser theory', see. J. Sumida, *In Defence of Naval Supremacy* (Boston: Unwin Hyman, 1989).

NOTES 339

9 Lambert, 'Admiral Sir John Fisher and the concept of Flotilla Defence, 1904–1910'.
10 The Grand Fleet was not just the name given to the Home Fleet. The Grand Fleet was in fact an abbreviation of a tactical idea. It was known when first conceived as the Grand Fleet of Battle, the notion of battleships working in conjunction with torpedo-armed flotilla craft, cruisers and ultimately submarines.
11 Lambert, *Fisher's Naval Revolution*, chapter 7.

15 'Defend the north': Commander Thring, Captain Hughes-Onslow and the beginnings of Australian naval strategic thought

1 For an example, see F. Cain, *The Origins of Political Surveillance in Australia* (Sydney: Angus & Robertson, 1983), p. 78.
2 See Thring's entry in, G. Searle (ed.), *Australian Dictionary of Biography 1891–1939*, vol. 12 (Melbourne: Melbourne University Press, 1990), p. 222.
3 For a recent review of this rivalry, see A. Gordon, *The Rules of the Game: Jutland and British Naval Command* (London: John Murray, 1996), pp. 365–8.
4 Cited in the diary of G.E. Morrison, an adviser to the Chinese Government and keen observer of Australian personalities, 3 January 1918. With thanks to Ross Lamont.
5 'Introduction', in *The Australasian Naval and Military Annual 1912–13* (Sydney: Angus & Robertson for the Australian National Defence League, 1913), p. ix.
6 W. Thring, 'The Pacific Problem', the *Naval Review*, 1914, p. 102.
7 For example, see letter, Admiralty to ACNB, 15 May 1913, NAA: MP 1049, 14/157 (13/173).
8 For a summary of Australian concerns see, 'Naval Defence', memorandum by the Minister for Defence, 13 April 1914, *CPP*, No. 1, 1914.
9 Diaries of Sir George King-Hall, 21 July 1913, NHD, Canberra.
10 'War Orders for HM Australian Naval Service', 1913, NAA: MP 1049, 14/157 (13/173).
11 C.H. Hughes-Onslow, *The Australian Naval Board Scandal* (Melbourne: Page & Bird, 1914), p. 3.
12 J. Sumida, *In Defence of Naval Supremacy: Finance, Technology and British Naval Policy, 1889–1914* (Boston: Unwin Hyman, 1989), p. 155.
13 *Recommendations by Admiral Sir Reginald Henderson, KCB*, 1

March 1911 (Melbourne: Government Printer, 1911).
14 Bob Nicholls, *Statesmen & Sailors: Australian Maritime Defence 1870–1920* (Balmain: published by the author, 1995), p. 174.
15 ibid., p. 218.
16 Diaries of Sir George King-Hall, 5 October 1913.
17 'Remarks by First Naval Member on Part II of Second Naval Member's Report' by Creswell, 27 August 1913, NAA: MP 1049/1, 15/054.
18 Hughes-Onslow, *The Australian Naval Board Scandal*, p. 13.
19 Nicholls, pp. 193, 257–9.
20 Melbourne *Punch*, 10 July 1913, cited in Hughes-Onslow, *The Australian Naval Board Scandal*, p. 14.
21 *Recommendations by Admiral Sir Reginald Henderson*, p. 8.
22 'Strategical Report with some notes on preparations for war', by Hughes-Onslow, July 1913 (hereafter 'Hughes-Onslow Report'), NAA: MP1587/1, 186K, p. 1.
23 ibid., p. 2.
24 See for example, Department of Defence, *Australia's Strategic Policy* (Canberra: Directorate of Publishing, 1997), p. 10.
25 H. Lea, *The Value of Ignorance*, cited in 'Report on the Naval Defence of Australia' by Commander W.H. Thring (hereafter 'Thring Report'), NAA: MP 1185, 186K, p. 3.
26 ibid., pp. 2–3.
27 Admiral Sir George King-Hall, 'Australia's Naval Policy', in *The Australasian Naval and Military Annual 1912–13*, p. 3.
28 'Memorandum on Strategic Reports' by Hughes-Onslow, 18 July 1913, NAA: MP 1049/1, 15/054.
29 'Introduction', in *The Australasian Naval and Military Annual 1911–12* (Sydney: Angus & Robertson for the Australian National Defence League, 1912), p. vii.
30 Hughes-Onslow Report, p. 6.
31 ibid., p. 8.
32 Remarks by Hughes-Onslow, undated, on paper 'Naval Policy of Australia', by Manisty, NAA: MP 1049/1, 15/054.
33 Hughes-Onslow Report, p. 6.
34 ibid.
35 J.S. Corbett, *Some Principles of Maritime Strategy* (Annapolis: Naval Institute Press, 1988, reprint of 1911 edition with an introduction by E. Grove), p. 310. Corbett listed the advantages of defence as: (1) proximity to base; (2) familiar ground; (3) facility for arranging surprise by counter-attack.
36 Hughes-Onslow Report, p. 10.
37 Corbett, p. 15.

NOTES 341

38 ibid., p. 239.
39 Thring Report.
40 J. Mordike, *An Army for a Nation: A history of Australian military developments 1880–1914* (Sydney: Allen & Unwin, 1992), p. 243.
41 'Remarks by 1st NM', 1 September 1913, NAA: MP 1049/1, 15/054.
42 One might note that in the 1990s the Jindalee over-the horizon-radar was described as having a similar role. See G. Ferguson 'Tripwire in the North...', *New Zealand Defence Quarterly*, Autumn 1998, pp. 13–15.
43 Hughes-Onslow Report, p. 5.
44 ibid., p. 12.
45 Corbett, p. 94.
46 Hughes-Onslow Report, p. 12.
47 Thring Report, Appendix 1.
48 Thring Report, p. 6.
49 Corbett, p. 231.
50 Thring Report, p. 6.
51 ibid., p. 24.
52 'Memorandum on Strategical Reports' by Hughes-Onslow, 18 July 1913, NAA: MP 1049/1, 15/054.
53 'Principles agreed upon by meeting of the ACNB', 17 July 1913, NAA: MP 1049/1, 15/054.
54 Memorandum, Manisty to Secretary Department of the Prime Minister, 12 August 1913, NAA: MP1049/1, 15/054.
55 'Remarks on Commander Thring's Scheme', by Creswell, 27 August 1913, NAA: MP 1049/1, 15/054.
56 For examples, see comments in King-Hall diaries, 9 and 19 August, 4 October 1913.
57 For these plans see, I. Cowman, ' "The Vision Splendid": Australia, Naval Strategy and Empire, 1919–23', in D. Stevens (ed.), *In Search of a Maritime Strategy: The Maritime Element in Australian Defence Planning since 1901*, Canberra Papers on Strategy and Defence No. 119 (Canberra: SDSC, 1997), pp. 55–9.
58 See 'Report of Admiral of the Fleet Viscount Jellicoe of Scapa on Naval Mission to the Commonwealth of Australia (May–August 1919), HMS *New Zealand* at Sydney, 12 August 1919', NHD Canberra.
59 Mount Creswell and the Clarkson Range remain on the latest edition of the chart (AUS 631), but Thring Harbour has been renamed Bwaguda Bay.
60 When assessing the need for a railway line to Bynoe Harbour, Thring noted that the single-line Siberian Railway had conveyed 400 000

troops to the front and maintained them for more than a year 6000 miles from their base. See Thring Report, p. 17.

16 Divergent paths: problems of command and strategy in Anglo–Australasian naval operations in the Asia–Pacific: August–November 1914

1. Research for this chapter, in the form of a BA (Hons) thesis, was facilitated by financial support from the School of History, University of NSW, ADFA.
2. 'The German Cruiser Squadron in the Pacific, 1914', *Naval Staff Monographs*, vol. 1, p. 52.
3. Minute, CinC China (Jerram) to Secretary of the Admiralty, Enclosure 1 'Plan of Operations in event of war with Germany',12 January 1914. PRO: ADM 137, HS 819, p. 289.
4. 'War Standing orders for Vessels Employed in the Protection of Trade', July 1914. PRO: ADM 137, HS 818, pp. 244–7.
5. P. Overlack, 'German Commerce Warfare Planning for the Australian Station, 1900–1914', in *War and Society*, May 1996, p. 18; 'Asia in German Naval Planning Before the First World War: The Strategic Imperative', in *War and Society*, May 1999, p. 10.
6. 'War orders for H.M. Australian Naval Service', 15 May 1913, pp. 1–2, NAA: MP 1049/1, 14/0157.
7. Minute, 'Amendment to War Orders issued by the Admiralty 15 May 1913 for HMAS *Australia*', 21 April 1914, ibid.
8. 'War Orders for H.M. Australian Naval Service', ibid.
9. Admiralty to Colonial Office, 15 May 1913, forwarded by Secretary of State for the Colonies, 16 May 1913, ibid.
10. A.W. Jose, *The Royal Australian Navy 1914–1918, The Official History of Australia in the War of 1914–1918*, Vol. IX (Sydney: Angus and Robertson, 1943), p. 8.
11. Telegram, Navy Office to RAC, 31 July 1914. AWM: AWM 35, 2/10; telegram, Macandie to Navy Office, 31 July 1914, NAA: MP 1049/1, 14/0299.
12. Letter, Thring to Bywater, 4 September 1934, Naval History Directorate: Thring papers.
13. Telegram, Navy Office to RAC, 0357 2 August 1914, AWM: AWM 35, 2/10.
14. Telegram, RAC to Navy Office, 3 August 1914, ibid.
15. Letter RAC to ACNB, 16 August 1914, AWM: AWM 36, 21/3; telegram, Navy Office to RAC, 4 August 1914, ibid.
16. 'The German Cruiser Squadron in the Pacific, 1914', pp. 80–1.

17 Telegram, Governor of New Zealand to the Secretary of State for the Colonies, 1430 2 August 1914, PRO: ADM 137, HS 4, p. 8.
18 Minute, DOD to COS, 2 August 1914, ibid.
19 Minute, COS to First Sea Lord, 2 August 1914, ibid.
20 'Australia: Preparation of defence schemes', PRO: CAB 38, 23/15; National Maritime Museum: RIC1/9 Richmond's Diaries, 5 and 14 August 1914.
21 Minute, COS to First Sea Lord, 2 August 1914, PRO: ADM 137, HS 4, p. 9.
22 Jerram's subsequent bombardment of Yap provides for the historian an important precedent for such a course of action, even though it was not strictly within the confines of international law.
23 NMM: RIC1/9 Richmond's Diaries, 5 August 1914.
24 Minute, M.P.A. Hankey to Prime Minister, 5 August 1914, PRO: CAB 21, 3.
25 'Proceedings of Sub-Committee of the Committee of Imperial Defence', 5 August 1914; 'Recommendations of the Sub-Committee of the Committee of Imperial Defence which considered the question of offensive operations against German Colonies', 6 August 1914, PRO: CAB 21, 3.
26 W.S. Churchill, *The World Crisis 1911–1914* (London, Thornton Butterworth, 1923), p. 283.
27 'Naval Notes on New Zealand's expedition to Samoa', Jackson, 7 August 1914, PRO: ADM 137, HS 4, p. 17; 'Naval Notes on joint expedition from Australia', Jackson, 7 August 1914, PRO: ADM 137, HS 5, p. 13.
28 ibid.
29 Telegram, Admiralty through Navy Office to RAC, 2007 4 August 1914, AWM: AWM 35, 2/10.
30 S.J. Smith, *The Samoa (NZ) Expeditionary Force 1914–1915* (Wellington, Ferguson & Osborn, 1924), pp. 12–15.
31 Minute Jackson to COS and First Sea Lord, 8 August 1914, PRO: ADM 137, HS 4, p. 22.
32 Note, COS, 8 August 1914, PRO: ADM 137, HS 4, p. 22.
33 Telegram, Admiralty through Navy Office to RAC and CinC China, 1230 9 August 1914, PRO: ADM 137, HS 4, p. 36.
34 Memorandum by Defence Minister, 8 August 1914, NAA (ACT): A 5854/69, 1755/3.
35 Telegram, Secretary of State for the Colonies to the Governor-General of Australia, 6 August 1914, AWM: AWM 51, 48, p. 1.
36 Telegram, RAC to Navy Office, 1008 8 August 1914, AWM: AWM 35, 2/10.

37 Memorandum by Defence Minister, 8 August 1914. NAA (ACT): A 5854/69, 1755/3.
38 Minute from ACNB to Minister, 9 August 1914, ibid.
39 Handwritten note by Thring, following Memorandum by Defence Minister, 8 August 1914, ibid.
40 Telegram, Governor-General of Australia to the Secretary of State for the Colonies, 10 August 1914, NAA: MP 1049/1, 14/0307.
41 'Admiral Patey's report on the participation by the Australian Seagoing Fleet in the operations in the Pacific', AWM: AWM 33, 18, pp. 9–12.
42 Letter, Patey to Charles and Helen, 10 August 1914, AWM: 2 DRL 795. Original emphasis.
43 AWM: AWM 33, 18, p. 12.
44 Telegram, CinC China to RAC, 1930 13 August 1914, AWM: AWM 35, 2/10.
45 Telegram, Governor New Zealand through SNO NZ to RAC, 12 August 1914, AWM: AWM 35, 2/10.
46 AWM: AWM 33, 18, p. 13; telegram RAC to Governor New Zealand, 2325 12 August 1914, AWM: AWM 35, 2/10.
47 Telegram RAC to ACNB, 1935 13 August 1914, ibid.
48 Letter, Lieutenant Warren to brother, undated, AWM: 1 DRL 597.
49 'The German Cruiser Squadron in the Pacific, 1914', pp. 70, 75.
50 Jose, *The RAN*, p. 51.
51 J.S. Corbett, *Naval Operations, Vol. I: To the Battle of the Falklands December 1914* (London: Longmans, Green & Co., 1920), p. 147.
52 K. Yates, *Graf Spee's Raiders: Challenge to the Royal Navy, 1914–1915* (Annapolis: Naval Institute Press, 1995), pp. 24–5; OU 6337 (40), 'Review of German Cruiser Warfare 1914–1919 (1940)', p 30.
53 Minutes of ACNB, 4 March 1914, NAA(ACT): A 2585, 1914/1919.
54 'HMAS *Australia* Ships Log 13 June 1914 – 15 March 1915, AWM: AWM 35, 2/1; 'HMAS *Melbourne* Ships Log 30 December 1913 – 19 December 1914', AWM: AWM 35, 17/1; and 'HMAS *Sydney* Ships Log 18 June 1914 – 9 June 1915. AWM: AWM 35, 24/2.
55 Cited in Jose, *The RAN*, p. 51.
56 Letter, RAC to Creswell, 21 August 1914, NAA(ACT): A 5954/69, 1755/3.
57 Telegram, ACNB to Admiralty, 15 August 1914, NAA(ACT): A 5954/69, 1755/3; telegram, Admiralty to ACNB, 15 August 1914, AWM: AWM 36, 21/3.
58 A. Gordon, *Rules of the Game: Jutland and British Naval Command* (London: John Murray, 1996), pp. 582–93.

NOTES

59 J. Hattendorf, 'Admiral Prince Louis of Battenberg (1912–1914)', in M.H. Murfett, (ed.) *The First Sea Lords* (Westport: Praeger, 1995), p. 85.
60 Minute, Churchill to First Sea Lord and COS, 20 August 1914, PRO: ADM 137, HS 5.
61 Telegram, Admiralty to CinC China, 2030 23 August 1914, PRO: ADM 137, HS 11, p. 371.
62 'The China Squadron, 1914, including the Emden Hunt', *Naval Staff Monographs*, vol. 5, pp. 52–4.
63 Minute, Churchill to First Sea Lord and COS, 24 August 1914, PRO: ADM 137, HS 11, p. 372. Original emphasis.
64 Telegram, CinC China to Admiralty, 24 August 1914, PRO: ADM 137, HS 1, pp. 80–1.
65 ibid., and Vice Admiral Jerram, letter, 29 August 1914, NMM: JRM/16/7.
66 Minute, First Sea Lord, 24 August 1914, PRO: ADM 137, HS 7, p. 348c-d.
67 Letter, Patey to Helen, 5 September 1914, AWM: 2 DRL 795.
68 Minute, Leveson to First Sea Lord, COS and Jackson, 2 September 1914, PRO: ADM 137, HS 1, p. 109.
69 Telegram, CinC China to Admiralty, 0120 12 September 1914, ibid., 148a-b.
70 Friedrich Wilhelmshafen was the main village of Friedrich Wilhelmshafen Land, the northern half of what is now Papua New Guinea. By September 1914, only 17 Europeans remained in residence there.
71 AWM: AWM 33, 18, p. 67.
72 ACNB to VAC, 5 October 1914, AWM: AWM 35, 2/17. This should actually have read that she was en route from the Marquesas to the Easter Islands.
73 Jose, *The RAN*, p. 123.
74 'Trade protection on and after the outbreak of the war', memo by First Lord, 14 April 1914, PRO: ADM 137, HS 818, pp. 172–4.
75 'The China Squadron, 1914, including the Emden Hunt', p. 113.
76 Note, First Lord to COS and First Sea Lord, PRO: ADM 137, HS 2, p. 62.
77 A.J. Marder, *The Portrait of an Admiral: The Life and Papers of Sir Herbert Richmond* (Oxford: Alden, 1952), 9 and 10 October 1914, pp. 112–16.
78 Corbett, *Naval Operations*, vol. I, p. 297.
79 Jose, *The RAN*, pp. 158, 161, 179–202.

80 C. Gray, 'Why strategy is difficult', lecture ADFA, Canberra, 30 July 1999.
81 Churchill, *World Crisis 1911–1914*, p. 295.

17 A strategy for the lower deck of the early Royal Australian Navy

1 NAA (ACT): A 5954/1, 1924/8.
2 G. Macandie, *The Genesis of the Royal Australian Navy* (Sydney: Government Printer, 1949), p. 58.
3 R. Parsons, *Navy in South Australia* (SA: self-published, 1974), p. 8. This monograph contains extracts from Creswell's diaries.
4 ibid.
5 J. Bach, *The Australian Squadron* (Sydney: UNSW Press, 1986), pp. 237–9. Bach states that from 1890 and 1913 there were 1500 ratings 'in a state of desertion' from the Australian squadron.
6 L. Batt, *Pioneers of the Royal Australian Navy* (NSW: self-published, 1967), p. 40.
7 Memorandum by Langdale Ottley, 'Admiralty views on the working of the Australian Naval Agreement', 27 February 1907, in N. Tracy (ed.), *The Collective Naval Defence of the Empire, 1900–1940* (London: Naval Records Society, 1997), p. 69.
8 NAA(VIC): MP 124/6, 463/201/113.
9 Naval Board Minutes, 1904–1919, No. 13, 11 July 1906, NAA(ACT): A 2585.
10 Admiralty Minutes, CinC Report to the Admiralty, 6 April 1904, PRO: ADM 1/7730, 6916. Australian Joint Copying Project, National Library.
11 C. Jones, *Australian Colonial Navies* (Canberra: AWM, 1986), p. 134.
12 H.J. Feakes, *White Ensign-Southern Cross*, (Sydney: Ure Smith, 1951), p. 120.
13 N. Lambert, 'Economy or Empire?', in G. Kennedy, and K. Neilson (eds), *Far Flung Lines* (London: Frank Cass, 1996), p. 58.
14 Macandie, p. 242. Australia agreed to pay approximately £750 000 to Britain for maintenance, pay and allowances for loan personnel, training and other associated costs.
15 D.A. Baugh, 'The Eighteenth Century Navy as a National Institution, 1690–1815' in J.R. Hill (ed.), *The Oxford Illustrated History of the Royal Navy* (Oxford: Oxford University Press, 1995), p. 155. Between 1818 and 1898 only two members of the lower deck had gained commissions.

16   J. Winton, 'Life and Education in a Technically Evolving Navy 1815–1925', ibid., p. 253.
17   A. Carew, *The Lower Deck of the Royal Navy* (Manchester: Manchester University Press, 1981), p. xiv.
18   Naval Board Minutes, 1904–19, No. 3, 24 June 1910, NAA(ACT): CP 78/22/1, 136/1912 and A 2585.
19   In 1914 Captain Gaunt became naval attaché in Washington and became a key figure in the British efforts to influence American opinion before their entry into the war.
20   'Diaries of Admiral Sir George King-Hall, 1911, 1912, 1913', 2 March 1912, unpublished, copies held by Naval History Directorate, Canberra.
21   Admiral Sir R. Henderson, *The Naval Forces of the Commonwealth—Recommendations*, pp. 24, 15. Henderson's plan was reported in the *Argus*, 14 and 15 March 1911.
22   *HMAS Cerberus 1997, Information Book for Personnel and their Families Posted to HMAS Cerberus*. The training establishment, also known as Flinders Naval Depot, was named *Cerberus* when the ironclad monitor was decommissioned.
23   *Commonwealth Parliamentary Debates* (*CPD*), vol. LXI, 9 November 1911, p. 2380. Fleet instruction continued to take place on board ships of the Australian Squadron.
24   *How to join the Royal Australian Navy* (Melbourne: Australian Navy Office, 1912), p. 16. If aged 17–19 the physical minimum requirements were a height of 5 ft 2 inches and a chest measurement of 33 inches.
25   R.C. Roberts, *Birth of a Navy* (Perth: Patersons, 1944), p. 21.
26   *Commonwealth Year Book*, vol. 12, 1919, p. 1015.
27   *CPD*, vol. LXXI, 2 October 1913, p. 1787. Between 1912 and 1927 some 3158 boys would receive the first elements of their naval training in *Tingira*.
28   The *Sydney Morning Herald*, 23 August 1913.
29   The *Navy*, November–January 1970–71, p. 55. He was serving in the RN at the time.
30   The *Sydney Morning Herald*, 1 November 1996.
31   R.Wilson, 'Memoirs', AWM: PR 84/26.
32   D. Phillipson, *Band of Brothers* (Cornwall: Sutton, 1996), p. 17.
33   ibid., HMS *Ganges* near Ipswich.
34   Wilson, 'Memoirs'.
35   A. Evans, *A Navy For Australia* (Sydney: ABC, 1996), p. 87.
36   J.W. Niesigh, *Neptune's Babies* (Melbourne: Government Printer, 1912), p. 10.
37   The *Argus*, 12 July 1911.

38 Macandie, p. 280.
39 *CPD*, vol. LXI, 13 October 1911, p. 1402, and vol. LX, 13 September 1911, p. 369.
40 Discussion can be found in *CPD*, vol. LXIX, 12–17 December 1912, pp. 6956–7267; vol. LXIV, 20 June 1912, p. 61; and vol. LXXI, 24 October 1913, pp. 2520–1.
41 *CPD*, vol. LXXII, 20 November 1913, pp. 3334–5.
42 C.H. Hughes-Onslow, *The Australian Naval Board Scandal* (Melbourne: Page & Bird, 1914), p. 5. Manisty returned to the United Kingdom in 1914 and eventually retired as Rear Admiral Sir Eldon Manisty, KCB, CMG. Hughes-Onslow established by personal contribution a relief fund for sailors in distress. See R. Hyslop, *Australian Naval Administration 1900–1939* (Melbourne: Hawthorn Press, 1973), p. 120.
43 J. Keegan, *The Price of Admiralty* (London: Hutchinson, 1988), p. 120; and Phillipson, p. 28.
44 NAA(ACT): A 471/1, 122.
45 NAA(ACT): CP 78/23/1, 19/89/679.
46 The *Evening Standard*, 30 June 1913; the *Dundee Courier*, 2 July 1913; and the *Irish Times*, 2 July 1913.

18 The Royal Australian Navy, the Constitution and the law—then and now

1 S. Keeva, 'Lawyers in the War Room', *ABA Journal*, December 1991, p. 52.
2 Imperial statute 63 and 64 Victoria, Chapter 12.
3 See Department of Defence (Navy), *An Outline of Australian Naval History* (Canberra: AGPS, 1976), pp. 22–6; M. McKernan and M. Browne (eds), *Australia Two Centuries of War and Peace* (1988), pp. 130–7.
4 Various indigenous laws may also have existed in 1788, but the nature and form of such laws is not germane to the substance of this chapter.
5 J. Baalman, in J. Malor (ed.) *Outline of Law in Australia* (3rd edition 1969), p. 17.
6 ibid., p. 18.
7 ibid., p. 19.
8 ibid.
9 G.J. Lindell, 'Why is Australia's Constitution Binding?', *Federal Law Review*, 16, p. 31.

10 A. Mason, 'The Australian Constitution 1901–1988', *Australian Law Journal*, 62, p. 753.
11 See I. Harris, 'Australia Acts end our last constitutional links with UK', in *Australian Law News*, April 1986, p. 21.
12 *Re Residential Tenancies Tribunal (NSW); Ex Parte Defence Housing Authority* 190 CLR 410.
13 *Commonwealth of Australia Gazette*, No. 1, 1 January 1901.
14 *Commonwealth of Australia Gazette*, No. 9, 20 February 1901.
15 N. Stephen, 'The Role of the Governor-General as Commander-in-Chief of the Australian Defence Forces', *Defence Force Journal*, November/December 1983, pp. 3–9.
16 ibid., p. 9.
17 For a more detailed analysis of these issues, see Mason, 'The Australian Constitution 1901–1988', and R.D. Lumb, 'The Bicentenary of Australian Constitutionalism: The Evolution of Rules of Constitutional Change', *University of Queensland Law Journal*, vol. 15, no. 1, pp. 3–32.
18 N. Lambert, *Australia's Naval Inheritance*, Papers in Australian Maritime Affairs No. 6 (Canberra: Maritime Studies Program, 1998), p. 9.
19 *Defence Act* 1903 (Commonwealth), No. 20 of 1903.
20 ibid., section 5.
21 While the *Defence Act* applied to both naval and military forces, further reference will be primarily limited to aspects affecting the naval forces.
22 *Defence Act* 1903, section 29.
23 Separate Acts of Parliament were subsequently passed to deal specifically with the RAN and the RAAF. These Acts are the *Naval Defence Act* 1910 and the *Air Force Act* 1923.
24 *Naval Defence Act* 1910, section 7(1).
25 ibid., section 18(1).
26 ibid., section 19.
27 ibid., sections 31–7.
28 Commonwealth of Australia, *Future Directions for the Management of Australia's Defence* (Canberra: AGPS, 1997).
29 Foreword in S. Blay, R. Piotrowicz and M. Tsamenyi (eds), *Public International Law—An Australian Perspective* (1997), p. v.
30 Full details of each case can be found at the International Court of Justice website at www.icj-cij.org.
31 Protocol Additional to the Geneva Conventions of 12 August 1949, and Relating to the Protection of Victims of International Armed Conflicts (Protocol I) of 8 June 1977, *Australian Treaty Series* 1991 No. 29.

32 S. Keeva, 'Lawyers in the War Room', pp. 52–9 provides an overview of the role played by United States forces legal officers in Operations DESERT SHIELD and DESERT STORM in 1990–91.
33 Extracted in D.J. Harris, *Cases and Materials on International Law* (5th edition 1998), p. 894.
34 T. McCormack, 'The Use of Force', in S. Blay, R. Piotrowicz and M. Tsamenyi, *Public International Law—An Australian Perspective*, p. 241.
35 Test enunciated by US Secretary of State Webster in exchange of correspondence with the United Kingdom: *The Caroline Case*. See fn 33.
36 ICJ Reports 1949, p. 4.
37 XXI *ILM* (1982), p. 1261.
38 International Convention on the Prevention of Marine Pollution by Dumping of Wastes and Other Matter, *Australian Treaty Series* 1985 No. 16.
39 T. Holden, *The Administration of Discipline in the Royal Australian Navy 1911–1964* (Canberra: Royal Australian Navy, 1982).
40 ibid., pp. 1–7.
41 *Naval Defence Act* 1910, section 36.
42 Holden, pp. 2–28 to 2–43. See also J. Goldrick, 'The *Australia* Court Martial 1942', unpublished MLitt thesis, University of New England, 1984.
43 ibid., pp. 2–37.
44 *Re Tracey ex Parte Ryan* (1989) 166 *CLR* 518, *Re Nolan ex Parte Young* (1991) 172 *CLR* 460 and *Re Tyler ex Parte Foley* (1994) 181 *CLR* 18.
45 Brennan and Toohey considered that when the jurisdiction of service tribunals was exercised it was not the judicial power of the Commonwealth, it was a power *sui generis* that was supported by Section 51 (vi) of the Constitution for the purpose of maintaining and enforcing service discipline. The Brennan–Toohey test was subsequently confirmed by the High Court in both *Re Nolan* and *Re Tyler*.
46 (1998) High Court of Australia 47.
47 Hembury was acquitted of two charges involving acts of indecency, but convicted on alternative charges involving conduct likely to prejudice army discipline and assault on a Defence Force member of inferior rank. The appellant was also convicted on a further charge involving disobedience of a lawful command.
48 Holden, pp. 2–43.

19 A fleet not a navy: some thoughts on the themes

1 J.T. Sumida, *Inventing Grand Strategy and Teaching Command: The Classic Works of Alfred Thayer Mahan Reconsidered* (Washington: Woodrow Wilson Center Press, 1997). See especially chapter 5 'National, Transnational and International Politics', pp. 80–98.
2 N.A.M. Rodger, *The Admiralty* (Lavenham, Suffolk: Terence Dalton, 1979), p. x.
3 See J.T. Sumida, *In Defense of Naval Supremacy: Finance, Technology and British Naval Policy, 1889–1914* (Boston: Unwin Hyman, 1989); and N.A. Lambert, *Sir John Fisher's Naval Revolution* (Columbia: University of South Carolina Press, 1999).
4 N.A.M. Rodger, *The Safeguard of the Sea: A Naval History of Great Britain, Vol. I, 660–1649* (London: Harper Collins, 1997). pp. 430–4.

Index

Page numbers in *italics* refer to photographs and maps

Aborigines, 237
Adelaide, 115
Aden, 100
AE1 (submarine), 256, *257*
AE2 (submarine), 256
Age, 143–4, 149, 152, 153, 157
air power, 22, 29
Alabama (ship), 128
Alagappa, Muthiah, 84
Albania, 286–7
Albert, Prince, 110, 113
Albert (ship), *134*
Allen, Colonel James, 124
The American Way of War (Weigley), 86
Amery, Leo, 200, 211
Amokura (ship), 121, 124
amphibious warfare, 15, 22, 29, 35, 38, 78–81
Amsterdam Treaty, 80
ANZAC convoy, 256–60, 260
Anzacs/Diggers, 89, 90, 92
Argus, 152, 210
Armed Constabulary Act 1867, 120
Arms, Anita, 84
Armstrong, Sir W.G., 132–3
Armstrong Whitworth (company), 172
Aslanbegoff, Rear Admiral, 131
asymmetric warfare, 92
Auckland, 119, 120–1, 122, 184–7, *186*, 196
Auckland Weekly News, 181
Australasian Naval Defence Act 1886, 136

Australia: American war plans for, 188–94, *189*; assesses defence requirements (1877), 129–30; British troops withdraw from, 100, 129; coastal flotilla proposed for, 151; confidence in Admiralty leadership falters, 259; Deakin issues statement on defence, 148–9; defence budget (1911–12), 232; Defence of Australia policy, 94; Department of Defence, 279; difficulty in maintaining pre-Federation vessels, 135; era of Australian Settlement, 87–8; floating defences (1905), 161–2; Forward Defence policy, 94; General Scheme of Defence, 133; Jose proposes navy for, 209; lack of aggression towards, 139; lack of maritime tradition, 92–3; legislation for local squadron introduced, 213; maritime strategy, 92–5; men available for naval service (1892), 135; military and naval manpower (1906), 164; naval forces before Federation, 125–39; objects to shelving of Singapore base, 62; offers to pay for Dreadnought for Britain, 206–8, 217–18; perceived vulnerability of, 141–7, 149–50, 152, 183; Permanent Force of Australia, 190; push for establishment of independent navy, 142, 149–50, 152–3, 157, 169; relationship between foreign and naval policy, 211–12; relationship between nation and navy, 292; relationship with

INDEX

Britain, 293–4; relationship with US, 181–2, 293; reluctance to question Admiralty judgement, 250; report on coastal defences (1914), 158; role in capture of German colonies, 247, 250; service of British ships in, 104–5; strategic culture, 86–9; subsidises Royal Navy, 143–5, 149, 154, 168, 199; way of warfare, 89–92; welcomes new destroyers (1910), 172–3; *see also* Australian Army; Royal Australian Navy
Australia Act 1986, 278, 279
Australia (ship): arrives in Sydney Harbour (1913), 1; in British strategic thinking, 159; in World War I, 243–5, 247, 249–54, 256–8, 295; near New Guinea, 257; ship's company, 272–4
Australia (II) (ship), 289
Australian Army, 93, 94, 164
Australian Constitution, 277, 279–81
Australian Defence Force, 90–5, 280
Australian Expeditionary Force, 256
Australian Fleet Unit, 1, 159, *293*
Australian Labor Party, 202, 203
Australian National Defence League, 200
Australian Naval and Military Expeditionary Force, 76
Australian Naval Cadet Corps, 172
Australian Naval Officers' Committee, 150
Australian Round Table, 157
Australia's Naval Inheritance (Lambert), 215
Australia's Strategic Policy, 94

balanced fleet, 21, 22
Barkly, Sir Henry, 103–4
Barton, Sir Edmund, *56*, 143, 145
Batt, Lofty, 169, 263
Batterham, Chief Petty Officer, 273
battle cruiser theory, 219, 220
Beachy Head, 13
Bean, Charles, 89, 90, 210
Beatty, David, 224
Beatty, Earl, 61, 73
Beazley, Kim, 87, 93
BEF, 29
Beresford, Admiral Charles, 218, 220, 226
Berlin, Isaiah, 42
Berlin Agreement (1996), 80
Bermuda, 101, 110, 113
Berrima (ship), 256, 258
Black Prince (ship), 196
blockade, 14, *16*, 21, 22, 233
blue-water control, 21, 22

Boer War, 26
Bogatyr (ship), 127
Bond, Sir R., *56*
Boomerang (ship), 146
Borden, Sir Robert, 64
Brassey, Lord, 141
Brennan–Toohey test, 290
Bridge, Carl, 90
Bridges, Lieutenant Colonel W.T., 148
Brisbane (ship), 266
Britain: ability to maintain navy questioned, 210; Admiralty deprecates French-style defence force, 169; Admiralty efforts to protect ANZAC troops, 256–60; Admiralty fails to uphold 1903 Agreement, 200; Admiralty hostility towards Australian navy, 214–16, 275; Admiralty offers concessions to Australia, 215–16; Admiralty orders Samoan expedition, 254–5; Admiralty policy after Australian Federation, 142–3, 150, 153–8, *156*; Admiralty policy in colonies, 57–8, 101–8, 114–15, 122–4, 135–9, 141; Admiralty proposes Pacific fleet, 227; Admiralty unconvinced by Fisher's arguments, 221–2; Admiralty war orders for Australian navy, 243–4, 245; America considers possibility of war with, 175–9; amphibious forces, 80, 82; Anglo–Dutch alliance, 18; Anglo–Dutch wars, 13; Anglo–French Entente, 146, 220; Anglo–French wars, 18; Anglo–Japanese alliance (1902), 146, 150, 154, 155–6, 176; Anglo–Japanese alliance (1905), 177, 179, 182, 183–4, 217; Anglo–Japanese alliance (1911), 227, 237; Anglo–Prussian alliance, 18, 20; arms race with France, 108; captures German Pacific colonies, 246–7, 249; co-operative arrangements with US, 78; Colonial Defence Committee, 133, 139; Colonial Office, 104, 139, 145, 149, 156–7; Committee of Imperial Defence, 58, 145–6, 148–51, 200, 204, 212, 215, 217, 222; defence strategy, 55–7, 62–3, 99–113, 116, 118; deploys 58th Regiment in New Zealand, 125–6; Dominion Fleet Units, 153; fears Germany's ship construction program, 216; 'Flying Squadron' strategy, 116–17; hands forts and barracks back to Australia, 100; Imperial Defence Committee, 166; in South Africa, 26; Joint Naval and Military Committee, 247; joint operations with Netherlands, 80–1;

proposes formation of Australian navy, 215; proposes Imperial Squadron, 157; relationship with Australia, 293–4; relationship with US, 63, 174; Report on Colonial Defence (1905), 148–51; seizes and burns *The Caroline*, 285–6, 287; strategic culture, 86; Strategic Defence Review, 37–8; *Times* derides Australian naval policy, 211; *Trent* crisis, 108–13, *109*, 114, 117; withdraws guarantee of Australia's defence, 211; withdraws support for minelaying in Australia, 165; withdraws troops from Australia, 100, 129; *see also* Royal Navy
Britannia (ship), 226
The British Way in Warfare (Hart), 86
Broeze, Frank, 93
Bulgaria, 129
Bull, Hedley, 23
Bulletin, 143, 144, 146
Bynoe Harbour, 235, 236, 240

cadet corps, 164
Cadiz, 15, *16*, 18
Cairns Naval Brigade, *137*
Calder, Sir Robert, 74–5
The Call, 205, 208
Callaghan, Sir George, 224
Callwell, Charles E., 33
Cambrian (ship), 1
Campbell-Bannerman, Sir H., 211
Canada: attacked by US, 108; attitude to independent navy, 57, 58; British forces in, 100, 109, 113, 115; complains about lack of consultation, 63–4; fishery protection cruisers, 168; in Battle of the Atlantic, 64; lack of defence against submarines, 65; launches assault on Dieppe, 65; policy towards NATO, 67–9, 70; promises to develop naval forces, 217; reaches agreement with Royal Navy, 59; relationship with Britain, 60–1; relationship with United States, 63, 67–70; Royal Canadian Army, 65; Royal Canadian Navy, 67, 68, 70
Canada (ship), 168
Caroline (ship), 285–6, 287
Cerberus (ship), 128, 131, *134*, 135, 138, 161, 173, 264
Challenger (ship), 263, 266
Chamberlain, Joseph, *56*
Chataway, Thomas, 269
Cheeseman, Graeme, 86–7
Chesapeake Bay, 12, 18

Childers, Civil Lord Hugh, 116–17
Childers (ship), *134*, 161, 166–7, 171
China, 78–9, 104, 105
Chirol, Valentine, 211
choke points, 23
Christmas Islands, 258
Churchill, Sir Winston, 155–9, 246–7, 255–6, 258, 260
Clarkson, Engineer Captain William, 229, *230*, 238, 271
Clausewitz, Carl von, 31, 39, 40–54, *41*, 86
Clowes, William Laird, 76
coastal defence, 22
Cobden, Richard, 110
Cobra (ship), 166
Code Napoléon, 50
Cold War, 29–30, 65–7, 78
Collingwood, R.G., 53–4
Collins, Captain R. Muirhead, 142
Collins class submarines, 292
Colonial Conference (1907), 216
Colonial Defence Act 1862, 120
Colonial Laws Validity Act 1865, 278
Colonial Naval Brigades, 274
Colonial Naval Defence Act 1865, 115, 122, 128
colonialism, demise of, 284
command capability, 46–7
commerce war, 8, 14–15, 16, 21, 34, 36
conscription, 197, 232
Constitution *see* Australian Constitution
The Constitution Act 1901, 279
continental–naval dichotomy, in strategy, 92–4
convoying, 14, 35, 117
Cook, Joseph, 87, 153
Corbett, Sir Julian: advocates joint maritime strategy, 94; as classical naval strategist, 3, 7, 9, 10, 21, 23, 28; defines maritime strategy, 34; influence of Clausewitz on, 54; on balanced fleets, 20; on defensive operations, 233–4; on failure to pursue *Emden*, 259; on influence of politics, 77; on maritime communications, 235; on naval and maritime strategy, 77; on the function of the fleet, 34; on the Samoan expedition, 252; on theory of war, 40–2; on war by contingent, 95; portrait of, *28*; understanding of Nelson, 13; view of land–sea interface, 75–6, 82
Corfu Channel case, 286–7
Coronel, Battle of, 242, 259, 260

INDEX

Countess of Hopetoun (ship), 161, 164, 166–7, *167*, 168, 171
Courier (ship), 172
courts-martial, 288–90
Craddock, Admiral, 242, 259
Creswell, Captain William Rooke: alarmed at cost of Thring's plan, 238; as commander of *Protector*, 263; as publicist, 167; at 1909 Imperial Defence Conference, 213; at odds with other naval officers, 203; compromised in Admiralty war orders, 244; derides Thring's concept of strategy, 234; enters South Australian Naval Forces, 166; faith in Australian seamen, 263; favours purchase of destroyers, 168; on a German–Japanese alliance, 154; on Australia's defence requirements, 151; on Bass Strait, 167; on priorities in the Pacific, 159; orders report on Thursday Island, 230; Patey complains to, 254; pleased at Deakin's stance on defence, 149; portraits of, *144*, *230*; proposes federal naval force, 93, 143, 145, 169–71, 199–200, 209, 242, 262; proposes primary naval base, 148; recommends establishment of navigation school, 264; refutes Foster's article in *Argus*, 210; relationship with Defence Ministers, 169–70; relationship with Naval Board members, 238, 271–2; sent to England (1906), 205; Thring appointed assistant to, 226; unwilling to increase workload, 229; vindicated by outbreak of war, 159
Creswell, Engineer Sub-Lieutenant 'Sparker', 173
Crimean War, 102, 113, 119
Cuban missile crisis, 68
Custance, Admiral Sir Reginald, 24
cyberspace, 37

Danzig, US Secretary of Navy, 78
Dardanelles, 18
Davis, Oscar King, 181–2
Deakin, Alfred: accepts Creswell's proposals, 172; asks Parliament to approve coastal fleet, 151; attitude to Admiralty policy, 160, 173; decides on composition of fleet, 204; insists upon interchangability of personnel, 222; introduces first defence bill, 212; issues statement on defence, 148–9; loses prime ministership, 171; manages naval policy, 3, 203–5; New Protection plan, 211; Norris on, 197; on coastal defence, 201–2; portrait of, *201*; proposes acquisition of submarines, 205–6; proposes rethink of defence strategy, 200, 203; suggests Royal Navy subsidise mail ships, 203, 204; supports visit by US fleet, 181–2; sympathetic to idea of Australian navy, 145; vacillates over offer of Dreadnought, 207–8, 217; wrings concessions from British Admiralty, 153, 216
Decisive Manoeuvre, 90–1
Defence Act 1903, 277, 282, 288, 289
Defence Act 1909, 121
Defence Efficiency Review, 284
Defence Force Discipline Act 1982, 289–90
Defence of Australia policy, 94
Defence Reform Program, 284
Defence (ship), 267
Delane, John, 111
Denison, Sir William, 103, 104, 106
Depression (1890s), 135
destroyers, 171, 172
Diefenbaker, Prime Minister, 67, 68
Dieppe, 65
Diggers, 89, 90, 92
diplomacy, 15–16, 22–3
discipline, 269, 271, 288–90
Drake, Sir Francis, 8, 15, 18, 19
Dresden (ship), *245*
Drummond, Captain James, 103
Dunedin, 121
Dutch West India Company, 14
Dyer, Rear Admiral K.L., 68

East Timor, 94
Eber (ship), *132*
Eccles, Admiral Henry E., 95
Edinburgh, Duke of, 105
Eisenhower, Dwight, 294
Electra (ship), 126
electromagnetic spectrum, 25–6
electronic warfare, 36
Elias, Stoker, 289
Elizabeth I, 8, 19, 20
Ellen Ballance (ship), 161
Elsick Ordnance Company, 133
Emden (ship), 79, 243, 246, 251, 257–60
Encounter (ship), 1, 243, 258
The End of Certainty (Kelly), 87
Esher, Lord, 74
ethnocentrism, 84
Europe, amphibious forces in, 79–81

European Maritime Force, 81
European Security and Defence Identity, 80
Evans, Gareth, 89
Evans, Rear Admiral Robley D., 179
Evening Post, 183
expeditionary operations, 75, 77, 82, 87, 88, 89

Falkland Islands, 100
Falklands, Battle of, *223*, 259
Fanshawe, Vice Admiral Sir Arthur, 264
Farncomb, Captain, 289, 290
Feakes, Sub-Lieutenant Henry, 264
Fiji, 123, 258
Fisher, Andrew, 153, 207, 208
Fisher, Admiral Sir John: appointed First Sea Lord, 181; backs appointment of Henderson, 228; on the Singapore base, 166; orders withdrawal from China Station, 146; portrait of, *218*; proposes fleet unit for Australia, 228; rivalry with Beresford, 226; vision of naval warfare, 218–24; welcomes Creswell in London, 170
Fitzherbert, William, 122
Fitzroy, Governor, 125–6
fleet engagement, 13, 22, 73, 75
flotilla defence theory, 219, 220
'Flying Squadron' strategy, 116–17
foreign policy, 59
Forrest, Sir John, 145
Fort Denison, Sydney, 102
fortifications, 102, 162, 165, 194
Forward Defence policy, 94
Forward From the Sea, 78
Foster, Colonel H., 210
Foxton, Colonel J.F.G., 149, 213
France: ambitions in Europe, 112; amphibious capability, 80, 81; Anglo–French Entente, 146; Anglo–French wars, 12, 14, 16, 18, 19; arms race with Britain, 108; fear of in colonial Australia, 128; forces rethink in British strategy, 102–3; policy towards NATO, 68; relationship with Japan, 166
Frederick the Great, 18
free market economics, 88
Freedman, Lawrence, 86
Fremantle, 115, 194
From the Sea, 78
Fuller, T.E., 56
'functionalist' principle, 64

Galatea (ship), *105*
Gallipoli, *91*
Garden Island, Sydney, 101
Gaunt, Captain, 266
Gayundah (ship), 133, 161, *162*, 167
George V, 266
Germany: America considers possibility of war with, 176–7; as a threat to Australia, 140–1, 147–9, 151–2, 154, 157–8; as a threat to Britain, 150, 154, 166, 216, 220, 232; constructs Dreadnoughts, 216; defeats Britain at Coronel, 242; East Asiatic Squadron, 146, 159, 242–3, *245*, 246, *248*, 249–53, 255–61; imperial ambitions, 147; in World War II, 35; maritime strategy, 34; Pacific colonies, 157, 159
Gladstone, William, 107, 116
globalisation, 87, 88, 89
Gneisenau (ship), 243, 249, 252, 255, 257–8
Gordon, Acting Leading Stoker, 289
Gordon, Brigadier General J.M., 230, 233
Gordon (ship), 161
Gower, Major General Steven, 90
graving docks, 101, 115
Gray, Colin, 9, 10, 14, 84, 260
Great Britain (ship), 114, 115, 127
Great Eastern (ship), 109
Greece, 81
Grey, Charles, 2nd Earl, 100
Grey, Sir George, 114
Grey, Jeffrey, 89
Griffith, Gavan, 284
Grigg, E.W.M., 210
guerre du course, 8, 14–15, 16, 21, 34, 36
gunboats, 131, 132, 135

Halifax, 110, 113
Halsey, Midshipman William F., 180
Hamilton, General Ian, 158
Hampshire (ship), 243, 257
Hancock, Sir Keith, 87
Hankey, Sir Maurice, 60, 247
Hanson, Victor Davis, 86
Harding, Sir Edward, 60
Hart, Liddell, 9, 75, 77, 86
Hastings, Battle of, 53–4
Hattendorf, John, 10, 255
Hawaii, 176
Hawaii Defence Plan, 179–80
Haworth-Booth, Captain, 157
Headquarters Australian Theatre, 90
Hellyer, Able Seaman John, 273

Hembury v Chief of the General Staff, 290
Henderson, Admiral Sir Reginald, 155, 157, 228–9, 237–8, 266, 268
Henderson's case, 279
Herald (newspaper), 148–9, 202, 203
Herald (ship), 101
High Court of Australia, 279, 280, 284, 289–90
historical school of thought, 24, 26
history, and theory, 47–9, 51–4
A History of Warfare (Keegan), 86
Hitler, Adolf, 35
Holden, Captain Tom, 288
Holland *see* Netherlands
Hong Kong, 65, 100
Hornby, Rear Admiral Sir Geoffrey, 117
Horner, David, 90
Hotham, Captain Sir Charles, 126
Howard, Sir Michael, 23, 85
Hughes-Onslow, Captain Constantine, 228–35, *230*, 237–40, 271–2
Hume, Sir A.H., 56
Hutton, Major General Sir Edward, 142, 169
Hygeia (ship), 160

Ibuki (ship), 259
Imperial Conferences: (1887), 122; (1902), 55–7, *56*, 123; (1909), 123, 153, 215, 221, 226, 227, 242, 292; (1911), 226; (1921), 57, 61; (1923), 60; (1930), 62
imperial defence strategy, 55–7, 99–113
Imperial Federation League of Victoria, 202
Imperial Naval and Military Defence Conference (1909), 213
Imperial Naval Discipline Act 1866, 289
India, 61, 62, 78, 237
Indiana (ship), 176
industrial revolution, 16–17
intelligence, 220
International Court of Justice, 285, 286
international law, 284–5, 286–7
internationalism, 87, 88, 89
Invincible (ship), *223*
ironclad steamers, 113

Jackson, Admiral, 247, 249, 256
Jackson, Commander J.M., 240
Janie Seddon (ship), 161, 163
Japan: America considers possibility of war with, 176, 178; Anglo–Japanese alliance (1902), 146, 150, 154, 155–6, 176; Anglo–Japanese alliance (1905), 177, 179, 182, 183–4, 217; Anglo–Japanese alliance (1911), 227, 237; as a threat to Australia, 141, 149, 154, 158, 182–3, 197, 200, 209, 211, 213, 226, 232–3, 235, 238; as a threat to Britain, 150, 217; as a threat to the US, 178–9, 184; battle plans for US Pacific Fleet, 36; expansion of influence in Asia, 141, 177, 232; in Hitler's strategy, 35; Japanese squadron visits Australia, 207; likely reaction to Anglo–US war, 195; migration of labourers to US, 177–8; naval building program, 61; naval strength (1927), 234; relationship with France, 166; Russo–Japanese War, 149, 166, 177, 197, 200
Jellicoe, Admiral Sir John, 61, 62, 75, 123, 240
Jerram, Vice Admiral T., 243, 249, 251, 252, 255–7
Jervois, Colonel Drummond, 129–30
Jervois, Sir William, 133
John Thorneycroft (company), 133
joint operations: British concept of, 80; involving Australia, 90, 92; Slater on, 72–3; UK–Dutch, 80–1; US–Canadian, 67, 68, 70; US–UK, 78
Jose, Arthur Wilberforce, 198–203, 205–12, 244, 252, 253–4
Jutland, Battle of, 36, 73, *74*, 75, 267

Kanimbla (ship), 79
Karrakatta (ship), 146
Kaskowhiski (ship), 122
Kennedy, John, 68
Kennedy, Paul, 18, 20, 27
King, William Lyon Mackenzie *see* Mackenzie King, William Lyon
King George Sound, 194
King-Hall, Admiral Sir George: as Commander of Australia Station, 1, 226; helps to establish Australian navy, v, ix–x; ignorant of Admiralty Pacific policy, 227; on protection of sea lanes, 140; on the 1903 Naval Agreement, 265; on the Royal Navy's sphere of influence, 232; sees colonials as troublemakers, 271; supports independent Australian navy, 266
Königsberg (ship), *221*
Korean War, 15
Kosovo, 26

La Nauze, J.A., 197
La Trobe, Governor, 126

labour deregulation, 88
Lady Loch (ship), 172
Lady Roberts (ship), 161, 163
Lambert, Nicholas, 264–5
Lamont, Ross, 292
land–sea interface, 15, 18–19, 23, 29, 38, 75–6, 77–82
Land Wars, New Zealand, 119, 122
Laurier, Sir Wilfred, 56, 57, 59
Lavarack, Colonel J.D., 93
Lavery, Brian, 13, 14
Law of the Sea Convention (1982), 287
League of Nations, 62
Legislative Councils, 278
Leichhardt, Ludwig, 93
Leipzig (ship), 243
Leveson, Rear Admiral Arthur, 246
Lewis, George Cornewall, 109
Lincoln, Abraham, ix, 112
Lindsay, Norman, *156*
Lisbon, 19, 113
littoral warfare, 94–5
London Dumping Convention, 287
Lonsdale (ship), 161
Lord, Carnes, 85
Loring, Captain William, 105
Louis, Prince of Battenburg, 220, 247, 255–6
Lusitania (ship), 136
Lyons, Lord, 110, 112–13

Macarthur, Douglas, 15
Macdonald, Ramsay, 62
Macedon (ship), *281*
Mackenzie King, William Lyon, 60, 64, 69
Mackinder, Sir Alfred, 27
Mahan, Rear Admiral A.T.: as an Anglophile, 174; as classical naval strategist, 3, 7, 21, 22, 27–8, 33, 34, 74, 76, 82; impact of Nelson on, 13; on blue-water strategy, 8; on commerce war, 36; on history of naval strategy, 10; on influence of politics, 77; on offence, 31; on silence of naval power, 17; on tactics, 9; on the defence of the Dominions, 142; on the place of sea power, 35; portrait of, *28*; reveals extent of British withdrawal from Pacific, 181, 183; Rodger's criticisms of, 33; Sumida on, 291–2
Malta, 100, 114
Manisty, Staff Paymaster Eldon, 229, *230*, 230, 237, 238, 271
Manoora (ship), 79
Maoris, 105–6, 119, 120

Maritime Contribution to Joint Operations, 80
The Maritime Military Struggle in the World Military Trend, 78–9
maritime strategy, 77–82, 83, 92–5, 291; *see also* naval strategy
Maritime Strategy, 78, 82
Maritime Strategy and Continental Wars, 78
A Maritime Strategy for the Next Century, 78
Mars (ship), 161
Marshall Islands, 252, 258
Mason, Mr (Confederate envoy), 108, 113
Massachusetts (ship), 176
Massalia (ship), 136
materialist school of thought, 24, 26
Mathews, James, 270
Maxfield, Midshipman Lewis, 178
May, William, 220
McCay, Lieutenant Colonel J.W., 93, 148, 169
McDougall, Allan, 269
McKenna, Reginald, 216
McLean, Lieutenant Commander Ridley, 191
Meaney, N., 197
Melbourne: American War Plan for, 192–4, *193*; fortifications, 162; harbour defences, 115; minefields, 163; scare of Russian invasion, 127
Melbourne (ship), 1, 243, 252, 256–7, 259, 266, 269, 287
Menon, Rear Admiral Raja, 78
merchant ships, 136, 157
Midge (ship), 161
Mildura (ship), 123
Militarism and the Citizen Tradition in Australia (Encel), 89
Militia Act (1858), 120
Millen, E.D., 1–2, 155–6, 159, 227, 244, 249–50
Mills Committee, 107, 109, 116
Milne, Rear Admiral Sir Alexander, 103, 110, 111, 112, 113
Miner (ship), 161, 163
mines and minelaying, 162–3, *163*, 165, 185
Minotaur (ship), 243, 257, 259
missiles, 36
Montcalm (ship), 258
Moore, Sir John, 15, 75
Morison, Samuel Eliot, 21
Mosquito (ship), 161

INDEX 359

multiculturalism, 88
Munich crisis, 62, 68
My Lai massacre, 285

Napoleon, 13, 15, 17, 35, 75
Napoleon III, 108, 112
nation states, 10
National Review, 156
nationalism, 57
NATO: air war against Yugoslavia, 70; amphibious forces, 80–1, 82; as a model of collective defence, 55; Canadian policy towards, 67–9, 70; Central Front, 37; during the Cold War, 30; in Kosovo conflict, 26; role of sea power, 29
Nauru, 247, 249, 256
Naval Agreements: (1887), 121–2, 122, 123, 142, 214; (1902), 143, 145; (1903), 148, 151, 168, 198–9, 202, 265; (1909), 154, 155, 156, 264
naval bases, 61, 62–3, 93–4, 99–101
Naval Defence Act 1910, 265, 277, 282–3, 288
Naval Defence Act 1913, 124
Naval Discipline Act, 288
Naval Discipline (Dominion Naval Forces) Act 1911, 288
Naval Loan Act 1909, 283
Naval Review, 239
naval strategy: Admiral Fisher's ideas on, 218–20; advantages of sea power, 31–2; as part of maritime strategy, 77; Australia's strategic dependence upon Britain, 199–200; balanced fleet, 21, 22; blockade, 14, 21, 22, 233; blue-water control, 21, 22; British (19th century), 118; classical strategists, 21; context of, 20–1, 23, 27; defined, 9; early Australian strategic thought, 225–41; element of risk, 20, 23; fleet engagement, 13, 22; 'forward policy', 231; history of, 7–23; human factors, 19–20; land–sea interface, 15, 18–19, 23, 29, 38, 75, 77–82, 92–4, 233; offensive versus defensive strategy, 233–4; power projection, 15, 36; relation to diplomacy, 15–16, 22–3; relation to history, 9; silence of naval power, 17; strategic geography, 18, 23; strategic importance of sea power, 24–39; World War I, 244–59
Naval War College (US), 178
Nelson, Horatio, 9–10, *11*, 13–14, 18–20, 73–5, 82

Nelson (ship), *117*, *134*, 135
Nepean (ship), 161
Netherlands: Anglo–Dutch alliance, 18; Anglo–Dutch wars, 13; Britain assumes alliance of Germany with, 243; demise as commercial power, 12; German plans to annex, 147; invades England (1688), 15; joint operations with UK, 80–1
Netherlands Amphibious Force, 80, 82
Netherlands Marine Corps, 80, 82
New Britain, 200
New Caledonia, 104, 106, 128
New Guinea, 147, 157, 247, 249, 250, 255–7, 258
New Hebrides, 200
New Left Australian isolationism, 86–7
New South Wales: acquires HMS *Wolverine*, 131–2; colonial government, 101, 102, 278; considers design for monitor, 128–9; floating defences (1905), 161; military and naval forces, 164, 214; Royal Navy protocol in, 137; suggests cost-sharing with Britain, 103; Voluntary Artillery, 126
New York Times, 182
New Zealand: American War Plan for Auckland, 184–7, *186*; armed forces (1906), 164; Britain deploys 58th Regiment in, 125–6; confidence in Admiralty leadership falters, 259; defence force (1908), 187; fears Japanese invasion, 183; floating defences (1905), 161; Naval Artillery Volunteer units, 120, 123; naval defence (1854–1914), 119–24; navy delays pursuit of Spee, 259; offers expeditionary force to Britain, 246, 249, 254–5; offers to fund battleships for Britain, 216–17; Permanent Militia, 120; role in capture of German colonies, 247; Samoan expedition, 251–4; subsidises Royal Navy, 168; supports Singapore base, 62; uses *Sparrow* as training ship, 168
New Zealand Herald, 181
New Zealand (ship), 123, *124*, 159
Newcastle, 115, 163
Newcastle, Duke of, 109, 114
Newcastle (ship), 243
Nicholson, Air Vice Marshal Peter, 91–2
Nickle, Sir Robert, 127
The Nile, Battle of, 13, 16, 17
Nineteenth Century (Brassey), 141–2
Nissin (ship), *212*
Nolan, Sidney, 93

NORAD, 67–8
Norman, Captain William, 127
Norris, R., 197
Norstad, General, 67
North American Air Defence Agreement, 67–8
Norway, 81
nuclear warfare, 30, 31, 37
Nünberg (ship), 243, 258

Official History of the First World War (Bean), 89
Ohm (ship), 161
On War (Clausewitz), 42–54
Operation DEEP FREEZE, 196
Operation DESERT SHIELD, 277
Operation DESERT STORM, 277
Oregon (ship), 176
Ottlet, Rear Admiral Charles, 56
Ozanne, Alfred, 271

Paget, Captain Lord Clarence, 116
Palmerston, Lord, 107, 109, 110–11, 112, 116, 196
Paluma (ship), 133, 161, *162*, 167–8
Panter, Lieutenant, 137
Papua, 235, 240
Paret, Peter, 44
Parkes, Henry, 129
Parramatta (ship), 1, 172–3, 252, 265, 269–71, *281*
Patey, Rear Admiral Sir George E., 1, 244–5, 249, 250–6, 258
Pax Britannica, 16–17
Pearce, George Foster, 153, 229, *230*, 265
Pearl Harbor, 64, 176, 179–80
Pearson, Lester, 64, 67, 69
Pedersen, Peter, 90
Pegasus (ship), *221*
Peninsular War, 15, 75
Philippines, 176, 180
Philomel (ship), 124, 259
Phoebe (ship), *117*
Picket (ship), 161
Pioneer (ship), 169, *221*
Pitt the Elder, 20
Pitt the Younger, 20
Playford, Thomas, 170
Poland, 81
politics, and war, 42–3
Poore, Admiral Sir Richard, 263
Port Arthur, 166, 240
Port Phillip *see* Melbourne
Portugal, 16, 17, 81

Pound, Captain Dudley, 57
Powell, General Colin, 277
power projection, 15, 36, 73, 117
Powerful (ship), 191
privateering, 14
Protector (ship), 133, 161, 166, 167, 263, *281*
Prussia, 18, 20
Psyche (ship), 124, 169, 264
Pyramus (ship), 124, 169, 259, 264

Quebec, 15, 113
Queensland: floating defences (1905), 161; military and naval manpower (1906), 164, 165; Queensland Marine Defence Force, 166; uses gunboats for coastal defence, 133
Quiberon Bay, 18
Quick, Sir John, 145

radar, 36
radio communications, 36
Rae, Arthur, 269
Rapke, Lieutenant, 290
Rawson, Admiral Sir H., 210
reconnaissance, 235
Reid, Sir George, 148, 171, 202, 273–4
religion, in naval strategy, 21
Report on Colonial Defence (1905), 148–51
Revolution in Military Affairs, 22, 26, 86
Richmond, Admiral Sir Herbert, 10, 29, 75, 93–4, 246–7, 258–9
Riley, Stoker, 289
The Rise and Fall of British Naval Mastery (Kennedy), 20
Robertson, Norman, 64
Rodger, Nicholas, 10, 33–4, 292
The Role of the Army in a Maritime Concept of Strategy (Evans), 79
Roosevelt, Theodore, 177, 178, 181–2, 192
Royal Australian Air Force, 90, 94
Royal Australian Naval College, 265, *283*
Royal Australian Navy: as a 'fleet in being', 235; as an independent force, 1–2; attitude towards British officers, 191; Boy Seamen entry scheme, 267; Citizen Naval Force, 265; command problems in World War I, 259–60; Commonwealth Naval Board, 226, 228, 229–31, *230*, 237–40, 243–4, 259–60, 265, 271–2; Commonwealth Naval Forces formed, 264, 265, 274; conceived of as model navy, 224; conditions aboard ship,

INDEX

272–3; dependence on Royal Navy infrastructure, 292, 293–4; discipline in, 269, 271, 288–90; early naval strategic thought in, 225–41; early recruiting strategy, 266–9; effectiveness in Pacific (1914), 261; favours blue-water imperial defence, 93; force structure of early navy, 236; impact of Royal Navy on, ix, 21; in strategic policy, 94; legal issues surrounding formation of, 276–7, 280–3; legal support for RAN operations, 283–7; messing system, 271; mixed British–Australian crews in, 274; Permanent Naval Force, 265; reneges on issue of deferred pay, 269–70; role in contemporary strategy, 90; Royal Navy officers in, 262, 263–4, 274; status within imperial navy, 227–8, 229; training of seamen, 262–6, 274; war-readiness in 1914, 242–4; works budget (1913), 238
Royal Canadian Navy, 67, 68, 70
Royal Gun Factory, 133
Royal Naval War College, 228
Royal Navy: agrees to Australian fleet unit, 222–3; aircraft carriers, 38; as part of collective defence force, 56–7; attitude towards Australian seamen, 136–7, *138*, 191, 263–4, 270–1, 275; Australian Auxiliary Squadron, 122, 123, 136, 138, 168–9; Australian Squadron, 101, 105, 121–2, 129, 146, 151, 168, 191, 215, 245, 254, 257; Australian subsidy of, 143–5, 149, 154; bases on foreign soil, 99–101; begins using River class destroyers, 165; China Squadron, 104, 105, 146, 243–4, 246, 251, 255–6, 257; command problems in World War I, 254–5, 259–60; construction program (1909), 220; *Corfu Channel* case, 286–7; defeated at Coronel, 242; desertions from, 263; distances itself from Australian colonial navies, 215; division between officers and lower deck, 265; East Indies Squadron, 101; fails to understand German strategy in Pacific, 243, 246, 249, 251, 257, 258, 259, 260; fleet rationalised (1904), 166, 181; history (1550–1880), 10–16, 19–20; impact on RAN, ix, 21; in World War I, 33, 242–61; in World War II, 33; lends cruiser to New Zealand, 124; likely reaction to Anglo–US war, 195; limitations of, 32; Naval Intelligence Branch, 244; new concept of operations, 80; pledges to defend Australia, 198–9; power of in 19th century, 118; pursues Russian fleet in Pacific, 119; role in imperial defence policy, 106–7; Royal Naval Reserve, 123, 136, 138, 168; sends sloop to protect gold ships, 126; strategic power, 113; strategy based on battleships, 218–19; trains Australian seamen, 199, 265; treatment of recruits, 267–8; uses Auckland as stores site, 121; uses gunboats for coastal defence, 132; withdraws from Pacific (1904), 181, 183
Royal Netherlands Marine Corps, 80
Royal Netherlands Navy, 80
Royal United Services Institute, 71
Russell, Lord John, 109, 110
Russia: as a threat to Australia, 126, 127–8, 131, 141, 202; averts war with Britain, 117; conflict with Ottoman Empire, 129; in the Crimean War, 113; Russian ships feted in Australia, 131; Russo–Japanese War, 149, 166, 177, 197, 200; wages conflicts at sea, 34

Samoa, 157, 246–7, 249, 251–4, 256, 258, 260
San Jacinto (ship), 108, *109*
Saracen (ship), 171
Scharnhorst (ship), 243, 249, 252, 255, 257–8
Schroeder, Rear Admiral Seaton, 179–80
Scratchley, Lieutenant Colonel Peter, 129–30, 132
'sea blindness', vii
Sea Dogs of Australia (film), *88*
sea lines of communication, 94
Second Boer War, 26
Seddon, R.J., 56
Seven Years War, 18, 20, 21
Sewa Bay, *239*, 240
Seymour, Admiral Sir Edward, 263
Seymour, Captain Frederick Beauchamp, 104, 106, 111, 114, 116
Shedden, Frederick, 93
Shenandoah (ship), 115, 128
'ships of the line', 36
Silburn, P.A., 142–3
Sims, William S., 174, 192
Singapore, 61, 62–3, 93–4, 166
Sino-Japanese War (1894–95), 141
Skelton, Undersecretary of State, 63–4
Slater, Admiral Sir Jock, 72–3, 75

Slessor, Sir John, 84
Slidell, Mr (Confederate envoy), 108, 113
Some Principles of Maritime Strategy (Corbett), 40
Somerset, Duke of, 107, 109, 110, 111–12
South Africa, 62, 143
South Australia: acquires gunboats, 133; bi-cameral parliament, 278; fears bombardment of Port Adelaide, 104; floating defences (1905), 161; military and naval manpower (1906), 164; South Australia Naval Forces, 166
Spain, 8, 12–15, 18, 81, 174
Sparrow (ship), 121, 161, 168
Spee, Vice Admiral Count Maximilian von, 159, 243, 249, 251–5, 258–60
Sperry, Rear Admiral Charles S., 178–9
St Malo agreement, 80, 81
The Standard, 210
Statute of Westminster 1931, 279, 289
Statute of Westminster Adoption Act 1931, 279, 288
steam power, 16, 17, 121
Stephen, Sir Ninian, 280
Stimpson, H.L., 73–4
strategic culture: Australia, 86–9; concept of, 84–6; relation to maritime strategy, 92–5; styles of warfare as part of, 89–92; United Kingdom, 86; United States, 84, 85, 86
strategic geography, 18, 22, 23
strategy, 44–5, 50, 99–101; *see also* maritime strategy; naval strategy; strategic culture
Sturdee, Vice Admiral, 246, 249, 256
submarines: Canadian lack of defence against, 65; *Collins* class, 292; Fisher's ideas for employing, 219; Jose opposes proposed purchase of, 205–6; replacement of minefields by, 165; Thring on use of, 236; use of by US against Japan, 34, 36
Suez Canal, 129
Sumida, Jon, 35, 76, 291
Sumner, Charles, 110
Sun Tzu, 86
Svetlana (ship), 127
Sweden, 81
Swift (ship), 171, 172
Sydney: American War Plan for, 188–92, *189*; as a British naval base, 100–1, 105; fortifications, 162; harbour defences, 115; minefields, 163; reaction to *Trent* crisis, 114

Sydney Mail, 154
Sydney Morning Herald, 153, 154, 155, 158, 174, 267
Sydney (ship): arrives in Sydney, 1; foul food served aboard, 271; patrols North Sea, *30*; role in World War I, 243, 250, 252, 256, 257–9; ship's company, 266, 269, *272*

tactics, Clausewitz on, 44
Taft, William H., 177
Taiwan Strait, 22–3
Taro, Katsura, 177
Tasmania: acquires torpedo boat, 133–4; bi-cameral parliament, 278; military and naval manpower (1906), 164, 165
TB No. 191 (torpedo boat), 133–4
technology, 22, 36–7, 92, 113, 121
telegraphy, 17, 115, 129, 157, 234, 235
theory, of war, 40–54
'Third Wave', of warfare, 30
Thring, Captain Hugh, 225–8, *227*, 230, 231–40, 250
Thring Harbour, *239*, 240
'Thring Line', 234, 238
Thursday Island, 230–1, 245
Tickell, Depot Captain, 173
The Times, 111, 150, 198, 200, 210–11
Tingara (ship), 267–8, *268*
Tirpitz, Admiral Alfred von, 147
Torch (ship), 124
torpedo boats: added to Australia Squadron, 122, 136; Britain deprecates Australia's request for, 145; Creswell favours, 170; cruise to Tasmania, 166–7; Fisher's ideas for employing, 219; New Zealand acquires, 121; role in naval warfare, 130, 133; Russian scare prompts colonies to buy, 131; Victoria acquires, 164
Torres Strait, 235, 236
Tracey case, 290
Tracy, Nicholas, 10, 14
Trafalgar, Battle of, 13, 17, 18, 19, 75
transnationalism, in defence, 55, 63–4
Trent crisis, 108–14, *109*, 117
Triumph (ship), 243
Tromp, Admiral Maarten, 18, 19
Trudeau, Pierre Elliott, 69
Tsushima, Battle of, 197, 220

United Nations, 55, 69, 284–5, 287
United States: as leader of collective defence structure, 65–6; attacks Canada,

108; Australian War Plans, 188–96, *189*, *193*; Civil War, 109, 122; co-operative arrangements with UK, 78; considers war with Japan, 176, 178–9; Hawaii Defence Plan, 179–80; influence on Canadian policy, 60; Japanese immigrants in, 177–8; maritime strategy, 78; New Zealand War Plans, 184–7, *186*; pressures Canada to assist in Vietnam, 69; relationship with Australia, 181–2, 293; relationship with Britain, 174; relationship with Canada, 67–70; SEA DRAGON program, 78; Spanish-American War, 174; strategic culture, 84, 85, 86; *Trent* crisis, 108–13, *109*, 114, 117; use of submarines, 34–5; War of Independence, 12, 14, 18, 19, 20; War Plan RED, 175–9, 195
United States Army, 85
United States Marine Corps, 78, 82
United States Naval War College, 175
United States Navy: Anglophiles in, 174; co-operative arrangements with Canada, 67, 68, 70; fleet visits Australia (1908), 152, 178, 181–2, *182*, 190–2, *192*, 204, *204*; in Battle of the Atlantic, 64; in Vietnam, 35–6; in World War II, 36; operational emphasis, 78; role of fleet aircraft carriers, 32; strategy, 12, 38

Veale, Stan, 172, 173
Victoria: acquires vessels for coastal defence, 126, 128, 133, 135; allows Confederate ship to resupply, 128; bi-cameral parliament, 278; defences for Port Phillip Bay, 103, 114, 115, *117*; floating defences (1905), 161; forced to sell gunboats, 138; forces inspected by Commodore, 137–8; military and naval manpower (1906), 164; naval forces, 214; Victorian Navy, 166; Victorian Rifles, 169
Victoria I, 109, 110, 113
Victoria (gunboat), *134*
Victoria (steam sloop), 104, 127
Victory (ship), 273
Vietnam, 35–6, 69
Vietnam War, 285
Voss (White), 93
Vulcan (ship), 161, 164

Wainwright, Rear Admiral Richard, 179
War of the Second Coalition, 17

War of the Spanish Succession, 16, 17
War Plan RED, 175–9, 195
Ward, Sir Joseph, 120, 123, 181–2
warfare: as part of strategic culture, 85, 86; asymmetric, 92; Australian way of, 89–92; future of, 39; theory of, 40–54
Warrego (ship), 1
Warren, Commander W.H.F., 252
Warrender, Sir George, 224
Warspite (ship), 104
Washington, Captain John, 111–12
water-planes, 236
weaponry, late 19th century, 121
Weekly Graphic, 183
Wellington, 121, 122
Wellington, Lord, 17, 75
West Australian, 147
West Indies, 115
Western Australia, 164, 165, 194
WEU, 55
White Australia Policy, 87, 88, 198, 211
Wilhelm II, 147
Wilhelmschafen, 258
Wilkes, Captain Charles, 102, 108, 112
Williams, Major General Dion, 178
Wilson, Admiral Sir Arthur, 222
With the Flagship in the South (Bean), 210
Wolfe, General James, 15
Wolverine (ship), 131
World War I: naval strategy in, 244–59; Royal Australian Navy readiness for, 159, 242–4, 294; sea power in, 29
World War II: Australia's maritime campaign, 94; Canadian naval forces in, 64–5; Hitler's strategy in, 35; Royal Australian Navy readiness for, 294–5; sea power in, 29, 35
The World's Awakening, 183
Wrong, Hume, 64, 66
Wynter, Colonel D.H., 93

xenophobia, 87
Xu, Colonel Weidi, 78–9

Yamamoto, Admiral, 36
Yap, 247, 249, 251, 256
Yarmouth (ship), 243
Yarra (ship), 1, 172, *257*, 265, 269–71, *270*, 281
Yorktown, 18
Yugoslavia, 285

Zelee (ship), 258